CAPE COD,
MARTHA'S VINEYARD,
& NANTUCKET

ACCESS®

D1017947

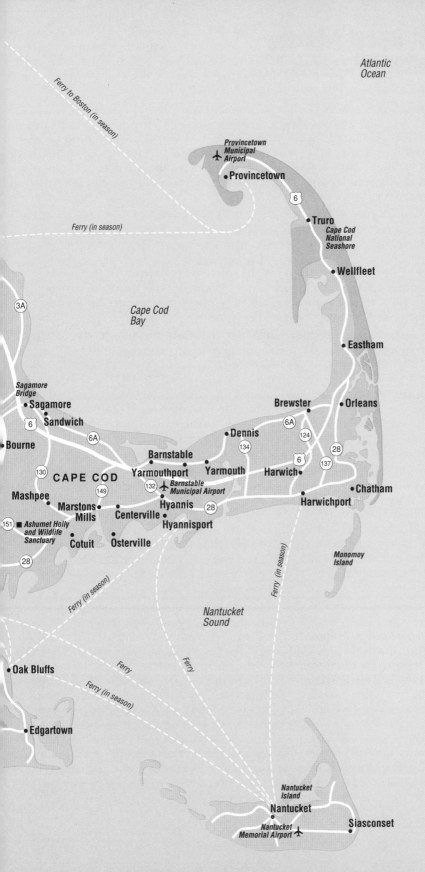

Orientation

A real-estate agent couldn't have dreamed up an easier sell than this lush peninsula some 60 miles long, crenulated with nearly 600 miles of shoreline, nearly half of it glorious beach. No wonder Cape Cod's praises have been sung by visitors as disparate as Henry David Thoreau and Patti Page.

Yet the Pilgrims were not much impressed when, on 11 November 1620, they pulled into what would someday become **Provincetown**, a protected harbor cupped in the hand of the Cape's "flexed arm." They moved on after a month, convinced the place would never amount to much. Since they were highly appreciative of profitable pursuits, they might be chagrined to learn that the Cape today attracts up to 13 million tourists a year and generates annual revenues in excess of $1.3 billion.

The early settlers themselves account for at least part of the Cape's mystique. The area is steeped in history—not just the brave exploits of the colonists and the largesse of the indigenous peoples who welcomed them, but the escapades of pirates and patriots, whalers, and farsighted entrepreneurs. And while modern innovations ultimately eclipsed many of their grand schemes (whale oil, for instance, was replaced by kerosene), the settlers left behind an extraordinary cache of architectural treasures, enhanced by unspoiled landscapes of surpassing beauty.

Just as Cape residents started migrating to Boston and Lowell, Massachusetts in search of factory work (the population declined by one-third between 1860 and 1920), city dwellers began arriving at Thoreau's "wild rank spot" for rustic vacations. By the turn of the century, more than 75 hotels had opened. The figure now runs to 10 times that, and tourism revenues make up about 60 percent of the area's economy. Even though commercial development has compromised the Cape's visual appeal—particularly along the southernmost shore—there remain great pockets of preservation lands where, as Thoreau wrote, "a man can stand and put all America behind him."

Thoreau was referring particularly to the "Back Side," a 30-mile-long stretch of wild dunes and pounding surf located on the ocean side of the **Outer Cape**, which has been under the protective stewardship of the **Cape Cod National Seashore** since 1961. Unencumbered by human habitation (beyond the occasional picturesque lighthouse or remote weathered shack), this seemingly endless beach knows no equal in New England. Though the access points fill up fast on fine days, walk a ways and you're on your own. The placid bays have their charms as well—surf gentle enough for a toddler, and miles of shell-strewn sands to explore at low tide.

The peninsula's idiosyncratic communities all distinguish themselves in some way. History buffs and those interested in fine architecture might start with a detour to **Plymouth** before they arrive at Cape Cod itself, then follow historic **Route 6A** from **Sandwich** (the Cape's oldest town, founded in 1637) to **Orleans**; houses lining this twisting road range from Colonial to Victorian in style. The western coast of the Cape offers a peaceful redoubt for families, while its southernmost tip, the tiny village of **Woods Hole**, a ferry port for **Martha's Vineyard** and home to a world-renowned scientific community, represents one of the hipper enclaves in these parts, with laid-back restaurants and watering holes. Old money has claimed the coastline along the **Nantucket Sound**, from **Falmouth** to **Hyannisport** by way of **Osterville** and **Centerville**, but there's no charge for gazing at these seaside estates, and you can even live like a lord or lady of the manor, if only for a night or two, by checking in at an elaborate mansion-turned-inn.

Route 28 east of **Hyannis**—unabashedly commercial and unapologe... crass—has been mucked up by overdevelopment, but you'll still find so... genteel pockets, such as **Harwichport. Chatham,** at the Cape's "elbow," ... an old-fashioned Norman Rockwell flavor. It's filled with inviting shops, and the weekly band concerts there draw standing-room-only crowds.

Past Orleans is a wind-scrubbed landscape where you're never more than a mile or two from the sea. Pretty **Wellfleet** is doing a good job of upholding the Cape's tradition of inspiring and supporting artists. Provincetown is regaining its former standing in the arts while it remains a haven for sensualists of all stripes, with a European sophistication and a New Orleans–style sense of fun. The Islands—**Nantucket** and Martha's Vineyard—are worlds unto themselves. They offer all the advantages of modern-day life (Nantucket's restaurants, in particular, regularly set new standards for the culinary vanguard), but with few of its stresses. Once you venture past the well-preserved whaling towns of **Nantucket** on Nantucket Island and **Edgartown** on Martha's Vineyard, you'll find yourself wandering amid rolling moors and scrub-oak forests, with only a few fellow escapists for company.

Except for a handful of larger towns (Falmouth, Hyannis, Provincetown) that remain active year-round, Cape Cod and the Islands recede into quietude every winter and swell again with visitors come summer. Don't underestimate the allure of the depopulated "shoulder seasons," however. In fall, the foliage casts a fiery glow across the marshlands and inland hills, and the cranberry bogs gleam with fruit. There's no pleasure so great as reveling in an all-but-empty beach on a warm Indian summer afternoon. Spring brings a fair amount of rain, but also cool bright days perfect for long walks along deserted shores.

But it's no wonder that the Cape attains its peak of popularity in summer. From Memorial Day to Labor Day, when the sand sizzles, activity heats up. Teens and young adults converge to enjoy the sun, sea, and social life; families with young children rediscover the many little miracles of surf and dune; and mature beach lovers return for their annual seaside sojourns.

Many of the Cape's visitors never make it to the attractions listed here, except perhaps during long spates of rain. They're too busy splashing in the surf, baking on the beach, engineering sand castles, or reading hefty paperback novels. It's remarkable how the days drift by, in a daze of sunny sensory pleasures. Writer Paul Theroux, who calls the Cape home for half

the year, summed up its charms succinctly in an essay for *Cape Cod Life:* "Anyone who grows tired of Cape Cod needs his head examined," he opined. "A perfect summer is a dream of childhood, idleness, and ice cream, and heat."

...cally
...ne
...s

...A'S VINEYARD,
...NANTUCKET ACCESS® is arranged so you can see at a glance where you are and what is around you. The numbers next to the entries in the following chapters correspond to the numbers on the maps. The text is color-coded according to the kind of place described:

Restaurants/Clubs: Red   **Hotels:** Blue

Shops/🌳 Outdoors: Green   **Sights/Culture:** Black

& Wheelchair accessible

Wheelchair Accessibility

An establishment (excluding a restaurant) is considered wheelchair accessible when a person in a wheelchair can easily enter a building (i.e., no steps, a ramp, a wide-enough door) without assistance. Restaurants are deemed wheelchair accessible *only* if the above applies *and* if the rest rooms are on the same floor as the dining area and their entrances and stalls are wide enough to accommodate a wheelchair.

Rating the Restaurants and Hotels

The restaurant star ratings take into account the quality, service, atmosphere, and uniqueness of the restaurant. An expensive restaurant doesn't necessarily ensure an enjoyable evening; however, a small, relatively unknown spot could have good food, professional service, and a lovely atmosphere. Therefore, on a purely subjective basis, stars are used to judge the overall dining value (see the star ratings at right). Keep in mind that chefs and owners often change, which sometimes drastically affects the quality of a restaurant. The ratings in this guidebook are based on information available at press time.

The price ratings, as categorized at right, apply to restaurants and hotels. These figures describe general price-range relationships among other restaurants and hotels in the area. The restaurant price ratings are based on the average cost of an entrée for one person, excluding tax and tip. Hotel price ratings reflect the base price of a standard room for two people for one night during the peak season.

Restaurants

★	Good	
★★	Very Good	
★★★	Excellent	
★★★★	An Extraordinary Experience	
$	The Price Is Right	(less than $10)
$$	Reasonable	($10-$15)
$$$	Expensive	($15-$25)
$$$$	Big Bucks	($25 and up)

Hotels

$	The Price Is Right	(less than $75)
$$	Reasonable	($75-$150)
$$$	Expensive	($150-$225)
$$$$	Big Bucks	($225 and up)

Map Key

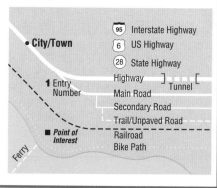

Area code 508 unless otherwise noted.

Getting to Cape Cod, Martha's Vineyard, & Nantucket

Airports

Logan International Airport (BOS)

If you are traveling by commercial airline to Cape Cod, **Boston** may be your first point of arrival. Boston's **Logan International Airport**, located three miles east of downtown, on a peninsula across the harbor from the city, services about 50 domestic and international airlines. Airlines listed below provide connecting flights or can arrange air links to points on the Cape.

Airport Services

Customs and Immigration..................800/973.2867

Ground Transportation Hotline 800/23.LOGAN

Lost and Found 617/561.1714

Police..617/561.1714

Travelers' Aid 617/567.5385

Airlines

Cape Air/Nantucket Airlines......................771.6944, ...800/352.0714

US Airways 617/428.4332, 800/428.4322

Getting to and from Logan International Airport

By Bus

Bonanza Bus Lines (548.7588, 800/556.3815) links **Logan International Airport** with **Bourne**, Falmouth, and Woods Hole. **Plymouth and Brockton Bus Lines** (775.5524) travels to Plymouth, Hyannis, and Provincetown.

LOGAN INTERNATIONAL AIRPORT (BOS)

Gate Locations for Major Airlines

A Cape Air
Colgan Air
Continental
Spirit
US Airways Shuttle
(to LaGuardia
in NY only)

B American/American Eagle
America West
Delta Shuttle
(to LaGuardia
in NY only)
Midway
Midwest Express
US Airways

C Delta
Delta Connection/
Business Express
Nations Air
TWA (domestic)
TW Express
United/United Express

D Charter Flights

E International Flights
Northwest (domestic)

Car-rental counters and baggage claim are located on the lower level.

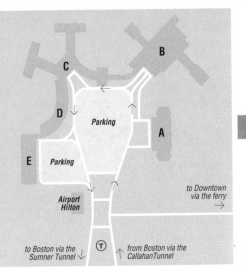

By Car
The trip from **Logan International Airport** to the bridges leading onto the Cape is about 55 miles; the distance all the way to Hyannis is about 70 miles, and traffic is often extremely congested. It's best not to plan on leaving or arriving at **Logan** during weekday rush hours, and getting onto the Cape Friday evening, or off the Cape Sunday evening, is particularly difficult.

Rental Cars
Shuttle buses will transport you from outside the terminals' baggage-claim areas to car-rental counters, which are open 24 hours a day. Car-rental companies offering services at the airport include:

Avis 617.561.3510, 800/831.2847

Budget 617/497.1800, 800/527.0700

Hertz 617/569.7272, 800/654.3131

National.....................617/569.6700, 800/227.7368

Thrifty 617/569.6500, 800/367.2277

By Limousine
You can arrange to travel from **Logan International Airport** to the Cape in style by contacting a limo service, such as **Boston Couch** (617/387.7676, 800/672.7676) or **Custom Transportation Service** (617/848.6803, 800/525.3767), or by calling the **Ground Transportation Hotline** (800/23.LOGAN). But be prepared to pay a high price for your comfort.

By Taxi
Cab stands are located at all the terminals, but fares to the Cape are expensive. At peak times, with traffic highly congested, a cab might be comparable in cost to a limousine.

Barnstable Municipal Airport
Located about a mile from **Main Street** in Hyannis, **Barnstable Municipal Airport** (775.2020) services flights from Boston and other cities and provides connections to other points on the Cape. Taxi service is available year-round, and in summer there is a trolley. **Avis** (775.2888), **Hertz** (775.5825), **National** (771.4353), and **Budget** (771.2744) provide car-rental service.

Airlines
Cape Air/Nantucket Airlines 771.6944,
....800/352.0714

Colgan Air 775.7077, 800/272.5488

Continental Express 800/525.0280

Delta 800/345.3400

Island 775.6606, 228.7575, 800/248.7779

US Airways 617/428.4332, 800/428.4322

Martha's Vineyard Airport
Martha's Vineyard Airport (693.7022) in centrally located **West Tisbury**, services flights from Boston and other cities and connecting flights to Cape points. Taxis are available, and cars may be rented from **All Island** (693.6868), **Budget** (693.7322), and **Bayside** (693.4777).

Airlines
Cape Air/Nantucket Airlines 771.6944, 800/352.0714

Continental Express 800/525.0280

United 800/241.6522

US Airways 617/428.4332, 800/428.4322

Nantucket Memorial Airport
Nantucket Memorial Airport (325.5300), located about three miles from the center of Nantucket, services flights from Boston and other cities (including Providence, RI), and to Cape points. There's taxi service into town; and cars may be rented from **Budget** (228.5666), **Hertz** (228.9421), and **Thrifty** (325.4616).

Airlines
Cape Air/Nantucket Airlines 771.6944,
....800/352.0714

Colgan Air	325.5100, 800/272.5488
Continental Express	800/525.0280
Delta	800/345.3400
Island	775.6606, 228.7575, 800/248.7779
US Airways	617/428.4332, 800/428.4322

Provincetown Municipal Airport

Located about four miles from the center of town, **Provincetown Municipal Airport** (487.0241) services flights to and from Boston; Cab service to town is available. **Budget** (487.4557) provides rental services at the airport; **U-Save** (487.6343) and **Thrifty** (487.9418), located in town, will bring the rental car to you.

Airlines

Cape Air/Nantucket Airlines .... 771.6944, ... 800/352.0714

Bus Stations (Long-Distance)

Bonanza Bus Lines (548.7588, 800/556.3815) provides service from New York City and intermediate points to the bus station in Hyannis; it also links Boston with Bourne, Falmouth, and Woods Hole. **Plymouth and Brockton Bus Lines** (775.5524) travels from Boston to Plymouth, Hyannis, and Provincetown.

Train Station (Long-Distance)

At press time there was no train service to the Cape from Boston or New York.

Getting Around Cape Cod, Martha's Vineyard, & Nantucket

Bicycles and Mopeds

Virtually flat, and crisscrossed by a growing network of bike paths, the Cape and Islands are ideal to explore by bike; see page 106 for further details. Mopeds are available for rental, too, but be forewarned: residents, especially islanders, hate them for their noise and road-hogging. Should you choose to indulge, expect some dirty looks.

Buses

Bonanza (548.7588, 800/556.3815) and **Plymouth and Brockton Bus Lines** (775.5524) connect the larger towns on the Cape. In addition, a growing number of towns operate their own free or minimal-cost shuttles during the summer. To date, these include **Dennis**, Falmouth, **Harwich**, Hyannis, Martha's Vineyard, **Mashpee**, Nantucket, Orleans, Provincetown, Woods Hole, and **Yarmouth**. Contact each town's chamber of commerce, or call the **Cape Cod Regional Transit Authority** (800/352.7155).

Driving

If you can manage without a car, you'll be doing yourself and the natives a favor, for glutted highways are one of the major headaches of summer on Cape Cod. If you do choose to drive, be forewarned: The hardest part about getting around the Cape is getting *onto* it. Only two rather narrow bridges—the **Sagamore** and Bourne—offer access. Common sense would suggest that, if possible, you avoid funneling on during the Friday-night crush, or exiting on a Sunday evening. Beyond that, a service called **SmartTraveler** (617/374.1234) uses remote cameras and airplane spotters to provide up-to-the-minute reports on congestion, as well as on parking availability at the ferry terminals.

Few people really need a car on the Islands, and getting one over by ferry is prohibitively expensive—that is, *if* you can get a reservation in the first place (see "Ferries," below). And make sure you've got return passage covered; in peak times, such as summer, reservations are often booked by early spring. All the island-bound ferries have ample pay-per-day parking available (some in satellite areas with a free shuttle bus), so car-free connections are

easy. Car rentals can be arranged on-island, if necessary, and off-the-road vehicles are permitted on certain stretches of beach at specified times; generally, a sticker is required.

The layout of the Cape, once you're on it, is not complicated, though the terminology is. While there are variations in the terms used, basically the Cape can be divided into the **Upper Cape, Mid-Cape, Lower Cape,** and **Outer Cape.** These designations have nothing to do with what's "higher" on the map; rather—as befits a nautical community—you follow the longitudes, going from upper to lower as you head east. The Outer Cape can be used to refer to the final northern sweep, reaching from the Lower Cape, or "elbow," through **Eastham** and Wellfleet up to Provincetown. Three main roads cover most of the territory. Scenic Route 6A, a historic preservation district also known as the "Army of the Grand Republic Highway," the "Cranberry Highway," and the "Old King's Highway," is the longest stretch of historic highway in the country; it started out as a native footpath and now winds leisurely along the biceps of the Cape's somewhat misshapen "arm." **Highway 6,** built for speed, not aesthetics, cuts east-west through the thickest part of the peninsula. Route 28, as you head south from the bridges, is similarly fast and utilitarian, while its sidekick, **Route 28A,** is much prettier; they join near Falmouth and then, combined as Route 28, scoop around the outer rim. At Orleans, the three main roads converge, and Highway 6 continues up the narrow forearm and into the "fist" of Provincetown (Route 6A reemerges briefly to skim the shore along **North Truro** and Provincetown). Innumerable secondary roads crisscross among the main drags, and the right zigzag could save you a lot of time—a key consideration if you're racing to catch a ferry.

Note: Beware the dreaded Massachusetts rotary, a device that strikes fear in most drivers. The rule is that those *in* the circle have the right of way and will think nothing of cutting you off. You may have to bide your time before entering. Another fiendish arrangement is the four- or even five-way stop; here diplomacy—and any instinct for self-preservation—rule.

Ferries

So beautiful are the views from these workaday vessels, tourists often take a day trip just for pleasure, even though the longer rides tend to be expensive—astronomically so if you want to bring your car. Only the **Steamship Authority** (see below) transports cars, but it and the other ferries welcome bikes, for a small fee. If you do plan to take a car, call for the **Steamship Authority**'s *Customer Service Handbook* (477.8600), as there is now a reservations-only policy for peak-summer travel (mid-May to early September) between Hyannis and Martha's Vineyard on weekends (Friday through Monday). Standbys are still allowed on the Hyannis-Nantucket run, but you'll be taking chances.

The trip to Martha's Vineyard from the Cape takes less than an hour; to Nantucket, a bit over two, unless you take the one-hour **Hy-Line** catamaran (778.0404, 800/492.8082). **Bay State Cruises** (617/457.1428) makes one six-hour round-trip from **Commonwealth Pier** in Boston to Provincetown, with a three-hour layover, daily late June through Labor Day, and Saturday and Sunday only from Memorial Day weekend through Columbus Day weekend (the latter time span is usually what is meant by "in season"). Travelers arriving from the south could take **Cape Cod Cruises** (747.2400) from Plymouth to Provincetown, in season, or **Cape Island Express** (997.1688) from **New Bedford** to **Vineyard Haven** on Martha's Vineyard. Those bound for the Vineyard from the Cape can leave from Hyannis on the **Hy-Line** *Grey Lady* catamaran to **Oak Bluffs**, in season; from Falmouth aboard the *Island Queen* (548.4800) to Oak Bluffs, in season (it boasts the quickest crossing time, only 35 minutes); from Woods Hole via the **Steamship Authority** (477.8600) to Vineyard Haven, year-round, and to Oak Bluffs (no cars allowed) in season.

Most Nantucket boats leave from Hyannis: Both the **Steamship Authority** and a **Hy-Line** catamaran run year-round. In addition, the **Freedom Cruise Line** (432.8999) runs a summer shuttle from Harwichport, and **Hy-Line** operates a ferry between Oak Bluffs and Nantucket, in season. **Cuttyhunk Boat Lines** (992.1432) makes one round-trip daily in summer to its tiny namesake island, and runs less often during the rest of the year.

Island ferries depart several times daily from Hyannis and Woods Hole, year-round; if you miss one, there's always another, or a good excuse to investigate a new bed-and-breakfast. However, rooms are virtually impossible to find in August, and nearly as hard to find in July; be sure to secure one before you show up.

Limousines

The Cape is a shirtsleeves kind of place, so there's not much call for limos. If you would like one (at the possible risk of being mistaken for a senior on prom night), **Cape and Islands Limo** in Hyannis (775.3028) serves the entire area. Provincetown is proud of its **Mercedes Cab** fleet (487.9434), which operates like regular taxis.

Parking

In addition to the lots maintained by the ferry lines, many private citizens who live near the ferry terminals convert their driveways and lawns into quick cash cows come summer. They're legitimate and usually charge slightly less than the official lots. You pay up front and estimate your time of return—a good idea in any case, lest you find yourself hemmed in. However, even these spaces tend to fill up by Friday night, so come early in the day, or arrange your trips for a less heavily traveled time. Short-term parking can be tight in many of the Cape's more heavily trafficked towns (such as Sandwich, Falmouth, and Hyannis); in Provincetown it's pretty much impossible.

Beach parking throughout the Cape, as well as on Martha's Vineyard, is a complex matter. Each town has its own sticker system, with information ordinarily available at the individual town halls (if not, your innkeeper can steer you in the right direction). You can pay by the day or week or season, but one way or another, you will pay, at all but a handful of beaches (usually not the best). The mammoth beaches within the **Cape Cod National Seashore** have fairly priced lots, but they fill up fast, so you'll have to show up early (by 10AM at least) or late in the day. Nantucket beaches are all fee-free, mirabile dictu, and depend on (1) scarce cars, and (2) careful parkers who neither block the way nor get mired in sand.

Taxis

Virtually all the towns on the Cape have cab companies; the Islands have many. Check the Yellow Pages of the phone book or ask your innkeeper. Most charge a set fee, rather than by the mile.

Tours

Among the dozen or so companies offering bus tours to the Cape and the Islands are **Brush Hill Tours** (617/986.6100), **Maupintour** (913/843.1211, 800/255.4266), and **Tauck Tours** (203/226.6911, 800/468.2825). On Martha's Vineyard, **Adam Wilson** of **AdamCab** (693.3332, 800/281.4462) gives an excellent van tour of the island. On Nantucket, the van to catch is that of sixth-generation native Gail Johnson of **Gail's Tours** (257.6557); islander **Andrea Dougan** (228.1861) gives walking tours.

Trolleys

Two towns offer narrated sight-seeing trolleys: Provincetown and Plymouth. In addition, a growing number of towns offer free or low-cost intra-town shuttles to ease traffic congestion.

Walking

The best way to take in the area's architectural riches is on foot. Among the more visually rewarding enclaves are Sandwich, Yarmouthport, and **Chatham on the Cape**, plus Oak Bluffs and Edgartown on the Vineyard, and the town of Nantucket. Beach and nature walks are available in virtually unlimited abundance.

FYI

Accommodations

Lodgings range from casual, sprawling resorts to exquisite little inns. Many bed-and-breakfasts operate like luxurious mini-hotels, with the hosts a combination of concierge, cook, cicerone, and (in some cases) newfound friend. They make up in personal attention for whatever they may lack in square footage, and the furnishings tend to feed fantasies of idyllic country life. Virtually every bed-and-breakfast on the Cape also packs a lot of history; many are on the National Register of Historic Places. The **Massachusetts Office of Travel and Tourism** (617/727.3201, 800/447.6277) offers a free statewide bed-and-breakfast guide.

Make reservations ahead of time, especially for accommodations during the peak summer season. **Destinnations** (800/374.4667), a reservation service representing several dozen outstanding inns throughout New England, can arrange an itinerary custom-tailored to special interests or just general enjoyment; a fee is charged. **Bed and Breakfast Cape Cod** (775.2772, 800/686.5252) can help you find lodgings from their listings of over 100 bed-and-breakfasts around the Cape; there is a booking fee. **Orleans Bed and Breakfast** (255.3824, 800/541.6226) serves the Lower and Outer Cape Cod, for a charge; call for a brochure. The **Provincetown Reservation System** (487.2400, 800/648.0364) will book restaurants as well as lodgings; no fee is charged.

Climate

The climate on Cape Cod is relatively mild in summer and winter. There's rarely more than a few inches of snow in January and February; then there's about an equal amount of rain every month for the rest of the year. Vacationers may not much relish the precipitation, but they do appreciate the fact that when inland Massachusetts broils through the dog days of August, the Cape and Islands generally stay breezy and cool. Old hands pack a cotton sweater and windbreaker even for summer jaunts, since a brisk wind off the ocean can chill you to the bone.

Months	Average Temperature (°F)
January-March	35
April-June	50-55
July-September	70
October-December	50-55

Drinking

The legal drinking age is 21, and IDs are checked for those whose age appears questionable. Should you be "carded," the only acceptable ID is a Massachusetts driver's license or a state liquor-identification card, issued by the state Registry of Motor Vehicles. At smaller restaurants without a liquor license, you're usually welcome to bring wine or beer (call ahead to confirm). On Martha's Vineyard, all the towns except Edgartown and Oak Bluffs are "dry," so bring your own if you want to drink.

Hours

Opening and closing hours for shops, attractions, coffeehouses, tearooms, etc., are listed by day(s) only if normal hours apply (opening between 8 and 11AM and closing between 4 and 7PM). In all other cases, specific hours will be given (e.g., 6AM-2PM; daily 24 hours; noon-5PM). The "season" on the Cape is generally defined as Memorial Day weekend to Labor Day; however, some use the term to include July and August only. It's a good idea to call ahead in June or September, and definitely in the off-season between September and June, when schedules may vary depending on customer demand, personal whim, and the weather.

Money

ATMs are ubiquitous throughout the Cape and Islands; among the largest banks is **BankBoston** (800/788.5000). **Fleet Bank** (800/841.4000) and **Cape Cod Bank and Trust** (800/458.5100) both have branches across the Cape. Foreign currencies may be exchanged at some Cape banks, but be sure to call ahead to confirm. Traveler's checks and credit cards are widely accepted.

Personal Safety

For the most part, the Cape and Islands are still so rural and peaceful that you might be tempted to leave your car unlocked—but it's not a good idea. Car theft may not run rampant here, but it's always a risk. The lifestyle is casual, so leave expensive jewelry and other valuables safe at home. In the more populous towns (e.g., Hyannis and Provincetown), you'll want to exercise the usual caution regarding pocketbooks and cameras.

A more pressing concern than pickpockets is another kind of parasite, the Lyme disease–carrying tick, prevalent in tall grass and brush, particularly in April through October. As a precaution when hiking, wear light-colored trousers (the better to spot the suckers) tucked into socks, and stick to the center of the trail. Spray your clothes (not skin) with a DEET-based insecticide, and inspect for ticks often. If you find one lodged in your skin, pull it upward from its head area with tweezers, taking care not to squeeze the body (which could spread the infection). Then disinfect the skin with alcohol and take the tick and yourself to a doctor. A rash consisting of a red-rimmed blotch(es) may signal an undetected bite. If you see signs of any rash, even later, have it checked out. For further information, contact the **Massachusetts Department of Public Health** (617/983.6800) or the **Lyme Disease Foundation** (860/525.2000). A milder threat is poison ivy, which you can avert by avoiding plants with a cluster of three shiny green leaves, and alleviate by thoroughly washing the affected area immediately after contact.

Publications

Cape Cod Life, a bimonthly, covers local issues and pleasures. Every June, Boston magazine publishes a well-informed, up-to-date guide to the Cape, with a table listing the relative merits of and facilities to be found at the public beaches (the latter information also is in the phone book). Other glossies include Provincetown Arts (an annual) and Martha's Vineyard and Nantucket magazines, which come out four times a year from spring through fall. The Cape Cod Times is the daily paper for the region, and Provincetown, Martha's Vineyard, and Nantucket have two worthwhile weekly papers apiece. Among the freebies you'll find, The Little Yellow Cape Cod Guide is worth picking up for its useful information and discount coupons.

Radio Stations

AM:

1170	WKPE	South Dennis	Easy Listening
1240	WBUR	Boston	National Public Radio

FM:

90.3	WCCT	Hyannis	National Public Radio
91.9	WOMR	Provincetown	Education/Variety
92.7	WMVY	Vineyard Haven	Album Rock/Jazz
93.5	WJCO	Hyannis	Adult Contemporary
94.9	WXTK	West Yarmouth	News and Talk
96.3	WRZE	Hyannis	Adult Contemporary
99.9	WQRC	Hyannis	Adult Contemporary
101.1	WWKJ	Falmouth	Classic Rock
101.9	WCIB	Falmouth	Easy Listening
102.9	WPXC	Hyannis	Classic Rock
103.9	WOCN	South Yarmouth	Pop Standards
104.7	WKPE	Orleans	Rock 'n' Roll
106.1	WCOD	Hyannis	Adult Contemporary
107.5	WFCC	Chatham	Classical

Television Stations

Cape 11 News originates in Yarmouth. Boston television stations also are received on Cape Cod.

Restaurants

The Cape's idea of fine dining used to be bland, boring "family" restaurants offering undistinguished seafood, but now its many outstanding dining rooms are in the forefront of the New American culinary revolution. However fancy and pricey the venue, jackets are almost never required (the four-star establishments might warrant a call just to check). Reserve well ahead in peak season, especially on weekends, or be prepared to eat either early (around 6PM) or late (around 10PM).

Shopping

T-shirt shops aside, the Cape and Islands offer top-quality shopping for clothing and decorative items. Among the better towns for browsing are Chatham, Edgartown, Nantucket, Provincetown, and Wellfleet. The stores that remain open late into the fall or winter are apt to offer fantastic discounts.

Smoking

Smoking ordinances vary from town to town (and sometimes, it would seem, from restaurant to restaurant). The larger restaurants all offer a nonsmoking section, and some of the bigger hotels offer nonsmoking rooms. An increasing number of bed-and-breakfasts are adopting no-smoking policies, so inquire before you book.

Taxes

In Massachusetts, a five-percent tax is charged on all purchases except services, on food bought in stores (not restaurants), and on items of clothing less than $175. There is also a hotel tax that can run as high as 9.7 percent, depending on the location.

Telephones

Local calls cost 25 cents from a pay phone; however, calls between counties are usually long distance. Long-distance credit calls can be initiated by dialing "0" before the area code and number. Some hotels charge extra for calls made from the room. Usually the fee is posted; if not, ask or look for a pay phone.

Time Zone

The region, like all of New England, is located in the Eastern Time Zone.

Tipping

The norm for restaurant meals is 15 percent of the pretax total; 20 percent signals appreciation for exceptional service, or a patron particularly mindful that tips account for a major portion of a worker's wages for the season. Personal services usually entail a tip of 15 to 20 percent. It's customary to give a dollar or more for help in carrying bags and leave a dollar or so per day for housekeeping services.

Visitors' Information Centers

Every town's chamber of commerce operates an information office and disseminates useful literature. For the name of each, call information, or start your inquiries with the umbrella organization, the **Cape Cod Chamber of Commerce** (362.3225). The Hyannis branch's information number (800/449.6647) is available year-round.

Cape Cod Indians used the largest of local clams, called a surf clam (Mactra solidissima), as a hoe for their gardens.

Phone Book

Emergencies
AAA Emergency Road Service 800/222.4357
Ambulance/Fire/Police 911
Cape Cod Hospital 771.1800
Coast Guard Search/Rescue 457.3210
Massachusetts Dental Society 800/342.8747
Missing Persons 800/622.5999
Outer Cape Health 487.9395
Poison Hotline 800/682.9211
Traveler's Aid 617/542.7286

Visitors' Information
American Youth Hostels 202/783.6161
Amtrak 800/872.7245
Massachusetts Office of Travel and Tourism
................................617/727.3201, 800/447.6277
SmartTraveler (for latest travel conditions)
....617/374.1234
Time 617/637.1234
US Customs 800/973.2867
US Passport Office 617/565.6990

Cape Cod on the Calendar

In the Cape's variegated townships, civic pride takes the shape of seasonal festivals—some held to celebrate a harvest, special date, or event, others (one can't help suspecting) mostly to attract tourists in the off-season. Motivation aside, these celebrations offer enjoyable occasions to mingle with the locals—and handy ways to keep the kids entertained.

April

Daffodil Festival During the last weekend of the month, **Nantucket** celebrates this event with masses of flowers and over 100 decorated antique cars that congregate in **Siasconset** for a colorful tailgate picnic, held after the seven-mile parade from Nantucket town. For more information, call 228.1700.

May

Cape Maritime Week Cultural organizations throughout the Cape mount special events during the second week of the month to highlight the region's illustrious oceangoing past. One such celebration is **Yarmouth Maritime Days,** which includes free admission to the historic **Winslow Crocker House** and **Captain Bangs Hallett House**. For more information, call 800/732.1008.

Figawi Sailboat Race The race from **Hyannis** to Nantucket is the largest gathering of its kind on the East Coast. It takes place on the last weekend in May and a celebratory victory tent is raised on Nantucket. For more information, call 228.1700 or 800/449.6647.

Spring Plant Festival in **Sandwich** This event celebrates the bloom of **Heritage Plantation of Sandwich**'s famous Dexter rhododendron. It's held on 28 May, when the Dexter is at peak color, and includes lectures, plant sales, and tours. For more information, call 888.3300.

June

Antique Show Over 50 top antiques dealers from around New England display their wares at the **Heritage Plantation of Sandwich** the first weekend of the month. For more information, call 888.3300.

Harborfest Held the first weekend of the month, this celebration brings in tall ships and mobs of chowder-tasters to Nantucket. There's also a **Pirate and Mermaid Parade** and sailboat or tugboat tours of the harbor. For more information, call 228.1700.

Cape Heritage Week Fifty historically significant sites and museums put together special tours, presentations, and exhibits throughout the Cape during the second week of the month. For more information, call 362.3828 or 888.1234.

Nantucket Film Festival Both shorts and feature-length films are shown during this five-day event in mid-month; there are also staged readings, panel discussions, and screenplay competitions. For more information, call 228.1700.

Provincetown Portuguese Festival This celebration of ethnic heritage on the last weekend of the month combines a **Blessing of the Fleet** with fado music, a block dance, a cultural bazaar featuring gifts and food, fireworks, and a parade with marching bands. For more information, call 487.3424 or 800/637.8696.

July

Mashpee Wampanoag Pow Wow All are welcome to observe traditional Native American dances and other time-honored rituals—including fireball soccer—in **Mashpee** on the Fourth of July weekend. For more information, call 477.0208.

Great New Bedford Summerfest Also on the Fourth of July weekend, this celebration includes fireworks, a carnival, a tall ships regatta, whale boat races, a concert, and a **Blessing of the Fleet.** For more information, call 800/288.6263.

dgartown Regatta This
ace, held the third
weekend of the
month, attracts the
sleekest of yachts.
For more
information, call
627.4361.

Barnstable County Fair An
old-fashioned agricultural gathering, complete with
livestock competitions, is the big attraction in **East
Falmouth** during the last weekend in the month.
Baking contests, a petting zoo, and horse pulls
are just a sampling of the activities. For more
information, call 563.3200.

Antique Auto Show and Competition The **Heritage
Plantation of Sandwich** attracts about a hundred
outstanding (and still operating) vintage cars from all
over New England on the last weekend of the month.
For more information, call 888.1222 or 888.3300.

August

Possible Dreams Auction The resident celebrities of
Martha's Vineyard turn out for this annual charitable
event on the first weekend of the month. Breakfast
with Carly Simon is one of the offerings. For more
information, call 693.7900.

Carnival Week The peak of the gay
summer season is observed with
entertainment, cocktail parties, and a
costume parade in Provincetown during
the third week of the month. For more
information, call 487.2313 or
800/637.8696.

**Martha's Vineyard Agricultural Society Livestock
Show and Fair** Held the third week of August, this

annual event at the **West
Tisbury Fairgrounds**
reveals how much hard
work goes on at the many
farms on the island in this
summer playground. For
more information, call
693.4343.

September

Provincetown Harbor Swim for Life The annual
charity swim, which benefits the local AIDS
organizations, is preceded by a **Celebration of Life
Concert** and followed by a **Mermaid Brunch** at the
Boatslip and then a **Festival of Happiness**, held at
Herring Cove Beach at sunset. It all takes place on
the first Saturday of the month. For more
information, call 487.3684.

October

Women's Week The Women Innkeepers of
Provincetown organization arranges a series of
activities, including entertainment, sports events,
excursions, and workshops, during the second week
of the month. For more information, call
800/933.1963.

Fantasia Fair Transvestites converge on
Provincetown the third week of the month for this
extravaganza. A costume ball and talent show are
featured, and there is a wine tasting at **The
Provincetown Art Association and Museum.** For
more information, call 800/637.8696.

Cranberry Harvest Festival Nantucket celebrates
the harvesting of this tart native fruit on the third
weekend of the month, as colorful leaves fall all
around. There is a bogs tour, cranberry cookery
contest, and open house at several historic inns. For
more information, call 228.1700.

Trash Fish Banquet A delectable
seafood feast that focuses
on underutilized species
is held on the third
weekend of the month in
Provincetown. Sponsored by the
town's restaurants, the banquet benefits
the Center for Coastal Studies. For more
information, call 487.3622.

Halloween For a transformative night, Provincetown
is the place to be on 31 October. For more
information, call 487.3424 or 800/637.8696.

November

Lighting of the Pilgrim Monument The ceremony,
which takes place on Thanksgiving eve, adds a
dramatic new highlight to the Provincetown skyline
when all 5,000 lights climbing the 255-foot
monument are illuminated. The lighting coincides
with the first landing of the Pilgrims in Provincetown.
For more information, call 487.3424.

Nantucket Noel The island's month of holiday
festivities begins the day after Thanksgiving with a
Christmas tree lighting ceremony for the trees lining
Main Street and community caroling. For more
information, call 228.1700.

December

Christmas Stroll Most of
Nantucket's shops,
restaurants, and inns reopen
briefly for the first weekend
of the month. Summerers
flock back in droves for
one last idyllic visit.
There's also seasonal
entertainment. Several
communities, such as Sandwich,
Falmouth, and **Orleans,** mount similar festivities.

Holly Days The **Ashumet Holly and Wildlife
Sanctuary** in Falmouth holds this event featuring
fresh-cut greens and refreshments during the first
two weekends of the month. For more information,
call 800/637.8696.

New Year's Eve Several towns, including Falmouth,
Hyannis, **Chatham,** Provincetown, and **Vineyard
Haven,** have caught **First Night** fever from Boston
and celebrate the changing of the year with free or
low-cost cultural events.

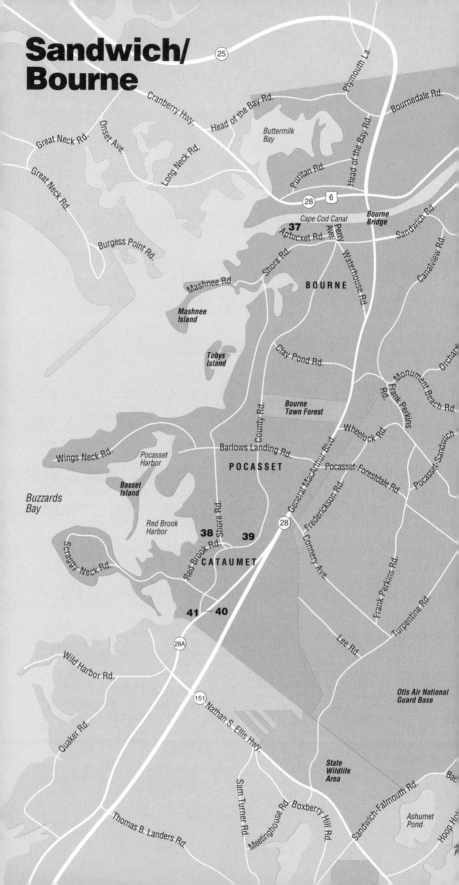

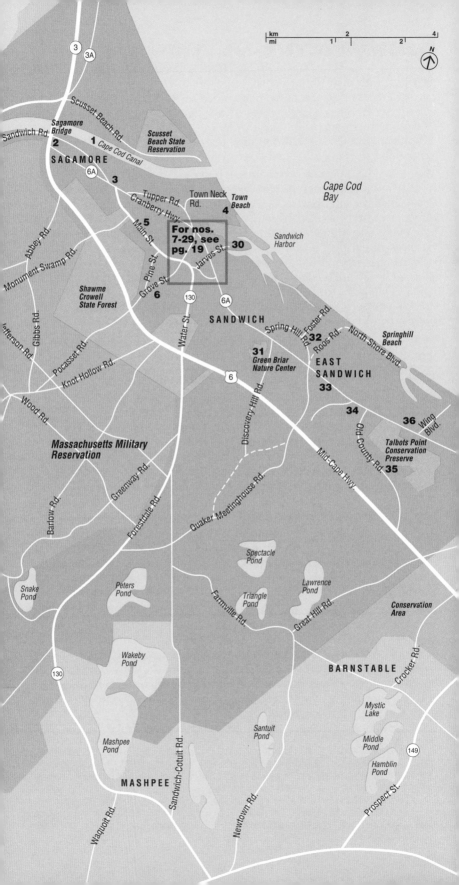

km
mi
1
2
2
4

N

③
3A

Scusset Beach Rd.

Sandwich Rd.

Sagamore
Bridge

1 Cape Cod Canal

Scusset
Beach State
Reservation

Cape Cod
Bay

2

SAGAMORE

6A

3

Tupper Rd.

Town Neck
Rd.

**Town
Beach**

Cranberry Hwy.

4

5

Main St.

For nos.
7-29, see
pg. 19

30

Sandwich
Harbor

Abbey Rd.

Pine St.

Jarves St.

Monument Swamp Rd.

Grove St.

6

130

6A

Shawme
Crowell
State Forest

SANDWICH

Spring Hill Rd.

Foster Rd.

32

Roos Rd.

North Shore Blvd.

**Springhill
Beach**

Jefferson Rd.

Gibbs Rd.

Pocasset Rd.

Water St.

6

31
Green Briar
Nature Center

**EAST
SANDWICH**

Knot Hollow Rd.

33

Wood Rd.

34

Old County Rd.

36

Wing Blvd.

**Massachusetts Military
Reservation**

Discovery Hill Rd.

Mid-Cape Hwy.

**Talbots Point
Conservation
Preserve**

35

Barlow Rd.

Greenway Rd.

Forestdale Rd.

Quaker Meetinghouse Rd.

Spectacle
Pond

Lawrence
Pond

**Conservation
Area**

Snake
Pond

Peters
Pond

Farmville Rd.

Triangle
Pond

Great Hill Rd.

Crocker Rd.

BARNSTABLE

130

Wakeby
Pond

Mystic
Lake

Mashpee
Pond

Sandwich-Cotuit Rd.

Santuit
Pond

Middle
Pond

149

Hamblin
Pond

MASHPEE

Waquoit Rd.

Newtown Rd.

Prospect St.

Sandwich/Bourne

Founded in 1637 by a splinter group of Puritans, Sandwich is the oldest town on Cape Cod. According to Plymouth Colony records, "tenn men from Saugust" (now the town of Lynn in Massachusetts) were granted "liberty to view a place to sitt down & have sufficient lands for three score famylies." Having found a site rich in local resources—plentiful fish, fresh water, and salt marsh hay as fodder for their livestock—these men did indeed "sitt down," naming their rough-hewn settlement for the town of Sandwich in Kent, England, also renowned for its salt marsh.

The New World Sandwich remained a bucolic retreat, favored for its prolific trout streams (statesman Daniel Webster purportedly hooked a few big ones here), until the 1820s, when Boston glass merchant Deming Jarves turned it into an industrial center virtually overnight. Jarves recognized in Sandwich an ideal glass-manufacturing site: It had plenty of virgin forest to fuel the furnaces, hay for packing the output, and if the local sand wasn't quite up to snuff, no matter; there was a good harbor, so the raw material could be shipped in. By mid-century, the tiny town had two factories that made every type of glassware, from purely decorative knickknacks to strictly functional drinking vessels. These companies eventually put Sandwich on the map as one of the foremost glass capitals of the world.

Sandwich's industrial boom was short-lived. In the 1860s and 1870s, competition from coal-powered plants in the Midwest cut into the market, diminishing the demand for the more expensive Cape Cod–produced glass, and in 1888 the Boston & Sandwich Glass Company shut down for good. But the town was rejuvenated when the first wave of automobile-borne tourists arrived in the 1920s. To the delight of visitors, Sandwich has a town center that is the very picture of a pristine New England village. Captains' houses of the Federal period—typically white clapboards with black trim—still lend a formal grace to the tree-shaded streets. And prescient planners and generous local benefactors have made sure colonial-era buildings such as the carefully restored **Hoxie House** and **Dexter Grist Mill** remain intact and open to the public.

Although Sandwich's bayside beaches don't begin to match the wild beauty of the vast, unspoiled oceanside stretches of the Outer Cape, they certainly suffice for sunbathing, swimming, and perhaps a sunset stroll. Sandwich attracts a more affluent and somewhat older beach-oriented crowd than the towns from Orleans up to Provincetown. A major draw are the exceptional museums, including the **Heritage Plantation**, a 76-acre complex encompassing noted collections of folk art, and the **Sandwich Glass Museum**.

West of Sandwich is the town of Bourne (which split off in 1864, naming itself for a New Bedford whaling magnate and philanthropist), a place that is primarily rural and decidedly private, making few concessions to attract tourists. Summer homes here have descended through generations, and the inhabitants are content to savor the simpler pleasures of Cape life—intensive gardening, swimming in the protected and relatively warm waters of **Buzzards Bay**, and bicycling along winding country roads. Focus on the quiet beauty of the place and you'll understand why Bourne residents are happy just to stay put.

---

1 Cape Cod Canal The idea of constructing this remarkable 17.4-mile waterway was under discussion as early as the 17th century, and was championed by such prominent figures as Myles Standish and George Washington. But it was New York financier Augustus Perry Belmont who finally saw the plan through. Having beat the completion of the Panama Canal by a scant, but significant, 17 days, Belmont captained the triumphant opening parade of boats on 29 July 1914. Among the notables on hand was Assistant Secretary of the Navy Franklin D. Roosevelt. (Though Belmont gave financial backing to the project, it never garnered him much monetary reward, and when it was sold to the US government for $11.5 million in 1928, the bondholders—who had put up $16 million—suffered a loss.)

Under the jurisdiction of the US Army Corps of Engineers (USACE) since 1917, the canal remains the world's widest sea-level canal—480 feet—and transports some 20,000 vessels yearly. Because of strong currents (and busy marine traffic), it's off limits to swimmers. The banks, however, have been turned into a greensward popular with bicyclists, who enjoy seven miles of paved paths on each side. The USACE staff offer "bike hikes" from the Buzzards Bay railroad bridge, guided walks around Sagamore Hill (starting at the entrance to **Scusset State Reservation**), and other interpretive programs. ♦ 759.5991 &

2 Christmas Tree Shops These giant emporia—with seven locations on the Cape, others elsewhere in New England—have nothing at all to do with Christmas, except in the spending sense. Off-price housewares crowd an outsized pseudo-Elizabethan thatch cottage, where you can pick up the odd bargain on such items as lawn furniture, gardening supplies, books, toys, even gourmet foodstuffs. How about some fluorescent shoelaces? ♦ Daily 8AM-11PM Apr–late Oct; daily 9AM-9PM late Oct–Mar. 9 Rte 6A (between Adams St and the Sagamore Bridge), Sagamore. 888.7010 & Also at: 655 Rte 132 (just west of Airport Rotary), Hyannis. 778.5521 &; Falmouth Plaza, Rte 28 (at Falmouth Heights Rd), Falmouth. 548.1414 &; Rtes 28 and 6A, Orleans. 255.8494 &

2 The Bridge ★★$$ You might not give this ho-hum–looking restaurant a second glance, but inside, the Prete family has been turning out excellent Italian food (homemade minestrone, tortellini, and more) since 1953. Chef and daughter-in-law Pon has added her Thai spring rolls and *padt ka prow gai* (chicken with basil, garlic, and peppers), as well as the refreshing *yum nuer* (sliced sirloin marinated in lemon, peppers, scallions, and spices, served cold with jasmine rice). ♦ Italian/Thai ♦ Daily lunch and dinner. 21 Rte 6A (between Adams St and the Sagamore Bridge), Sagamore. 888.8144

CRYSTAL BY Pairpoint

2 Crystal by Pairpoint Combining 18th-century techniques introduced by Deming Jarves, founder of the Boston & Sandwich Glass Company, and by Thomas J. Pairpoint, a leading glass designer of the 1880s, the Pairpoint line has been prized by collectors practically since its inception. Among the less expensive items are commemorative "cup plates." Ascending the price scale are handblown candlesticks and decorative koi fish. It's fascinating to watch this ancient craft applied to tomorrow's collectibles. ♦ Daily. Glassblowing demonstrations: M-F. Rte 6A (opposite rear of Christmas Tree Shop), Sagamore. 888.2344, 800/899.0953 &

3 Sagamore Inn ★$$ For your first glimpse of "corny old Cape Cod" (an increasingly scarce commodity), duck into this classic 1920s roadhouse with wooden booths and tin ceiling. The food may not be anything to write home about, but it's cheap and plentiful, and you can't go wrong with the steamers—longneck clams to be dunked in their own broth, then in melted butter. For connoisseurs of classic diner fare, there's pot roast and grapenut pudding. ♦ American/Takeout ♦ M, W-Su lunch and dinner Apr-Nov. 1131 Rte 6A (between Tupper and Sandwich Rds), Sagamore. 888.9707 &

horizons on cape cod bay

4 Horizons on Cape Cod Bay ★★$$ Make a beeline for the bay, and this is the first scenic eatery you'll find. The airy interior is generic collegiate, with pennants decorating the rafters, but the deck basks in a broad bay view that is spectacular at sunset. Try a fried clam roll, the Cape's ubiquitous low-cost delicacy. And if you have a large group, you can arrange to have a traditional New England clambake, right on the beach. ♦ American ♦ Daily lunch and dinner Apr–late Oct. 98 Town Neck Rd (at Freeman Ave), Sandwich. 888.6166 &

4 Bay Beach B&B $$$ This modern six-bedroom bed-and-breakfast offers all one could ask in terms of setting, privacy, and luxury. It's right on a private stretch of **Town Beach,** with a view of the marsh boardwalk and (on a clear day) Provincetown. The unobtrusive owners live next door. There are two sitting rooms: One doubles as an exercise room, with a Stairmaster and Lifecycle, and the other suits more sedentary types who prefer a good book, comfortable couch, and crackling fire. Rooms are spacious and thoughtfully equipped, right down to the CD players and Jacuzzis-for-two. ♦ 1-3 Bay Beach La (off Freeman Ave), Sandwich. 888.8813, 800/475.6398

5 Dillingham House $ Built by one of the town founders, this circa 1650 house—a three-quarters Cape—reputedly harbored a backroom bar during Prohibition. The former tack room, with its wood stove, grand piano, and loads of books, games, and puzzles, is a great place to hang out when the weather's uncooperative. When the outdoors beckon, guests have the use of house bicycles. There are four not too fancy, but nice enough—and well-priced—guest rooms. ♦ 71 Main St (near Burbank St), Sandwich. 833.0065

6 Heritage Plantation of Sandwich You could—and probably should—devote at least a half-day to savoring this complex's various components. Set on 76 acres of landscaped grounds, these museums showcase a strange and enchanting amalgam of Americana assembled by relatives and friends in honor of Josiah Kirby Lilly, of pharmaceutical fame.

For instance, a reconstructed Shaker round barn (copied from the real thing in Hancock, Massachusetts) houses antique automobiles from the era when cars were dazzling chariots of steel. Among the holdings is Gary Cooper's snazzy 1930 Duesenberg. The military museum features an exhibit of Native American artifacts, including a striking Haida blanket made of gray and red wool and decorated with mother-of-pearl buttons. The high point of the art museum is a free, working indoor carousel (circa 1912) with 32 hand-carved creatures, including a giraffe and a goat. An ostrich, frog footman, and other peculiar turn-of-the-century mounts are stationed around it in the glassed-in room.

An open jitney carts visitors around the property, but the grounds, with labeled flora, invite self-propelled exploration on foot. This is especially true in May and June, when the carefully bred rhododendrons burst forth in infinitely varied shades of delicate pink. ♦ Admission. Daily mid-May–Oct. Grove St and Shawme Rd, Sandwich. 888.3300 &

Within the Heritage Plantation of Sandwich:

Carousel Cafe ★$ This gourmet snack bar offers soups (including chowder and gazpacho), salads, and overstuffed sandwiches. Enjoy it all under a striped green tent. Grab a tasty cranberry cookie for a portable dessert. ♦ Snack bar ♦ Daily lunch and snacks. 888.3300 &

7 Old Cemetery Point It stands to reason that the Cape's oldest town would have some of its most ancient graves. This knoll overlooking Shawme Pond has lots of well-kept tombstones (dating from 1683) sporting pithy admonitions and winged death's heads. Most are hand-hewn. You may find it interesting later to match up the various "Here lyes ye body of" with figures whose family names are still bandied about town. ♦ Grove St (between Shawme Rd and Main St), Sandwich

8 H. Richard Strand Antiques This fine 1800 emporium carries only the best furniture, china, and glass, all beautifully arrayed in formal settings. Early in the season it looks almost like a person's house rather than a shop—albeit a house inhabited by an incurable collector. The quantity of holdings gradually diminishes as the summer progresses, but the quality remains constant. ♦ Daily. 2 Grove St (between Academy Rd and Main St), Sandwich. 888.3230

9 Town Hall Built in 1834 at a cost of $4,138 to accommodate Sandwich's boomtown business, this plain and boxy Greek Revival beauty with four Doric columns as understated decoration was made to last. It's still in use as the center of town government. ♦ Main St (at Water St), Sandwich. 888.0340 &

10 The Inn at Sandwich Center $$ This 1750s saltbox, aggrandized with an 1850s Federal roofline, has five inviting bedrooms decorated in bold bright colors. Owners Eliane and Al Thomas serve all homemade foods for breakfast—scones, muffins, breads, pastries, even homemade butter. Ask to see the beehive oven's chimney, crafted of clamshell plaster. Centrally located right across the street from the **Sandwich Glass Museum**, the inn is peacefully situated on its own hillock. ♦ 118 Tupper Rd (at Main St), Sandwich. 888.6958, 800/249.6949

11 Sandwich Glass Museum Half the history of the town is encased in this extensive collection of glassware, much of it displayed to optimal effect along banks of sunny windows. A good succinct video introduction explains the rise and fall of the business from 1825 to 1888. Deming Jarves's glass-production system, utilizing local resources and a mostly immigrant workforce, initially worked

---

Restaurants/Clubs: Red   Hotels: Blue

Shops/ 🎋 Outdoors: Green   Sights/Culture: Black

so well that even citizens of modest means could afford glassware. His enterprise went swimmingly, until coal-powered Midwestern plants undercut and outproduced him. Jarves's ill-timed recourse was to attempt a return to handblown glassmaking just as his labor force was beginning to bridle after decades of exploitation. His business crashed and burned—but the glassware it created lives on, to be prized by collectors. Even non-aficionados will find much to admire in the products on display, from dolphin-motif candlesticks to pressed "lacy" glass.

The museum is owned and staffed by the nonprofit Sandwich Historical Society, and the volunteer docents are happy to fill in with local lore. A gift shop on the premises features related literature and reproductions of Sandwich classics, as well as contemporary work by Cape Cod artisans. ♦ Admission. Daily Apr-Oct; W-Su Feb-Mar, Nov-Dec. 129 Main St (at Tupper Rd), Sandwich. 888.0251 &

12 First Church of Christ Built in 1847 by **Charles Bulfinch** associate **Isaac Melvin** of Cambridge, and evidently influenced by the designs of **Sir Christopher Wren** (the spire resembles **Wren**'s masterpiece, St. Mary-le-Bow in London), this elegant church counterposes ornate Corinthian columns (two sets, one miniaturized in the cupola) and a chunky geometric design. The result is at once down-to-earth and celestial. ♦ Service: Su 10AM. 136 Main St (at Water St), Sandwich. 888.0434 &

13 Dexter Grist Mill During the glass factories' heyday, this circa 1640 mill, built by Thomas Dexter, was one of several turbine-powered workhorses. Its output became obsolete in the 1880s (coal-powered Western mills could provide flour more cheaply), and it sat idle until the 1920s, when Alice Harvey turned it into a tearoom to attract the new wave of motoring tourists. In the late 1950s, the defunct mills surrounding it were demolished, and in 1961 it reopened as a working mill—and tourist attraction.

Using a cypress wood waterwheel and wooden gears (the oldest form of milling machinery in the country) powered by pond overflow, today town miller (and school-teacher) Leo R. Manning churns out cornmeal. In addition to colonial staples like johnnycakes and Indian pudding, the organically grown cornmeal sold here in cloth bags makes terrific polenta. Ask for recipes. The mill is also a popular spot with Shawme Pond's feathered friends: a dozen or so swans, geese, and ducks are usually in attendance. ♦ Admission. M-Sa; Su 1-4:45PM mid-June–mid-Sept. Sa-Su 1-4:40PM mid-May–mid-June, mid-Sept–mid-Oct. Off Water St (south of Main St), Sandwich. 888.1173

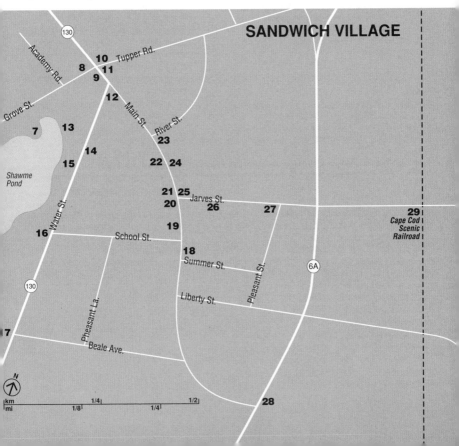

SANDWICH VILLAGE

Shawme Pond

Cape Cod Scenic Railroad

14 Dunbar House $$ Mike and Mary Bell, teachers from Somerset, England, rescued this 1741 house from two decades of dereliction in 1990. They've made the most of its prime location (opposite the **Dexter Grist Mill** and Shawme Pond), turning the house into a charming bed-and-breakfast. Each of the three guestrooms is pleasantly, if not dazzlingly, decorated, and guests are treated to home-cooked breakfasts as well as afternoon tea. ♦ 1 Water St (between School and Main Sts), Sandwich. 833.2485 &

On the grounds of the Dunbar House:

Dunbar Tea Shop ★★$ This carriage house–turned–tea shop boasts a wonderful blend of antiques, gifts, British comestibles, and new and old books. The tearoom, with its wood stove, couldn't be cozier in winter; come summer, tables are set up in the unstudied splendor of the garden. Lunches feature savories, quiches, and such specials as vol-au-vent (pastry shell filled with a ragout of meat or fish); sweets include pies, scones, Scottish shortbread, and wickedly rich "Trafalgar squares." ♦ Tearoom ♦ Daily. 833.2485 &

15 Thornton W. Burgess Museum Local boy and avid conservationist Thornton W. Burgess (1874-1965) wrote 15,000 children's stories and 170 books, some of which may seem a bit musty to modern eyes. But little children love this tiny museum with its original illustrations by Harrison Cady, puzzles and games, gift shop, and, best of all, live-animal story times (with a real critter on hand) during the summer.

The 1756 cottage, known as the **Eldred House,** was the home of Burgess's eccentric aunt, Arabella Eldred Burgess, a teacher who claimed to communicate verbally with both wildlife and plants. A "tussie-mussie" garden shaped like a nosegay and an inviting "touch and smell" garden filled with aromatic herbs flourish outside. The museum, along with the **Green Briar Nature Center & Jam Kitchen,** is currently operated by the T.W. Burgess Society, a nonprofit organization conceived by local bookseller Nancy Titcomb to commemorate his works and keep alive his philosophy. ♦ Donation. M-Sa, Su 1-4PM Apr-Nov. 4 Water St (south of Main St), Sandwich. 888.4668

16 Hoxie House Built circa 1675 by Reverend John Smith and named for whaling captain Abraham Hoxie, who bought the house in 1860 for $400, this archetypal saltbox is one of the oldest houses on the Cape. It is difficult to date many of the Cape's "first period" houses—those built between 1620 and 1725—with precision because an 1827 fire at the **Barnstable County Court House** destroyed many ancient deeds. The remarkable thing about this saltbox is that it was occupied as is, without benefit of modern amenities, up into the 1950s. In 1960 the house was disassembled, de-Victorianized, and, with about 50 percent of its original materials intact (including some two-foot-wide planks), opened to the public. A few of its exquisitely sparse furnishings, faithful to the era, are borrowed from Boston's Museum of Fine Arts. ♦ Admission. M-Sa; Su 1-5PM mid-June–mid-Sept. 18 Water St (south of Main St). 888.1173

17 Quail Hollow Farm The produce and gourmet foods displayed at this picturesque, nicely weathered 1840 barn look almost too attractive to eat, and the prices (unposted) make them seem too expensive to buy. But this is a good place to go if you're willing to splurge. Try the locally made canned goods (such as jalapeño-pepper jelly or amaretto-chocolate topping). Don't miss the tea cakes, usually available in lemon or blueberry; they're moist, dense, and super sweet. ♦ M, Th-Su late May–mid-Oct. Water St (between Shawme Rd and Main St), Sandwich. 888.0438

18 Isaiah Jones Homestead $$ Victorian decor can sometimes be lugubrious, but this 1849 sea captain's home is unabashedly bright and cheery, with its ornate trim painted cream, dusty rose, and slate blue. Inside are five nicely decorated guest rooms, two with Jacuzzis. Try the **Deming Jarves Room,** with its demi-canopy bed draped in burgundy damask. A gourmet breakfast is served by candlelight, and fireside tea or lemonade on the porch is offered according to the season. ♦ 165 Main St (at Summer St), Sandwich. 888.9115

19 Summer House $$ Aptly named and decorated, this circa 1835 Greek Revival house is spacious, airy, and supremely refreshing. Four of the five large corner rooms have working fireplaces, and all have private baths. The breakfast room is a dazzler, with Chinese-red walls and black-and-white checkerboard floor. Expect some rather elaborate eye-openers at this first meal of the day: puff pastries, coffee breads, and home-baked muffins—*plus* a hearty entrée, something along the lines of eggs Benedict. Complimentary afternoon tea, with fresh cookies or British biscuits, is served on the sunporch. And the hammocks in the English-style garden are so inviting you may wish that Sandwich didn't have quite so many alluring activities. ♦ 158 Main St (at School St), Sandwich. 888.4991

20 Home for the Holidays Ltd. The front parlor of this 1850 home-turned-shop observes Christmas year-round; other rooms honor holidays in passing, with seasonally appropriate presents. There's one room set aside for gifts for babies and children, and the repertoire tends to classic delights, such as Steiff stuffed animals. Among the big-ticket items for adults is a Thomas B. Swain & Co. picnic hamper, fully accoutred, available for slightly short of four figures. Whether you're buying a gift, or simply treating yourself, the choices here are truly select. ♦ M-Sa; Su noon-5PM late May–Dec; off-season by appointment. 154 Main St (between School and Water Sts), Sandwich. 888.4388

21 Captain Ezra Nye House $$ Yet another house to make you wonder why sea captains ever left home. This 1829 Federal manse, hosted by Elaine and Harry Dickson, has six appealing bedrooms, including one in blue calico with a working fireplace. A typical breakfast might feature a homemade apple-cinnamon quiche or soufflé. ♦ 152 Main St (between School and Water Sts), Sandwich. 888.6142, 800/388.2278; fax 833.2897 ♿

22 The Weather Store, Inc. An interest in meteorological matters is not a prerequisite for enjoying this store: "Weather" is interpreted broadly to incorporate giant lobster weather vanes, brass lanterns, compasses, maps, globes, etc. If you are a weather nut, all the better. Paraphernalia ranges from handsome Maximum instruments (a must for the home or yacht) to the "weather stick,"

an "easy to install, no maintenance" device that lets you know when a storm's brewing. Customers seeking a gift for the already overequipped rarely leave empty-handed. ♦ M-Sa May-Dec; call for off-season hours. 146 Main St (between School and Water Sts), Sandwich. 888.1200, 800/646.1203

23 Yesteryears Doll Museum Housed in the somewhat shabby **First Parish Meetinghouse** (illustrated above; an 1833 Gothic Revival structure that replaced the 1638 original) is a fabulous collection of dolls from the past three centuries, lovingly presented in glass cases raised on old church pews. The effect, especially when you happen upon the life-size dolls in the old altar area, is more than a little spooky, as is the parade of forgotten childhood favorites.

Among the holdings is an elegant Queen Anne doll from the 17th century; more recent exemplars include a panoply of Shirley Temples, a bouncy Betty Boop, and "literary dolls" like Eloise. Barbie shares a case with G.I. Joe. But it's the infinite variety of 19th-century German and French bisque dolls that steals the show. New exhibits are organized yearly, and there's a consignment shop/doll hospital in the basement for collectors with a niche to fill or a poppet to put to rights. ♦ Admission. M-Sa mid-May–Oct. Main and River Sts, Sandwich. 888.1711

24 The Dan'l Webster Inn $$$ This large but sensitively landscaped complex—operated since 1980 by the Catania family, owners of the Hearth 'N Kettle chain of restaurants—expertly fulfills the role of town nexus. There are 46 luxurious, reproduction-appointed rooms (including eight suites with canopy beds and fireplaces in nearby historical houses). A small outdoor pool with a gazebo, access to a local health club, and truly delectable food (meal plans are available) round out the amenities. Because of its modernity, it's not as evocative as the many historic little inns in town, but the four-star service more than compensates. ♦ 149 Main St (between Jarves and River Sts), Sandwich. 888.3623, 800/444.3566; fax 888.5156

Building Character: The Architecture of Cape Cod and The Islands

We tend to imagine that the Pilgrims, immediately upon landing in the New World, constructed the plain plank houses with which they've come to be associated, but in fact, arriving in the bitter cold of winter, they were desperate to put together whatever temporary shelter they could. At first they copied Native American wigwams made of arched saplings covered with bark, hides, cornstalks, grass—anything that lay at hand. As soon as they were able, the settlers began to replicate familiar English styles, adapting them to the harsh seaside environment. The simple yet effective post-and-beam method of construction, initially filled in with wattle and daub, later with interior walls of wide vertical planking, more than sufficed for most people's needs well into the early 1800s.

The archetypal Cape Cod cottage (circa 1630-1720), of which many exemplars survive, was a one-and-a-half story building, with a steep (60°) side-gable roof designed to deflect wind and precipitation. (The settlers had to replace thatch, which blew away with the first gust of a northeaster, with native slate; the pitched roofs also helped distribute this added weight.) The early one-room structures—usually about 16 feet square, in accordance with the English measurement known as a rod—were erected around massive fieldstone fireplaces cemented with clay. Perpendicular to the fireplace, transecting the ceiling, was a "summer beam" (possibly derived from the Latin *summus,* meaning "uppermost," or the French *sommier,* for "cross beam"). This huge beam, set athwart the ground floor, supported the upper floor, which was usually low-ceilinged and served as a children's bedroom or storage area.

Such an arrangement, with two windows and the door set to one side, would today be classified as a "half-Cape." The design proved adaptable as families' needs—and sizes—grew. A "three-quarter" house extended far enough to permit an additional window

on the other side of the door. A "full Cape," large enough to accommodate farming families, was about 30 feet deep by 34 feet wide, with a central door and hearth, and two front rooms—the "hall," or master bedroom, and the parlor—each with two front windows. The back of the house became a "keeping room"—a combination cooking and all-purpose living room. Its sun-warmed southwest corner was typically walled off as a small "borning room," which could also serve the sick or the elderly. The cold northeast corner housed a pantry and a buttery.

As the settlers prospered and multiplied, many a half-Cape grew to a full Cape and then some, incorporating connected outbuildings referred to as "warts." Some houses grew upward as well as out—into the "saltbox" style, imported from Kent, which resembles the slope-lidded boxes in which colonists stored that precious commodity. The roof declines precipitously from the second floor to just above the first-floor windows in back. The result was greater height but limited living space. By the mid-17th century, however, builders realized that the walls could support roofs at a 45° angle. Extending the roof over rear lean-tos, they achieved the "colonial mansion" style, spacious enough for two large front-corner rooms and a kitchen extension in back. Usually the second floor boasted two corner bedrooms, but to create even more space, builders introduced the gambrel roof, which flares out before dropping downward, much like a barn's roof.

Eager to optimize the sun's warmth, the colonists quickly abandoned casement windows for 6- by 8-inch panes of glass shipped from England. Depending on their net worth—glass was extremely expensive—homeowners arranged these double-hung windows in multiples of four across, as in "eight over twelve" or even "twelve over sixteen."

By the close of the 17th century, all of these hastily improvised styles were beginning to coalesce.

M. BLUM

Around the same time, English builders—challenged by the fire that flattened London in 1666—were traveling abroad and returning with bold new ideas about classical proportions, inspired by the work of 16th-century Italian architect **Andrea Palladio,** which they encoded into "pattern books." Gradually, religiously motivated asceticism gave way to a new trend toward self-expression and a deliberate aesthetic—embraced most readily by the affluent, cosmopolitan seafarers along the colonies' coast. Whereas Georgian England (circa 1714-1830) built its grand symmetrical mansions in brick and stone, New England favored stylized wood, sometimes carved or painted to resemble brick. Decorative variations ran rampant and were often superimposed right over the plainer, homespun colonials. Doorways grew especially ornate, flanked by fluted pilasters and topped with rectangular, triangular, and even elliptical pediments; when the latter began to frame glass, the graceful fanlight was born. By now, larger panes were available, locally produced, so that Georgian windows generally ran in units of three across (as in "six over six," etc.). Even windows got the pediment treatment, sometimes in a showy sampling of assorted styles.

American builders developed and refined their own architectural vocabulary in the Federal period (1775-1820), so named for its association with the fledgling US government, and returned to the well of classical inspiration during the Greek Revival of 1820-60. Beginning in 1860, religious camp meetings spawned cottages of a modest Greek Revival mien, which soon blossomed into the no-holds-barred ornamentation of Carpenter's Gothic; marvelous examples survive in **Oak Bluffs** on **Martha's Vineyard.** The continental, and specifically Victorian, influence continued late into the 19th century, as the moneyed classes embraced the Second Empire (1865-80) and Queen Anne (1885-1920) modes. By the late 19th century, New England architects had grown sufficiently self-assured to create their own vernacular, the Shingle style, which peaked from 1880 to 1920 and produced many a grand summer house, hotel, and place of worship. These mammoth wooden buildings, made of humble materials, may have seemed a case of back-to-basics "reverse snobbery," but with their flowing open spaces and airy verandas, they were actually easier to maintain than their more formal predecessors, and far cooler in summer.

Low-slung, veranda-fronted bungalows—modeled on the heat-deflecting Indian *bangla* and suited to the modest means of the middle class—popped up throughout the Cape between 1890 and 1930. With the Depression came a revival of the plain, cost-cutting Cape Cod cottage design from colonial days; modern clones carpeted new suburban developments from coast to coast, as well as on the Cape itself. It was the building booms of the 1960s through 1980s that introduced characterless structures that have never—and will never—fit in well with the landscape, much less the legacy of the venerable dwellings surrounding them. Responding to zoning and design restrictions, as well as the potential for profitability, developers in recent years have shown an interest in reviving and respecting the aesthetics that inform the older, more traditional Cape.

Within The Dan'l Webster Inn:

The Dan'l Webster Inn Dining Rooms
★★★$$$ The **Conservatory, Morgan Room, Webster Room,** and **Heritage Room** are all served by the same kitchen, with executive chef Robert Catania at the helm. The **Devil n' Dan Tavern,** a casual bar and grill with a colonial ambience, serves a special burger topped with Canadian bacon, barbecue sauce, and vegetables; it's a local favorite. The other four rooms are for more serious dining. You might choose the **Conservatory,** skylit and fronting a meticulously tended garden; the wood-paneled early-American–style **Heritage Room;** or the cozy, intimate alcove in the **Morgan Room.** Or, for a very formal dining experience, try the chandeliered **Webster Room,** with its peach background and Queen Elizabeth chairs. At dinner the chef pulls out the stops: In addition to traditional favorites (broiled seafood in white wine, scallopini of veal with béarnaise sauce), Catania composes a monthly menu to take advantage of seasonal offerings. So dedicated is he to fresh ingredients that the inn has its own aquaculture farm, yielding freshwater fish and hydroponic vegetables. The desserts are elaborate and invariably exquisite. ◆ New American ◆ Daily breakfast, lunch, and dinner. 888.3623

25 The Brown Jug Antiques Art glass (particularly the local product), Staffordshire china, and French and English cameos are the specialties at this homespun little shop, in business since 1935. ◆ M-Sa; Su noon-5PM May-Oct. By appointment Mar-Apr, Nov-Dec. 155 Main St (at Jarves St), Sandwich. 833.1088

26 Village Inn at Sandwich $$ This 1837 Federal-style bed-and-breakfast looks welcoming on the outside, with its broad lawn and wraparound porch, and inside it's even prettier. New owner Susan Fehlinger has retained the furniture and decor of a past era—the handmade chairs and tables look like freshly minted Victoriana. The eight bedrooms have bleached floors, feathered comforters, swaths of fabric, and imaginatively angled wooden beds. The whole effect is dramatic and romantic, with a contagious sense of style. A unique aspect of the inn are workshops given by various artists. ◆ Closed

January through March. 4 Jarves St (between Main and Pleasant Sts), Sandwich. 833.0363, 800/922.9989

27 Madden & Company Located in a restored late–19th-century chapel, this shop showcases Americana in great variety: antique country furniture (including Nantucket lightship baskets), lanterns, and scrimshaw; folk art carvings of whirligigs; marine paintings; sconces; and oil lamps. ♦ M-Sa; Su by appointment May-Dec. 16 Jarves St (at Pleasant St), Sandwich. 888.3663 &

28 Sandwich Minigolf Trust Sandwich to have a *tasteful* miniature golf course. Built on a former cranberry bog, this 18-hole beauty incorporates the architectural vernacular of the region—shingled windmills, covered bridges—as well as nautical wonders, into the hazards. There's a whale and a sea horse to maneuver around, plus the world's only floating golf green. ♦ Admission. Daily 10AM-10PM mid-June–mid-Sept; Sa-Su 10AM-10PM mid-May–mid-June, mid-Sept–mid-Oct. 157 Rte 6A (between Dewey Ave and Liberty St), Sandwich. 888.1905

28 Maypop Lane Pretty much a flea-market–style hodgepodge, this group store (which is stocked by seven dealers) is just the kind of place that hints at surprise pickings—particularly in the area of dolls, quilts, or costume jewelry. ♦ Daily. 161 Rte 6A (between Dewey Ave and Liberty St), Sandwich. 888.1230 &

29 Cape Cod Scenic Railroad (CCSR) Board a vintage train in Sandwich for a day trip into Hyannis (about 40 minutes away) or a brief 10-minute jog west to Sagamore. ♦ Four departures Tu-Su June–late Oct; limited schedule May, late Nov–late Dec. Jarves St (between Rte 6A and Factory St), Sandwich. Main office: 252 Main St (at Center St), Hyannis. 771.3788 &

Restaurants/Clubs: Red   Hotels: Blue
Shops/♥ Outdoors: Green   **Sights/Culture:** Black

30 Sandwich Boardwalk When Hurricane Bob blew this 1,350-foot-long, 117-year-old landmark away in 1991, undaunted locals raised $80,000 for a board-by-board replacement. Sponsored "personalized planks," inscribed with messages, were pounded in place under the supervision of the Department of Conservation. The delicate wooden walkway arches over the marsh and toward the sea. Look for great blue herons stalking their dinner in the shallow tidal pools. ♦ Off Factory St, Sandwich

L.L.B.

31 Green Briar Nature Center & Jam Kitchen You'll know you've come to the right place when the aroma of slowly simmering jam envelops you like a sweet fog. Ida Putnam founded her jam kitchen in this late–18th-century house in 1903 and expanded it in 1916 to make room for a new line of "sun-cooked" preserves. Her recipes, and those of kindred canners, are sold in the on-site shop and by mail order to this day. Author Thornton W. Burgess, who traipsed the surrounding woods as a boy, commended her efforts, writing, "It is a wonderful thing to sweeten the world, which is in a jam and needs preserving." Visitors are sure to agree.

Not only can you wander through the cheerful kitchen with its 20 Glenwood burners performing sugary alchemy, but there's also a little nature library, a classroom with skulls, stuffed animals, tiny dioramas of wildlife performing human domestic chores, and other neat stuff. There's also a 57-acre nature preserve named for Burgess's fictive environment, the **Old Briar Patch.** A take-along trail map identifies local flora, and afterward you can visit the wildflower garden or have a nibble—alongside "Peter Rabbit" in his hutch—overlooking "Smiling Pool." Visit the shop for take-home goodies: pear butter, Mae's mincemeat, or maybe just a jug of Squanto's Secret fertilizer and a rubber snake. ♦ Donation. M-Sa; Su 1-4PM mid-Apr–Jan. Tu-Sa Jan–mid-Apr. 6 Discovery Hill Rd (off Rte 6A), East Sandwich. 888.6870 &

32 1641 Wing Fort House Accruing around a basic "peak house" (steep-roof dwelling) built by the family of Reverend John Wing circa 1641, this three-quarters Colonial is the oldest house in America owned and lived in continuously by the same family. No Wings are in residence at present, but caretaker David Wheelock can provide an in-depth tour, showing how successive generations "recycled" parts of the structure to suit their changing needs. In the Victorian parlor are "gunstock posts" that resemble upright rifles, barrels to the ground—early builders thought the extra thickness on top might bear more weight, a precaution later proven unnecessary. A "press bed" and half-tester bed, both of which fold up flat to the wall, are the space-saving precursors of a Murphy; their rope underpinnings, which required constant cranking to prevent sagging, may have given rise to the expression "sleep tight." ♦ Nominal admission. Tu-Sa mid-June–mid-Sept. 69 Spring Hill Rd (at Foster Rd), East Sandwich. 833.1540

32 Quaker Meeting House The oldest Quaker Meeting House in continuous use in North America was established on this site in 1657. This third incarnation of the house, erected in 1810, is plain inside and out—shingled exterior and simple pews arranged around a wood stove. The building is flanked by carriage barns. ♦ Service: Su 11AM. Spring Hill Rd (at Foster Rd), East Sandwich. 398.3773 &

33 Pine Grove Cottages $ This cluster of 10 shingle-sided cottages, family-run for three generations, includes some one-roomers scarcely bigger than a birdhouse. Owner Kathy Bumstead has freshened them up with lots of white paint, stenciling, and chenille bedspreads. Most visitors head straight for the beaches, but if you want to hang around, there's an aboveground pool, as well as badminton and croquet. Children are certain to find peers to play with. ♦ 348 Rte 6A (between Atkins and Quaker Meetinghouse Rds), East Sandwich. 888.8179

34 Bee-Hive Tavern ★$$ 🐝
Dark paneling, booths, banker's lamps, old paintings and prints, and even a gaping salmon displayed over the bar are among the decorations at this roadhouse. The food runs along more standard lines— burgers, salads, sandwiches (including Middle Eastern roll-ups), and plenty of steaks and chops. For a unique treat try one of the traditional fish dishes—such as baked stuffed quahogs, a dish rendering the giant native clam palatable by means of micro-dicing and seasoned stuffing. ♦ American/International ♦ M-Th lunch and dinner, F-Su breakfast, lunch, and dinner mid-May–mid-Oct; daily lunch and dinner mid-Oct–mid-May. 406 Rte 6A (between Old County and Atkins Rds), East Sandwich. 833.1184 &

34 Titcomb's Book Shop This well-stocked three-story barn houses new and used books; specialties include regional, maritime, genealogical, and children's titles. There's usually quite a bit of vintage Thornton W. Burgess on hand: Owner Nancy Titcomb spearheaded the revival of interest in his work, and the establishment of the museum and nature center dedicated to his memory. It's also a good place to load up on maps and guidebooks. ♦ M-Sa; Su noon-5PM. 432 Rte 6A (between Old County and Atkins Rds), East Sandwich. 888.2331 &

35 Nye Family Homestead Home to early Sandwich settler Benjamin Nye, this 1685 peak house–turned saltbox–turned full Cape colonial is not a must-see, but it's sufficiently interesting if you have a bit of spare time. Marring the whole effect are a modern overhead light fixture, a 1940s quilt, and some rather overzealous renovations: The stenciling in the back "borning room," though lovely, looks as if it had been retouched yesterday, as does the mustard-colored painted paneling in the parlor. Among the more interesting artifacts are small wood-and-iron stilts, apparently once used to maneuver through mud, and a house-keeper's tie-on pocket (colonial clothes had none, fabric being scarce). The small room beneath the stairs was installed simply to help ventilate the fire, but it's become known to generations of children as "the Bugaboo room." ♦ Admission. M-F noon-4:30PM mid-June–mid-Oct. 85 Old County Rd (between Holt Rd and Rte 6A), East Sandwich. 888.4213

When the head honchos of the Plymouth Colony checked up on their satellite town of Sandwich in 1655, they found it intolerably lax: many men had taken to wearing their hair below their ears! The Puritans put up stocks and a whipping post, and soon the "teenaged" town was set to rights.

Settlers misnamed Buzzards Bay, mistaking the native osprey for the scavengers.

Sometimes the early settlers went overboard in their search for meaningful Biblical names: Nathan Bourne of Sandwich, for instance, named his ninth son (born in 1770) Mahershalallashbaz.

WINGSCORTON FARM INN 1758

36 Wingscorton Farm Inn $$ This 1758 Federal farmstead, named for the Quaker abolitionist Wing family, was once a key stop on the Underground Railroad. Ask owner Dick Loring to see the secret room concealed behind a fireplace panel in the library, where fugitive slaves hid until they could be escorted to the beach under cover of darkness. The farm remains a working one; its seven secluded acres harbor horses, a donkey, sheep, pygmy goats, free-range chickens, assorted cats, a pet turkey, and a potbellied pig. There are only two upstairs suites, each with a king-size canopy bed (the only nod to modernism); an adjoining single room; plus a two-story carriage house with its own kitchen and sundeck. All four bedrooms have working fireplaces and stunningly pared-down period furniture.

Guests invariably partake of the multicourse farmhand breakfast (with nut breads fresh from the oven) at the plank table in the main house. The "keeping room," now a com-fortable living room, features what is thought to be the largest colonial hearth in New England: It's nine feet long, with a mantel that showcases an array of antique pewter. The inn is as well suited to romantic getaways as it is to family holidays; children delight in this lively domestic zoo. For a memento, buy some fresh eggs or a free-range chicken from the fridge in the barn, where they're sold on an honor system. ♦ 11 Wing Blvd (off Rte 6A), East Sandwich. 888.0534

37 Aptucxet Trading Post Museum
Centuries ago (before the Cape Cod Canal), two rivers almost met at this site; the portage route between them made a natural trading ground, especially with the Wampanoag tribe encamped nearby, and the Dutch accessible to the south.

The Pilgrims built their first trading post here in 1627, using polished fragments of quahog shells (known to the Indians as *wampumpeake* or wampum) as currency. The year before (in the first official treaty signed in North America), they had assumed the debts of their English backers in exchange for a monopoly on trade with the natives. The original post was destroyed by hurricane, and a second, erected in 1635, lasted only a few decades. However, references in Bradford's account enabled a pair of archaeologists to locate the site and excavate it in 1926. The dig yielded not only arrowheads, tools, and shards, but the original building's foundation.

Today, there's a replica of the trading post, ably explicated by curator Eleanor Hammond. One room is arranged as it might have been in the days when two paid hands worked the property; the other displays the artifacts found on-site, plus the stone threshold to an Indian church built in the late 17th century. This so-called "Bournedale stone," when turned over, reveals nearly illegible inscriptions. No one is sure whether these are Phoenician or Viking—or neither.

The modest complex, operated by the nonprofit Bourne Historical Society, contains a couple of other oddities as well, from a small Victorian train station built in 1892 for the personal use of President Grover Cleveland to the windmill that served his fishing buddy, actor Joseph Jefferson (renowned for his portrayal of Rip Van Winkle), as an art studio; it's now a gift shop. A shaded picnic area overlooks the canal and the Vertical Lift Railroad Bridge, which lowers a 554-foot-long span of track to permit trains to pass. Built in 1935 at a cost of $1.5 million, it's the second-largest bridge of its kind, but no longer very active. The best time to try to catch the *Seagull Express* in action is evenings between 6 and 7PM. ♦ Nominal admission. M-Sa; Su 2-5PM July-Aug. Tu-Sa; Su 2-5PM May-June, Sept–mid-Oct. 24 Aptucxet Rd (off Perry Ave), Bourne Village. 759.9487 ♿

38 Chart Room ★★$$ Now a comfortably broken-in bar and restaurant, this rehabbed railroad barge used to be a machine shop that produced vessels for use in the Korean War. It's one of the few places where you can watch Cataumet residents disport themselves—tastefully, of course. It's tucked away amid an active marina, and specialties include swordfish slathered with anchovy butter. ♦ American ♦ Daily lunch and dinner mid-June–early Sept; Th dinner, F-Sa lunch and dinner, Su lunch mid-May–mid-June, early Sept–early Oct. Cataumet Marina, Shipyard La (off Shore Rd), Cataumet. 563.5350 ♿

"Ice King" Frederick Tudor of Bourne (1763-1864) earned fame and fortune shipping ice to the West Indies and India. His inventor son, Frederick Jr., built the Monument Beach mansion that would become Gray Gables, Grover Cleveland's "summer White House."

39 Wood Duck Inn $ Staying in either of the two suites at this 1848 house overlooking a working cranberry bog is like having a place of your own (each has a private entrance). One has a small deck (where innkeeper Maureen Jason will gladly bring you breakfast), and both have a full living room with kitchenette and chintz-covered armchairs, a bathroom with stenciled ivy trailing from the skylight, and a cozy bedroom with comforters. Basically, no amenity is overlooked, and if you're interested in the "real" Cape, there's no better place to experience it. Maureen and her husband, Dick, who carves decoys (hence the inn's name) can direct you to conservation lands in the area, where you may get to mingle with the nonhuman population. ♦ 1050 County Rd (between Red Brook Harbor and Valley Farm Rds), Cataumet. 564.6404

40 Courtyard Restaurant and Pub $$ All-American favorites predominate at this casual family spot, indigenous fare having expanded to include *pizzette* and chili. Kids get a crack at their favorites, too, such as peanut butter and jelly sandwiches. Among the specialties are such yummy *Joy of Cooking* throwbacks as seafood medley topped with crumbled Ritz crackers. The bar, paneled in barn board with Oriental rugs, can be a comfortable hideout when the weather's discomfiting. ♦ American/International ♦ Daily lunch and dinner Apr-Oct; Tu-Su lunch and dinner Nov-Mar. Cataumet Square, 1337 County Rd (at Rte 28A), Cataumet. 563.1818 &

40 Cataumet Fish Step right up and watch your dinner being gutted, or pluck a live lobster from the tank. This quaint little market looks antique, thanks to the vintage iceboxes and stove used to display designer pasta and Common Crackers, but the fish is as fresh as this morning. Check out the board of nautical knots to see how your Scout training holds up. ♦ Daily. Cataumet Square, 1360 Rte 28A (at County Rd), Cataumet. 564.5956. Also at: Deer Crossing, Rte 28 (just south of the Maspee Rotary), Mashpee. 477.4116 &

41 Emack & Bolio's One of Boston's favorite ice-cream emporia has a well-situated outpost here. Try the "Cosmic Cataumet Crunch," a gooey delight shot with caramel. ♦ M-Th noon-8PM, F-Su noon-9PM mid-Apr–mid-Oct. 1356 County Rd (at Rte 28A), Cataumet. 564.5442. Also at: 2 Kent Pl (between Main and Cross Sts), Chatham. 945.5506; Oracle Square, Rte 6A, Orleans. 255.5844 &

41 Thunder Mine Adventure Golf Follow the yellow diamonds to this 18-hole Astroturf minigolf course with a Gold Rush motif. En route or afterward, you can pick up some penny candy or add to your baseball card collection. ♦ M-Th 10AM-10PM, F-Su 10AM-11PM late May–mid-Oct. Rte 28A and County Rd, Cataumet. 563.7450

Bests

Joyce Zavorskas
Artist, Zavorskas Studio

Coffee at the **Hot Chocolate Sparrow** in **Orleans,** freshly brewed morning to night.

Watching *Star Wars,* or any movie, under the stars at the **Wellfleet Drive-In,** just like the good old days.

Walking the **Salt Pond Trail** at the **Cape Cod National Seashore's Salt Pond Visitor Center** in **Eastham,** for the astounding overlook that changes by the hour, day, season, etc.

Walking the **Inner Dunes** in **North Truro,** panoramic views of dunes and ocean.

Dinner at the **Nauset Beach Club** in **East Orleans,** best Northern Italian food, casual atmosphere.

Lunch at the **Land Ho!,** ordering kale soup and watching owner John Murphy shine up the tables and talk to all the regulars.

Taking a class at the **Creative Art Center, Chatham,** very supportive for their artists and students, unique exhibitions and classes throughout the year.

Walking down **Commercial Street, Provincetown,** in winter; and walking the **West End** jetty at low tide.

Taking a printmaking class at **Truro Center for the Arts** at **Castle Hill.**

Buying fresh produce at **Phoenix Fruit** in Orleans.

Eating fried clams at **Arnold's** in Eastham.

Arthur S. Harris, Jr.
Editor/Travel Writer

Walking to a secluded part of a **Cape Cod National Seashore** beach in **Truro** where your feet sink deeply into the hot sand and you can strip everything off and swim and sun naked—well, this is paradise. Tall sand dunes form the backdrop to this hedonistic pleasure. Although technically it is illegal, lots of naked sun worshipers appear along the shoreline. Also in **Provincetown,** there is some sun bathing *au naturel* at **Herring Cove Beach**—face the sea from the parking lot and walk left.

As my wife and I are vegetarians, we like the good veggie cuisine at **Napi's** in Provincetown; and **Terra Luna** in Truro.

Falmouth/ Mashpee

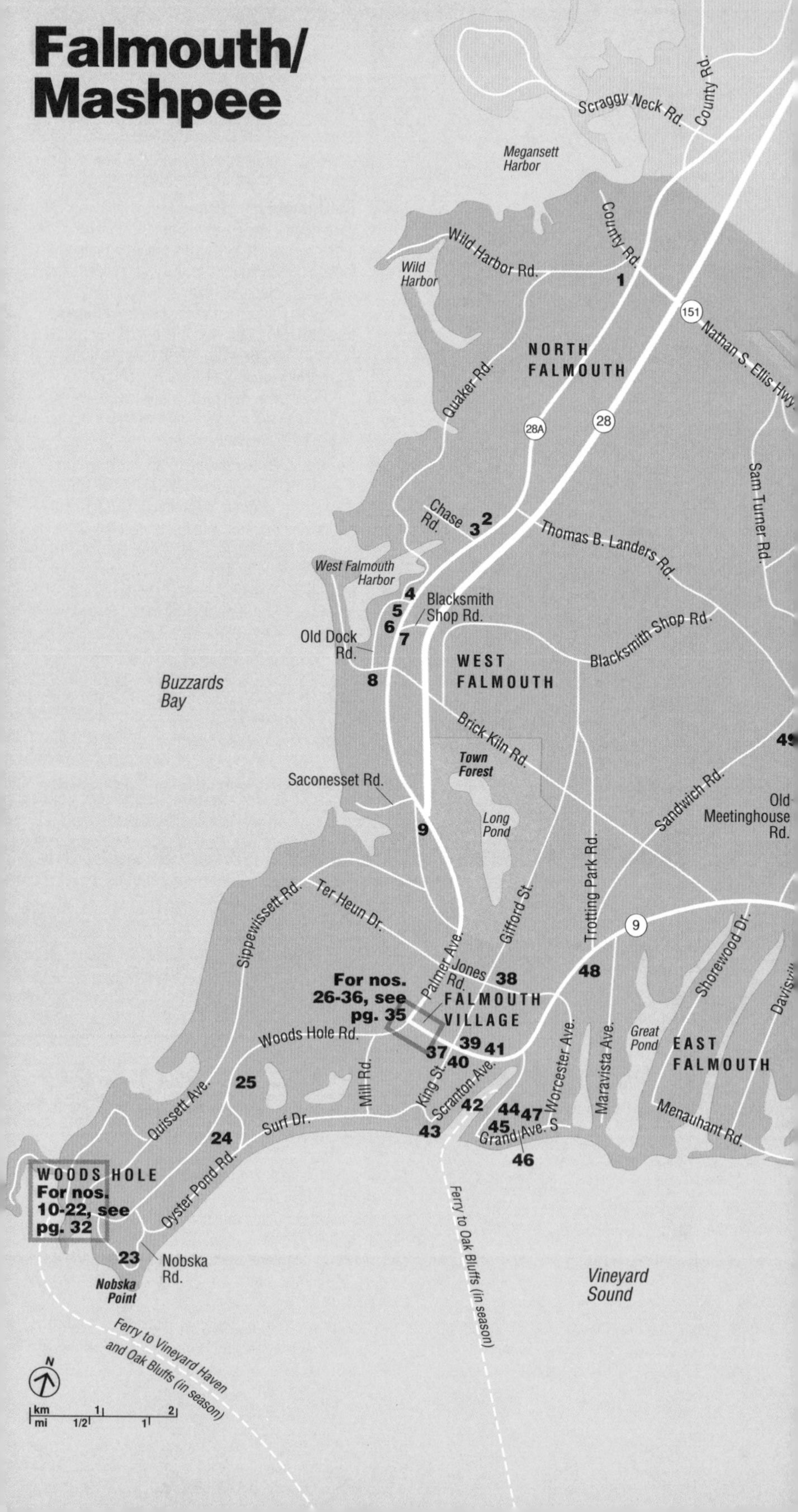

Scraggy Neck Rd.

County Rd.

Megansett Harbor

Wild Harbor Rd.

Wild Harbor

County Rd.

1

151

NORTH FALMOUTH

Nathan S. Ellis Hwy.

Quaker Rd.

28A

28

Sam Turner Rd.

Chase Rd.

3 2

Thomas B. Landers Rd.

West Falmouth Harbor

4

Blacksmith Shop Rd.

5
6
7

Old Dock Rd.

WEST FALMOUTH

Blacksmith Shop Rd.

8

Buzzards Bay

Brick Kiln Rd.

Town Forest

4 9

Saconesset Rd.

Long Pond

Sandwich Rd.

Old Meetinghouse Rd.

9

Sippewissett Rd.

Ter Heun Dr.

Gifford St.

Trotting Park Rd.

9

Palmer Ave.

Jones Rd.

38

48

Shorewood Dr.

Davis

For nos. 26-36, see pg. 35

FALMOUTH VILLAGE

Woods Hole Rd.

37
40

39 41

Worcester Ave.

Maravista Ave.

Great Pond

EAST FALMOUTH

Quissett Ave.

25

Mill Rd.

King St.

Scranton Ave.

42

44 47
45

Grand Ave. S.

Menauhant Rd.

24

Surf Dr.

43

46

Oyster Pond Rd.

WOODS HOLE
For nos.
10-22, see
pg. 32

23

Nobska Rd.

Nobska Point

Ferry to Oak Bluffs (in season)

Vineyard Sound

Ferry to Vineyard Haven and Oak Bluffs (in season)

N

km   1   2
mi   1/2   1

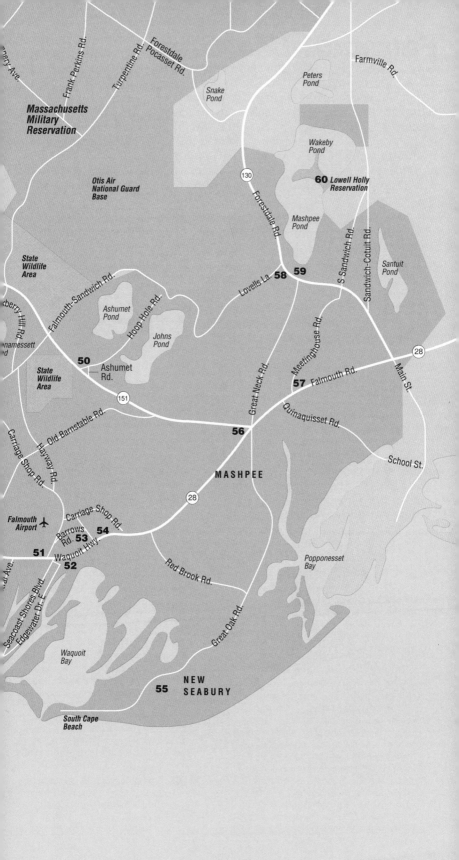

Falmouth/Mashpee

Among the most staid and content of Cape towns, Falmouth takes its allure for granted. For those passing through en route to the Island ferries, it may appear as nothing more than a nuisance, a logjam designed to entrap impatient vacationers. But take the time to savor Falmouth like a native—its timeless **Town Green**, its narrow but scenic beaches, and its lively mix of shops and exceptional restaurants—and you'll find it to be a worthwhile destination in and of itself. The area of **West Falmouth** along **Route 28A** is especially restful, untouched as yet by tacky tourist traps. **Falmouth Heights,** a cluster of weathered shingle houses on a bluff facing distant Martha's Vineyard, seems to have dozed off at the turn of the century; the nostalgia element here is genuine.

Falmouth, or rather the eight villages it comprises, was established in 1660 by about a dozen Congregationalists driven out of Barnstable for advocating Quakers' rights. It flourished briefly as a whaling port in the early 1800s, after which the population began to plummet, largely because of the lure of new industry near Boston. The town rebounded when tourists discovered it: They began arriving by the trainload in the late 19th century. The railroad reached the tiny port of **Woods Hole** in 1872, a year after the US Commission of Fish and Fisheries had set up a small seasonal collecting station to study marine specimens; the settlement has blossomed into a year-round scientific community of international stature.

Adjacent to Falmouth is Mashpee, which served as a summer campground for a number of Native American tribes (its native name meant "land near the great cove") for millennia before the colonists arrived. In 1660, moved by the impassioned speeches of missionary Richard Bourne, the Plymouth General Court set aside 10,500 acres in the region of Mashpee, or "Marshpee" as it was then known, as an Indian "plantation"; the arrangement was meant to last in perpetuity. However, much of the territory has passed out of native hands, and the area is now riddled with suburban developments. Only 800 or so Wampanoags still live on the Cape, but a great many more Native Americans, representing other tribes, gather for the annual Fourth of July weekend Wampanoag Powwow, a spectacular event featuring traditional rites and foods.

1 Silver Lounge Restaurant ★★$$
Popular since it opened in 1956 (one of the longest sole restaurant ownerships on Cape Cod), Bill eatery is loved by tourists, who line up for a table in summer, and by locals, who take it over in winter. Ask for one of the ten tables in the restored caboose, and try the house special marinated black dia-mond steak or the baked scallop casserole (no fried foods are available). The prices are reasonable and the nautical artifacts along the walls are actual antiques. ♦ American ♦ Daily lunch and dinner until 1AM. 412 Rte 28A (between Winslow and County Rds), North Falmouth. 563.2410 &

Next to the Silver Lounge Restaurant:

Uncle Bill's Country Store There's an eclectic look to this post-and-beam store that features a colorful mix of gifts, flowers, and antiques. ♦ Daily. 564.4355

2 Haland Stable Those who can "sit English" will be well prepared for the escorted trail ride through woods and past cranberry bogs; beginners will need a half-hour lesson before they start. Instructor Hazel Shaw, who grew up here, opened the stables in 1964, and has transformed many a novice into a devotee. ♦ M-Sa (weather permitting). Reservations required. 878 Rte 28A (between Chase Rd and Forman La), West Falmouth. 540.2552

2 Whistlestop Ice Cream It's not much more than a shack decorated with old railroad trappings, but the offerings are locally made and delicious. Try a cone of one of the different specials, such as cookie dough or "death by chocolate." ◆ Daily noon-10PM mid-May–mid-Oct. 854 Rte 28A (between Chase Rd and Forman La), West Falmouth. 540.7585. Also at: 171 Clay Pond Rd (near Shore Rd), Monument Beach. 759.4010

3 Sjoholm $$ More casual than some and welcoming of children, this 19th-century farmhouse with 15 rooms (including a few in a converted carriage house) is an eminently affordable bed-and-breakfast. The Swedish name, a legacy of former owners, means "safe place set near water," and it fits. Among the breakfast treats new innkeepers Barbara and William White offer are Swedish pancakes and fruit-topped hot cereals. ◆ 17 Chase Rd (off Rte 28A), West Falmouth. 540.5706, 800/498.5706

4 Europa Imports of West Falmouth Unusual clothing, African straw bags, embroidered T-shirts, offbeat jewelry—it's worth seeking out this out-of-the-way outpost for world-beat womenswear (there's great stuff for little kids, too). ◆ M-Sa; Su noon-6PM. 628 Rte 28A (between Old Dock and Cordwood Landing Rds), West Falmouth. 540.7814. Also at: 37 Barnstable Rd (at North St), Hyannis. 790.0877

5 Village Barn This former barn now houses eight antiques dealers with a spectrum of aesthetic slants. One person is keen on quilts, another on Quimper and glass paperweights—you get the picture. There's also a "junk room" up in the hayloft. It's reassuring to know that even pros will pick a dud from time to time, and some of their rejects may strike your fancy. ◆ Daily late May–mid-Oct; F-Su mid-Oct–late May. 606 Rte 28A (between Chapoquoit and Old Dock Rds), West Falmouth. 540.3215

6 Chrisalis Country Home A combination home furnishings/antiques store, this place has some exquisite stock. The intriguing selection is arranged by owner Dorothy Donlan in happy groupings; she has an eclectic eye and unerring taste. ◆ Daily Mar-Dec. 550 Rte 28A (at Chapoquoit Rd), West Falmouth. 540.5884

7 Inn at West Falmouth $$$ New owner/manager Karen Calvacca is gifted as a decor-ator and it shows in this 1900 shingle-style summerhouse overlooking Buzzards Bay (flowers are everywhere, inside and out). The inn has had many incarnations—it served as a private residence, a piano camp, a home for unwed mothers, and even as a 1950s bachelor pad. A 1985 renovation brought it back into its own, as the kind of rural retreat city dwellers dream of.

Five of the six rooms are furnished with unusual European antiques and hand-embroidered linens; one has an Oriental cast, with grass-paper wall coverings and bold Korean accoutrements, which are also ancient. Several rooms have fireplaces and/or private balconies, and all adjoin Italian marble bathrooms with whirlpool baths. Breakfast is served buffet style until late morning, so no one need stir who doesn't care to. There's a jewel-like heated pool set in the deck, and below, on the quiet, bloom-strewn grounds, a clay tennis court. You don't even need to pack a good book; Karen lays in stacks of the latest best-sellers. The beach is a 10-minute stroll away. ◆ 66 Frazar Rd (between Rte 28A and Blacksmith Shop Rd), West Falmouth. 540.7696, 800/397.7696; fax 548.6974

8 Chapoquoit Grill ★★★$$ It's hard to tell, without that telltale final "e," whether a grill is just the local watering hole or one of those newfangled wood-fired places. This California-style bistro is definitely the latter. Designer pizzas are crisped in a brick oven, and the seafood specials—usually swordfish or salmon—emerge with a smoky flair, accompanied by the likes of mango chutney salsa. This quiet corner of the Cape has been somewhat slow to respond to current culinary trends, so naturally the place has been a big hit since day one. ◆ New American ◆ Daily dinner. 410 Rte 28A (between Charles La and Little Neck Bars Rd), West Falmouth. 540.7794 ♿

9 Peach Tree Circle Farm ★★$ This pleasant little farmstand-cum-lunchroom looks as though it has been there forever, but it's actually a mid-1980s innovation. Drop by to pick up some cut flowers or produce fresh from the field, and, odds are, you'll want to linger for a light lunch of fresh garden vege-table soup or salad. The deli can fix you up with homemade jams and jellies, the bakery with strawberry-almond bars and other treats. ◆ American ◆ Daily lunch. 881 Old Palmer Ave (just south of Rte 28A), Falmouth. 548.2354 ♿

10 Woods Hole Gallery Edith Bruce has found a select group of area artists, and has been showing their work since 1963, making fresh discoveries every year. (She restores Old Masters, so knows what to look for in a work of art.) Among her finds, for instance, are the compact dunescapes of Beth Pykosz, who with smudges of intensely hued pastels conveys a fragile, complex world. "All the artists have won awards—they have to," says Bruce. "It's my house, so I can be picky." ◆ M, Th-Sa; Su 2-5PM late June–mid-Sept. 14 School St (between Water and Millfield Sts), Woods Hole. 548.7594

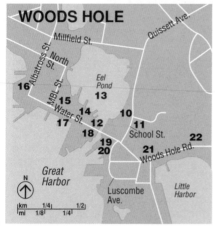

WOODS HOLE

11 Woods Hole Oceanographic Institution Exhibit Center (WHOI)

The largest independent oceanographic research institution in the United States, WHOI (pronounced *Hoo-ee* by locals) was founded in 1930 with a $3-million grant from the Rockefeller Foundation. It is dedicated to the study of all aspects of marine science and engineering, and to the education of marine scientists and engineers. There are over a thousand employees, students, and scientists conducting research in the labs here on everything from climate change to coastal erosion and aquaculture. A modest exhibition hall that documents the institution's highly successful history educates tourists who visit the facility.

Originally seasonal, the institute began operating year-round during World War II when it performed research on underwater explosives and submarine detection. Since then, the facility has grown and changed and gone on to explore the seven seas with a phalanx of research vessels, from the 279-foot *Knorr* (which has been cut in half and lengthened like a stretch limo) to the 25-foot *Alvin*, a 1964 submersible built for three and capable of descending to depths of over 14,750 feet. The latter earned headlines in 1966 when it retrieved an unexploded hydrogen bomb in the Mediterranean, and again, in 1986, when it probed the *Titanic*. Little *Alvin* (named for resident scientist/inventor Allyn Vine) has been especially effective in exploring pitch-dark ocean depths where unsuspected forms of life have been found.

The physical exhibits at the visitors' center may not be extensive (check out the pickled "cookie-cutter" shark, and the full-scale model of *Alvin*'s personal sphere with videos projected through its three portholes), but the stop may be the next best thing to a *20,000 Leagues Under the Sea* voyage of your own. ♦ Free. Tu-Sa; Su noon-4:30PM May-Oct. Call for off-season hours; closed January through March. 15 School St (at Maury La), Woods Hole. 289.2252; fax 457.2180 &

12 Black Duck ★$$ A cafeteria by day, restaurant by night, this casual spot has a deck overlooking Eel Pond and a repertory of some 60 soups, chowders, and stews, of which a handful are available at any given time. The rest of the menu is filled out with fairly standard seafood fare. ♦ International ♦ Daily breakfast, lunch, and dinner June–mid-Oct; call for off-season hours. 73 Water St (between School and MBL Sts), Woods Hole. 548.9165 &

12 Cap'n Kidd ★$$ Seafood dominates the bill of fare at this popular bar/restaurant (primarily bar). A crude mural (circa 1946) depicts the namesake pirate who, legend has it, was brought ashore in Woods Hole en route to his hanging in England. The hand-carved mahogany bar with its hefty marble railing is thought to be about 150 years old; as for the institution itself, no one seems to know. Customers sit on stools at barrel tables and in winter the glassed-in deck, with its wood stove, is a magnet of social activity. ♦ American ♦ Daily lunch and dinner. 77 Water St (between School and MBL Sts), Woods Hole. 548.9206 &

Within Cap'n Kidd:

The Waterfront ★★$$$$ Cap'n Kidd has a civilized side, which comes out only in summer. When the warehouse-size adjoining dining room fills up, diners push out onto a pier in the pond. Chef Frank Belfiore's menu is an exercise in unabashed fishploitation: broiled swordfish gets the "Pier House" treatment (braised with mango and papaya, with Champagne beurre blanc) and the seafood *en croute* gets its kick from vermouth, brandy, and cream. As for service, the official line is: "The only thing we overlook is the water." ♦ International ♦ Daily dinner early June–late Sept. Reservations recommended. 548.8563 &

13 Susan Jean Captain John Christian's 22-foot shallow-draft *Aquasport* is usually moored in Eel Pond, but pickups can be arranged virtually anywhere along the shore. A native Cape Codder with over 30 years of experience on the water, Christian will lead a maximum of three very serious fish-seekers on a hunt for trophy bass along the Elizabeth Islands. (In this company, anything under three feet or so is tossed back.) He knows all the best spots, from Quick's Hole to the "hallowed" Sow and Pigs Reef at Cuttyhunk, and trips—typically eight hours in length—are timed to take advantage of tides and climatic conditions, even if that means embarking in the middle of the night. "There's a lot of beauty out there," says Christian. "Some days we'll see the moon set as the sun rises—something you can't get with a boat that leaves at six in the morning." ♦ Reservations required. Eel Pond (off Water St), Woods Hole. 548.6901

14 Shuckers World Famous Raw Bar & Cafe ★★$$ "Never eat lobster in a place where you have to wear a shirt," advises Glen Waggoner, whose rounds as dining critic for *New England Monthly* earned him the nickname "The Man Who Ate New England." He'd feel right at home at this tiny restaurant, which has room for maybe a dozen people inside and another 100-plus spilling over onto cafe tables lining the periphery of Eel Pond. Start with clam chowder—a modest misnomer packed with fresh crab, shrimp, and whatever marine surplus the chef cares to toss in. Appetizers include "crabcraves" (crab and cheese sauce on toast points), and marinated grilled eel, about which the menu warns: "You order it, you bought it." Entrées run the gamut between cioppino and "traditional lobster boil," consisting of clams, mussels, lobster, and corn on the cob. Wash it down with a Nobska Light, a beer brewed right in Falmouth. ♦ International ♦ Daily lunch and dinner early May–late Oct. 91A Water St (between School and MBL Sts), Woods Hole. 540.3850 &

15 Marine Biological Laboratory (MBL) Founded in 1888, the nonprofit MBL (whose offices are housed in a converted 1836 granite spermaceti candle factory) has a somewhat broader mandate than WHOI: The approximately 800 scientists who work here study simple marine organisms as a key to "fundamental biological processes common to all life forms." (Research on sea urchins, amazingly enough, led to such reproductive breakthroughs as in vitro fertilization, and may someday spawn a birth control pill for men.) The MBL is happy to show visitors around, provided they reserve ahead. The two-hour programs feature a slide presentation and a guided tour of the holding tanks for a look at the "creepy-crawlies" (e.g., eels, squid, sponges, coral, crabs, and dogfish aggressively nosing the surface). ♦ Free. M-F afternoon mid-June–Aug; call for hours. Reservations required (preferably a week in advance). MBL and Water Sts, Woods Hole. 289.7623 &

16 National Marine Fisheries Service Aquarium (NMFS) Set up in 1871 as a summer sampling station by the US Commission of Fish and Fisheries (the NMFS's predecessor), this is the oldest aquarium in the country and a wonderfully sloppy place in which to experience close encounters of the piscine kind. Little kids revel in the "touch tank" tide pools, and taller tanks painted in bright colors hold further surprises. In the wall-mounted tanks you can observe the graceful glide of loggerhead sea turtles or the scuttling of a natural blue lobster. You might even get to watch a toothy wolffish devour a hapless crab. Two seals from **Buttonwood Park Zoo** in New Bedford have taken up residence in a street-side tank; feedings are at 11AM and 3PM. A new display commemorates the 125th anniversary of the founding of the Commission of Fisheries; it features a section on Rachel Carson, who studied in Wood's Hole before writing *Silent Spring,* and old and new photographs. ♦ Free. Daily mid-June–mid-Sept; M-F mid-Sept–mid-June. Albatross and Water Sts, Woods Hole. 495.2001 &

Marine Education, Woods Hole, MA

17 Ocean Quest Geared for all ages, these half-hour marine biology excursions through Great Harbor are intriguing enough to merit a detour. Participants board a fully equipped research vessel to take actual readings on water temperature, turbidity, and the like; they also get to study live specimens dragged up from the depths. On board, professional scientists, educators, and mariners guide you through a hands-on look into modern oceanography. ♦ M-F 10AM, noon, 2PM, 4PM mid-June–Labor Day. Reservations recommended. Water St (between Railroad Ave and Albatross St), Woods Hole. 457.0508, 800/376.2326

18 Woods Hole Handworks This small but distinguished shop, an artisans' co-op, carries the work of 16 contributors—most notably, manager/weaver Gunjan Laborde, whose colorful chenille shells and shawls drape as beautifully as they glide through the day. Keep coming back: the artists are always evolving, along with the stock. ♦ Daily May-Oct; call for off-season hours. 68 Water St (between Railroad Ave and Albatross St), Woods Hole. 540.5291

19 Fishmonger's Cafe ★★$$ As a footnote on the menu advises, it's a mere "262 leisurely paces" from here to the ferry gangplank, but it's worth missing the next boat, if you must, to savor the ebullient natural foods served at "the 'Monger." Operated by chef/owner Frances Buehler since 1974, this lively sunny-yellow harborside cafe, with exposed beams and kitchen, features treats throughout the day. The breakfast special might be lemon-ricotta–soufflé pancakes with raspberry sauce; always on the menu are California omelettes (guacamole, salsa, and sour cream) and Thai crab-and-pork sausage, packing peanuts, cilantro, and coconut milk. Check the blackboard as the day progresses; you might come across such delicacies as Portuguese kale soup or fresh trout with pesto cream sauce. A folksinger often performs at night. ♦ International ♦ Daily breakfast, lunch, and dinner mid-June–mid-Oct; call for off-season hours; closed December–mid-February. 56 Water St (between Railroad Ave and Albatross St), Woods Hole. 548.9148 &

20 Landfall ★$$$ Run by a local family since the 1940s, and built almost entirely of salvage, this harborside eatery serves the usual seaside offerings: clams, lobster, swordfish, etc. Surrounding you are relics from shipwrecks and long-gone grand hotels; the massive beams overhead came from a Gloucester pier, the glass panels from horse-drawn trolleys that used to traverse Harvard Square. Successive hurricanes, from Carol to Bob, have battered the restaurant, but it keeps bouncing back. ♦ American ♦ Daily lunch and dinner Apr-Nov. 2 Luscombe Ave (at Woods Hole Rd), Woods Hole. 548.1758

21 Bradley House Museum Captain William Bradley bought this house for $339 in 1821 before he was lost at sea; it now houses the *Woods Hole Historical Collection*. What's on view at any given time varies, except for a diorama of the town circa 1895 and a "spritsail" boat made at the turn of the century by local builder Eddie Swift. There's a potluck quality to the exhibits. If you'd prefer something more substantial, try one of the free walking tours of town Tuesday at 4PM during July and August; reservations are required. ♦ Free. Tu-Sa mid-June–mid-Sept. 573 Woods Hole Rd (at Water St), Woods Hole. 548.7270 &

22 Nautilus Motor Inn $$ This establishment doesn't exactly exude ambience; it has the somewhat drab personality of a stereotypical scientist-nerd (in fact, visiting scientists account for a good portion of the clientele). However, the 54 rooms are fine, and the views —on the waterside—are pretty spectacular. There are also free tennis courts and a nicely situated pool. ♦ Closed November–late April. 539 Woods Hole Rd (between Harbor Hill and Nobska Rds), Woods Hole. 548.1525, 800/654.2333; fax 457.9674

Within the Nautilus Motor Inn:

The Dome ★$$$ Buckminster Fuller built this dome when he was at MIT in 1953, and it is a curiosity—it's the oldest geodesic structure in the country. The food, frankly, doesn't warrant the tariff. If you just want to get a peek at the retro-futuristic interior, draped in circuslike swathes of mauve, mint, ivory, and bronze fabric, duck in for a drink before you commit. The overall effect can be a bit creepy, unless you're a true fan of 1950s kitsch. ♦ American/Continental ♦ Tu-Su dinner late Apr–Oct. 548.0800 &

23 Nobska Lighthouse This classically proportioned tower, listed on the National Register of Historic Places, is an 1876 replacement for the 1828 original; it consists of four impervious cast-iron shells. Operation of the facility has been automated since 1985 but with or without a keeper on hand, the view of the nearby Elizabeth Islands is romantic. ♦ Nobska Rd (off Woods Hole Rd), Woods Hole. 547.3219

24 Marlborough House $$ From the road it looks like your ordinary, if rather prepossessing, oversized Cape. You'd never guess there was a jewel-like pool hidden behind it, and alongside that a tiny romantic cottage with a large bed, a love seat, and its own backyard. All the rooms—there are five guest rooms in the main house—are air-conditioned and accoutred with fluffy quilts and abundant cut flowers. Enjoy new owner Al Hammond's gourmet breakfasts: quiche, French toast strata, and hot cereals. ♦ 320 Woods Hole Rd (between F.R. Lillie and Oyster Pond Rds), Woods Hole. 548.6218, 800/320.2322; fax 457.7519

25 Woods Hole Passage $$ Owners Todd and Robin Norman have brought a Southwestern flair to this five-bedroom bed-and-breakfast. The living room in the main building (a converted 19th-century carriage house) has wrought-iron and pastel furniture and a view of the spacious back garden. Four of the bedrooms were carved from a century-old barn; the upstairs rooms, with their cathedral ceilings, are particularly appealing. The fifth room is in the main house and is decorated with hand-

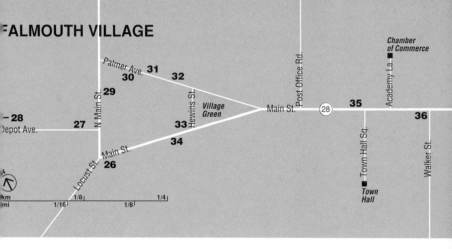

painted furnishings. Daylong traffic along the main route to Woods Hole might be a deterrent, but you'll probably be out all day anyway, enjoying the area's many attractions. Should you run out of things to see and do, the Normans can suggest some little-known destinations, such as nearby **Spohr's Garden** and the **Knob.** In any case, they'll send you off with a hearty breakfast with Southwestern touches—green chile soufflé, perhaps; or quiche with some fresh salsa on the side (that's not jam for the muffins!). For those with an early ferry to catch, they'll pack a breakfast-to-go. ♦ 186 Woods Hole Rd (between Oyster Pond and Ransom Rds), Woods Hole. 548.9575, 800/790.8976; fax 540.4771

26 Inn at One Main $$
Known since the 1950s as "the Victorian," this 1892 decorative shingled house with Queen Anne accents features six guest rooms that draw on owners Mari Zylinski and Karen Hart's blithe spirits and romanticism. Lace and wicker abound, especially in the turret room, which boasts a brass bed. Breakfasts are creative too, with such dishes as cranberry pecan waffles and gingerbread pancakes. ♦ 1 Main St (at Locust St), Falmouth. 540.7469, 888/281.6246

27 Market Bookshop Housed in a century-old former butcher shop, this bookstore is an integral part of the community and a delight for transient browsers. A massive maple table sits by a hearth (roaring in winter), and the books are arranged in logical groupings on high oak shelves. Owner Bill Banks is proud to have mentored preschoolers straight through college over the past two decades plus. The store offers an out-of-print search service ($2 per title), and same-day follow-through on contacting publishers with special orders. You'll probably find all you need right here, though, particularly if it's Cape Coddiana

you're after. ♦ M-Sa 8AM-9PM, Su noon-5PM late June–mid-Sept; call for off-season hours. 15 Depot Ave (off N Main St), Falmouth. 548.5636 & Also at: 22 Water St (between Woods Hole Rd and Railroad Ave), Woods Hole. 540.0851

Behind the Market Bookshop:

Market Barn Gallery The century-old barn out back, with its whitewashed interior, is a great place to show New England artists, as well as to conduct readings and signings. There's also an outdoor sculpture garden. ♦ M-Sa; Su noon-5PM late June–mid-Sept. 540.0480, 548.5636 &

28 Highfield Theatre The 650-acre **Beebe Woods** estate, where two brothers had built matching mansions in the 1870s, was about to fall prey to developers when a local bene-factor, the late Josiah K. Lilly, stepped in and bought the property for the town in 1972. The buildings were deeded to the Cape Cod Conservatory, and although one mansion was too far gone to survive, the other, **Highfield Hall** remains—a glorious, hulking if uninhabit-able relic. The real prize, however, was the estate's former horse barn, already converted into an Equity theater back in the 1940s. In 1969, Oberlin administrator Robert Haslun came up with the idea of an intercollegiate theater company, culled nationwide, and the **College Light Opera Company (CLOC)** was born. Each season, this independent, nonprofit educational institute plucks its 32 players from universities across the country, along with 17 musicians to fill out the full-size orchestra pit. The young hopefuls—many of whom go on to tackle Broadway—mount an astounding nine musicals in as many weeks, much to the delight of what are usually capacity crowds. During the off-season, the theater is used for Conservatory exhibits and recitals, and for productions by the enthusiastic amateur **Falmouth Theatre Guild.** ♦ CLOC perform-ances: Tu-W, F-Sa 8:30PM; Th 2:30PM, 8:30PM late June–Aug. Highfield Dr (west of the railroad tracks), Falmouth. 548.0668

29 Food for Thought ★$$ Housed in a small-scale shopping arcade of pleasing shingled facades, this little eatery is nothing to make a special trip for, but convenient if you're in the neighborhood and in need of a nosh. Breakfast specials run from regional staples like cranberry-granola muffins to such unusual early morning choices as burritos. Dinners are usually a panoply of ethnic specials. ♦ International ♦ Tu-W breakfast and lunch; Th-Sa breakfast, lunch, and dinner; Su breakfast. 37 N Main St (between Main St and Palmer Ave), Falmouth. 548.4498 ♿

29 Enseki Antiques The stock here runs from big, bold pieces, such as the stray carousel horse (clocking in at around $6,000), to more modest, but still charming, items like a 1930s Deco kitchen clock. Gary Enseki was an antiques dealer in England before opening this shop in 1992, and in this short space of time he's made other area antiques shops look pretty pallid. ♦ Daily; call ahead to confirm. 43 N Main St (between Main St and Palmer Ave), Falmouth. 548.7744

30 The Coffee Obsession ★$ The menu at this spare, cathedral-ceilinged cafe consists of "mostly coffee"—e.g., seven different brews of the day, or perhaps iced cappuccino—plus the odd pastry and biscotti. The walls are hung with the works of local artists (and the ceiling, with coffee sacks). Games, books, and newspapers are there for your use. An expanded retail area has the latest in coffee brewing machines and paraphernalia. ♦ Cafe ♦ M-Sa 6:30AM-9PM, Su 7AM-8PM. 110 Palmer Ave (between Hewins and N Main Sts), Falmouth. 540.2233 ♿

Ꭿᴜᴿᴏᴿᴀ Ᏼᴏᴿᴇᴀʟɪꜱ Ꭿᴨᴛɪqᴜᴇꜱ

30 Aurora Borealis Chinaware is the predominant focus of this quirky shop, much of it labeled and exhaustively annotated, so you can educate yourself as you poke around. Strongest in British ceramics, the shop also carries nautical antiques (like telescopes and sextants), Japanese woodblock prints, and vintage local postcards. The prices are reasonable. ♦ Th-Sa 11AM-3PM May–early Sept; or by appointment (548.8280). 104 Palmer Ave (between Hewins and N Main Sts), Falmouth. 540.3385

31 Palmer House Inn $$ Though perhaps a bit fussy for some tastes, this turreted 1901 Victorian establishment offers a cosseting experience. Lavish furnishings make up for the dark original woodwork, and each of the dozen rooms has some special feature: a sleigh bed here, a canopy there. There's also a private cottage set in the garden out back. Complimentary bikes can be used for exploring the vicinity. Innkeeper Joanne Baker's breakfasts (high teas, too, weekends off-season) are lovely and offer such indulgences as Finnish pancake with strawberry soup or chocolate-stuffed French toast with vanilla cream. ♦ 81 Palmer Ave (between Main St and Katherine Lee Bates Rd), Falmouth. 548.1230, 800/472.2632; fax 540.1878 ♿

32 Falmouth Historical Society Museums Set in a formal colonial garden researched by landscape archaeologists and maintained by the Falmouth Garden Club, the three structures in this complex synopsize the high points of Falmouth's history. Guided tours are given of the **Julia Wood House**, cute as a dollhouse, with its tiny, pillared two-tier porch. It was built in 1790 by Dr. Francis Wicks, a smallpox inoculation pioneer who had served as a medical corpsman in the Revolution. His vintage office, where he also practiced dentistry and veterinary medicine, has been reconstructed, and it's fascinating, if sobering.

The **Conant House** (pictured above), originally a half-Cape, was home to Reverend Samuel Palmer, minister of the neighboring First Congregational Church (which harbors a 1796 Paul Revere bell) from 1730 to 1775. Today it's used to display such seagoing memorabilia as harpoons, sailor's valentines (folk sculptures fashioned from shells), and exquisitely embroidered mourning pictures. One room commemorates Katharine Lee Bates, the **Wellesley College** professor and Falmouth native who in 1893 penned the poem/anthem "America the Beautiful." Born at 16 Main Street in 1859, Bates spent her girlhood in Falmouth.

The **Dudley Hallett Barn** houses a 19th-century sleigh, along with assorted farm implements and several grand old flags draped from the hayloft. The **Village Green** that the complex fronts served as a grazing ground for horses into the early 19th century. It was initially laid out, in 1749, as a militia training field—just in time for the skirmishes of 1776 and 1812. Historical Society docents lead free, informative walking tours Tuesday at 4PM, July through August. ♦ Admission. W-Su 2-5PM mid-June–mid-Sept. 55-65 Palmer Ave (between Main St and Katherine Lee Bates Rd), Falmouth. 548.4857

33 Village Green Inn $$ This plain 1804 Federal house got gussied up with fancy shingling in the Victorian fervor of 1894 and is all the prettier for it. Each of the four rooms and one suite has some unusual feature, such as a bathroom with pressed-tin walls. The roomy bay-windowed suite has a full-size desk, helpful for those who can't leave the workaday world behind. Business will fade soon enough, as you lounge on the porch of this bed-and-breakfast, sipping lemonade and surrounded by red geraniums. Breakfast features such delights as apple cinnamon French toast, accompanied by freshly baked blueberry almond bread or raspberry cream coffee cake. ♦ 40 Main St (at Hewins St), Falmouth. 548.5621, 800/237.1119; fax 457.5051

Mostly Hall
BED & BREAKFAST INN

34 Mostly Hall $$ Built by Captain Albert Nye to please his New Orleans–born bride in 1849, this plantation-style house—unique on Cape Cod—got its name more than a century ago from a young visitor who marveled, "Why Mama, it's mostly hall!" By rights it should be called Mostly Headroom: soaring ceilings leave plenty of space for queen-size canopy beds in each of six corner rooms. Officially classified as a "Greek Revival raised cottage," it sits on granite pillars, generously set back from the street. Hosts Caroline and Jim Lloyd have made it a first-class inn. It's not just the breakfasts, though the cheese blintz muffins, eggs Benedict soufflé, and peach–poppy-seed muffins have already prompted a cookbook. The Lloyds go overboard to ensure that you're happily occupied, listing their various concierge services on a slate should you be too shy to ask. They offer badminton, croquet, six free bikes (the **Shining Sea Bikeway** is nearby), and an entire bureau stuffed with brochures and menus, backed by firsthand reports. Pore over the options in the parlor, with its blue-velvet love-seat set, or retire to the widow's walk, equipped with a VCR. ♦ Closed January–mid-February. 27 Main St (between Town Hall Sq and Locust St), Falmouth. 548.3786, 800/682.0565; fax 457.1572

35 Quarterdeck Restaurant ★★$$ You might not think to venture into this Main Street hideaway, which looks like just another dim watering hole from the outside. The interior, however, is surprisingly atmospheric, with modern stained glass and exposed wooden beams. And Culinary Institute of America grad Rob Pacheco offers innovative dishes ranging from pan-blackened scallops with Siberian garlic sauce to succulent specials borrowed from his wife's Azorean background. ♦ International ♦ Daily lunch and dinner. 164 Main St (between Academy La and Post Office Rd), Falmouth. 548.9900

35 Laureen's Just the place for a pick-me-up, Laureen Iseman's snazzy shop/cafe appeals to your senses the second you walk in. Even if you don't decide on a cup of designer coffee (it's delicious), you can't miss the aroma. The deli counter is open from breakfast through nighttime. There's also a great array of gift items—everything from Boyajian caviar (order a day ahead) to books, baskets, spaetzle-makers, and American Spoon Foods by the case, which is how these nonpareil delectables from the wilds of Michigan tend to get consumed. ♦ Daily June-Oct; M-Sa Nov-May. 170 Main St (between Academy La and Post Office Rd), Falmouth. 540.9104, 800/540.9104 ₺

36 Ben & Bill's Chocolate Emporium Look for the kids invariably clustered outside, raptly indulging in piled-high ice-cream cones. The two dozen fresh-cranked flavors would be lure enough, but candy is also made on the premises, in huge copper pots, and you get to watch, surrounded by glass cases filled with the end results. ♦ M-Th 9AM-10PM; F-Su 9AM-11PM. 209 Main St (at Walker St), Falmouth. 548.7878

The 1796 Paul Revere bell that tops Falmouth's First Congregational Church bears an upbeat inscription, in keeping with the fire-and-brimstone bent of his era: "The living to the church I call, and to the grave I summon all."

Child's Play

1 Swirl astride an antique carousel horse at the **Heritage Plantation of Sandwich** or **Flying Horses**.

2 Puzzle over the "driftwood zoo" at the **Jericho House and Barn Museum**.

3 Encounter nature up close at the **Cape Cod Museum of Natural History** and **Wellfleet Bay Wildlife Sanctuary**.

4 Grind corn at the **Dexter Grist Mill** or **Stony Brook Grist Mill**.

5 Hang out with "real" Pilgrims at **Plimoth Plantation**.

6 Practice professional marine biology with **Ocean Quest**.

7 Drool as spuds turn into snacks at the **Cape Cod Potato Chips** factory.

8 Take in a matinee at the **Cape Cod Melody Tent**.

9 Roller-disco at the **Charles Moore Arena**.

10 Drive—for real!—at **Bud's Go-Karts**.

37 Cape Cod Chicken ★★$ A close cousin to the popular Boston Chicken now stalking the nation, this rotisseried-unto-utmost-tenderness bird is a great budget dinner choice, especially with tarragon carrots or perhaps a brown-sugared butternut square on the side. A small, plain, tin-ceilinged space divided by booths, the restaurant is made surprisingly attractive by wall decorations that range from antique valentines to cable skis and bongos. ♦ American ♦ Daily lunch and dinner. 237 Main St (between King and Walker Sts), Falmouth. 457.1302 ₺ Also at: 1671 Rte 28, Centerville, 771.1302 ₺

38 Coonamessett Inn $$$ This inn, which grew from the nucleus of a 1796 homestead, first opened beside the river of the same name (Algonquian for "place of the large fish") back in 1912. Owner Edna Harris moved it to its present site in 1953, and when the property came up for sale in the mid-1960s, an anonymous benefactor—Josiah K. Lilly, by all accounts—bought it to keep it just the way it was. Surrounded by seven acres of gardens and bedecked with blooms (maintained by the full-time "flower lady" on staff), the inn is staid in the best sense of the word, and only a short distance from the bustling town center. There are 16 traditionally decorated suites and eight guest rooms. ♦ Jones Rd (at Gifford St), Falmouth. 548.2300; fax 540.9831 ₺

Within the Coonamessett Inn:

Coonamessett Inn Restaurant
★★★$$$$ Three dining rooms accommodate up to 300 guests, or conference groups. The largest, the **Cahoon Room**, features playful primitive paintings by the late Cape artist Ralph Cahoon (whose commemorative museum is located 10 miles east in Cotuit) and chandeliers resembling hot-air balloons. Chef Richard Cole, a Culinary Institute of America graduate, generates excitement with his napoleon of house-cured salmon, and it's worth turning up in May for his lobster sautéed with spring vegetables, tossed with fettuccine and herbed butter. The pastry chef's creations are hearty yet subtle and also make maximum use of local bounty. ♦ New American ♦ Daily lunch and dinner. Reservations recommended. 548.2300

Eli's ★★$$ The tavern, a handsome blend of blond wood, brass, and hunter-green trim, serves solid Yankee staples like chowder and pot roast; more exotic fare, such as grilled portobello mushroom appetizer or seafood *pappardelle* (with broad noodles), make regular appearances on the menu. ♦ American/International ♦ Daily breakfast, lunch, and dinner. 548.2300

39 Peking Palace ★★$$ Most towns think their Chinese restaurant is tops, but this one really is a winner. It's apparent right from the entryway—bamboo lines the alley to the parking lot, and a small, perfect garden graces the narrow setback. Etched-glass windows and rosewood tables are among the opulent decorative touches. But the best proof is in the dishes themselves—hundreds of them, encompassing Mandarin, Szechuan,

Cantonese, and Polynesian specialties. The shrimp in various sauces are invariably plump, and the dish called "Blessed Family Happiness in the Nest" is aptly named. ♦ Chinese/Takeout ♦ Daily lunch and dinner (until 2AM in summer). 452 Main St (between Lantern La and Gifford St), Falmouth. 540.8204; fax 540.8382 ⑤

40 Betsy's Diner ★★$ This 1957 diner, imported from Pennsylvania by Larry Holmes in 1992, is perfectly packaged nostalgia, down to the neon cup of coffee "steaming" in the window. The fixtures are original, and an added-on dining room features enamel-top tables and vintage advertising art. The jukebox is stocked with period platters (from "Hound Dog" to "Chapel of Love"), and the prices feel like rollbacks, too. Breakfast is served anytime, and the pastries, including meringue pies, are made fresh on the premises. No wonder the joint is jumping from dawn into the night. ♦ American/Takeout ♦ Daily breakfast, lunch, and dinner. 457 Main St (between Nye Rd and King St), Falmouth. 540.0060 ⑤

41 Falmouth Artists Guild Stemming from an informal interest group in the early 1950s, the guild coalesced into a nonprofit corporation in 1969 and set up shop in the **Old Town Infirmary.** Some 8 to 10 shows are held a year, half of them juried, and the work is, as a rule, superior to what you'll see in many more moneyed galleries. It's a great place to catch rising stars. At least 60 percent of the purchase price goes to the artist, reversing the typical commission ratio imposed by commercial galleries. ♦ M-Sa 10AM-3PM. 744 Main St (between Dillingham Ave and Lantern La), Falmouth. 540.3304 ⑤

the FLYING BRIDGE

42 The Flying Bridge ★★$$ This longtime local favorite sparkles with harbor light and is enthusiastically staffed. Enjoy a water view while eating out on the wraparound deck. The menu is extensive (the blackboard specials are your best bet). There's in-house entertainment weekend evenings—and on Thursday nights in summer, you can stroll to the nearby **Harbor Band Shell** for a bit of patriotic oompah-pah. ♦ American/Continental ♦ Daily lunch and dinner Mar-Dec; call for hours Jan-Feb. 220 Scranton Ave (between Clinton Ave and Main St), Falmouth. 548.2700 ⑤

42 Cape Parasailing An instant formula for feeling on top of the world: let a parasail gently lift you aloft from a speeding winch boat (we're told the landings are perfectly soft—but you be the judge). Boats head out

hourly with room for five intrepid fliers. ♦ Fee. Daily July-Aug; call for schedule June, Sept. Falmouth Marine, 220 Scranton Ave (between Clinton Ave and Main St), Falmouth. 457.1900

The Regatta

43 The Regatta of Falmouth By-the-Sea ★★★$$$$ Brantz and Wendy Bryan are widely credited with awakening the Cape from its culinary doldrums. Their airy perch at the mouth of Falmouth Harbor, decorated in ever paler shades of mauve and pink, sets a standard of elegance that only their other restaurant, **The Regatta of Cotuit at The Crocker House,** can hope to match. The plates, for instance, are not just Limoges, but a Limoges design of Wendy's own devising, with two entwined roses. Of course, it's what goes *on* the plates that counts. **The Regatta** classics include corn-and-lobster chowder, wild mushroom strudel, and lamb *en chemise,* stuffed with chèvre, spinach, and pine nuts, wrapped in puff pastry, and served in a Cabernet Sauvignon sauce. Afterward, try the dessert sampling, or perhaps the "chocolate seduction." ♦ International ♦ Daily dinner mid-May–Oct. Reservations recommended. 217 Clinton Ave (between Scranton and Sheridan Aves), Falmouth. 548.5400 ⑤

43 Patriot Party Boats This three-vessel fleet has something for everyone. The magnificent *Liberté,* modeled after a 1750s Pinky schooner, sails the Vineyard Sound; the speedy *Minuteman* was custom-designed to serve expert sportfishers; and the homely *Patriot Too,* with its fully enclosed deck, is ideal for families who want to try "bottom fishing" for scup, bass, fluke, and the like. Tackle and instruction are included, and kids under five ride free. The *Patriot Too* also goes out on scenic cruises, and with any luck Bud Tietje, who started the business, will ride along; he knows every house along the shore. Son Jimmy Tietje's current fleet also conducts bird-watching day trips to the Elizabeth Islands with the Audubon Society, and fills in as a backup ferry to Martha's Vineyard. ♦ Daily 7:30AM-7PM late May–early Sept; call for off-season hours. 227 Clinton Ave (at Scranton Ave), Falmouth. 548.2626, 800/734.0088 ⑤

At Patriot Party Boats:

Clam Shack ★★★$ It's nothing fancy, but has repeatedly garnered *Cape Cod Life*'s "best clam shack" award. This rustic joint consists of one long counter, five drop-down tables suspended by chains, and a million-dollar view. The bellied clams served here are the Cape Codder's homegrown delights. ♦ American ♦ Daily lunch and dinner late May–mid-Sept. 540.7758

44 Holiday Cycles Bob Mollo stocks and services all the regular bikes, from three-speeds to ten-speeds, spanning six-speed "cruisers" with extra-wide handles. He also has tandems and bright-red Italian-made "surreys" with fringe on top, capable of transporting a family of four to six with two or four people doing the peddling (these he rents only by the hour, because, cute as they are, "they do have some weight to them"). The tiny shop, where you can leave your car for free, is located a short jog from the Falmouth Heights beach, and Mollo is happy to steer seasoned cyclists to a 23-mile loop through bucolic Sippewissett that ends on the Shining Sea Bikeway, with the wind (and sun) to their backs. ♦ Daily mid-May–mid-Oct. 465 Grand Ave (off Falmouth Heights Rd), Falmouth Heights. 540.3549 &

44 Food Buoy ★$ Carbo-depleted cyclists aren't the only ones piling into this classic road stand. Anyone in need of a good feed can appreciate the rock-bottom prices on Cape classics like fried clams, and, for the choles-terol-conscious, veggie-burgers. ♦ American/Takeout ♦ Daily breakfast, lunch, and dinner late June–mid-Sept; call for off-season hours; closed mid-Oct–mid-May. 465 Grand Ave (off Falmouth Heights Rd), Falmouth Heights. 540.0080

Inn on the Sound

45 Inn on the Sound $$ This 1880 shingled cottage enjoys a perfect setting, inside and out. The 10 breezy rooms are decorated in a casual beach-house style; the common room is graced by a substantial stone fireplace and several couches arranged so that you can drink up the bluffside sea view, straight out to Martha's Vineyard. This is a relaxed and comfortable kind of place, and the beach is just a short stroll down the bluff. ♦ 313 Grand Ave S (off Falmouth Heights Rd), Falmouth Heights. 457.9666, 800/564.9668

"Never was there a lovelier town than our Falmouth by the sea," wrote "America the Beautiful" author Katharine Lee Bates of her birthplace, continuing, "Tender curves of sky look down on her grace of knoll and lee."

46 The Wharf Restaurant ★★$$ If you favor seafood with a touch of sea breezes, head straight for this waterfront eatery—as generations have since the turn of the century. Their photos line the entryway, and a moosehead with a seen-it-all smile presides over the usual nautical artifacts. The recently revamped menu includes such items as broiled fresh tuna, shark steak, and pasta. Owner Bill Sweeney is committed to fish that's as fresh as possible: The restaurant's fishing boat, *Casino*, may even be seen offloading the day's catch while patrons inside order one of these fresh delicacies. ♦ American ♦ Daily lunch and dinner May-Dec. 281 Grand Ave S (off Falmouth Heights Rd), Falmouth Heights. 548.0777 &

Within The Wharf Restaurant:

Captain Bill's Bluefish Cafe Outside the surf is pounding, and inside the music's throbbing. While the bands aren't big names, the college crowds who flock here couldn't care less. ♦ Cover. F-Su 8PM-1AM May-Sept. 548.2772

47 Lawrence's ★$$ Back in the 1890s, when this was **Lyman Lawrence's Sandwich Depot**, the house specialty came on bread baked on the premises and cost a nickel apiece. Expanded in 1930 by architect **Gilbert E. Boone** in a vaguely Tudor style (dark beams, herringbone brick), this local institution has subjected its menu to some contemporary items. You can still get lobster pie and the like, but the steaks now come with portobello mushrooms, and there are lots of light, budget-priced items, like "beach sticks" (grilled skewers of chicken, beef, and seafood), for after a day in the sun. ♦ American/Continental ♦ M-F dinner; Sa-Su lunch and dinner June–mid-Oct. 24 Nantucket Ave (off Grand Ave), Falmouth Heights. 540.9600 &

48 Iguana's ★$$ With no formal ties to Mexico, this restaurant carries off its south-of-the-border theme with surprising authenticity. Typical dishes like enchiladas and burritos are tastefully done, but be sure to try one of the more unusual plates, including Kokopelli chicken (roasted with pecan bread crumbs and topped with a kiwi-pineapple sauce), or fried ice cream—its contradictory description alone makes it worth a try. The cacti are real, and so is the iguana. ♦ Mexican/Southwestern ♦ Daily lunch and dinner. 31 Rte 28 (between Worcester and Maravista Aves), Falmouth. 540.6000 &

49 Tony Andrews Farm and Produce Stand East Falmouth was once the strawberry capital of the world; this is one of the few farms left where you can still "pick your own" if you feel up to it. Tony Andrews has been nurturing fruit here since 1927, and the scent hangs heavy in the shimmering heat. ♦ Picking: daily 8AM–noon mid-June–mid-Aug. Farmstand: daily mid-June–Nov. 398 Old Meetinghouse Rd (between Old Barnstable and Carriage Shop Rds), East Falmouth. 548.5257 &

50 Ashumet Holly Reservation and Wildlife Sanctuary A 45-acre preserve whose Wampanoag name means "water near a spring," this sanctuary contains more than 1,000 holly trees (some 65 varieties) cultivated by the late Wilfred Wheeler, the state's first commissioner of agriculture, who was concerned by the attrition among native hollies caused by excessive holiday harvesting. Following Wheeler's death in 1961, the property was placed in trust under the aegis of the Audubon Society by Josiah Lilly. Well over a hundred species of birds have been spotted passing through, and about four dozen swallows have returned to nest in the barn every April since at least 1935. In fall, the most sought-after sight is a blooming franklinia— a member of the tea family and named for Benjamin Franklin—which produces large white flowers. Walkers can follow a self-guided map through wildflowers and heather, and around a glacier-formed kettle pond abloom every summer with Oriental lotus flowers. ♦ Admission. Daily dawn-dusk. 286 Ashumet Rd (off Rte 151), East Falmouth. 563.6390 &

51 Oysters Too ★★$$ Just another ranch-style roadside restaurant? Look again, because the decor is quite tasteful—lots of dark wooden booths, illumined by hanging Depression-style glass lamps—and the dishes are delectable and attractively priced. Try the sea scallops, flash-broiled and brushed with lemon-butter, or the sautéed shrimp and chicken with curry cream sauce, topped with peanuts over a bed of rice. Or consider the grilled swordfish New England, served stuffed with crabmeat and topped with sun-dried tomatoes. ♦ American/Continental ♦ Daily dinner. 876 Rte 28 (just west of Fresh Pond Rd), East Falmouth. 548.9191 &

52 Waquoit Bay National Estuarine Research Reserve Estuaries, where freshwater rivers meet the ocean, are among the most fertile—and fragile—segments of the coastal environment. Traditionally dredged, filled, and otherwise manipulated to suit commercial needs, these delicate ecosystems have come under the protective scrutiny of the National Estuarine Research Reserve System (NERR), created by an act of Congress in 1972. One of only a handful of such sanctuaries in New England, the Waquoit Bay property (added to the NERR roster in 1988) is a shallow embayment covering 2,250 acres, including a 500-acre state park at South Cape Beach. The old **Swift Estate** mansion is gradually being turned into a headquarters with exhibition space; meanwhile, you can find your own living exhibits by walking its paths. During summer, resident naturalists offer guided walks (covering such topics as birds, plants, and dune ecology) and "Evenings on the Bluff," family-oriented educational programs. ♦ Tu-Sa July-Aug; call for off-season hours. 149 Waquoit Hwy (between Seacoast Shores Blvd and Takemmeh Way), East Falmouth. 457.0495 &

Bed & Breakfast
Of Waquoit Bay

53 Bed & Breakfast of Waquoit Bay $ Tom and Janet Durkin's four-bedroom bed-and-breakfast, set back on several acres of tree-shaded grounds along the bucolic Child's River, reflects the couple's interests in jazz and other lively arts. The 1920s-era "great room," which resembles a cross between a chapel and an arts-and-crafts bungalow, is adorned with bold paintings by their daughter, and has a piano for visiting musicians/friends. Janet's "Waverly fabric fetish" has resulted in some very handsome rooms. Europeans who've discovered this hideaway appreciate the private baths, complete with bidets; off one bedroom there's also a secluded roof deck, suitable for sunbathing au naturel. Omelettes, French toast and bacon, pancakes, and homemade cranberry muffins are the breakfast offerings. ♦ 176 Waquoit Hwy (between Baptiste La and Cross Rd), East Falmouth. 457.0084; fax 457.0084

54 Moonakis Cafe ★★$ If it's not past 2PM, try stopping at this low-key roadside restaurant. Unless you're doing the bed-and-breakfast route, where breakfasting is a competitive sport, you won't come across repasts like these anywhere. Omelette varieties include lobster-asparagus, bacon-and-brie, and smoked shrimp–red onion–chèvre, to name just a few of the more unusual combos. Or perhaps you'd prefer chicken-apple sausage, pumpkin-nut pancakes, or Belgian waffles with kiwi? Lunch is good, too, if a bit more predictable (sandwiches and burgers), and you can always finish up with a rousing apple brown Betty. ♦ American ♦ M-Sa breakfast and lunch; Su breakfast. 460 Waquoit Hwy (between Cross and Carriage Shop Rds), East Falmouth. 457.9630 ♿

55 New Seabury, Cape Cod $$$$ The subject of a long and so far futile land rights battle initiated by the Wampanoag tribe, who were granted most of Mashpee in 1660, this enormous resort development—some 1,700 condos spread over 2,000 acres—contains about 170 rentable units, as well as three miles of private beach on Nantucket Sound, two 18-hole golf courses, two swimming pools, 16 all-weather tennis courts, and an indoor recreation complex. The condos are sorted into more than a dozen "villages," of which four are open to transients: **Tide-watch,** a 1960s-era hotel complex adjoining the country club; **The Mews,** made up of California-modern villas and houses, along with a Nautilus center; **SeaQuarters,** golf-side villas with Jacuzzi solaria; and **Maushop Village,** modeled on Nantucket cottages, with rose-entwined white picket fences and crushed-clamshell walkways—and named for the mammoth Wampanoag sea deity. ♦ Great Oak Rd (south of Red Brook Rd). 477.9111, 800/999.9033; fax 477.9790 ♿

Within New Seabury, Cape Cod's Maushop Village:

Popponesset Marketplace Within this cluster of white-shingled buildings are about a dozen shops, mostly offering resortwear and staples, and the casual **Marketplace Cafe** (477.9111), good for a quick bite. Special events appealing to kids are scheduled through the summer months. ♦ Shops: M-Sa; Su noon-5PM late June–early Sept. Sa; Su noon-5PM late May–late June, early Sept–mid-Oct. Restaurant: daily breakfast, lunch, and dinner late June–early Sept; Sa-Su breakfast, lunch, and dinner late May–late June, early Sept–mid-Oct. 477.9111 ♿

Popponesset Inn ★★★$$$ Since taking over in 1988, co-owner Linda Zammer has lightened up the decor of this venerable 1940s inn-turned-restaurant with a color scheme that's predominantly white (down to the painted Windsors) with washes of pale blue.

The whole place—and it's large, accommodating as many as 500 in enclosed decks and tents—seems to embrace the sea, and vice versa. Executive chef David Schneider is a veteran of the RockResorts circuit (Carambola, Williamsburg, Woodstock) and does right by local bounty, wrapping seafood *en papillote* and smothering lobster in a brandied cream Newburg. If your wallet or cholesterol level make you wary, try the lighter fare in adjoining **Poppy's** or just sip a "Poppy Codder" (Absolut vodka, with cranberry juice and a splash of Triple Sec) while imbibing the sea breezes. ♦ Continental ♦ Daily lunch and dinner Apr–mid-Oct. Reservations recommended. Mall Way (off Shore Dr). 477.1100 ♿

56 Mashpee Commons The principals of Fields Point Limited Partnership (the same company that developed New Seabury) have gone to great pains to create a 30-acre mall that looks like a traditional New England town. They went so far as to measure and replicate the sidewalks and streets of Woodstock, Vermont, in order to create a pedestrian-friendly "town center" encompassing some 50 shops and eateries. The buildings erected to date (designed by such firms as **Prellwitz/ Chilinski, Ellenzweig Associations, Orr & Taylor,** and **A.E. Ferragamo**) are indeed handsome. But nearly two decades into its master plan (formalized in 1979), the complex still has a sterile, reconstituted feel. The current phase, with input from Miami architects **Andres Duany** and **Elizabeth Plater-Zyberk** of Seaside, Florida fame, involves an influx of neo-traditional dwellings ranging from half-Capes to "captain's houses" and "courtyard apartments." Scheduled for completion in 1999 is the **Boch Center for Performing Arts,** endowed by automobile mogul Ernie Boch, who summers on Martha's Vineyard, and designed by noted Cambridge architect **Graham Gund.**

If the development-oriented ethos doesn't disturb you too much, there are several appealing shops worth browsing here. **Signature** (539.0029) features chic—as opposed to cutesy—crafts. There's a de rigueur **Gap** (477.6668), as well as an **Irresistibles** (477.5853), a women's clothing chain that carries cottons (especially hand-knit sweaters) and the Segrets line of vividly printed sportswear. There's also a six-screen movie theater—concealed behind a tasteful curved arcade—and on Wednesday and Friday nights in summer there are free outdoor concerts. ◆ Shops: daily. Rte 151 and Falmouth Rd, Mashpee. 477.5400 ♿

Within the Mashpee Commons:

Gone Tomatoes ★★$$ Who would expect to find haute Northern Italian cooking in a mall? This handsome bi-level restaurant, with creamy walls, teal accents, and terra-cotta floors, does a great, undeniably rich ravioli carbonara. Seafood generally turns up in the daily specials, and there are at least a half-dozen types of grilled focaccia pizza always available. Service is friendly and efficient—helpful if you're trying to catch a movie next door. ◆ Italian/Takeout ◆ Daily lunch and dinner. 477.8100 ♿

57 Old Indian Meetinghouse Built in 1684 on Santuit Pond and moved here in 1717, this is one of the oldest church buildings in America, and is still used for worship and meetings. Converted by British missionary Richard Bourne (the son of a wealthy shipping merchant), the "Massapee" tribe—spellings varied widely early on—was welcomed into the Congregational fold in 1670. In the mid-1800s, after a succession of indigenous preachers, the Mashpee people decided to become Baptists. Volunteer curators can fill you in further; you might also want to buy a copy of Russell M. Peters's excellent history, *The Wampanoags of Mashpee.* The interior of the building is plain, except for an improbable Victorian chandelier, and much smaller in scale than comparable structures erected by the colonists. ◆ Donation. Service: Su 11AM; once a month in July and August; call for dates. Meetinghouse Rd (at Falmouth Rd), Mashpee. 477.0208

58 Wampanoag Indian Museum Housed in a 1793 half-Cape, this collection of tools, baskets, mementos, etc., is not impressive in and of itself; one must read between the lines, or better yet, read some of the historical literature to put the collection into perspective. When Captain John Smith came reconnoitering in 1614, the Wampanoags of eastern Massachusetts may have numbered more than 30,000. In 1617, after Lieutenant Thomas Hunt had kidnapped six men from the tribe and sold them into slavery, a small band boarded an unoccupied ship in retaliation—and there encountered plague, which swept through the community. People died by the thousands, and the whole fabric of society unraveled. (This is why the Pilgrims were able to take over an abandoned farm site when they arrived a few years later.) Uninformed visitors have been known to dismiss this modest museum, but much can be learned from the meager artifacts if one is willing to delve. ◆ Donation. M-Sa 10AM-2PM. Rte 130 (between Great Neck Rd and Lovells La), Mashpee. 477.1536

59 The Flume ★★★$$$ This pared-down yet striking restaurant is named for the ladder that fish climb to spawn. Co-owner Earl Mills is both Chief Flying Eagle of the Wampanoag tribe and an extraordinary chef. Here he serves such New England classics as clam chowder, codfish cakes, scalloped oysters, baked beans, pot roast, apple-stuffed duckling, and an authentic Indian pudding. In addition, at press time Mills had just had his book, *Son of Mashpee,* published. Get your copy autographed. ◆ American/Takeout ◆ M-Sa lunch and dinner; Su dinner late May–mid-Sept; call for off-season hours; closed December through March. Lake Ave (off Rte 130), Mashpee. 477.1456

60 Lowell Holly Reservation This 135-acre woodland preserve was bequeathed by former Harvard University president Abbott Lawrence Lowell to the trustees of the reservation in 1943. It's the oldest private land trust in the country, having been founded in 1891 by Harvard president Charles Eliot, and now includes tens of thousands of acres of exceptional scenic, historic, and ecological value. In addition to some 500 holly trees, the reservation—an unspoiled peninsula jutting into Cape Cod's largest freshwater ponds, Mashpee and Wakeby—harbors stands of native American beech untouched for centuries. Wildflowers to be seen include beechdrops (a brown parasite that blooms under beeches), silverrod (a slim cousin of goldenrod), and pink lady's slipper, a native orchid that blooms in spring. ◆ Free. Daily late May–mid-Oct. Off S Sandwich Rd (between Rte 130 and Sandwich-Cotuit Rd), Mashpee. 617/921.1944

Bests

Richard P. Carpenter
Associate Travel Editor, *Boston Globe*

These, in no particular order, are a few of my favorite things.

Main Street, Hyannis—Being as touristy as I wanna be, as I poke through the varied shops.

Thornton W. Burgess Museum, Sandwich—Revisiting the heroes of my childhood reading, including Grandfather Frog and Peter Rabbit.

The **Cape Cod Scenic Railroad**—Returning to an earlier and more relaxed era, especially on the railroad's delicious dinner excursions.

The **seashore**—Strolling in the sand before the crowds of summer arrive, or after they're gone.

Chatham Bars Inn—Admiring the Old Cape Cod ambience of the stately main building and the cottages by the sea.

The Wampanoag, who maintained summer camps in the area that is now Falmouth, called the region Suckanesset, which translates roughly as "where the black wampum is found."

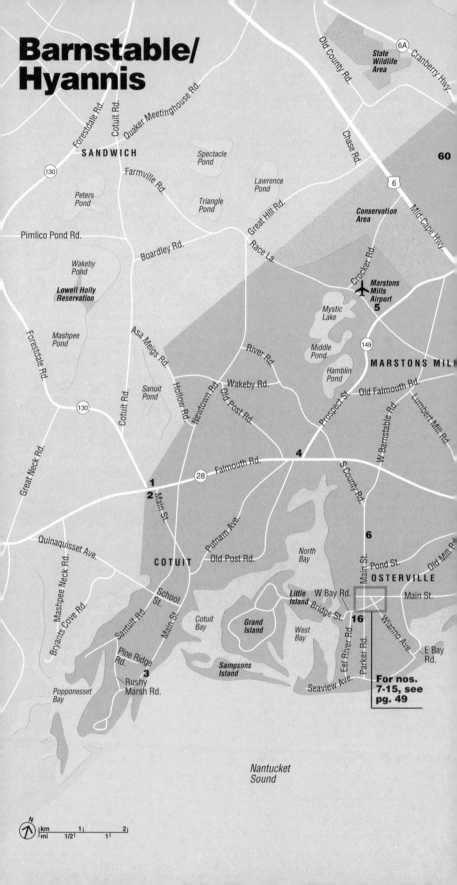

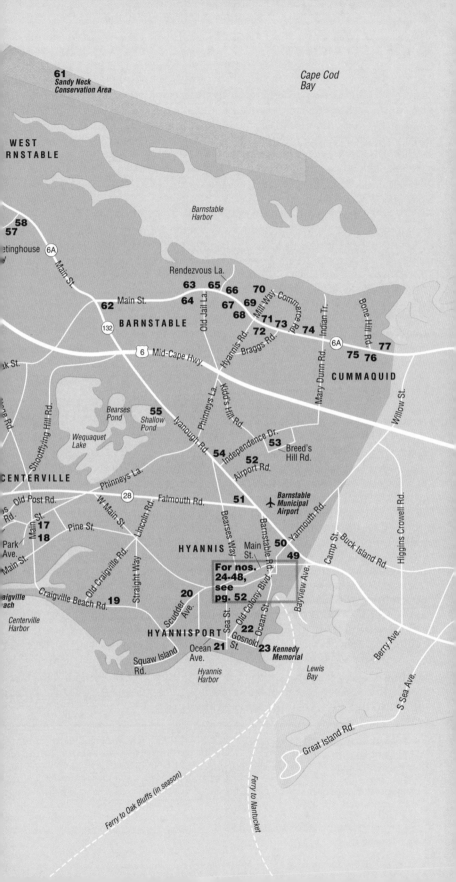

Barnstable/Hyannis

Barnstable County is a study in contrasts. One of the oldest communities on the Cape (it was founded by the parish of English Congregational minister John Lothrop in 1639), it's also a nexus of commercial activity—particularly in Hyannis, the Cape's transportation hub and "unofficial capital city." With the introduction of the **Cape Cod Mall** in 1970, strip development ran rampant along **Routes 132** and **28**, while the town center of Hyannis slipped into shabbiness. In the early 1990s, however, local boosters teamed up with Barnstable semiretiree **Benjamin Thompson** (the architect who masterminded Boston's Faneuil Hall Marketplace) to develop the notion of a "Main Street Waterfront District." Thompson had been pushing this plan, to no avail, since the early 1960s; now, however, the citizenry is paying attention, and results are accreting quickly.

Even a few years ago, the waterfront was just a big outdoor waiting room for the hundreds of thousands of ferry passengers who pass through yearly. Now they can wait in style, tided over with snacks and meals at the dozen or so appealing restaurants that line an attractive harborfront park. The ambience of **Main Street**, the principal thoroughfare, has never been quite as cosmopolitan as Kennedy fans expect. In fact, the allure of the Kennedy family compound, hidden beyond hedges in nearby Hyannisport, brought in T-shirt shops and other forms of commercialization that made things worse. But a better balance is being struck now. Restaurants like **Alberto's** have restored some cachet to an evening on the town, the rose-clustered patio at the **Asa Bearse House** fosters the fine art of people watching, and several intriguing shops, such as **Plush & Plunder**, reward the determined browser. Even those die-hard Kennedy-peepers now have a healthy outlet: The **John F. Kennedy Hyannis Museum**, a small but stirring audiovisual display at **Old Town Hall**, shows the human side of the legend that has captivated so many.

West of Hyannis is a cluster of seaside communities—full of sleepy, old-money charm—scarcely touched by the relentless commercialism that infects Route 28. Take a detour into **Cotuit**, so popular among academics since the turn of the century (Erik Erikson summered here) that it earned the nickname "Little Harvard"; it's also renowned for its oysters. Meanwhile, **Osterville**, bought from Native Americans in 1648 for two copper kettles and some fencing, and originally known as "Oysterville," has evolved into the Cape's most affluent community, harboring such names as Cabot, Mellon, and du Pont. You won't find a whole lot to do here, except perhaps to gaze at the real estate (much of it cloistered behind broad gates and long drives) and pretend-shop for your own mythical multimillion-dollar mansion. **Centerville**, a site of Christian Camp Meeting Association gatherings since 1872, has the appeal of an old-fashioned town; it also harbors the popular (and usually packed) **Craigville Beach**, where the water, warmed by the sound, hovers in the comfortable mid–70-degree range.

Tradition-seekers can head north to the bayside villages of **Barnstable**, a tidy trail of historical sites and bed-and-breakfasts. They'll also discover a couple of radical enterprises, such as the **Pinske Gallery**.

---

1 Cahoon Museum of American Art
The 1775 Georgian Colonial farmhouse in which this little museum is located is an artwork in its own right, especially the

1810 stairway stenciling. The top floor, with a flip-up wall, could be converted into a ballroom, handy in the house's tavern days. Bought by naïf artists Ralph and Martha Cahoon in 1945, the house has served as a nonprofit museum since the mid-1980s.

The core collection of the Cahoons' work is of limited appeal, though apparently of considerable value; it consists of "contemporary primitive" pastiches of Cape Cod icons (mermaids, lighthouses, and the like) rendered in a fashion perhaps better suited to furniture decoration, the craft in which they started out. But the changing special exhibits, five or six a year, are much stronger. Some draw on a permanent collection of lesser-known but nonetheless noteworthy American artists, from itinerant portrait painters to Impressionists. Contemporary artists are shown as well; a standout exhibit in 1996 featured the pastel artist Jane Lincoln, and her pieces showing the four seasons of a cranberry bog. The curatorial notes, posted alongside the artwork, are singularly jargon-free and thought-provoking. ♦ Free. Tu-Sa Jan, Apr-Dec. 4676 Falmouth Rd (between Santuit-Newtown Rd and Rte 130), Cotuit. 428.7581 &

1 Isaiah Thomas Books & Prints How often do you see a rare book from the 17th century just sitting on a shelf for anyone to leaf through, or a priceless first edition plunked on the counter? Owner James S. Visbeck, who in 1991 moved his 60,000 tomes to this circa 1860 house, is clearly a book-lover, not just an accumulator. His wares *have* tended to pile up, forming stalagmites on the floor and even encroaching onto the sofa. But no matter—many pleasurable hours could be spent poking around among the miniatures, maps, prints, "books on books," and other subspecialties too numerous to list. ♦ M-Sa; Su noon-5PM June-Oct. Tu-Sa; Su noon-5PM Nov-May. 4632 Falmouth Rd (between Santuit-Newtown Rd and Rte 130), Cotuit. 428.2752 &

The Regatta

2 The Regatta of Cotuit at The Crocker House ★★★$$$$ Brantz and Wendy Bryan's branch restaurant has all the allure of their summers-only waterside landmark in Falmouth, plus its own unique charms. The eight intimate dining rooms in this converted circa 1790 stagecoach inn have a variety of decors, ranging from delicate florals to clubby burnished wood. The unifying thread is chef Heather Allen's unsurpassable seasonal fare, supplemented by an astute sprinkling of herbs and garnishes from the kitchen's *potagère* (garden). She might pair sautéed Plymouth rainbow trout, encrusted in pistachios, with orange-cilantro butter sauce, for example, or grilled *poussin* (young chicken) with fresh rosemary and thyme. For all the finesse poured into the preparation and presentation, this is not a stiff, pretentious place—in fact, the dress code is "attractively formal or attractively informal," and the atmosphere pleasantly festive. ♦ New American ♦ Daily dinner. 4613 Falmouth Rd (between Main St and Bowdoin Rd), Cotuit. 428.5715 &

3 Samuel B. Dottridge Homestead There are more exciting historical museums on the Cape, but if you're in the neighborhood, take a quick look around this circa 1790 home, which was occupied during the early 19th century by a carpenter and his family. A barn museum out back, also maintained by the Historical Society of Santuit & Cotuit, contains all sorts of odd flotsam from several centuries of domestic and agricultural endeavor. ♦ Free. Tu, Th, Sa-Su 2:30-5PM mid-June–mid-Sept. 1148 Main St (near Ocean View Ave), Cotuit. 428.0461

4 Inn at the Mills $$ It's hard to imagine a more idyllic spot than this 1780 house (on the National Register of Historic Places; illustrated above), overlooking a placid pond complete with swans, geese, and a gazebo. It's a natural for weddings—indeed, for celebrations of any sort. Owner Bill Henry used to run the restaurant at the old **Popponessett Inn,** and leftover celebrity photos line a side stairwell off a rustic yet elegant dining area. The front room is a formal parlor with wingback chairs and crystal decanters. It's attached to a wicker-filled sun porch with a white baby grand, and a swimming pool just outside. Up the semi-circular staircase are five rooms with pencil-post, four-poster beds or canopied twins, plus the "hayloft" room, which seems to go on forever. Even with no advertising (not so much as a sign), the inn tends to be booked up solid through the summer, but it's just as lovely and, if possible, even more restful when the greenery's gone and the fireplaces are glowing. ♦ 71 Rte 149 (between Rte 28 and River Rd), Marstons Mills. 428.2967; fax 420.0075

Cape Cod Soaring

5 Cape Cod Soaring If you've ever wondered what it's like to fly like an eagle, here's your chance to find out. Coasting in a sleek white glider along the sea breezes "takes no more training than watching TV," claims pilot Randy Charlton. That's because he does the driving. A light plane tows the glider to anywhere from 1,000 to 5,000 feet up (depending on length of flight), then you ease on down in absolute silence, perhaps performing a few "aerobatics," if you wish, along the way. You could stay up as long as six to eight hours, but rides generally run 20 to 40 minutes, with the fees rising concomitantly. Should you really get hooked, Charlton also provides rentals and instruction for getting a glider license (teenagers have done solos). ♦ Daily Apr-Nov; by appointment Dec-Mar; weather permitting. Marstons Mills Airport, Race La (at Rte 149), Marstons Mills. 540.8081, 800/660.4563

6 Appleseed's "Suburban classics" sums up the feminine image evoked here. This relatively small, New England–based chain and mail-order outfit has the well-heeled matron pretty well cased. It offers cotton and florals, in every reasonable combination, and in sizes up to 20. ♦ Daily. 1374 Main St (between Pond St and Bumps River Rd), Osterville. 428.6081 &

6 The Farmhouse Carolyn and Barry Crawford have set up their antiques store to resemble a lived-in house, but with price tags. Over half the stock is here on consignment, so there are many treasured objects. The shop was recently expanded to add 700 square feet of antiques. The overall effect is an intentional mishmash, with stray architectural elements to lend intrigue. ♦ M-Sa; Su noon-4PM. 1340 Main St (between Pond St and Bumps River Rd), Osterville. 420.2400

6 Oak and Ivory This is the only place off-island where you're apt to encounter authentic Nantucket lightship baskets. Bob Marks, a Nantucket native, studied with master basket-maker Bill Sevrens. Each creation takes around 40 hours to put together, and prices range from a few hundred dollars for a simple ice-bucket design to a few thousand dollars for an exquisite Nantucket basket candlestick table. The store also stocks a few rare antique baskets, as well as compatible home furnish-ings, such as nubby Kennebunk Weavers throws and 18th-century reproduction furni-ture. ♦ M-Sa; Su noon-5PM May-Dec. Call for off-season hours. 1112 Main St (between Pond St and Bumps River Rd), Osterville. 428.9425 &

7 Joan Peters The "Joan Peters look," featured in design showrooms from Boston to Dallas, is not so much a look as a world, a pastel-hued, light-drenched landscape where no unpleasantness—much less tastelessness —could possibly intrude. The atelier here produces her signature fabrics and ceramics, and the showroom represents a cohesive portfolio, from throw pillows that resemble little fairy-tale cottages to pale, floral-splashed matching comforters, cushions, tablecloths, and chair covers. You could even commission

a complementary sink, at a price. ♦ M-Sa. 885 Main St (between Bay St and Meadow Lark La), Osterville. 428.3418

8 Country Store Here is an unspoiled general store that looks, sounds, and even smells as a general store should (a blend of venerable dust and wax). Charlie Kalas grew up in this circa 1890 emporium and hasn't seen a need to change it much. Sure, penny candy costs more like 15 cents now, but kids still come around, attracted also by the assortment of ice-cream pops. ♦ Daily 7:30AM-8:30PM. 877 Main St (at Bay St), Osterville. 428.2097

9 A. Stanley Wheelock Antiques A semi-retired, Parsons-trained interior designer, Wheelock pretty much buys to suit himself these days, which works out well since his taste is right on target. Among the covetable objects that have been on sale: a cast-zinc French shop sign in the shape of a horse head and a lacquered Regency table. Strong suits include Orientalia, silver, and a general mélange of "very decorative things." ♦ M-Sa Apr-Dec; by appointment Jan-Mar. 870 Main St (between Tower Hill Rd and Blossom Ave), Osterville. 420.3170

9 Eldred Wheeler The company's self-description—"Handcrafters of Fine 18th Century American Furniture"—may be a bit oxymoronic, unless these artisans have managed to master time travel. But their reproductions are almost as nice as the real thing, a little less fragile, and a whole lot cheaper (80 percent or more). Bigger modern bodies appreciate a bed in a noncolonial size, like queen or king, and if you're embarrassed to buy this kind of thing, you could always rough it up a bit and pretend it belonged to your great-great-great-grandfather. ♦ M-Sa. 866 Main St (between Tower Hill Rd and Blossom Ave), Osterville. 428.9049 &

10 Joseph's Restaurant ★★$$ This informal cafe, with bookshelves trailing ivy, encourages you to take your time with chef Joe Murray's hearty Italian dishes. Though he has come up with an ingenious faux Alfredo (using cottage cheese and skim milk) for the faint or sensible of heart, the offerings are mostly peasantlike and plentiful: baked ziti with five cheeses, for example, or roast vegetables *al forno*. Lunch features subs (including grilled chicken pesto with fontina) and custom-made pizzas. ♦ Italian ♦ Daily breakfast, lunch, and dinner. 825 Main St (between Wianno Ave and Parker Rd), Osterville. 420.1742 &

OSTERVILLE

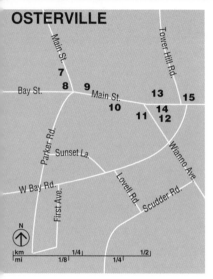

Main St.

Tower Hill Rd.

Bay St.

7

8 **9** Main St. **13** **15**

10 **14**

11 **12**

Parker Rd.

Sunset La.

Wianno Ave.

W Bay Rd.

First Ave.

Lovell Rd.

Scudder Rd.

N

km		
mi	1/4	1/2
	1/8	1/4

11 Mark, Fore & Strike Purveying to ultra-preps since 1951, this Florida-based chain remains a beacon of unchanging mores. Women can choose among *Provençale*-print garment bags and traditionalist fashions from such designers as David Brooks; meanwhile, men can browse through the emblem belts (whales, ducks, and so on) and a rainbow of Eric Holch ties. ♦ M-Sa; Su noon-4PM late May–Dec. 21 Wianno Ave (between W Bay Rd and Main St), Osterville. 428.2270 & Also at: 482 Main St (between Chatham Bars Ave and Blackberry La), Chatham. 945.0568 &

12 Talbot's This is the only post on the Cape for this preppy outfitter, and it's perfectly situated in the epicenter of classicism. The company may be owned by a Japanese conglomerate now, but it keeps churning out the most appropriate business and social fashions for folks on the East Coast—which is to say, a bit over-formal at times but always in impeccable taste. ♦ M-W, F-Sa; Th 9AM-8PM; Su noon-5PM. 32 Wianno Ave (between W Bay Rd and Main St), Osterville. 428.2204 & Also at: Harwich Commons, 114 Rte 137 (at Rte 39), Harwich, 432.8900 &

13 Natural Image Everything you see is made of natural fibers, but of a rarefied caliber. Designer Jackie McCoy's dresses fashioned from antique linen tablecloths, and wedding gowns of handmade lace, are pretty (and expensive), while still off the rack. Custom work is also available, at even higher prices. ♦ M-Sa May-Oct. 812 Main St (between Tower Hill Rd and Blossom Ave), Osterville. 428.5729 &

Operating from 1860 to 1923, the West Barn-stable Brick Company churned out as many as 100,000 bricks a day. Today, these collectibles fetch up to $35 apiece.

14 Clothes Encounters The Cape is full of thrift shops that may do wonders for charity but do little for one's clothes closet. At Ann Marie Ross's shop, however, the women's hand-me-downs are all in impeccable condition and tend to that timeless look that never goes out of fashion. She has two daughters who "never wear anything twice"; they should consider going into the garment business. ♦ Tu-Sa Apr-Dec; Sa Jan-Mar. 805 Main St (between W Bay Rd and Wianno Ave), Osterville. 428.9265

15 Wimpy's Seafood Cafe & Market ★$$ This modest and moderately priced restaurant was founded in 1938 to serve workers imported to install the town's water mains in 1938; with only six stools, they had to eat in shifts. After numerous expansions, it now comfortably seats 200. The decor is semi-colonial (huge stone fireplace, lots of wood trim) except for the cheery solarium toward the back. The menu is fittingly traditionalist, from the signature jumbo Wimpy's burger to "Mother's" chicken pot pie. The retail store next door offers all kinds of goodies, including the freshest of seafoods and homemade chowders, pasta, and salads. ♦ American ♦ Restaurant: daily lunch and dinner. Market: daily. 752 Main St (at Tower Hill Rd), Osterville. Cafe 428.6300, market 428.3474 &

16 Captain John Parker House Serving as the main museum for the ever-grow-ing collections of the Osterville Historical Society, this 1824 house exhibits an intriguing array of China trade spoils. There's an especially nice collection of dolls and toys upstairs. Next door, past historically accurate plantings maintained by the Osterville Garden Club, is the 1728 **Cammett House,** a "one-pile-deep narrow house" (only one room straight through). It was never expanded; the owners couldn't afford to add on. Rescued when a condominium development threatened it with demolition, the house is a valuable repository of early building techniques; down in the cellar, archaeological fragments are displayed. Completing the trio of historic properties is the 19th-century **Herbert F. Crosby Boat Shop,** where owners of antique boats can research their boats' roots and less-nautical types can admire such vessels as a *1922 Catboat Cayuga* and a *Wianno Senior,* favored by John Fitzgerald Kennedy. ♦ Nominal admission. Tu, Th, Su 1:30-4:30PM mid-June–mid-Sept. 155 W Bay Rd (between Parker and Eel River Rds), Osterville. 428.5861

17 The Inn at Fernbrook $$$ The Cape is rife with historic inns, but few with such a star-studded past as this onetime showpiece estate, which is on the National Register of Historic Buildings. Howard Marston of Boston's Parker House had it built in 1881, commissioning renowned landscape architect Frederick Law Olmsted to design the sunken sweetheart garden of pink and red roses, pocked with water lily ponds and ringed with exotic trees. After Marston's son gambled away his legacy, the house was bought in the 1930s by chemist Dr. Herbert Kalmus, co-inventor of Technicolor, who hosted such notables as Walt Disney, Cecil B. DeMille, and William B. Mayer. When Kalmus left the property to the Catholic church, it became a summer retreat for Cardinal Francis Spellman, who entertained both Nixon and Kennedy here. The house had fallen on hard times when Brian Gallo and Sal DiFlorio (both escapees from the mega-hotel trade) took it on; they restored it to its Queen Anne grandeur and filled it with period furnishings.

Among the five rooms and suites at this luxurious bed-and-breakfast (there's also a pleasant garden cottage), two are knockouts. The **Olmsted Suite,** on the dormered third floor, has two bedrooms with queen-size brass beds, a living room with a fireplace, and at the end of a staircase so steep you practically have to crawl up, a little balcony with a telescope, leading to a private roof deck. The **Spellman Room,** adapted from a chapel, is atmospheric to say the least, with a private entrance, stained-glass windows, a tile fireplace, and a massive Victorian canopy bed. Breakfast entrées include such delights as Dutch baby (a German-style pancake made like an egg puff) and egg linden (baked in a muffin tin with two different cheeses, white pepper, and heavy cream), both served with homemade muffins, toast, fresh fruit, and bacon or sausage. ◆ 481 Main St (between S Main St and Briarcliff La), Centerville. 775.4334; fax 778.4455

17 Centerville Historical Society Museum Heavily endowed by native son Charles Lincoln Ayling, this collection is more extensive than most, running to 14 rooms. Among the treasures: Reginald Fairfax Bolles's 1922 portrait of Mrs. Ayling wearing an embroi-dered, moss velvet Fortuny gown, with the gown itself displayed alongside; some 350 other gowns, plus accessories; a great cache of dolls and toys; carvings of native Cape birds by Anthony Elmer Crowell; currency dating back two centuries, along with some lottery tickets that helped finance the Revolution; and many military and marine artifacts. Also on display are old cranberrying and carpentry tools and a "colonial revival" kitchen as envisioned by Victorians inspired by an exhibit at the 1876 World's Fair. "Of course, in colonial days they never would have had so much *stuff,*" says director/curator Barbara Friling, gesturing to the shelves packed with now-rare crockery. There's so much to see, you really do need a guide to make sense of it all, so viewing is by tour only, with the last group leaving at 3:30PM. ◆ Admission. W-Su 1:30-4:30PM mid-June–mid-Sept. 513 Main St (between S Main St and Briarcliff La), Centerville. 775.0331

18 Four Seas A smithy and garage around the turn of the century, this classic ice-cream parlor—in business since 1934—has seating for only a couple of dozen customers at a time at its blue-and-white counter stools, booths, and bentwood chairs, but it still manages to serve some 3,000 people a day all summer long. Fans range from the Kennedys (they opened a charge account) to delighted critics from *Food & Wine* magazine and the like. As the authors of *The Best Ice Cream and Where to Find It* wrote: "The Four Seas is to Cape Cod what the White House is to Washington: Every VIP who passes through the area finds time for a brief visit." The store got its name from the "four seas" that surround the Cape (Buzzards and Cape Cod bays, the Atlantic Ocean, and Nantucket Sound), and its reputation from butterfat-packed, super-premium concoctions in delectable flavors that include rum butter toffee and cantaloupe. It's all made fresh daily, and once a year owner Richard Warren whips up his own unique variety, Cape Cod beach plum. ◆ Daily 10AM-10PM late May–early Sept. 360 S Main St (at Main St), Centerville. 775.1394 ও

19 Craigville Pizza & Mexican ★$ Other than the heavily laden nachos, don't bother with the Mexican fare here. The tomato sauce is more at home on the regular or whole-wheat pizzas, piled with vegetables, meats, and even on such entrées as chicken fajitas. This small bustling place tends to get packed, even early in the evening. ♦ Italian/Mexican ♦ Daily lunch and dinner. 618 Craigville Beach Rd (between Old Town Rd and Marie Ave), Hyannisport. 775.2267 ♿ Also at: 4 Barlows Landing Rd (just west of Rte 28), Pocasset. 564.6306

20 Simmons Homestead Inn $$$ A variety of animal motifs accentuate and differentiate the 12 rooms at this 1820s captain's house, and owner Bill Putman has a certain Tigger-like quality himself. He positively bounces with enthusiasm—over his inn, over this corner of Cape Cod, over life in general. A former ad man, Putman sees his role here as that of not only innkeeper but also "purveyor of timely tidbits of information," and he has compiled detailed tipsheet/maps covering all there is to do, see, and eat in the region. While he professes to be a terrible cook, guests—including such notables as Carly Simon, James Woods, and Dinah Shore—have had no complaints about the delicious blueberry pancakes or homemade French toast served for breakfast. As for those animals—stuffed, wooden, needlepointed, painted, every which way but real—you'll probably find them either delightful or de trop. ♦ 288 Scudder Ave (between Smith St and the West End Rotary), Hyannis. 778.4999, 800/637.1649; fax 790.1342

21 Sea Breeze Inn $$ This shingle-sided house has been spiffed up to the hilt, with picket fence, gazebo, picnic tables, and wooden swing. The 14 rooms may not be antiques-laden, but they're cheery and fresh. You can enjoy an expansive continental breakfast, and then there's the scent of the sea, which is just a short walk away. ♦ 397 Sea St (just south of Ocean Ave), Hyannis. 771.7213; fax 862.0663

22 Up the Creek ★★★$$ Off the beaten track but worth a short detour, Jimmy Dow's marginally anti-mainstream restaurant offers an inviting and affordable alternative to the hurly-burly of downtown Hyannis. The place has a timeless look, with a cream and forest-green color scheme, and encircling the tables are six ample booths. Among the more popular dishes is a seafood strudel served with hollandaise; daily specials are apt to include as ambitious a dish as veal Savoyard, with sun-dried tomatoes, feta, and Marsala demiglace. Best of all, you feel as if you've left the strip-mall joints of Routes 28 and 132 far behind. ♦ American/International ♦ M-F lunch and dinner, Sa dinner, Su brunch and dinner May-Oct; M, Th-F lunch and dinner, Sa dinner,

Su brunch and dinner Nov-Apr. 36 Old Colony Rd (between Gosnold and Nantucket Sts), Hyannis. 771.7866 ♿

23 Kennedy Memorial "I believe that it is important that this country sail," President John F. Kennedy once said, "and not lie still in the harbor." But this pretty garden spot, where a stone wall frames a brass plaque installed in 1966 by the townspeople, invites one to stay put for a while. It sits on Veteran's Beach, a narrow strip of sand overlooking the placid harbor, where facilities include parking, a snack bar, rest rooms, and a children's playground. ♦ Ocean St (between Kalmus Park Beach and Harbor Bluff Rd), Hyannis

24 Steamers Grill & Bar ★$$ You can't go far wrong with the namesake dish; take a mess of clams, dip in broth, plop in drawn butter, and you have it. Instant gratification is pretty much the name of the game at this harborside spot catering primarily to the young and carefree, where live bands play weekends in season. The other motif is mesquite grilling; try a slab of swordfish or shrimp stuffed with spinach, garlic, cheese, and pine nuts. At dusk the deck is packed. ♦ American ♦ Daily breakfast, lunch, and dinner May–late Dec; call for hours late Dec–Apr. 235 Ocean St (at Nantucket St), Hyannis. 778.0818 ♿

25 The Moorings ★★$$$ With a captive audience waiting for the **Hy-Line** ferry, this eatery is sitting pretty. You can join them in a skylit interior spruced up with white latticework and ocean-view dining on both the upper and lower decks. Recently renovated by owners Don and Sharon Buckley, this dining spot offers such dishes as scallops sautéed with ginger and garlic in a creamy lemon sauce over angel hair pasta, and grilled swordfish seasoned with coriander red-pepper vinaigrette. ♦ American ♦ Daily breakfast, lunch, and dinner May-Aug; daily lunch and dinner Apr, Sept-Dec. 230 Ocean St (at Channel Point Rd), Hyannis. 771.7177 ♿

25 Hesperus It's a classic beauty, this 50-foot John Alden sloop, and it can cut along quickly with cooperative winds. Although cruising Lewis Bay and the Hyannis Harbor happens to be the only way to cop a discreet peek at the **Kennedy Compound,** your motives don't have to be quite so base; what's wrong with a couple of pleasant hours on the sparkling water? The captain will even let you hoist the sails or take the wheel for a while. The *Hesperus*

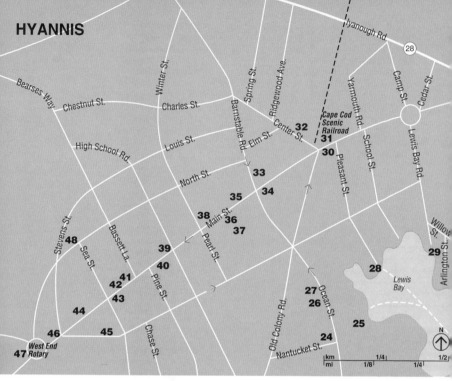

accommodates up to 22 passengers and, in summer, heads out a couple of times during the day, again at sunset, and sometimes under the moonlight, too. ◆ Call for schedule; closed November through April. Pier 16, Ocean St Dock (off Ocean St, between Channel Point Rd and South St), Hyannis. 790.0077

26 Hyannis Harborview Resort Motel $$ Spiffed up to fit in with the revitalized waterfront, this rather large complex—136 handsomely furnished rooms—includes outdoor and indoor pools, an exercise room, and a bar. Ask for a room in the front with views of the fishing boats, island ferries, and seafood restaurants. At press time there were plans to add a restaurant. ◆ 213 Ocean St (between Nantucket and South Sts), Hyannis. 775.4420, 800/676.0000; fax 775.7995 &

27 The Black Cat ★★$$$$ This waterfront venue aims at a more civilized air than the typical fishhouse. It also branches out a bit—about half the entrées are premium steaks (including a formidable 22-ounce porterhouse) or pasta (such as the ultrarich "straw and hay," made of spinach and egg fettuccine with prosciutto, peas, mushrooms, sausage, cream, and blended cheeses). The decor is middling

upscale; it features a handsome mahogany-and-brass bar, pillars painted with flowers, and a row of brocade banquettes, overseen by some pretty silly cat portraits in Elizabethan garb. The daily ferry schedule is posted on a blackboard by the door—or you can just look out and watch them coming in. ◆ New American ◆ M-Sa lunch and dinner; Su brunch and dinner. 165 Ocean St (between Nantucket and South Sts), Hyannis. 778.1233 &

28 Baxter's Boat House Club and Fish-N-Chips ★$$ Opened in 1955, this place is so near the water it's actually over it, atop pilings. This is a something-for-everyone kind of place. Over-21s can hang out in the diner-size lounge, where there's a roving raw bar and usually some good blues piano. The underaged and their families can order great seafood meals—the fried clams are tops, and the conch fritters tasty—and take them out on the deck. ◆ American/Takeout ◆ Daily lunch and dinner Apr–mid-Oct. 177 Pleasant St (south of South St), Hyannis. 775.4490, 800/507.8354 &

29 Tugboats ★$$ Haute it's not, but the food here is fun—especially bar snacks like Cajun swordfish bites or beer-and-corn–batter onion rings. And the two roomy decks are perfect at day's end for catching the last rays of the sun. Toast a day well spent with "sunset cocktails" packed with plenty of ice cream. ♦ American ♦ Daily lunch and dinner Apr-Oct. 21 Arlington St (between Columbus and Willow Sts), Hyannis. 775.6433 ♿

30 Road Kill Cafe ★$$ No, it's not real road kill, and yes, it's part of a chain. This eatery can be fun for kids, because on the menu the ingredients are intentionally absent for sandwiches with names like "The Chicken That Didn't Make It Across The Road" or "Porky Pig Meets Elsie" (ask your server for details). One hint: "Oh Deer" is a venison steak with salad, rice, and vegetable, and it's not bad. ♦ American ♦ Daily lunch and dinner. 247 Main St (between Pleasant St and Old Colony Rd), Hyannis. 771.7379 ♿

31 Cape Cod Scenic Railroad (CCSR) Three vintage cars—the *Nobscot, Sconset,* and *Monomoy*—chug the 42-mile round-trip to Buzzards Bay and back in a bit under two hours, with soothing scenery and informative commentary en route. The special *Dinner Train* makes the same circuit in three hours, adding a sunset stopover at the canal, and tables of four (or fewer, for an additional fee) can enjoy a catered five-course meal. Though it's not quite "the ultimate dining experience" it's billed as (as the *Boston Globe* found it lacking in "culinary distinction"), a ride on the *Dinner Train* is romantic, and as popular with those planning proposals as those celebrating anniversaries. **CCSR** also offers occasional "ecology discovery tours," with an on-board naturalist and a half-hour stopover at **Talbots Point Conservation Preserve** in Sandwich for a guided walk through the marsh. ♦ Sight-seeing trips and Dinner Train: Tu-Su June-Oct; call for Feb-May and Nov-Dec schedule; closed in January. Reservations required; jacket required for Dinner Train. 252 Main St (at Center St), Hyannis. 771.3788, 800/872.4508 ♿

32 Cape Cod Storyland Every putter tells a story? Perhaps they will after playing miniature golf over these two intensively landscaped acres of waterfalls, caves, and miniaturized reproductions of Cape and the Islands landmarks. Or for a refreshing splash, take out a couple of molded-plastic bumper boats and bash one another around. ♦ Admission. Daily 8AM-11PM mid-June–mid-Sept; call for off-season hours; closed mid-October–late March. 70 Center St (between Main St and Ridgewood Ave), Hyannis. 778.4339

33 Sophie's ★$$ The main course is the nightly music, featuring such forward-fringe acts as the Strangemen, self-described "sci-fi rockabilly surf rockers." If you should get bored, which is unlikely, you can pick nonchalantly at the affordably priced, retro–home-style food. ♦ American ♦ M-F

lunch and dinner; Sa-Su breakfast, lunch, and dinner May-Oct; call for Nov-Apr schedule. 8 Barnstable Rd (between Main and Elm Sts), Hyannis. 775.1111

34 Penguins SeaGrill ★★★$$ Meat-lovers can get their Black Angus fix here, but it's the fish-lovers who'll have a real field day. You can opt for a "Sampler Extravaganza" including clams casino, oysters Rockefeller, scrod, fillet of sole, stuffed jumbo shrimp, and half a baked lobster stuffed with crab and topped with sea scallops. Or you pick out your own fish from the daily fish board, and have it either brushed with herb butter and wood-grilled, topped with sherried crumbs and baked, nut-crusted and served with tropical fruit salsa, or "pan-bronzed" with herb beurre blanc. The space, though inland, is elegant; one room is sheltered by a giant Roman parasol. ♦ International ♦ Daily dinner mid-Feb–early Jan. Reservations recommended. 331 Main St (at Ocean St), Hyannis. 775.2023 ♿

35 Alberto's Ristorante ★★★$$$ Owner-chef Felisberto Barreiro was only 23 in 1984 when he opened the first incarnation of this delightful restaurant on Ocean Avenue and introduced Cape Codders to the joys of homemade pasta. Patrons were so plentiful that in 1993 he was able to move to expanded quarters on Main Street. The place is both contemporary and romantic, with creamy, pale pink walls (echoed in the table linens) and flattering sconces. Though large (it seats about 160), the restaurant is broken up into a series of gallerylike rooms, maintaining a sense of intimacy.

Choices on the menu range from an antipasto featuring marinated fresh mozzarella and sevichelike scungilli to veal chops Porto Fino, with morels, porcini, and shiitake mushrooms, served in a sauce of shallots, brandy, and cream. The treatments are not of the exquisite, anemic sort, but robust and

53

flavorful; any meal is bound to feel like a celebration. ◆ Italian ◆ Daily lunch and dinner. Reservations recommended. 360 Main St (between Barnstable Rd and Winter St), Hyannis. 778.1770 ♿

36 John F. Kennedy Museum There is absolutely nothing to see at the **Kennedy Compound** on Irving Avenue in Hyannisport other than a high wooden fence and lots of hedges. However, with hordes arriving every year hoping to see *something,* the Hyannis Chamber of Commerce finally opened this minimuseum in **Old Town Hall.** In its first six months of operation in 1992, it logged 40,000 visitors. Beyond a 10-minute video narrated by Walter Cronkite, the exhibit consists mostly of photos from 1934 to 1963—blown-up snapshots exuding charisma. There's also an annotated aerial view of the compound to satisfy some of that indefatigable curiosity, but it's the unposed pictures of family life that really touch the heart. An exhibit on the Kennedy family tree and a gift shop are recent additions. ◆ Nominal admission. M-Sa; Su 1-4PM. 397 Main St (between Ocean and Pearl Sts), Hyannis. 790.3077 ♿

37 Guyer Barn Gallery Initiated by the Barnstable Cultural Council in 1986 and run by volunteer Chris Green, this community arts center reflects plenty of youthful enthusiasm. Green is delighted to give fledgling artists, some still in their early 20s, their first shows; as he says, "There's a lot of good energy around, and it's good to have a place to put it." The 1865 wood-frame barn was added to the National Register of Historic Places in 1988, and if you're wondering about the "action painting" on the floor, it dates from the building's previous tenure as a municipal works warehouse—dozens of lifeguard stands got their yearly coating here. Saturday evenings in the summer the gallery is transformed into the "Driftwood Coffeehouse," with an impressive roster of folk musicians drawn from all over the East Coast. ◆ Exhibits: free. Concerts: cover. Gallery: daily (hours vary) June-Oct. Concerts: Sa 8:30PM June–mid-Sept. 230 South St (behind Old Town Hall, between Ocean and Pearl Sts), Hyannis. 790.6370 ♿

Hyannis boasts an Octagonal House, built in 1850 on South Street by Captain Rodney Baxter. It has eight concrete exterior walls 18 inches thick; inside are two square rooms and many smaller rooms with closets tucked into oddly angled corners. It's a private home today, not open to the public.

Restaurants/Clubs: Red   **Hotels:** Blue
Shops/ ❦ Outdoors: Green   **Sights/Culture:** Black

38 Caffé e Dolci ★★$ This spiffy Neo-Italianate cafe suffused with heady aromas debuted in 1993, as one of the first harbingers of a resurrected Main Street. The coffee's superb (you can load up on arcane paraphernalia, too), and the gelato, granita, and chocolate-laden *tartuffo* are well worth sampling. ◆ Daily 8AM-11:30PM July-Oct; daily 8AM-6PM Nov-June. 430 Main St (between Barnstable Rd and Winter St), Hyannis. 790.6900

39 Hyannis Antique Co-op The oldest group shop on the Cape, this is not, however, among the most distinguished; it's really more like an indoor flea market. There's plenty of Depression glass, should you have a set that needs filling out. Among the few items that might be worth a closer look are the ornately inlaid "ship boxes" (fashioned by bored sailors). But you'll have to hunt to find other quality goods here. ◆ M, W-Su. 500 Main St (at High School Rd), Hyannis. 778.0512

40 The Egg & I $ Describing this place as "no frills" would be an understatement, but Hyannis night owls, early birds, and lie-abeds don't mind, as long as they can breakfast past noon—even all night, if they like. The "Create an Omelet" options span over a dozen ingredients including *linguica,* and specials include such Southern rarities as chicken-fried steak with green onion corn bread. As has been true since 1971, the clientele consists largely of collegiate types earning some spending money on the Cape, and if these frugal souls gather here, you know it's a good deal. ◆ Coffee shop ◆ Daily breakfast 11PM-1PM. 517 Main St (between High School Rd and Pine St), Hyannis. 771.1596 ♿

41 Maggie's Ice Cream It's easy to see why this place, operated by the eight-member Sweeney family, is a local favorite. It's a cheerful place, white splashed with Kelly green, and the ice cream's made fresh, including some fascinating custom blends. Try a "Cape Cod Mud" cone—coffee ice cream with chocolate chips, smashed Oreos, almonds, and fudge swirls. ◆ Daily 11AM-11PM Apr-Oct; daily 11AM-9PM Nov-Mar. 570 Main St (at Bassett La), Hyannis. 775.7540 ♿ Also at: 5 Mashpee Commons, Rte 151 and Falmouth Rd, Mashpee. 477.6442 ♿

TIBETAN MANDALA

42 Tibetan Mandala Providing one-stop shopping for that "been there" look, this store sells crafts, jewelry, and clothing from India and Nepal. Owner Lhakpa T. Sonam, who opened this branch of his Greenwich Village shop in 1992, says he also does a brisk trade in such items as Tibetan "singing bowls" and cymbals, imported tapestries, and music tapes. ♦ Daily 11AM-9PM Mar-Dec. 580 Main St (between Bassett La and Sea St), Hyannis. 778.4134 &

43 Plush & Plunder Ute-Barbara Gardner has enough hats to open a museum if she wanted to; instead, they line the ceiling of her exceptionally well-stocked vintage clothing store. She's been at it since 1981 and has found jackets, silk ties, alligator shoes, petticoats, rhinestone-studded cat-glasses, slinky dresses, all in mint condition. Over the years, this store has garnered encomia from such disparate celebrities as Joan Baez and Cyndi Lauper. Demi Moore shops by mail, and husband Bruce Willis is another big fan—as you're sure to be, too, the minute you step inside. ♦ Daily. 605 Main St (between Pine and Sea Sts), Hyannis. 775.4467 &

44 Sweetwaters Grille ★★$$ Hankering for Tex-Mex food? The fajita fixings here are char-grilled over a fruitwood fire and served with sage rice; appetizers include such unusual variations as white chili (made with white beans and chicken), "snakebites" (jalapeño peppers stuffed with cream cheese, then beer-battered and deep-fried), and "painted desert pizza" (which resembles a giant nacho). This cool sage-green eatery is an oasis for the hungry vacationer. ♦ Southwestern ♦ Daily lunch and dinner. 644 Main St (between Sea and Stevens Sts), Hyannis. 775.3323 &

45 Roadhouse Cafe ★★$$$ The decor may say old boys' club—especially the dark and inviting bar, with burgundy banquettes and bar stools and an old-fashioned phone booth—but the menu says, "Stop and smell the garlic." Owner Dave Columbo offers such

savory Italian specialties as cioppino (a seafood stew) and a *linguine aglio e olio* dressed up with pignoli, artichoke hearts, and sun-dried tomatoes. The prize dessert, though, gets its inspiration from the Irish: a creamy cheesecake flavored with Bailey's. ♦ American/Italian ♦ Daily dinner. 488 South St (between Sea and Main Sts), Hyannis. 775.2386 &

46 Harry's Restaurant & Bar ★★$$ Basically a bar, with a postage-stamp dance floor, this place brings a little bit of New Orleans north. Among the specialties are barbecued ribs, blackened fish, and four kinds of Southern-style rice: Hoppin' John (with black-eyed peas), jambalaya (with andouille), "dirty" (with chicken livers), and red beans and rice slow-cooked with ham hocks and herbs. Seating consists of six park-bench booths. What looks like a Shaker wall of drawers is strictly decorative, though the bartender jokes, "That's where we keep all the money." Evenings, the joint jumps with jazz, blues, rock, or any combination of the above. ♦ Southern/Takeout ♦ Daily lunch and dinner. 700 Main St (at Stevens St), Hyannis. 778.4188

47 The Paddock ★★$$$ The place has a kind of hokey grandeur, with its valet parking, impersonal facade, and heavily paneled interior (the summer-porch room, with a palm court effect, is a little less oppressive). However, no one, least of all the spillover crowds from the **Cape Cod Melody Tent,** complains about the bountiful spread, which stresses continental standards and derivatives—such as sole Oscar. It has been run by the Zartarian family since 1970, and they take a proprietary interest in their customers' well-being. ♦ Continental ♦ Daily lunch and dinner Apr–mid-Nov. Reservations recommended; jacket required. West End Rotary (between Scudder Ave and W Main St), Hyannis. 775.7677 &

47 Cape Cod Melody Tent It's a tent, all right, a big blue one, and you'll get as up close to household-name musicians and comedians as you could hope. British actress Gertrude Lawrence built her big top in 1950, inspired by America's first summer theater-in-the-round at Lambertville, New Jersey. Today's roster spans a wide range of tastes, from the Temptations to Mary Chapin Carpenter. There's also a special children's theater program Wednesday mornings at 11AM. All proceeds from the performances are channeled by the nonprofit South Shore Playhouse Associates to fund education and the arts on the South Shore and Cape. ♦ Admission. Schedule varies, late June–early Sept. W Main St and West End Rotary, Hyannis. 775.9100 &

48 Copacabana ★★$$ You're sure to have a good time at this Brazilian restaurant where the staff aims to please. Chef Carlos Barbosa from Rio de Janeiro will bring skewers of freshly grilled steak, pork loin, and chicken breasts to your table if you order Brazilian barbecue, the house special; nobody leaves hungry (because he won't stop filling your plate until you plead for him to stop). Be sure to try one of the soups, including *canjiquina*, in which yellow corn grits are mixed with chicken and kale, and *sopa de feijão preto*, where bacon bits and green onion settle in a black bean broth. ◆ Brazilian ◆ Daily dinner mid-May–mid-Sept; Tu-Su mid-Sept–mid-May. Village Marketplace, 243 Stevens St (between Bassett La and North St), Hyannis. 790.8227 ᕵ

49 Play It Again Sports Surf's up, and you forgot your board? Don't worry; you can always pick up a cheap one at this second-hand sporting goods franchise. In fact, virtually every conceivable sport and pastime is covered, from tennis to in-line skating. Golf is especially big; there's an extensive selection of clubs and bags. ◆ Daily. 25 Iyanough Rd (between E Main St and Yarmouth Rd), Hyannis. 771.6979 ᕵ

50 Boxcar Willy's Bar and Grill ★$ The food—or perhaps grub is a more accurate term—is pretty much an adjunct to the liquor, but it sure is cheap, for those times when filling up takes precedence over fine dining. In addition, these two rehabbed train cars, with wooden booths and bookshelves in place of luggage racks, make for an inviting, laid-back atmosphere. ◆ American ◆ Daily lunch and dinner. 165 Yarmouth Rd (at Rte 28), Hyannis. 775.4421 ᕵ

The Pilgrims had been settled in Plymouth for only six months when young John Billingham wandered off in the woods. The search party traced him as far as Barnstable Harbor, and from there Chief Iyanough led them to Nauset, where the boy had been happily assimilated into tribal life. Two years later, stirred by Myles Standish's alarums of an "Indian conspiracy," the English herded Iyanough and several other native leaders into a pestilential swamp, where all died, most likely of smallpox. Some settlers regretted the action enough to mark the chief's grave, in Cummaquid. Of Iyanough, Edward Winslow of the *Mayflower* wrote that he was "personable, gentle, courteous, and fair-conditioned; indeed, not like a savage except in his attire."

50 Pufferbellies Formerly **Jammers,** a club for the college crowd, this old railroad round-house is the biggest nightclub on the Cape (capacity 1,500). Patrons now are older and wider in girth, which may or may not refer back to the club's present name. The building is divided between two sides: **Little Texas,** for line and square dancing; and **Flashbacks**, where you'll hear Top 40 oldies from the 1960s to the 1980s. In the warmer months, the outdoor **Beach Bums** revs into gear with volleyball games played near a welcoming bar; after the game is over tanned pufferbellies can quench their thirst. ◆ Cover. W-Su 3PM-1AM late May–mid-Sept; Th-Sa mid-Sept–late May. 183 Iyanough Rd (between Yarmouth Rd and Ridgewood Ave), Hyannis. 790.4300, 800/233.4301 ᕵ

51 Starbuck's ★★$$ Good wholesome fun in the Friday's vein, this is a bar where you'd feel comfortable taking the family. The children's menu, topping out at $2.97, is a steal. But the adult prices are pretty sporting, too, and there's a wide variety. The menu globe-hops from fajitas and pasta to Oriental treats like Thai hot-peppered shrimp. Plenty of people come in just to drink; a 27-ounce margarita ought to do the trick, or, for novices, something silly and sweet like a Frozen Girl Scout Cookie. Kids love the "Prohibition Specials," otherwise known as virgin coladas and fruit daiquiris. This cavernous barn of a place has enough room in the rafters for all sorts of flotsam, including an entire *Fokker D-7* plane. ◆ International ◆ Daily lunch and dinner. 645 Iyanough Rd (between Rte 28 and Picture Pond Rd), Hyannis. 778.6767 ᕵ

52 Pain d'Avignon If it's not quite like any French bread you've ever tasted, that's because it's Slavic. Bakers Vojin Vujosevic and Branislav Stamenkovic have concocted breads that look like fantastical folk sculptures. Among the more recognizable offerings are skinny baguettes strewn with coarse salt, rolls topped with oats, and flatbreads baked with cheese and caramelized onion. ◆ Daily. 192 Airport Rd (off Rte 132), Hyannis. 771.9771

53 Cape Cod Potato Chips Having invented a "kettle cooking" method to impart richer flavor and greater crunch—which it does—Chatham resident Steve Bernard started up this company on a $30,000 grubstake in 1980; in 1985, he sold it to Eagle Snacks Inc. for a neat $7 million (he's now into croutons). Many snackers swear by the chips; they're sliced thicker than most and are said to taste more substantial. You can be the judge, since free samples are given away at the end of the self-guided tour along a glass-walled corridor flanking the assembly line. ♦ M-F. Breed's Hill Rd (at Independence Dr), Hyannis. 775.7253 &

54 Sam Diego's ★★$$ Papier-mâché toucans and colorful serapes adorn this popular roadside restaurant, and the setting sun glows through stained glass onto innumerable hanging plants twinkling with Christmas lights. The fare is fairly standard Americanized Mexican (strong on burritos, enchiladas, chimichangas, quesadillas, fajitas), but it's all done well, and the atmosphere is pleasant and lively. You might go for the native cod, either baked under a blanket of *salsa cruda* and cheese or *naranja*-style, in an orange sauce flavored with cilantro, garlic, and Triple Sec. And if you've never tried deep-fried ice cream, it's a must, a real junk-food masterpiece. ♦ Mexican/Southwestern ♦ Daily lunch and dinner. 950 Iyanough Rd (between Independence Dr and Phinneys La), Hyannis. 771.8816 &

55 Eastern Mountain Sports The only on-Cape outpost of New England's premier outdoor outfitter has doubled its retail space in this brand new building set beside a pond where you can paddle its canoes and kayaks. The store offers everything you could possibly need to survive—and thrive—in the wild: clothing, gear, and perhaps most important, counsel. You can rent if you're not ready to buy (from tents and sleeping bags to boats and kayaks), and the store offers all sorts of paddling clinics and guided excursions; call for details. ♦ M-F; Sa 10AM-9PM; Su noon-6PM June–mid-Sept. Call for off-season hours. Rte 132 (between Phinneys La and Huckins Neck Rd), Hyannis. 775.1072 &

British forces were all set to land in Hyannis during the War of 1812, but they were frightened away by rumors—no doubt fabricated by villagers—that the town was in the throes of a smallpox epidemic.

56 West Parish Meetinghouse

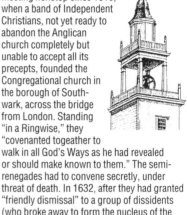

This fellowship has been meeting nonstop since 1616, when a band of Independent Christians, not yet ready to abandon the Anglican church completely but unable to accept all its precepts, founded the Congregational church in the borough of South-wark, across the bridge from London. Standing "in a Ringwise," they "covenanted togeather to walk in all God's Ways as he had revealed or should make known to them." The semi-renegades had to convene secretly, under threat of death. In 1632, after they had granted "friendly dismissal" to a group of dissidents (who broke away to form the nucleus of the Baptist church), they were caught at worship by officers of the king. Forty-two were imprisoned, including pastor John Lothrop. (While he was in jail, his wife died and his children were reduced to begging.) Released under pain of exile in 1634, Lothrop led some 30 families to the New World aboard the *Griffin.* (The pewter sacramental vessels they brought with them are in the church today.) After securing a grant from the General Court of Plymouth Colony, Lothrop and 22 of his followers set out from Scituate for the promising territory of "Mattakeese." This Native American name meant "plowed fields," and indeed the settlers were lucky enough to get land that had already been cleared, near an enormous salt marsh offering plenty of salt hay as fodder. They named their settlement Barnstable (probably for its resemblance to the English harbor of Barnstaple) and erected their first meetinghouse in 1646. The present building went up in 1717-19; a few years later, the bell tower, with its gilded rooster weather vane from England, was added on, and in 1806, patriot Paul Revere was commissioned to cast the half-ton bell.

During the early days of the nation, there was scant separation of church and state (in fact, Massachusetts towns levied taxes to support local churches until 1834), and for many years this meetinghouse doubled as a town hall. In 1852, the deteriorating building underwent a Neo-Classical remodeling that totally obscured its plain-spun beauty; what was worse, in the 1880s, someone saw fit to add wallpaper bordered with what parishioners considered "immodest cherubs." It took the lifelong efforts of one Elizabeth Crocker Jenkins (1874-1956) to restore the church to its original form and intent.

In the 1950s, drawing on funds Jenkins had raised and a great deal of "architectural sleuthwork," the firm of **Andrews Jones**

Biscoe & Goodell was able to uncover the church's original adzed oak framework and curved buttresses, its pine beams and posts. Workers restored or replicated the extensive woodwork, from high pulpit and "sounding board" to galleries, stairs, and pews. Historical significance aside (it's the oldest public building on the Cape and one of only two surviving "First Period" meetinghouses in New England), the restored church is quite simply a work of art. ◆ Service: Su 10AM. 2049 Meetinghouse Way (between Hwy 6 and Cedar St), West Barnstable. 362.4445 &

TERN STUDIO

57 Tern Studio A practitioner of the age-old art of "turning," Albert O. Barbour has a knack for finding the sculpture hidden in a hunk of wood. For his vases and bowls, he uses only native woods, whether staples like oak, elm, and maple, or rarer woods such as apple, cherry, box elder, and mulberry. He compares his process of wood turning to that of a pottery wheel. Each piece is varnished till it shines like polished stone, but the naturally occurring flaws are what lend these works their inimitable beauty; Barbour has no way of knowing, when he starts out, just what forms and patterns are going to emerge. ◆ Daily. 2454 Meetinghouse Way (between Church St and Rte 6A), West Barnstable. 362.6077

West Barnstable Tables

57 West Barnstable Tables Those centuries-old planks—of pine, oak, and chestnut—that don't find their way into historic renovations may end up here as trestle tables fetching thousands of dollars. You can also find unwanted window frames turned into mirrors. ◆ Daily. 2454 Meetinghouse Way (between Church St and Rte 6A), West Barnstable. 362.2676

One of the Cape's more fleeting get-rich-quick schemes was the manufacture of faux pearls from fish scales. French chemist Edward I. Petow came up with a formula during World War I and moved to Hyannis to set up a factory. Business boomed for a time, with revenues peaking at 50 million a year. However, the Depression, along with Japan's introduction of synthetic pearls, knocked the bottom out of the market, and the product—guaranteed to last five years—definitely didn't last much longer before starting to discolor and flake.

58 Prince Jenkins Antiques Hitchcock couldn't have invented a more archetypal antiques store. The original owner, Dr. Alfred A. King, died in 1997, but this shop continues to be a unique and interesting place to explore. Everything from a skeleton in a coffin to a highly valuable Chinese urn can be found on the premises. Also note the neighboring house, which King also owned. He claimed the nucleus of the structure was the 1626 home of Governor William Bradford (although he did concede that the shingled front part, with swan pediment painted with witch silhouettes and no fewer than seven weather vanes spinning on the captain's walk more likely dates from 1635-57). ◆ Daily Mar–mid-Nov. 975 Main St (at Rte 149), West Barnstable. No phone

59 Salt & Chestnut Weathervanes Former schoolteacher Marilyn E. Strauss admits to being a "frustrated museum director," which is why she doesn't mind if browsers come just to marvel over her extraordinary collection of antique weather vanes—as well as her own replica of the first known weather vane, from 48 BC Greece. A fascinating array crowds three rooms and two side gardens. She employs 29 area sculptors either to create their own work or to carry out her designs, such as copper "lighthouses" to decorate unsightly air vents. The modern work ranges from the understated to the absurd (a plump pig tooting a trumpet, for example), and there's also a collection of elaborate whirligigs, such as a shark with a swimmer mid-gulp and a foot-tapping jazz band. ◆ Daily. 651 Main St (between Willow and Maple Sts), West Barnstable. 362.6085

60 Black's Handweaving Shop You could say that weaving runs in this family. Bob Black's parents wove, as do his wife, children, and grandchildren. He started at 14, attended the Rhode Island School of Design, and is currently the only person in the country designing double-sided jacquard patterns, an all but lost art requiring a mathematician's precision. Working on commission, Black will weave custom designs into each coverlet or panel he makes (one couple celebrating their Cape summers wanted a lawnmower and greenhead flies worked in); with the signature and date, each is a potential future museum piece. But you don't have to order ahead—the shop is fully stocked with colorful throws, shawls, scarves, baby blankets, place mats, and ties; the rainbow chenille scarves are especially appealing. ♦ Daily. 597 Main St (between Maple St and Old County Rd), West Barnstable. 362.3955

60 Honeysuckle Hill $$ New owners Richard and Judith Field have restored this 1810 Victorian country house, transforming one of the three original guest rooms into a two-bedroom suite. White wicker furniture, handmade quilts, feather beds, and fresh flowers adorn the rooms. The breakfasts are buffet-style, so you may help yourself to coffee, juice, and pastries at the hour you deem civilized. Pets are no longer accepted. ♦ 591 Main St (between Maple St and Old County Rd), West Barnstable. 362.8418, 800/441.8418; fax 362.4854

61 Sandy Neck Conservation Area They make an improbable battleground, these pocky dunes (some up to 100 feet high) covered with beach grass and low-bush blueberries. But it's here, along a 6.5-mile-long barrier beach protecting Barnstable's 8,000-acre Great Marsh (one of the largest on the East Coast), that the endangered piping plover is fighting extinction. The state's coastline is at the center of the plovers' breeding range, and in the summer of 1996, naturalists recorded that 29 nesting pairs successfully produced over 2 chicks per pair, a substantial increase from the past. But plovers need constant monitoring to come back to their full numbers—they are subjected to such predators as gulls, foxes, and coyotes.

The birds dig a simple depression in which to lay their eggs, and it's up to the hatchlings—"about the size of a half-dollar with wings," according to the *Boston Globe*—to feed themselves, which they do by immediately scooting down to the intertidal zone. Beyond their natural predators, the biggest threat the plovers face is from off-road vehicles cruising the dunes (although over five miles of the area are closed to vehicular traffic during the plovers' breeding season—Memorial Day through June). You can park in the lot (for a fee, in summer), walk as far as your curiosity and feet will take you, and applaud the fact that the State Division of Fisheries and Wildlife has done the right thing by keeping four-wheeled vehicles at bay during breeding season. ♦ Sandy Neck Rd (off Rte 6A), West Barnstable. 362.8300

62 Pinske Art Center You may not like what Barre Pinske considers art, but you can't ignore it. The 6,000-square-foot gallery he created from a fishing supply/hardware store on prim-and-pretty Route 6A announces its presence with an oversize mailbox fashioned from an old fuel tank. In 1992, when the gallery and mailbox were unveiled, locals protested, claiming the mailbox violated local sign ordinances. But while signs along this historic highway are, indeed, strictly regulated, there proved to be no law setting limits on mailboxes—or on public art, for that matter.

Pinske's work runs the gamut from brash graffiti-style impastos to what he calls "highbrow" chain-saw art. Although he has attracted such well-heeled patrons as The Artist Formerly Known as Prince and Steve Tyler of Aerosmith, he keeps his output modestly priced. Whatever the marketing strategy, this is a brash, energetic place, much like its namesake, and a welcome respite from trite conventions often found in more "tasteful" venues. P.S.: About a half-mile east of Pinske's, look for some unusual graffiti on a railroad underpass—prototypical "goddesses" painted by artist Edith Vonnegut in her youth; they seem so lovely that no one has wanted to cover them over. ♦ M-Sa; Su noon-5PM. 1989 Main St (between Captain Franks Way and Rte 132), Barnstable. 362.5311 &

63 Charles Hinckley House $$ You'll pass through some 100 varieties of wildflowers, lovingly cultivated by innkeeper Miya Patrick, to get to the pilaster-framed front door of this 1809 Federal house. It's on the National Register of Historic Places, and the interior is furnished accordingly, with hand-picked antiques. But there's nothing posed or formal about the four very individual rooms. From the "library room," with its well-stocked bookcases, to the summer kitchen, they suggest an inspired touch.

Patrick does have inspiration, as you'll immediately deduce from her English breakfasts—perhaps poached eggs on crab cakes or French pancakes with homemade raspberry butter and maple syrup. She's an accomplished caterer, and her husband, Les, is a contractor specializing in period restoration. They started fixing up houses in Bucks County, Pennsylvania, turned around another Cape bed-and-breakfast, and have put their all into this one since 1983. In summer the bay beach is an enjoyable stroll down a quiet country lane; in winter, a flickering fire, those books, and the breakfasts are all anyone needs. ◆ 8 Scudder La (at Rte 6A), Barnstable. 362.9924; fax 362.8861

BEECHWOOD

64 Beechwood $$ So enveloping is the shade offered by century-old beech trees that your eyes might need to adjust to the sight of this mammoth 1853 Victorian painted butter-yellow and celery-green. It's even cooler and darker inside, past the wraparound porch set with rockers. Of the six rooms of this bed-and-breakfast, a few are quite extraordinary. Up the tight curl of a brass-handled captain's stairway, **Cottage** features a painted bedroom set in the style of the 1860s, and **Eastlake** embodies that 1880s aesthetic, with William Morris wallpaper, a spoon-carved bed, and matching marble-topped dresser. In the tin-ceilinged dining room, innkeeper Debbie Traugot serves blueberry-streusel muffins and apple-puff pancakes. ◆ 2839 Main St (between Old Jail and Aunt Hatch's Las), Barnstable. 362.6618 ♿

65 Olde Colonial Courthouse Built in 1772 as Barnstable County's second courthouse, this white clapboard building now houses Tales of Cape Cod, an organization founded by Louis Cataldo in 1949 to collect and preserve the Cape's folklore and oral history. The organization publishes historical materials and was responsible for acquiring such sites as **Iyanough's Gravesite** in Cummaquid and, for the grand sum of one dollar, the **Trayser Museum and Old Jail.** Tuesday evenings in summer, Tales hosts lectures by experts on Cape Cod arcana and popular topics such as famous Cape visitors "from Thoreau to Theroux." The courthouse is closed to the public except for lectures. ◆ Admission for lectures. 3018 Main St (at Rendezvous La), Barnstable. 362.8927

66 Sturgis Library If you think you might have a Pilgrim or two in your family tree, this is a good place to find out. Ancestor-hunters from across the country flock here to consult the outstanding genealogical collection, founded as a bequest of shipping merchant Captain William Sturgis (1782-1863). Left with no means of support after the death of his father, Sturgis, at 15 years of age, signed on as a cabin boy aboard the Orient-bound *Caroline;* four years later he returned as master of the ship. To compensate for his lack of formal education, he tackled a Harvard reading list borrowed from boyhood friend Lemuel Shaw

(later chief justice of Massachusetts). Retiring from the sea in his late twenties after some hair-raising adventures (including an attack by Cantonese pirates), Sturgis learned to maneuver just as cleverly in the tricky waters of entrepreneurship; his Boston-based firm, Sturgis and Bryant, cornered about half the China trade.

Though he never again lived in Barnstable, Sturgis cared enough about his roots here—Reverend John Lothrop was an eighth-generation forebear—to buy back his birthplace and leave it to the town as a library, along with a $15,000 endowment. The southeast portion of the building, a 1644 half-house, had in fact been built by the congregation to serve as Lothrop's home and, for two years, a meetinghouse. The library is thus both the oldest surviving building used for worship in North America and the oldest to house a library.

Though the library has been extensively renovated and expanded, the half-house's summer beam and deep window seats are still visible; also on display is Lothrop's tallow-burned Geneva Bible, which he painstakingly patched up with paper and rewrote from memory. In addition to its genealogical records (cross-indexed over the decades by local volunteers), the library also houses the *Kittredge Maritime History Collection,* begun with a legacy from St. Paul's headmaster William Crocker Kittredge, a library trustee and prominent Cape Cod historian. His collection of rare and out-of-print books, along with 1,500 maps and charts, is of interest not only to other historians but also to shipwreck researchers seeking hidden treasures.

Meanwhile, the townspeople of Barnstable can enjoy this place simply as a local library. It is complete with a well-stocked periodicals room and an inviting children's corner. ◆ Call for hours. 3090 Main St (between Mill Way and Rendezvous La), Barnstable. 362.6636 ♿

67 Crocker Tavern Bed and Breakfast $$ Built circa 1750, this tavern was a handy stopover on the Boston-Provincetown stagecoach route. It was also favored by attorneys working at the local courthouse and, during the Revolution, by Whigs. Owners Sue and Jeff Carlson have furnished the tavern with elegant antiques, and preserved many Colonial features, including wood plank floors, exposed beams, window seats, and working fireplaces. The five bedrooms are big and comfortably appointed, and the quiet back bedroom features an interesting bathroom fashioned from a colonial pantry. A hearty continental breakfast is served on china and crystal on a large trestle table of antique wood. ♦ 3095 Main St (between Hyannis Rd and Old Jail La), Barnstable. 362.5115, 800/773.5359; fax 362.5562 &

68 Barnstable Comedy Club Housed in **Village Hall,** a 1910 cedar-shingled building of pleasing proportions, the oldest surviving amateur theater group in the country has long adhered to its mission: to "produce good plays . . . and remain amateurs." Members have managed to do so since 1922, turning nonprofit in 1975. (Long before then, profits for many a season stayed in the single digits—though popular plays brought in everyone's family and friends.) In 1993 the club initiated **Imagine Theatre for Children**—"for, by, and about" would be more accurate. Kids usher, build the sets, and act, performing eight times a week through the summer. Each year the adult company puts on four major productions from fall to spring, plus a workshop, which could be anything from high drama to absurdist farce (for example, *Invasion of the Killer Carrots*). One notable alumnus of the group is Kurt Vonnegut, who played in a production of *Tiger at the Gates* (1971) clad in a leopard skin. Admittedly sentimental about it all, Vonnegut has given the club blanket permission "to make dramatic use of anything whatsoever of mine throughout all Eternity." ♦ 3171 Main St (between Hyannis Rd and Old Jail La), Barnstable. 362.6333

CHARLES M. HARDEN II

68 Barnstable Superior Courthouse Barnstable has been the seat of county government since 1685. This 1831-32 granite Greek Revival building, attributed to Bullfinch protégé **Alexander Parris** (who had recently completed Boston's masterful Quincy Market), boasts four fluted Doric columns and a wooden pediment and cornice that convincingly simulate stone. Looming over the little village, it sets a suitably pompous tone. The second-story courtroom is imposing, too, with its slightly arched and magnificently stenciled ceiling; two decorative columns, limned in gold, frame the judge. Walk in and listen in on the proceedings—it's justice in action, if not

always the most riveting entertainment. The cannons on the courthouse lawn, incidentally, were hauled by oxen from Boston to protect the town's saltworks from the British during the War of 1812. ♦ M-F. 3195 Main St (between Hyannis Rd and Old Jail La), Barnstable. 362.2511 &

69 Barnstable Tavern & Grille ★$$$ This early–19th-century tavern has been revamped and restored, and features a rustic inn decor, complete with the original wide pine floors. While some of the fare is a bit unimpressive, such catch-of-the-day dishes as halibut with herb-lime crumb topping and grilled sword-fish may well catch your fancy. At least it's all palatable and well priced. ♦ American/ Takeout ♦ Daily lunch and dinner. Reservations recommended. 3176 Main St (between Mill Way and Rendezvous La), Barnstable. 362.2355 &

69 Dolphin Restaurant ★★$$$ A locals' mainstay for decades, this little restaurant with an unassuming interior has more to offer than one might suppose. The menu includes such items as filet mignon with mushroom Merlot sauce, sautéed veal with a sauce of toasted hazelnuts, and Amaretto bread pudding. Sure, you can get a fried seafood platter, but you could also enjoy a fancy entrée for far less than it would cost in the big city (i.e., Hyannis). ♦ Continental ♦ Daily lunch and dinner. 3250 Main St (between Mill Way and Rendezvous La), Barnstable. 362.6610 &

West Barnstable produced one of the Revolution's most fiery orators. In 1761, lawyer James Otis resigned as customs agent to protest the British writs of assistance—search warrants permitting British soldiers to break into the homes of suspected smugglers. "A man's home is his castle," Otis declared at Boston's Old South Meetinghouse, "and whilst he is quiet, he is well guarded as a prince. His right to his life is his liberty, no created being could rightfully contest." But British loyalists believed otherwise, contending that the king had the right to do as he pleased. When Otis made the mistake of stopping in at a Tory tavern in 1769, he was beaten to within an inch of his life. His sanity compromised by the injuries, he burned all his papers and never again preached sedition. But the revolution he helped start rolled on without him.

Among the multitudes of birds that frequent the Atlantic flyway are occasional "vagrants"—those that took a wrong turn somewhere. In 1983, a brown-chested martin, the first ever seen north of Costa Rica, was spotted living among barn swallows, and a western reef heron, never before sighted in North America, drew bird-watchers from around the country.

Lights, Camera, Action:
Cape Cod and The Islands on Film

With its seafaring history, scenic landscapes, and summer homes for the wealthy, Cape Cod and the Islands have long been popular places for moviemakers. Among the films that have brought producers, directors, actors, and crew to Cape Cod and the Islands are the following:

Carly Simon, Live From Martha's Vineyard (1987) Shot on the seafront on **Martha's Vineyard,** this video of the singer's first concert after a seven-year hiatus includes such hits as "Anticipation," "Nobody Does It Better," and "You're So Vain."

Down to the Sea in Ships (1923) Clara Bow's first film, this silent movie deals with a romantic conflict in a Quaker whaling family. It features some rare footage from an actual whaling ship at sea.

The Inkwell (1994) A young African-American faces conflicts between his city ways and the country life while he and his family vacation at the traditionally black beach near **Oak Bluffs** on Martha's Vineyard.

Jaws (1975) This shark-on-the-prowl movie, shot on Martha's Vineyard, was an adaptation of a novel by Peter Benchley (son of Nathaniel Benchley—see *The Russians Are Coming,* below).

One Crazy Summer (1986) An early Demi Moore/John Cusack production, this movie about a teenage misfit's summer on **Nantucket** features abundant scenes of island living.

The Russians Are Coming! The Russians Are Coming! (1966) Alan Arkin made his star debut in this film about a Russian submarine crew that landed on Nantucket. The script was adapted from the novel, *The Off-Islanders,* written by longtime Nantucket resident, Nathaniel Benchley.

Sabrina (1995) This remake of the original 1954 Billy Wilder movie succeeds in updating the Cinderella myth. It features Julia Ormond in Audrey Hepburn's chauffeur's daughter role, and a marvelous vacation sequence on Martha's Vineyard in the company of the older—and richer—Harrison Ford.

To Gillian, On Her 37th Birthday (1996) Modern American moviemakers are infatuated with ghosts who return to advise us, and this film is certainly of that genre, with Michelle Pfeiffer as the deceased wife. But there's no mistaking Nantucket's **Polpis Road,** leave-takings on the **Hy-Line** ferry, the sand castle contest, and the most wonderful beach house imaginable.

Tough Guys Don't Dance (1987) This one-man show was directed by Norman Mailer from his mystery novel of the same name, and set in and around his own house in **Provincetown.** Ryan O'Neal plays the drinker who may have committed murder, but can't recall his actions.

War of the Roses (1989) Danny DeVito directed this blockbuster hit about a couple (Michael Douglas and Kathleen Turner) who meet on Nantucket, marry, and go through divorce court warfare over the property settlement—destroying the holdings in the process.

Antiques • Art Gallery • Design

69 Harden Studios A stellar addition to the array of fine antiques shops along the King's Highway, this family enterprise deserves immediate election to the first rank. Architect **Charles M. Harden,** who renovated this circa 1720 deaconage, has been in the business for years, mostly wholesaling to dealers at the Boston Design Center. There are some truly splendid museum-quality pieces on display; and prices are surprisingly reasonable—an antique corner cupboard or tiger maple slant-front desk, for instance, might go for a few thousand dollars. While overhauling, Harden also retrofitted an adjoining barn as a showcase for his son's highly skilled naturalist etchings, produced on the premises, and complementary work by area artists. ♦ M, W-Su; Tu by appointment. 3264 Main St (between Mill Way and Rendezvous La), Barnstable. 362.7711; fax 362.0217

70 Hyannis Whale Watcher Cruises If you're not going all the way to Provincetown, but still want to see these amazing mammals, hop on board this 100-foot supercruiser for an informative four-hour excursion. (The trip out of Provincetown to Stellwagen Bank takes about half the time, but before that you'd have to battle Highway 6 for a good while.) You can relax and sun yourself on deck while you wait to get splashed by one of those 50-foot whales. There's plenty to eat and drink, and a naturalist on board each trip helps to explain what's going on. ♦ Call for Apr-Oct schedule; closed November through March. Barnstable Harbor (off Mill Way), Barnstable. 362.6088, 800/287.0374; fax 362.9739

70 Mattakeese Wharf ★★$$$ Located next to the **Hyannis Whale Watcher Cruises** dock, this rambling harborside restaurant has everything you could hope for—broad decks with a sunset view, nautical decor, and bountiful seafood. Bob and Claire Venditti, owners since 1966, make the most of pasta and shellfish, offering fettuccine or linguine heaped with shrimp, mussels, scallops, and clams (singly or all at once), and sauces ranging from *bianco* (white), Alfredo, and carbonara to Dijon, marinara, or *fra diavolo* (spicy). Fresh slabs of broiled fish can't be beat; for something more elaborate, try sole Florentine, wrapped around spinach and romano and baked with a Mornay sauce. Or perhaps, with the bay breezes gently blowing, you could go ahead and order a lobster. ♦ American/Italian ♦ M-Sa lunch and dinner, Su brunch and dinner May-Oct. 271 Mill Way (off Main St), Barnstable. 362.4511 ⅙

71 Unitarian Church The much-younger "twin" of the **West Parish Meetinghouse,** this 1907 building designed by **Guy Lowell** (right before he took on Boston's Museum of Fine Arts), replaced an 1836 church that had burned down (and which itself had replaced the original early-1700s East Precinct meetinghouse). The church became Unitarian in 1825. **Lowell**'s design is suitably understated; two small windows are set high in the dove-gray facade, and two Ionic columns flank the recessed doorway. ♦ Service: Su 10:30AM. 3330 Main St (between Commerce Rd and Mill Way), Barnstable. 362.6381 ⅙

72 Donald G. Trayser Memorial Museum Built in 1856 as a customhouse, and used for that purpose for 37 years before serving as a post office from 1913 to 1959, this Italian Renaissance edifice of red-painted brick with white trim, now on the National Register of Historic Places, has perhaps found its true calling as a museum for the Barnstable Historical Commission. Heralded as the Cape's first fireproof building (fire had already destroyed all the county records once, in 1827), it's also among the grandest, with wrought-iron balustrades, lofty ceilings, and hefty pillars whose leafy crowns conceal heating ducts. From his office on the second floor, the customs collector (the first was Washington-appointee General Joseph Otis, brother of famed revolutionary orator James Otis) kept tabs on ships entering Barnstable Harbor and made sure the government got its due.

The museum housed here today is named for Donald G. Trayser, a well-regarded local historian. It contains collections ranging from native and colonial artifacts to China trade booty and children's toys. Among the odds and ends are a fringe-topped wicker baby carriage and a velvet-covered barber's chair. Also on the grounds is a carriage shed housing antique fishing implements, a horse-drawn hearse, and a pair of remarkable bicycles—an 1869 velocipede (with that huge front wheel) and a 1900 bike, seemingly ordinary but for its wood frame. Next door is a quaint circa 1690-1700 wooden jail—the oldest such wooden "gaol" in the United States that's still extant. ♦ Donation. Tu-Su 1:30-4:30PM mid-June–mid-Oct; call for off-season hours. 3353 Main St (between Braggs La and Hyannis Rd), Barnstable. 362.2092 ⅙

73 Cape Cod Art Association (CCAA)

Founded in Hyannis in 1947, this nonprofit community arts group bounced from site to site before finding a permanent home here in 1972. Local architect **Richard Sears Gallagher,** a CCAA member who had designed the **Parish Hall** addition to the **Unitarian Church** in 1960, came up with the plan for an adjoining pair of catercorner skylit saltboxes, which not only show off the artwork to best advantage but also provide excellent studio facilities. The spaces are so airy and open you have the sense of being on the water, though in fact the complex is well inland. Classes are given year-round, and shows are continually mounted. Although the caliber varies—there are over 400 associate and artist members today—it's clear that the organization is doing its best to respond to its charter and to "promote a high standard of fine art on Cape Cod." ♦ M-Sa; Su noon-5PM Apr-Nov. 3480 Main St (between Commerce Rd and Mill Way), Barnstable. 362.2909 &

Ashley Manor

74 Ashley Manor

Ashley Manor $$$ This bed-and-breakfast, a 1699 colonial mansion hidden behind a towering privet hedge, has it all: historicity, comfort, and, above all, enchantment. Donald Bain (an ex-New York lawyer) has been hosting since 1987, and he doesn't miss a trick. The breakfasts, served in a wainscoted dining room featuring built-in corner cupboards, are especially lavish (quiche, homemade granola, crepes with strawberry sauce), and the two rooms and four suites are charmingly decorated, with spackle-painted, wide-board floors and cheerful, floral-print wallpapers. All of the suites feature working fireplaces and canopied queen-size beds, and some have whirlpool baths. The living room is at once elegant and comfortable, with midnight-blue velvet couches and a grand piano. The two-acre grounds, redolent with boxwood, encompass a gazebo and a Har-Tru tennis court. Bikes are available, as is a croquet set. ♦ 3660 Main St (between Indian Trail and Commerce Rd), Barnstable. 362.8044, 888/535.2246; fax 362.9927

75 Fox Glen Manor

$$ The driveway seems to go on forever, past a corral of frisky Morgan horses and finally up to a porticoed, turreted pale yellow manse. It looks old, but isn't, though it's packed inside with a proliferation of decorative antiques. Nor has host Doug Kelly stinted on the three bedrooms. Two can be joined for a self-contained suite, which is just what a visiting Kennedy once did, apparently preferring this secluded manor to a perfectly good family compound down in Hyannisport. A full breakfast is served. Note: The inn is closed for renovations until 1999. ♦ 4011 Main St (between Marstons La and Mary Dunn Rd), Cummaquid. 362.4657; fax 362.3382

76 Owl's Nest Antiques

Nancy and David Galloni's barn is full of stuff you can actually use—complete sets of china, for instance, and a number of nonmuseum-quality (but very attractive) quilts. Textiles are a specialty including clothing and a good selection of vintage wedding dresses. An increasingly strong suit is dolls, along with the wardrobes they require. ♦ Daily May-Nov; call for an appointment in off-season. 4083 Main St (between Marstons La and Mary Dunn Rd), Cummaquid. 362.4054 &

77 Acworth Inn

$$ Cheryl and Jack Ferrell bring an irresistible affability, as well as a definite flair, to innkeeping. Forget any preconceived notions of uptight Olde Cape Cod tradition; the predominant style here, right from the notably spare sunroom entrance, is light and relaxed. To make you feel welcome, the owners will ply you with concoctions like Cape Cod spritzers (cranberry juice and seltzer), come up with customized suggestions for activities and map out local routes, and offer a complimentary bike. In your prettily decorated room, you also may encounter some homemade candy left as a pillowside lagniappe—just a preview of the pampering breakfast still to come. ♦ 4352 Main St (between Mill La and Bone Hill Rd), Cummaquid. 362.3330, 800/362.6363

Barnstable's West Parish Meetinghouse harbored a school from 1863 to 1883, and in the course of renovations some old papers were discovered behind the plaster, including a composition-on-composition by one Darius Howland. "Composition is something a scholar has to write and puzzle over till he gets a few words put together so as to make sense—or nonsense—which describes the subject he has to write about," Howland wrote. "The first thing in writing a composition is to think of a subject and then to tell something about it. . . . My stock of knowledge on the composition subject is exhausted so I will close with the truthful lines: Compositions are hard and tough, I've written these lines and that's enough."

Cranberries possess unique compounds that block infectious bacteria from clinging to the cells lining the urinary tract and bladder. The only other berry found so far to have similar capabilities is the blueberry.

The Cape and The Islands by the Book

you have time for some reading before you visit the pe, or perhaps on the side while you're there, any the following books should prove worth your ile. Many are available by mail order from **Cape d Life** (800/645.4482; fax 564.4470), or try **rnassus Books** (362.6420).

Vineyard Light by Rose Styron (Rizzoli, 1995) ese evocative poems are enhanced by Craig ipp's atmospheric photos.

ape Cod by William Martin (Warner Books, 1991) artin's doorstop best-seller chronicles the saga of o Cape families, several centuries removed.

ape Cod by Alan Nyiri (Down East Press, 1992) This ew of the Cape features strikingly attractive otographs, including panoramic aerial views.

ape Cod by Henry David Thoreau, with a foreword Paul Theroux (Penguin, 1987) Cape denizens and eir peculiar ways brought out the humorist in this rnest, perspicacious pilgrim of the 19th century.

ape Cod Architecture by Clair Baisly (Parnassus prints, 1989) Here is a handy, simply illustrated imer on the Cape's evolving housing styles over ree centuries.

he Cape Itself by Robert Finch, with photographs Ralph MacKenzie (Norton, 1991) Finch, a well-formed naturalist and gifted writer, offers insight to the fragile balance to be maintained between the rces of nature and human demands.

ape Light: Color Photographs by Joel Meyerowitz ullfinch Press, 1979) The distinctive beauties of the ape are captured in these pictures, as if in poetry.

ommon Ground: A Naturalist's Cape Cod by obert Finch (Godine, 1981) Here are some early eanderings by a writer and naturalist intimately miliar with the Cape and its natural beauties.

hosts of Nantucket by Blue Balliett (Down East ooks, 1984) This book is a good read—but don't try alone at night on **Nantucket.**

Guide to the Common Birds of Cape Cod by Peter rull (Shank Painter Publishing, 1992) Simple and oncise, this 72-page paperback provides an troduction to the pleasures of bird watching on ape Cod.

ighthouses of Cape Cod, artha's Vineyard, Nantucket: heir History and Lore by dmont G. Clark (Parnassus prints, 1992) Lots of details e offered here for those who annot resist the lights' lure.

oby Dick by Herman elville (Viking Penguin, 992) The literary giant ad never even visited antucket when he undertook to rite about it in part of his 1851 epic ovel; he had, however, set out whaling from

the town of Fairhaven, across the river from New Bedford.

Nantucket: Seasons on the Island by Cary Hazlegrove, with an introduction by David Halberstam (Chronicle, 1995) This collection of photographs captures the quintessence of Cape Cod—and it's enhanced by appreciative comments from a Pulitzer Prize–winning journalist and island devotee.

Of Plimoth Plantation by Governor William Bradford (McGraw-Hill, 1981) This classic provides a firsthand account of the trials endured by the Pilgrim pioneers centuries ago.

Old Provincetown in Early Photographs by Irma Ruckstuhl (Dover, 1987) More than a hundred vintage photographs and the detailed text offer fascinating glimpses into a rough-hewn past.

The Outermost House: A Year of Life on the Great Beach of Cape Cod by Henry Beston (Holt, 1992) This journal of a natural-born naturalist, and spellbinding writer, is well worth your attention.

The Pirate Prince by Barry Clifford, with Peter Turchi (Simon & Schuster, 1993) A recount of pirate Sam Bellamy's last adventure north aboard the *Whydah,* along with the modern story of how his wreck was found off the beach at Wellfleet.

A Place Apart: A Cape Cod Reader edited by Robert Finch (Norton, 1993) Finch's anthology offers a wide array of thematically arranged selections by authors ranging from Governor Bradford to Annie Dillard.

Provincetown as a Stage by Leona Rust Egan (Parnassus Imprints, 1994) Here is an in-depth recap of the heady summer of 1916, when this beachside Bohemia produced Eugene O'Neill's first play.

Short Bike Rides on Cape Cod, Nantucket and the Vineyard by Edwin Mullen & Jane Griffith (Globe Pequot, 1994) This book introduces you to 34 different rides, ranging from the leisurely to the highly vigorous, and from 7 to 27 miles.

Up Island by Anne Rivers Siddons (HarperCollins Publishers, Inc., 1997) **Martha's Vineyard** is shown off in exquisite prose in this journey of self-discovery made by a middle-aged Georgian woman facing divorce who finds serenity in a tiny shack on the resort's up island. Even the portrayals of harsh winters here make one want to sample its splendors.

Vineyard Summer by Alison Shaw (Little, Brown, 1994) These intense color compositions capture the essence of the isle.

Walks & Rambles on Cape Cod and the Islands: A Naturalist's Hiking Guide by Ned Friary and Glenda Bendure (Countryman Press, 1992) Friar and Bendure offer maps and descriptions of 35 scenic and/or historic trails.

Yarmouth/Dennis

It's in the midsection of the Cape, where Yarmouth and Dennis are ensconced, that the disparity between **Route 6A**, running along the bayside of the peninsula, and **Route 28**, near the southern coast, is most egregious—almost schizophrenically so. While Route 6A is rich with greenery and history, Route 28 is congested with traffic and tacky buildings. Most discerning travelers will want to plow through the latter as fast as possible—

ishing, like Thoreau, to concentrate only on "those features of the ape . . . in which it is peculiar or superior" to the mainland. But there re, fortunately, a few unspoiled stretches along the southern shore, and ome historical preserves, that are worth slowing down for, and even aking a detour.

has been widely claimed, though never proven, that the Vikings, led by eif Ericksson, sailed up **Bass River** around the first millennium and built a camp (now private land) in **Blue Rock Heights** five miles upriver. A number of tribes—including the Wampanoag, Satuit, Mattakee, Nobscusset, Monomoyick, and Cummaquid—were already settled in the area when the first known European colonists arrived in the 17th century, but the Native Americans died by the thousands during the smallpox epidemic of 1770. The colonists' first house was built in Yarmouth by Stephen Hopkins in 1638; the town (possibly named for the English port Great Yarmouth, from which some of the Pilgrims may have sailed) was incorporated the next year. Among its earliest settlers was *Mayflower* passenger Giles Hopkins. Farming in the region gradually gave way to shipping—at one point, Yarmouthport's milelong "Captains' Row" housed 50 prosperous skippers. Shipping, in turn, eventually gave way to tourism.

The town of Dennis, originally part of Yarmouth, was first settled by English cattle farmers. Incorporated in 1793, it was named for Reverend Josiah Dennis, who had served as an area minister for 38 years. Either the early residents had a poor sense of direction or they let the cows dictate divisions, given that West Dennis is southeast of Dennis proper, while East Dennis is northwest of South Dennis. Make no assumptions, and keep your map open at all times.

Map labels:
ration Rd. · Seaside Ave. · hing St. · Elm St. · 41 · Dr. Lord Rd. · **EAST DENNIS** · *Shiverick Shipyard* · Bridge St. · Airline Rd. · 38 · 40 · 42 · *Scargo Lake* · 37 · 39 · 43 · 44 · Scargo Hill Rd. · 45 · 6A · 33 · 31 · 0 · Old Bass River Rd. · East-West Dennis Rd. · Satucket Rd. · lins nd · 134 · Airline Rd. · Old Chatham Rd. · Kelleys Bay · 6 Mid-Cape Hwy. · **SOUTH DENNIS** · Great Western Rd. · 27 · 21 · Upper County Rd. · Center St. · Swan Pond · Grand Cove · Main St. · Baxter St. · Old Main St. · 20 · Depot St. · **WEST DENNIS** · Trotting Park Rd. · Swan Pond Rd. · Swan Pond River · Main St. · 26 · 28 · Lighthouse Rd. · 25 · Uncle Stephan's Rd. · 22 · Lower County Rd. · Shad Hole Rd. · Sea St. · 23 · 24 · Belmont Rd. · **DENNISPORT** · Old Wharf Rd.

Traditional fishers may have some peculiar superstitions (e.g., that whistling summons the wind), but their meteorological tricks are surprisingly reliable. For instance, birds wheeling in small circles generally augur a coming storm. "Sundogs"—small rainbows spotted at dawn— may suggest where the wind will come from next.

1 Abbicci ★★★$$$$ The interior of this 1775 house has been subjected to an ultrachic renovation—black steel bar, harsh track lighting, blown-up black-and-white maps of Italy as wall decoration—and what it has gained in modernity, it has somewhat sacrificed in charm. All is forgiven, though, once you dip into the *ostriche calde* (a half-dozen Cotuit oysters baked on a bed of sautéed leeks with fennel and star anise cream sauce) or the *sogliola fritta* (panfried sole with lemon, caper, and anchovy butter). ♦ Italian ♦ M-Sa lunch and dinner; Su brunch and dinner. Reservations recommended. 43 Main St (between Willow St and Marstons La), Yarmouthport. 362.3501 ♿

2 Wedgewood Inn $$ Set back from the road on a triple-tiered lawn, this lovely Federal house, built in 1812 for a maritime attorney, was the first in town to be designed by an architect; among the special touches is a beautiful built-in hall clock. Innkeeper Gerrie Graham greets you with a tea tray; you'll find a bowl of fresh fruit in your room. The corner rooms are formal, four-poster beauties; the downstairs ones come with both fireplaces and screened-in porches for year-round comfort. But it's the two third-floor rooms, tucked at odd angles under the eaves, that are wildly romantic; you're in your own little world. In addition to these six rooms, three deluxe (and more expensive) suites in the renovated barn were recently added to the inn. Each features a fireplace, luxury bathroom, and private deck. Breakfast here can include Belgian waffles with strawberries and whipped cream, pecan pancakes, or French toast made with French bread. ♦ 83 Main St (between Summer and Willow Sts), Yarmouthport. 362.5157; fax 362.5851 ♿

Cape waters have snagged thousands of wrecks, starting with the Jamestown-bound *Sparrowhawk*, out of Plymouth, England, which foundered off Nauset Beach in 1626. Chatham historian Joseph A. Nickerson (a descendant of town founder William Nickerson) estimates that some 2,000 ships have foundered off the Atlantic Coast between Monomoy Island and Eastham. One of the largest in recent history was the 470-foot Maltese freighter *Eldia,* which ran aground off Nauset Beach in 1984.

3 Hallet's Nostalgia fans should head straigh for this 1889 drugstore, which hasn't change appreciably since early in the 20th century, except there's now a museum upstairs that's full of old apothecary items, photos, and archives. Thacher Taylor Hallet has long ago ceased dispensing drugs, mail, and justice-of-the-peace services, but his granddaughte Mary Hallet Clark now serves sandwiches from behind the same carved-oak divider. The marble soda fountain still dispenses frappes, freezes, floats, and ice-cream sodas Sit at a stool or in one of the heart-shaped, wrought-iron chairs as a fan whirs beneath the pressed-tin ceiling and try an egg cream— it's the real thing. ♦ Daily 7:30AM-9PM late May-mid-Sept; call for off-season hours. 13 Main St (between Summer and Willow Sts), Yarmouthport. 362.3362

3 Town Crier Antiques Six dealers share this homelike storefront, as well as an interes in dolls. Among the other finds are vintage evening bags, christening dresses of sheeres cotton batiste, and comfortably weathered quilts. ♦ M-Sa mid-May-mid-Oct. 153 Main St (between Summer and Willow Sts), Yarmouthport. 362.3138

3 Inaho ★★★$$$ Co-owner and chef Yuji Watanabe has created a tranquil oasis in this plain old clapboard house. Several small dining rooms, separated by rice-paper screens and awash with soothing flute riffs, form a restful, private setting. True aficionados, though, will want to sit center stage—at the sushi bar—to watch Watanabe perform his magic. On the regular menu are "Tails in the Air," tempura shrimp wrapped with avocado and fish roe in rice and seawee along with more substantial dishes, such as *shabu shabu* (thin slices of beef cooked in so broth), but it's hard to pass up this chance to sample the freshest of raw fish. ♦ Japanese ♦ Tu-Su dinner. Reservations recommended 157 Main St (between Summer and Willow Sts), Yarmouthport. 362.5522 ♿

3 Design Works If you're still searching for the Scandinavian antique pine armoire of your dreams, you may get lucky here. There's an ample selection of linens, lamps, and crockery as well. ♦ M-Sa; Su 1-5PM. 159 Main St (between Summer and Willow Sts), Yarmouthport. 362.9698

3 Jack's Outback ★★$ Be prepared: This local landmark, the dominion of Jack Braginton-Smith, is not big on hospitality. Hi motto is "Great food, lousy service!" and he means it. You write your own order off the scrawled posters that approximate a menu (expect such creative spellings as "Roobin on Wry" or "Tappeeyolka Puddin"), then schlepp your plate to the pine-paneled dining room. Prices are rock-bottom, and there's a children's menu, listed as "For Brats Under 12." ◆ New England ◆ Daily breakfast and lunch. 161 Main St (between Summer and Willow Sts), Yarmouthport. 362.6690 ♿

AARDVARK CAFE

4 Aardvark Cafe ★★$$ Co-owners Peter Watson and chef Missy Minor Watson got recognition from the Yarmouth Historical Commission for the accurate restoration of this circa 1850s Victorian gingerbread house (wide-plank pine floors, wood moldings, high ceilings). Four rooms on the first floor are reserved for the restaurant, with additional tables outside. Try the miso-basted Atlantic salmon over cashew *somen* noodles, or Moroccan chickpea stew with toasted, hand-ground coriander and cumin and other spices, served over citrus-zested couscous. And pastry chef Peg Schultz makes an amazing angel food cake with lemon glaze and a homemade blueberry sauce that's, as hard as it is to believe, fat-free. **Java Port** on the enclosed porch serves coffee and delicious baked goods. ◆ New American/International ◆ Daily breakfast, lunch, and dinner June-Oct; Tu, Th-Su lunch and dinner, W dinner Oct-June. 134 Main St (between Thacher St and Vesper La), Yarmouthport. 362.9866; fax 375.0823

Nickerson Antiques

5 Nickerson Antiques This is one of the few places on the Cape where you can find substantive antiques—so many, in fact, that it's hard to squeeze your way around the jam-packed rooms. If prices seem reasonable, it's because many of the pieces are British transplants (England produced more furniture in the 17th and 18th centuries than the beleaguered colonies ever did). Since the American and British styles are compatible, no one need ever know the true origin of your find. ◆ M-Sa; Su noon-5PM. 162 Main St (between Thacher St and Vesper La), Yarmouthport. 362.6426

6 Peach Tree Designs From its dramatic showroom on the second floor, where a white bedstead and bold floral prints are accented against black rubberized wallpaper, to its eclectic selection of home furnishings, this store equals excitement. The wide array of merchandise includes everything from false-front books, blankets, and lamps to fanlight mirrors, flowery hats, and even esoteric foods. ◆ M-Sa; Su noon-5PM. 173 Main St (at Summer St), Yarmouthport. 362.8317. Also at: Mashpee Commons, Rte 151 and Falmouth Rd, Mashpee. 477.3920

7 Parnassus Books Ben Muse, proprietor of this stacked-to-the-gills bookstore—featuring "hand-picked" new, used, and rare books—may appear irascible but is really gentle as a lamb. As for the store's lack of signs to help you around—the idea, they say, is to let book-lovers dig around on their own, and experience "the fun of discovery." Muse has been stock-piling books since the 1950s and selling since 1960. Specialties include Cape and Islands titles and rare first editions, as well as art, the sea, antiques, and ornithology. Prices start at $1 and can run well into the thousands. There's a 24-hour honor-system rack outside, in case you run out of reading material at bedtime. The building was constructed in the 1840s as a combination arket/Swedenborgian church; services were held upstairs, where thousands of books now await their turn on the packed shelves below. ◆ M-Sa; Su noon-5PM. 220 Main St (between Thacher St and Vesper La), Yarmouthport. 362.6420; fax 362.7440

8 Winslow Crocker House Of the dozens of properties owned and maintained by the Society for the Preservation of New England Antiquities (SPNEA), this is the only one (to date) located on the Cape. In the 1930s, Mary Thacher, a descendant of Anthony Thacher, Dennis's first land grantee, bought a Georgian house built around 1780 by Winslow Crocker—a West Barnstable trader, speculator, and alleged rumrunner. She moved it here to display her growing collection of antiques. The magnificent furniture ranges from an 1800 tiger-maple case clock to a japanned William and Mary chest-on-chest. Two longtime site administrators, Sara Porter and Jim McGuiness, can fill you in on stories—how Thacher's 1690 family cradle, for instance, is thought to resemble one that Anthony Thacher and his wife clung to when they were shipwrecked in 1635 off what is now Thacher's Island in Rockport, Massachusetts (tragically, all four children were drowned). Mary Thacher spent her life pursuing beauty and distributing largesse. She gave Corporation Beach to Dennis, and her house to SPNEA in exchange for the promise that she'd be allowed to live out her years here. ◆ Admission. Tu, Th, Sa-Su noon-4PM June-mid-Oct. 250 Main St (between Church and Thacher Sts), Yarmouthport. 362.4385

8 New Church Swedenborgian fervor swept through Yarmouthport in the early 1800s, instigated by a young Harvard graduate named Caleb Reed. The search for a church site culminated in this 1870 building flanking the village green. Three small triangular windows, with stained glass in a trefoil pattern, adorn each side; the cloverleaf motif is repeated in the carved and painted roof trusses. A William Clarke tracker organ helps dispel the gloom. ♦ Services: Su 10:45AM July–early Sept. 266 Main St (at Church St), Yarmouthport. 362.3364

9 Captain Bangs Hallet House This 1840 Greek Revival house, maintained by the Historical Association of Old Yarmouth, faces the Village Green but is easier to reach from the back (just drive up behind the post office). Named for the daring China trade captain who lived here from 1863 to 1893, it's decorated with original period pieces, including a Hepplewhite sofa, Sheraton secretary, Chippendale frames, Hitchcock chairs, etc. For all its riches, however, it's more show than soul. Adjoining the property is the two-mile Yarmouth **Nature Trail;** it leads to the simple-style shingled **Kelley Chapel,** which was built by a Quaker in 1873 for a daughter left bereft by the loss of a child. ♦ House: Nominal admission. Trail: donation. Chapel: Free. House: Th-F, Su 1-4PM July-Aug; Su 1-4PM June, Sept. Trail: daily dawn until dusk. Chapel: daily 1-4PM July-Aug. 11 Strawberry La (just south of Rte 6A), Yarmouthport. 362.3021

Josef Berger's *Cape Cod Pilot,* written under the aegis of the WPA in 1937, contains the following instructions for a traditional clambake: "You will require a good supply of stones as big as your two fists. You must have enough of these to fill in a circle, six feet in diameter, of two layers. On top of your stones build a fire of driftwood and race it for an hour, covering all the stones. *You* do the direction, and let the others in your party bring piles of wet seaweed, washed as clean as possible of sand. Rake the embers off your hot stones and pile the weed on to a depth of 18 inches. Spread your clams over the weed, with your lobsters, potatoes, corn, or anything else you want to bake. Keep everything well away from the edge, and bunched towards the center. Then cover with more weed, to a depth of three feet. Then batten all down with an old piece of sailcloth, tucking in the edges all round, to retain the steam, and on top of this pile plenty of sand. Your work is finished now, except for the hardest chore of all—to keep everybody else away from the bake for at least 45 minutes, and to argue down those in the party who insist that half an hour is long enough, and they know because they tried it once on Long Island. Tell them this is Cape Cod. Explain that they do everything wrong here. That's why the baked clams taste so good."

10 Clancy's ★★$$$ This eatery has quickly become a year-round destination for casual dining in an amiable ambience of warm wood and brass furnishings. The dishes are tasty—try chicken Theresa, in which medaillons of meat, broccoli, and sun-dried tomatoes are sautéed in garlic and olive oil with a white wine and romano cheese sauce; or steak Lucifer, a New York sirloin topped with lobster meat, asparagus, and béarnaise sauce. On weekend nights you might hear solo guitarist Brian Kelly in all his nimble-fingered glory. ♦ American ♦ Daily lunch and dinner June-Oct; F-Sa lunch and dinner Nov-May. 175 Rte 28 (between Standish Way and E Main St), West Yarmouth. 775.3332 &

ZooQuarium
CAPE COD EDUCATION CENTER

11 ZooQuarium Although this facility in recent years has become more environmental/educational than exploitative or exhibitionistic, it still features performing sea lions. The trainers, however, are careful to explain that the captive stars would be unable to survive in the wild, and are trained by means of rewards rather than punishments. Other sheltered wildlife, as well as farm animals, can be visited out back. The facility continues to home in on fauna indigenous to the region—there is even a pair of rather formidable bobcats. Both animal and aquatic displays are designed to reflect the natural environment and are accompanied by informative signs. It's definitely worth a visit, with or without a child in tow. ♦ Admission. Daily 9:30AM-8PM July-Aug; daily mid-Feb–June, Sept–late Nov. 674 Main St (between Frank Baker and Winslow Gray Rds), West Yarmouth. 775.8883 &

12 Lobster Boat ★★$$ Imagine a collision between an enormous lobster boat and a Cape Cod cottage and you have an idea of what this place looks like. Irresistible to tourists, this rambling restaurant boasts a waterside setting (on Parkers River), the nautical pastiche of buoys, traps, flags, and nets, and the predictable seafood medley, offered at people-pleasing prices. The place gets mobbed the minute the doors open. "It's a zoo," says the maîtresse d', affectionately. ♦ American ♦ Daily dinner Apr-Oct. 681 Main St (between Seaview and South Sea Aves), West Yarmouth. 775.0486 &

13 Pirate's Cove Adventure Golf The decor is tasteless, not to mention morbid (a mock gravestone legend reads: "Dead Cats Don't Meow"), but if you have a cottageful of mutinous kids, set them loose for a few rounds of 18-hole miniature golf. ♦ Admission. Daily 9AM-10PM June-Aug; call for hours mid-Apr–May, Sept–mid-Oct. 728 Main St (between Frank Baker and Winslow Gray Rds), South Yarmouth. 394.6200 &

14 Jake's Bakes The usual seafood is offered at standard prices here, but what sets this caterer/take-out place apart is the clambake-to-go. This multicourse feast consists of chowder, barbecued chicken, lobster, steamers, mussels, Italian sausage, corn on the cob, red bliss potatoes, and steamed onions. It's all cooked by Jake and his staff under a layer of seaweed. Top off the meal with watermelon. ♦ Daily May-Oct. 57 Neptune La (between Pawkannawkut Dr and Rte 28), South Yarmouth. 394.0331

15 Captain Farris House $$$ This handsome inn, an 1845 Greek Revival, was completely restored in 1992 by its former owner. Stephen and Patty Bronstein took it over a year later and further refurbished the property. The eight spacious rooms are hand-painted in a subtle palette and have stylish and sturdy antique furnishings; all but one guest room has a Jacuzzi. Dishes in the three-course breakfast might include stuffed French toast, frittatas, and quiches. ♦ 308 Old Main St (at Mill La), South Yarmouth. 760.2818, 800/350.9477; fax 398.1262

16 Nineteenth Century Mercantile "I used to go to those places like Sturbridge and wonder, 'Why can't I take this stuff home?' " says Barbara Amster, who eventually did just that. Her store sells reproduction home furnishings, remedies, and household necessities. If you yearn for a slower, more considered life, look over the shelves filled with such essentials as moustache combs and killer hatpins, rosewater cologne and homemade piccalilli, long johns and reticules. "It's a true general store," says Amster, who dresses in period costume when on the job. "We have everything from food to plumbing supplies." ♦ Tu-Sa; Su noon-5PM. 2 N Main St (at Rte 28), South Yarmouth. 398.1888

17 Water Safaris It's not the Zambezi, but the Bass River has some pretty interesting wildlife of its own (terns, egrets, herons), and getting out onto the water is a cool way to explore it. The *Starfish,* a custom-built 1985 minibarge, accommodates 49 passengers, and Captain Cliff Smith provides a running commentary on the sights—from windmills to captain's homes—during the 1.5-hour cruise. ♦ Four departures daily mid-June–early Sept; two departures late May–mid-June, early Sept–mid-Oct. Rte 28 (at Bass River Bridge), West Dennis. 362.5555

17 Cape Cod Boats If you'd prefer to paddle your own canoe or self-propel your own motorboat, sailboat, or Windsurfer, you can rent by the hour to the week here. Bait, tackle, and licenses can be obtained from the shops in this complex. ♦ Rte 28 (at Bass River Bridge), West Dennis. 394.9268

We∫t Dennis on Cape Cod, Massachusetts

18 Lighthouse Inn $$$ The centerpiece of this old-fashioned beachside resort, opened by Everett Stone in 1938 and now run by his grandson, is an 1855 lighthouse decommis-sioned in 1914 and relit in 1989 in time to celebrate the bicentennial of US lighthouses. Starting with a cluster of cold-water cabins, the Stones expanded their accommodations to 61 homey rooms, suites, and cottages. The complex also includes a pool, tennis and volleyball courts, miniature golf, shuffleboard, horseshoes, and a gameroom. If this isn't enough to keep the children busy, you can enroll them in a structured play program. The Modified American Plan offers a refreshing nouvelle menu at enticing prices, and after dinner, there's action at the **Sand Bar** club. ♦ Closed January–mid-May, mid-October–December. 4 Lighthouse Rd (between Uncle Stephan's Rd and S Main St), West Dennis. 398.2244 &

Within the Lighthouse Inn:

Lighthouse Inn Restaurant ★★★$$$ Seated in this barn-size dining room that's cooled by sea breezes, you can enjoy such nouvelle Cape Cod fare as grilled salmon in a balsamic reduction. For dessert look for such satisfying specialties (in season) as raspberry torte truffle or blueberry cobbler. ♦ American/ Continental ♦ Daily breakfast, lunch, and dinner mid-May–mid-Oct. Reservations recommended for dinner. 398.2244 &

19 The Beach House $$ Set in a sleepy community of weathered cottages, this seven-room bed-and-breakfast is a definite sleeper itself. It's right on the beach, and kids are not only welcome, they're catered to, with an elaborate beachside playground. Among the other niceties: a complete kitchen (including two microwaves) for guests who want to cook in, as well as a cookout deck and picnic tables. The rooms are very pretty and have private decks to take advantage of the view. When the weather's nice, continental breakfast is served buffet-style on the outdoor porch. ♦ 61 Uncle Stephan's Rd (off Lighthouse Rd), West Dennis. 398.4575

20 Jericho House and Barn Museum This 1801 full Cape was built by Captain Theophilus Baker, whose 1834 trainee Richard Henry Dana would turn his maritime adventures into the novel *Two Years Before the Mast.* Baker's descendants lived here until 1954. The house was rescued from dereliction by Virginia Gildersleeve, former dean of Barnard College. It's filled with period furnishings—including, in the cramped upstairs bedrooms, a fur rocking horse and an assortment of jet-beaded capes. Peek into the musty attic to see the pegged rafters. The 1810 museum contains a race cart left over from the days when off-duty sea captains were avid fans of harness racing. There's also a miniature model saltworks, extensive carpentry and farm implements (including cranberrying tools), and a pretend blacksmith shop and country store. The prize, though, is a 20th-century folk-art extravaganza: a 150-creature "driftwood zoo" fashioned in the 1950s by retired ad executive Sherman M. Woodward. Woodward, who had a sense of humor as well as a good eye for flotsam, made everything from sea serpents to King Kong; kids are likely to find the collection fascinating. ♦ Donation. W, F 2-4PM July-Aug. Trotting Park Rd (at Old Main St), West Dennis. 398.6736

21 South Parish Congregational Church Erected in 1835, this chapel is famous for its Sandwich glass chandelier and Snetzler rosewood organ. The latter, built in London in 1762 and installed here in 1845, is the oldest pipe organ still in use in America. ♦ Service: Su 10AM. 234 Main St (between Center St and Hidden Shores La), South Dennis. 394.5992 &

22 Swan River Seafood ★★$$ To get fish any fresher, you'd have to head out on a boat with your hibachi. In concert with its on-site fish market, this 1950s institution serves fresh-sliced slabs, such as shark steak au poivre or scrod San Sebastian (simmered in garlic broth). The sweeping view takes in a marsh and windmill. ♦ International ♦ Daily lunch and dinner late May–Sept. 5 Lower County Rd (at Swan Pond River), Dennisport 394.4466 &

23 Woolfie's Home Baking Every beachside community has its favorite doughnut-and-muffin shop, and it's easy to see why Dennisport residents prefer this one. The muffins are huge and moist, and range from chip-studded double chocolate to wholesome cranberry-walnut. The Danish, strudel, and coffee cakes are light and flavorful. ♦ M-F, Su 7:30AM-4PM May-Sept. 279 Lower County Rd (between Sea St and Shad Hole Rd), Dennisport. 394.3717

24 Sundae School Created in 1976 by Paul Endres, a former Milton Academy history teacher, this barn-turned–ice-cream parlor is part museum, with vintage posters and paraphernalia, including a nickelodeon and Belle Epoque marble soda fountain. Choose from traditional flavors or more exotic ones, like Amaretto nut or Kahlua chip. All the usual toppings are on tap, or you can treat yourself to a seasonal sundae smothered in fresh blueberries or raspberries. ♦ Daily 11AM-11PM mid-Apr–mid-Oct. 387 Lower County Rd (at Sea St), Dennisport. 394.9122 & Also at: 210 Main St (between Beach and Great Oak Rds), East Orleans. 255.5473

24 Bob Briggs' Wee Packet ★★$$ It's tiny all right—a score of lemon-yellow Formica-top tables are crammed into a space not much bigger than a garage. But the down-home cooking (all the seafood staples, plus some classic diner fare) has been packing them in since 1949. As a special bonus, there are such satisfying homemade desserts as fudge cake, blueberry shortcake, and bread pudding with lemon sauce. ♦ American/Takeout ♦ Daily breakfast, lunch, and dinner May-Oct. 79 Depot St (at Lower County Rd), Dennisport. 398.2181 &

25 Main Street Antique Center Proprietors Vince Hinman and Richard White have gone upscale since they moved from their former shop, **Ellipse,** in Dennis, where they offered mostly Fiestaware. At this classy co-op,

Hinman and White represent 110 antiques dealers featuring a mix of early Americana and collectibles—including Fiestaware, paintings that range in price from $5 to $10,000, rare books, Shaker furniture, Native American art, and even the likes of a $9,000 grandfather clock made by Walter Durfee in Providence, Rhode Island, in 1890. ◆ M-Sa; Su noon-5PM. 691 Main St (between Belmont Rd and Depot St), Dennisport. 760.5700 ⚊

26 Cape Cod Discovery Museum & Toy Shop
You can't help applauding this venture, a viable alternative to the mind-numbing pastimes typically foisted on vacationing children. This place is a full-scale, 6,400-square-foot exploratorium with challenges and delights galore for the 12-and-under set. (Actually,

Cape Cod
DISCOVERY MUSEUM

adults could also have fun with a lot of the stuff.) One of the founders, Kate Clemens, is an award-winning curriculum developer, so it's not surprising her selections are state-of-the-art. Among the sensory treats in store are an "international diner" for pretend food play; a "baby pit" where under-threes can bumble about freely; a puppet theater and music room, with a see-through piano; a shadow room where your outline "freezes" on the wall; games, puzzles, and a cooperative (four-handed) maze; a recycled art corner; and the popular frosty sailboat exhibit that kids can climb into. If you're planning to be in the area for a while, by all means spring for the family membership—it's only $50 per annum, grandparents included. ◆ Admission. Daily 9:30AM-7:30PM mid-June–early Sept. W-Sa; Su noon-4:30PM early Sept–mid-June. 444 Main St (between Sea and Baxter Sts), Dennisport. 398.1600 ⚊

27 Cape Cod Braided Rug Company This factory showroom is operated by the great-grandchildren of Romeo Paulus, who in 1910 produced the first machine-made braided rug in the US. Wool/acrylic blend or rag rugs start at about $20 for throws and go on up for color-coordinated custom work. ◆ M-Sa. 259 Great Western Rd (between Depot and Thayer Sts), South Dennis. 398.0089 ⚊

28 Pewter Crafters of Cape Cod Former computer executive Barrie Cliff changed careers in 1977 to delve into the all-but-lost art of pewter making. His creations come in two finishes, satiny or shiny, and in two distinct lines: traditional (porringers, tea sets, bowls, and candlesticks, some with a signature scallop-shell motif) and contemporary (especially striking geometric bud vases). ◆ Tu-Sa. 927 Main St (between Satucket and South Yarmouth Rds), Yarmouthport. 362.3407 ⚊

28 Northside Crafts Gallery Paulette Cliff, wife of pewter maker Barrie, runs this contemporary American crafts gallery. A bird-carver herself, she has an eye for exceptional pottery in lush glazes. Also featured are glass, fabric, woodwork, and baskets. ◆ M-Sa May-Dec. 933 Main St (between Satucket and S Yarmouth Rds), Yarmouthport. 362.5291 ⚊

29 Captain Frosty's ★★$ It's your better-than-average clam shack, with all frying conducted in heart-friendly canola oil. Mike and Pat Henderson, a naval officer and schoolteacher before they started the business in 1976, are picky about their fish, purchasing hooked cod (not gill-netted) from Chatham, and sea (not bay) scallops and clams. The especially generous lobster roll is refreshingly filler-free. ◆ American ◆ Daily breakfast and dinner Apr-Sept. 219 Main St (at South Yarmouth Rd), Dennis. 385.8548 ⚊

30 Antiques Center of Cape Cod
"Dolls to Deco, Baskets to backdate"—that's just a sample of what you'll find at the largest co-op shop on the Cape. Founded in 1991, it features more than 135 dealers and their wares, and the pickings are often splendid—everything from primitive blanket chests and colonial shoe buckles to a solid copper bathtub and a 1922 slot machine. The big stuff is upstairs, the small down; depending on how acquisitive you're feeling, you might want to allow an hour or more for each. ◆ Daily. 243 Main St (at South Yarmouth Rd), Dennis. 385.6400 ⚊

31 Gingersnaps Stop in at Ginger Nunez's cottage bakery to pick from a delicious assortment of Danish, muffins, croissants, and fresh-baked breads and pies. You could also try the "chocolate white-out" devil's food cake—or, of course, a big sack of those signature cookies. ◆ Tu-Sa; Su 8AM-noon late May–early Sept; call for off-season hours. 467 Main St (between South Yarmouth and Old Bass River Rds), Dennis. 385.4200

32 Grose Gallery Even if you're leery of art galleries featuring the work of the proprietor, you should make an exception and check out the exquisite wood engravings of David T. Grose. Known for his illustrations of naturalist John Hay's trio of Cape Cod studies, *The Run*, *Nature's Year*, and *The Great Beach*, Grose can provide a new take on images as simple as compass grass (so-called because, when

windblown, it draws a circle in the sand).
Some works shown in this slaughterhouse-turned-studio are less skilled than others,
but you're not likely to be disappointed.
Depending on what's on the schedule for
that day, you might also be able to watch
the printing process. ♦ Daily Feb-Dec; by
appointment Jan. 524 Main St (between
Longfellow Dr and New Boston Rd), Dennis.
385.3434 ♦

33 Olde Towne Antiques of Dennis
Proprietors Ruth and Walt Jensen offer a
good selection of collectibles; their many
interests include antique sporting equipment
(baseball, golf, fishing), toy soldiers, books,
and pinups. ♦ Daily. 593 Main St (between
Black Ball Hill and Old Bass River Rds),
Dennis. 385.5202

33 Armchair Bookstore This enjoyable new
store is fun to stroll through, even if you're
not in the market for a book. Shelves are
scattered around three rooms—one totally
devoted to children's books, games, and
toys on the first floor, with lots of nooks and
crannies available for reading a few chapters.
Other specialties of the shop include
gardening guides (there are horticultural
gifts as well), books on Cape Cod, and a
"Discovery Shelf" of works by new authors.
A great card collection and custom-designed
dog paraphernalia—inspired by Chaps and
Buzz, the resident golden retrievers—are also
reasons to stop here. ♦ Daily. 619 Main St
(between Black Ball Hill and Old Bass River
Rds), Dennis. 385.0900

34 Gina's by the Sea ★★$$$ Note that it's
by, not *on,* the sea, but it's only a stone's
throw away. Located in Dennis's own version
of "Little Italy," this white clapboard restaurant
has been pleasing locals since 1938. Under
Larry Riley's ownership, the word is beginning
to spread farther. Small, lively, and convivial,
this dining spot serves the kind of Italian fare
that will weather any wave of chic (cannelloni
Florentine, for instance), while giving a nod to
the trendy—for example, smoked mozzarella
ravioli with pimiento. A specialty is scampi à la
Gina (with plenty of garlic); and for dessert try
Mrs. Riley's Chocolate Rum Cake. ♦ Northern
Italian ♦ Daily lunch and dinner July–mid-Sept;
daily dinner Apr–June, mid-Sept–Nov. 134
Taunton Ave (at Dr. Bottero Rd), Dennis.
385.3213 ♦

During the 1880s, the waters around the Cape
averaged a shipwreck every two weeks.

35 Isaiah Hall B&B Inn $$ The 1857 home of
cooper Isaiah B. Hall, who patented the
original cranberry barrel (his brother, Henry
Hall, was the first to cultivate the fruit), this
rambling farmhouse has been an inn since
1948—ever since the **Cape Playhouse** got
rolling again after World War II. Over the
years, it served as the theater's unofficial
residence, hosting a panoply of stars and
directors; if you come in summer, you might
find several staying here. Innkeeper Marie
Brophy is a ready-for-anything sort of hostess
and the inn reflects her friendly spirit.
Breakfast (cranberry breads, banana-nut
muffins) is offered buffet-style, at a massive
table-for-12; and the cathedral-ceilinged great
room in the carriage house makes a comfortable place to socialize come evening. The 10
rooms range from small, pine-paneled, and
quite inexpensive to expensive, beautifully
appointed, and still a good deal. ♦ Closed
mid-December–mid-March. 152 Whig St
(between Nobscusset and Corporation Rds),
Dennis. 385.9928, 800/736.0160; fax
385.5879 ♦

**36 Josiah Dennis Manse and Old West
Schoolhouse** The 1736 saltbox home of
the town founder is now a museum staffed
by friendly history buffs; you can wander
both floors on your own, and they'll volunteer
information. In addition to an unusual step-up
borning room, there's a maritime collection
with a beautifully made model of Dennis's
Shiverick Shipyard. (Active from around 1849
to 1863, this was the only facility on the Cape
large enough to produce clipper ships, sloops
and schooners.) The one-room schoolhouse,
dating from 1770, is sure to summon images
of braids dipped in inkwells—of which, in fact
there's an interesting collection. ♦ Donation.
Tu 10AM-noon, Th 2-4PM July-Sept. 77
Nobscusset Rd (at Whig St), Dennis.
385.2232

37 Emily's Beach Barn This mostly–bathing-suits sportswear store has suits by the thousands, plus coverups. Here is the fastest, most efficient way to get suited up for summer, with an unusually wide range of choices. ◆ M-Sa; Su noon-5PM Apr-Dec. 708 Main St (between Nobscusset Rd and Hope La), Dennis. 385.8328

37 Ice Cream Smuggler Yet another very worthy contender in the "finest homemade" category. You'd have to concede bonus points for the Turtleback Sundae (hot fudge *and* hot butterscotch), and for inventive flavors like apple pie. But a tester's work is never done. ◆ Daily 11AM-11PM mid-May–early Sept; daily noon-9PM Apr–mid-May, early Sept–Oct. 716 Main St (between Nobscusset Rd and Hope La), Dennis. 385.5307 &

37 Michael Baksa Goldsmith Baksa found his calling early in life; as a teenager, he apprenticed himself to a jeweler, and that was it. Now, as an adult, he's enough of a master to keep pushing the limits of the form. The symmetry he finds is not of the mirror-image sort, but something more satisfying; many of his pendants and earrings perform an almost Calderlike balancing act. He's also adept at offsetting colors, comparing the placement of gems against gold to the application of pigment to canvas. To broaden his palette, he's open to trying unconventional stones, such as cobalt calcium crystal (a blazing hot pink) and cool green-gray tourmaline, and he's fond of freshwater pearls in all shapes and hues. If you're contemplating custom work, you couldn't find a more accomplished accomplice. The gallery also features sensuous figurative sculptures in semi-translucent alabaster by his wife, Laura Baksa. ◆ M-Sa June–mid-Sept; Tu-Sa mid-Sept–late May. 766 Main St (at Mercantile Pl), Dennis. 385.5733, 800/357.5733 &

37 The Mercantile This elaborate deli (pictured above) offers the likes of avocado, mango, and shrimp salad or chocolate-zucchini cake, along with more traditional staples. It's a great place to piece together a picnic or a cafe meal. You can sit communally at a massive table at the center of the store and catch up on your reading with the complimentary magazines handily stored on a wooden helix. ◆ Daily 7:30AM-6PM July–early Sept. M-Sa 7:30AM-4PM; Su 7:30AM-3PM early Sept–June. 766 Main St (at Mercantile Pl), Dennis. 385.3877 &

B. Mango & bird

37 B. Mango & bird Cape Cod gift shops have a tendency toward triteness, but not this one. Odds are you won't have seen any of this stuff before—not the nubby cotton Steinweinder pillows or hand-painted valises, or the floor-model "pinnacle chime." Kids get some fun stuff, too—magnetic marbles, wind-up toys from the 1930s. The roster of artisans (some local) represented has surpassed the 200 mark, making this a shop to watch. ◆ Daily late June–early Sept. M-Sa; Su noon-5PM early Sept–late June. 780 Main St (between Mercantile Pl and Hope La), Dennis. 385.6700 &

38 Cape Playhouse America's oldest continuously operating professional summer theater was founded here in 1927 by Californian Raymond Moore, who had come to Provincetown in the early 1920s as a painter/playwright and got caught up in the theatrical fervor spawned by the **Provincetown Players.** After producing one barn-theater season in Provincetown, Moore—a man of vision at age 28—set his sites on the circa 1838 **Nobscusset (Unitarian) Meetinghouse** in Dennis, which had already undergone several lives as a livery stable, tin shop, smithy, barn, slaughterhouse, and garage. He bought it for a few hundred dollars, spent another $1,200 for 3.5 acres of farmland on which to relocate it, and had up-and-coming architect **Cleon Throckmorton** of New York City renovate, adding a stage, proscenium, and lofty fly gallery.

When the brave new venture opened 4 July 1927, with Basil Rathbone performing in *The Guardsman,* the roof leaked, but patrons persisted, popping up umbrellas. The next year they got to see a young Henry Fonda perform opposite an ex-usher determined to turn actress, Bette Davis. Not every season has been so stellar, but an endless roster of luminaries have passed through this "cradle of stars." These days artistic director Carleton Davis keeps things lively with a steady influx of fresh material and talent. ◆ Early June–late Sept; call for schedule. 36 Hope La (off Rte 6A), Dennis. 385.3911; fax 385.8162 &

On the Cape Playhouse grounds:

Cape Cinema It looks like a remodeled church, but, in fact it's a copy—Raymond Moore asked architect **Alfred Easton Poor** to replicate the exterior of Centerville's Congregational Church. The interior is decidedly original, featuring a 6,400-square-foot Art Deco ceiling mural of Prometheus, designed by Rockwell Kent and executed by set designer Jo Mielziner; their collaboration is a marvel of midnight blues, out of which fiery figures loom. Kent also designed the stage curtain, as a golden sunburst that folds back like a Japanese fan. Even the seats (of which there are only 92) are out-of-the-ordinary; they're black leather armchairs with white linen antimacassars. This luxury cinema, which opened on 1 July 1930, was subsequently chosen to host the world premiere of *The Wizard of Oz*. The cinematic fare is still select, hand-picked by well-known Boston art-house booker George Mansour. The refreshments fit right in—home-baked brownies and cookies, gourmet coffee, esoteric chocolates. And you can experience all this for no more than you'd pay at the local multiplex. ♦ Three shows daily early Apr–Oct; call for schedule. 385.4477 &

Cape Museum of Fine Arts This adjunct to the **Cape Playhouse** complex, which opened in 1985, has over 750 permanent works by Cape artists from 1898 to the present, ranging from some bad Arthur Diehl (a self-vaunting "speed painter" of the early 20th century, he did produce some museum-worthy work) to a Paul Resika—a characteristically understated landscape titled *Long Point and Black Roof* (1988). The newly renovated lower level galleries show everything from portraits by Robert Douglas Hunter to an untitled still life by Earl Pierce, a student of Hans Hoffman. The museum also organizes classes, tours, and regional art discovery field trips. ♦ Admission. Tu-Sa 10AM-5PM; Su 1-5PM. 385.4477; fax 385.7933

39 Scargo Café ★★$$ This rehabbed sea captain's house doesn't stand on ceremony. The rooms have been opened up into honey-paneled parlors, and there's also a pleasant glassed-in porch. The menu is divided into traditional and adventurous, convenient for parties of mixed persuasion. The conservative might order baked stuffed sole or quiche; for trailblazers there are dishes like "wildcat chicken" (sautéed with sweet Italian sausage, mushrooms, and raisins flambéed in apricot brandy). A fitting finish for both is the grapenut pudding, superb enough to have made an appearance in *Bon Appetit*. This is Cape Cod's only smoke-free restaurant, lounge, and bar. ♦ American/International ♦ Daily lunch and dinner. 799 Main St (between Old Bass River Rd and Pickering Way), Dennis. 385.8200 &

40 Red Pheasant Inn ★★★$$$ Since 1977, this marvelously atmospheric restaurant, an 18th-century ship's chandlery, has managed to remain cutting-edge contemporary. With chef-owner Bill Atwood Jr. in the kitchen (his father founded the restaurant) and his wife, Denise, seeing smoothly to the front, customers can relax and enjoy an extra-ordinary culinary experience. The decor is simplicity itself—low lighting, white tablecloths, a glassed-in garden room bursting with plants, and two hearths for the winter. The menu is inventive yet never overwrought; Atwood's specialties include cherrystone and scallop chowder scented with fresh thyme, carpaccio of venison, and an orange duck with green peppercorn reduction. Customers keep returning year after year. ♦ International ♦ Daily dinner; closed two weeks in March; call for exact dates. 905 Main St (between Pickering Way and Scargo Lake Rd), Dennis. 385.2133, 800/480.2133 &

41 Four Chimneys Inn $$ Russell and Kathy Tomasetti took over this bed-and-breakfast (the 1881 home of Dr. Samuel Crowell) in 1993 and have rapidly put it to rights. It offered some nice material to work with, including big, airy spaces with 11-foot ceilings. The eight rooms of varying sizes have been spiffed up with stencilwork and wicker; for the location (Scargo Lake is across the street, the bay beach a 10-minute walk away), they're very reasonably priced. An abundant continental breakfast is served on the outdoor porch, weather permitting. ♦ Closed January through April, November through December. 946 Main St (between Elm St and Seaside Ave), Dennis. 385.6317, 800/874.5502; fax 385.6285

42 Scargo Stoneware Pottery and Art Gallery At this woodsy studio, Harry Holl has had his hand to the wheel for years, while also rearing four daughters to join him in his craft. Their output spills out of the glass-topped showroom and into the bamboo-ringed grove—birdhouses camouflaged as castles, mosques, and basilicas; giant platters and planters; and sculptural pieces in an array of clays and glazes from delicate porcelain to earthy stoneware. Even if you're not in the market, you may want to take a look; the handiwork is fascinating. ♦ Daily. 30 Scargo Lake Rd (off Rte 6A), Dennis. 385.3894 &

43 Scargo Tower From atop this 28-foot stone tower, built on a 160-foot-high hill, you can see the entire sweep of the Cape's "arm," up to the clenched fist that is Provincetown. Constructed as an observatory for the Nobscusset Hotel, which was dismantled in the 1930s, it was donated to the town as a memorial to the hotel owners. Bring your binoculars if possible, or someone special to horizon-gaze with. Stretched out below is Scargo Lake, subject of dueling native legends. One version holds that the giant deity Maushop dug it to be remembered by. He piled the earth into a hill, where afterward he sat and smoked his pipe; the smoke created fog, and the ashes and spring rain nurtured nearby pines. A more romantic myth holds that an Indian princess received a pair of fish from a brave who was going away on a dangerous mission. When the fish outgrew their hollowed-out pumpkin bowl, she had four of her tribe's strongest braves shoot arrows to delineate the boundaries of a pond, which the squaws then dug out with clamshells. The fish prospered and multiplied, and her beloved returned home safe and sound. The question of origin aside, the lake does support abundant fish, including small-mouth bass and trout. ♦ Daily 6AM-10PM. Off Scargo Hill Rd (between Paddocks Path and Featherbed La), Dennis. No phone

44 Ross Coppelman In 1969, when he was just out of Harvard, Coppelman started making "hippie jewelry" and found he had a rare affinity for soft, malleable 22-karat gold, which can be worked into seamless, fluid shapes and beveled settings. He selects gems for their arresting depths of color—e.g., aquamarine, Australian opal, "watermelon" tourmaline—and frames them in illustrious settings. Known for his unusual pearl clasps, Coppelman enjoys reversing expectations with such creations as a "pearl" necklace fashioned of matte black onyx. His work is featured at the best Cape crafts galleries, and has also been shown at the Smithsonian. ♦ Daily July-Aug; Tu-Sa Sept-June. 1439 Main St (between East-West Dennis and Scargo Hill Rds), East Dennis. 385.7900

45 Webfoot Farm Antiques This eclectic shop, housed in a 19th-century captain's house, has a wilder assortment than most. It's located right next door to Eldred's, one of the Cape's premier auction houses, but owners George and Diane King look far and wide for their goods. There's quite a vast showing of Orientalia (including some antique kimonos), and among the larger pieces is a striking Spanish colonial desk with bowed, almost froglike legs. With prices ranging from $10 to $25,000 or thereabouts, there are ample choices for any budget. Depending on your interests—outdoor accessories are also a forte—you could putter around contentedly for quite some time. ♦ Daily June-Sept; M-Tu, Th-Su Oct-May. 1475 Main St (between East-West Dennis and Scargo Hill Rds), East Dennis. 385.2334; fax 385.2334

Bests

Patty Barnes
Author, Bookstore Owner, Armchair Book Store

Waking early Saturday morning, grabbing a cup of coffee, and shopping the jam-packed booths of the **Wellfleet Drive-In** flea market.

Experiencing breakfast and Jack at **Jack's Outback** in **Yarmouthport.** Misspelled menu selections are tacked to the wall, self-service means you do everything but cook, and owner/chef/cashier Jack Smith tries to be as crabby as his motto: "Great food, lousy service." Illustrator Edward Gorey eats here daily, along with the other locals who know that Jack's a great, big mush.

Driving **Route 28** along **Pleasant Bay** between **Orleans** and **Chatham** while listening to classical **WFCC 107.5FM**.

Reading the morning paper with a cup of toasted praline coffee on **Chatham Cookware**'s private side deck.

At sunset, going to **Nauset Light Beach** and watching people surf cast into a sky the color of heather, while the rest of the Cape gathers at the Bay.

Having dinner at **Joe's Beach Road Bar,** the grill at the **Barley Neck Inn** in Orleans. Lots of food for little dollars, and a "five-star" crème brûlée. Morgan, part of a great staff, salts the meals she serves with a dash of wit.

Treating oneself to a Saturday evening artist reception at **Addison Holmes Gallery** in Orleans.

Everett Potter
Writer

Spending an afternoon fishing on a small boat at the mouth of the **Pamet River** in **Truro** when the bluefish are in a feeding frenzy.

Walking the **Provincetown** beaches in early spring, when finback whales can be seen from shore.

Surf casting for stripers at **Wasque Point** on **Chappaquiddick.**

Brewster/Harwich/
Chatham/Orleans

Cape Cod Bay

Sea St.

6A Main St. **1**

2

Stony Brook Rd.

Red Top Rd.

3

Newcomb Rd.

6

4 **5**

**WEST
BREWSTER**

Satucket Rd.

Upper Mill Pond

Walkers Pond

Run Hill Rd.

Slough Rd.

W. Gate Rd.

7 8

Paines Creek Rd.

Lower Rd.

9
10

Brier La.

12

11

6A

Tubman Rd.

Great Fields Rd.

Seymour Pond

Hinkley Pond

Swamp Rd.

14

13

Breakwater Rd.

15 16

Cathedral Rd.

Main St. **20**
19

Foster Rd.

23

21
22

Underpass Rd. **18**

137

17

Long Pond Rd.

Snow Rd.

BREWSTER

124

Sheep Pond

Harwich Rd.

Long Pond

Long Pond Dr.

Freeman Way

Millstone Rd.

Hawks Nest Rd.

137

Long Pond Rd.

6 Mid-Cape Hwy.

Queen Anne Rd.

124

HARWICH

Orleans-Harwich Rd.

Depot Rd.

Great Western Rd.

Main St.

Main St

34

Pleasant Lake Ave.

39

Chatham Rd.

Morton Rd.

Swan Pond

**WEST
HARWICH**

Lothrop Ave.

Sisson Rd.

39

Forest St.

Long Rd.
40

Bank St.

Depot Rd.

28

Depot St.

Belmont Rd.
Bells Neck Rd.

30

29

Riverside Dr.

28

Main St.

32
33

Earle Rd.

Lower County Rd.

HARWICHPORT

Hoyt Rd.

Main St.

Uncle Venie's Rd.

35

37

36 38

39

41

Ayer La.

Wychmere Harbor

Saquatucket Harbor

31

**Nantucket
Sound**

Ferry to Nantucket (in season)

N

km   1   2
mi 1/2   1

104 Rock Harbor Rd.

ORLEANS

Skaket Beach Rd.

103

innell Rd.

—Crosby La.

27 (6A) Main St.

102 West Rd.

EAST BREWSTER

101

Eldredge Park Way

(28)

Mid-Cape Hwy.

(6)

Nook Rd.

as Rd.

(6A) Town Cove

For nos. 89-100, see pg. 102

88 Main St. **102**

81 River **82 83 84**
Rd.

80

Monument Rd.

South Orleans Rd.

Areys La.

Namequoit Rd.

SOUTH ORLEANS

Quanset Rd.

Orleans-Harwich Rd. **79**

Tarkiln Rd. **78**

Pleasant Bay Rd. **77**

Kendrick Rd.

CHATHAMPORT

Fox Hill Rd. **76**

Training Field Rd.

42

(28) Orleans Rd.

Ryder's Cove

CHATHAM

Sam Ryders Rd. Old Comers Rd.

George Ryder Rd. Old Queen Anne Rd.

Chatham Municipal Airport

47

46

(28) Main St. **48** **49**

WEST CHATHAM

uling Beach

Barn Hill Rd.

Oyster Pond

Cedar St. **52**

Stage Harbor Rd.

Bridge St. **54**

Morris Island Rd.

Harding Beach

Stage Harbor

Morris Island

Stage Island Rd.

Meetinghouse Rd.
Great Oak Rd.

87 86 Beach Rd.

Tonset Rd. Brick Hill Rd.

EAST ORLEANS

Barley Neck Rd.

Little Pleasant Bay

Sipson Island

Pleasant Bay

Crows Pond

Bassing Harbor

Strong Island

Stony Hill Rd. **75**

Crowell Rd. **74** Tern Island

Old Harbor Rd.

51 **73** Seaview St.

50 **72**

Main St.

Shore Rd.

Cross St. **55**

For nos. 56-71, see pg. 93

Chatham Breach

53 Monomoy National Wildlife Refuge **South Beach Island**

Nauset Harbor

Nauset Heights Rd. **85**

Nauset Beach

Sampson Island

Hog Island

Cape Cod National Seashore Park

Atlantic Ocean

Nauset Beach

Brewster/Harwich/ Chatham/Orleans

Near the Cape's elbow are several small summer colonies. Among the prettiest are Brewster, Harwich, Chatham, and Orleans. Each town boasts a unique history and character, and, for the most part, each has escaped much of the commercial invasion that has spoiled great stretches of the Mid-Cape. The traditions are just too entrenched and the economy too sturdy to brook much in the way of heavy-handed development—with the exception of Orleans, which sometimes appears to be flooded with tourist traffic.

Brewster/Harwich

Brewster (named for *Mayflower* passenger Elder William Brewster of the Plymouth Colony) was part of Harwich until 1803, when the towns split apart at the instigation of Brewster's prosperous sea captains, who wished to dissociate from their poorer neighbors to the south. Harwich went on to pioneer the cranberry industry, however, which took off as the maritime trades began to decline, so the towns' fortunes eventually evened out.

Despite the incursion of condominiums (most of which are, fortunately, relatively inconspicuous) and the proximity of the hugely popular—and, as a result, often overpopulated—**Nickerson State Park,** Brewster retains an air of calm gentility. Its hills and dales and scattering of small ponds make it seem more like open country than a seaside resort. The waters off Brewster's eight bay beaches are shallow and gentle, just right for little kids. At low tide the ocean recedes by as much as two miles, leaving behind a huge salty playground striated with colorful "garnet" sand, so named for its reddish streaks.

Harwich, which enjoys the slightly livelier surf of **Nantucket Sound,** has resisted the development that plagues the more westerly stretches of **Route 28** and is quite charming and graceful.

1 The Spectrum Two **Rhode Island School of Design** grads started this enterprise in a country schoolhouse in 1966 and quickly developed it into a premier chain of crafts shops, with branches as far-flung as Palm Beach. The split-level store is very late–1960s in style, with its sculpture gardens and expanses of plate glass. The stock is accessible and appealing, from Josh Simpson's glass-marble "planets" to Thomas Mann's totemic "techno-romantic" jewelry. ◆ Daily May-Sept; M-Sa Oct-Apr. 369 Main St (between Drummer Boy Rd and Sea St), West Brewster. 385.3322, 800/221.2472. Also at: 342 Main St (at Barnstable Rd), Hyannis. 771.4554; 26 Main St (between Union and Orange Sts), Nantucket. 228.4606

2 Kingsland Manor Antiques There's only one thing to be said about Doris and Norman Schepps's ivy-cloaked antiques shop, which offers an array of goods from tin to Tiffany— you'll either love it or hate it. This place is over the top, with Oriental carpets layered knee deep, and oddities as varied as matching baby elephant foot ashtrays ($350 a pair) and an antique medical exam table (slightly shy of $3,000). You might even splurge on a carved Victorian bar—for a mere $20,000. Mixed in with the outrageous items are some impressive big pieces with equally big price tags. ◆ Daily. 440 Main St (between A. Percie Newcomb and Stony Brook Rds), West Brewster. 385.9741, 800/486.2305

3 Underground Art Gallery In this amazingly light and airy studio/bunker, 10 massive tree trunks support 200 tons of earth, plus a sprinkling of wildflowers. Karen North Wells creates realistic watercolors, lithographs, and greeting cards of local sights; underground architect/avatar Malcolm Wells fills mail orders for his enormously successful books (from 1977's best-selling *Underground Design* to his delightful booklet *Sandcastles*) and executes impressionistic landscapes in plain latex house paint. His paintings sell for $40 to $1,000, but occasionally he puts a "free" tag on, "just to lighten things up a bit." ◆ Daily noon-5PM. 673 Satucket Rd (at A. Percie Newcomb Rd), West Brewster. 896.6850 &

4 High Brewster Inn $$$ This 1738 homestead on 3.5 acres shows its history in its intimate, low-ceilinged rooms. There's limited common space beyond the dining rooms (and the rock garden overlooking Lower Mill Pond), so you might consider staying over purely as a postprandial treat— unless you reserve one of the three roomy cottages, which are full-scale country retreats. The three rooms in the inn itself are a steep hike upstairs, and, although charmingly decorated, they are far from spacious and a bit pricey for the square footage. However, inn guests do get to indulge in the rather spectacular breakfasts. ♦ Closed January through March. 964 Satucket Rd (between Canoe Pond Dr and Stony Brook Rd), West Brewster. 896.3636, 800/203.2634 ⅃

Within the High Brewster Inn:

High Brewster Restaurant ★★★$$$$
The five-course, prix-fixe dinner changes seasonally to take advantage of local offerings, but chef Steve Arden's creations are invariably bold and robustly flavored. In early summer, for instance, you might partake of pan-seared duck breast with a peach *demi-glace,* perhaps accompanied by local greens tossed with sweet marjoram vinaigrette and garnished with pea tendrils and chive flowers. The inventiveness meets its match in artful, yet unfussy presentations. The three small dining rooms, with ladderback chairs, antique paneling, ceilings close enough to touch, and glowing candlelight are romance incarnate. ♦ New American ♦ Daily dinner mid-June–mid-Sept; call for off-season hours; closed January through March. Reservations recommended. 896.3636 ⅃

5 Stony Brook Grist Mill and Museum The 1663 original, the oldest water-powered mill in America, is long gone, and this circa 1873 model, built of saltworks salvage, started grinding corn only after it had exhausted its usefulness in the manufacture of overalls and ice cream. In other words, the building is not especially venerable, but it is one of the few vestiges of the **Factory Village** that thrived here in the 19th century. Also, the volunteer grinders are so enthusiastic, and so good at involving young children in the process ("You could run this place!" they're often told), that families might want to make a special stop. Upstairs is a pleasantly musty, eclectic museum featuring everything from a five-inch quartz arrowhead (tools dating back 10 millennia have been unearthed nearby) to a monumental 19th-century loom; you might catch a weaving demo in progress. There's a pretty walkway around the millpond, and in spring, thousands of herring can be seen leaping the natural rock ladder to spawn. ♦ Free. Th-Sa 2-5PM July-Aug; F 2-5PM May-June. 830 Stony Brook Rd (between Run Hill and Satucket Rds), West Brewster. No phone

6 Punkhorn Bookshop Unlike most of its ilk, David L. Luebke's rare and used bookstore is extremely tidy and well organized. Instead of languishing in dusty piles, his stock sits upright on ample shelving, grouped by the Dewey Decimal system and wrapped in protective translucent covers by his wife, Irene, a bookbinder. Specialties include natural history and New England regional titles; there's also a section featuring decorative bindings, and an intriguing selection of prints. ♦ Tu-Su late May–Oct; by appointment anytime. 672 Main St (between Paines Creek and A. Percie Newcomb Rds), Brewster. 896.2114

6 Brewster Farmhouse Inn $$ Carol and Gary Concors run this small, luxurious inn. The Greek Revival facade, with its striped awnings, may look a trifle stodgy, but step inside and you'll feel as if you've been transported to California—the space is awash with light and inviting down-filled sofas in soft neutral tones; a pool and hot tub beckon from beyond the expansive wooden deck. The five rooms share the same restful color scheme and center on dramatic canopied or hand-carved beds. Breakfasts are a feast, featuring such delicacies as homemade croissants and cheese blintzes with raspberry puree and fresh figs; teatime summons a fresh parade of treats, such as nectarine *clafouti* (tart). The only difficulty will be tearing yourself away to enjoy some sight-seeing. ♦ 716 Main St (between Paine Creek and A. Percie Newcomb Rds), Brewster. 896.3910, 800/892.3910; fax 896.4232

7 Harris-Black House and Higgins Farm Windmill That an entire family fit in this 1795 one-room half-Cape house, only 16 feet square, is amazing enough; then consider the fact that barber/blacksmith Nathan Black managed to raise 10 children here. The 30-foot-tall octagonal windmill, also built in 1795, is remarkable not only for its smocklike silhouette (popular in England when the Pilgrims set sail) but for its unusual boat-shaped cap, curved like a ship's hull. Knowledgeable members of the Brewster Historical Society are on hand to answer your questions. ♦ Free. Tu-F 1-4PM July-Aug; Sa-Su 1-4PM May-June, Sept-Oct. 785 Main St (between Paines Creek and Drummer Boy Rds), Brewster. 896.9521

CAPE COD MUSEUM OF NATURAL HISTORY

8 Cape Cod Museum of Natural History Founded in 1954 by a group of local naturalists, among them writer John Hay, this marvelous museum has long been in the vanguard of interactive exhibits. Children and adults alike will be fascinated by the "live hive" (a see-through working beehive) and the "window on the marsh," where myriad birds come to feed. For an even more active experience, venture out to the museum's 82 acres, transected by three trails: the quarter-mile **North Trail** crosses a salt marsh; the half-mile **South Trail** wanders through cattails, cranberries, and beech trees; and the 1.3-mile **John Wing Trail** (named for the town founder) leads to an untouched bay beach. In addition to permanent exhibits (the whale display is especially strong, enlivened with a tape of leviathan vocalizations), the museum schedules numerous special events, including children's and family programs, lectures, concerts, "eco-treks," and cruises of Nauset Marsh and the Monomoy Islands; there's even a sleepover at a Monomoy lighthouse, billed as "the ultimate Cape Cod experience." ♦ Admission. M-Tu, Th-Sa; W 9:30AM-7:30PM; Su noon-4:30PM July-Aug. Daily Sept-June. 869 Main St (between Paines Creek and Drummer Boy Rds), Brewster. 896.3867, 800/479.3867 &

9 Cook Shop If it has anything to do with food, you're likely to find it here: picnic hampers, cookbooks, professional-caliber pots and pans, blocks of French sink soap, weighty Italian pottery, tortilla warmers—no culinary tool is too exotic for inclusion. There's also an extensive and tempting array of gourmet staples. ♦ Daily. 1091 Main St (between Brier La and Paines Creek Rd), Brewster. 896.7698 &

10 Wysteria Antiques etc. Walking into this new shop in a fabulous, lavender Victorian home from the 1860s is like stumbling upon a pirate's treasure chest. The place sparkles with vintage costume jewelry, glass, china, and lace, arranged by Ken DiCarlo to be viewed like an intricate work of folk art. Visitors are greeted by DiCarlo and partner Clay O'Connor, who assure them that "We have something for everyone, but if this is not for you, we understand." Most visitors react with enthusiasm. ♦ Daily, depending on whim. 1199 Main St (between Brier La and Paine Creek Rd), Brewster. 896.8650

11 Beechcroft Inn $$ This handsome clapboard building started out as the town's 1828 Universalist meetinghouse. After being moved and having its steeple lopped off, it became an inn in 1852. Having submitted to much-needed renovations in the early 1990s, it's now an up-to-date country inn with a timeless air. The 10 rooms, of varying sizes and prices, are adorned with wicker,

stenciling, and little decorative touches. Guests enjoy the benefit of a bountiful country breakfast. ♦ 1360 Main St (at Tubman Rd), Brewster. 896.9534; fax 896.8812

Within the Beechcroft Inn:

Beechcroft Inn Dining Room ★★$$ Cross New England seafood with a country bistro, and you might get dishes as delicious as these—a hearty lobster-scallop pie, or scrod Sebastian (flanked by mussels and baked, with herbs and lemon). Seasonal vegetables see to the good-for-you aspect of the meal, soon to be undone by the naughty desserts. ♦ American ♦ Tu-Sa dinner mid-May–mid-Sept; call for off-season schedule. Reservations recommended. 896.9534

12 New England Fire & History Museum There's an endearingly homespun quality to the exhibits here, from the mannequins representing firefighters through the ages (since 22 BC) to a diorama of the Chicago Fire of 1871. In addition to the 30-odd antique fire engines (including a 1929 Mercedes Benz model valued at $1 million) and longtime **Boston Pops** maestro Arthur Fiedler's helmet collection, there are a few unrelated exhibits such as a reproduction smithy and apothecary shop. Adults who are not confirmed "sparkies" may find themselves underwhelmed, but children invariably lap it up. The gift shop features, not too surprisingly, fire chief hats and toy engines. ♦ Admission. M-F; Sa-Su noon-4PM late May–early Sept. Sa-Su noon-4PM early Sept–mid-Oct. 1429 Main St (between Brier La and Swamp Rd), Brewster. 896.5711

13 Brewster Ladies' Library Stirred to action by two public-spirited 17-year-olds, Augusta Mayo and Mary Louise Cobb, a dozen Brewster women established a "library"—rather, a shelf of books available for loan—in Miss Mayo's home in 1852. With financial assistance from local sea captains, they were able to move the growing collection into this picturesque yellow Victorian in 1868. The building has since expanded several times, but the two original front parlors, each with a fireplace, stenciled stained glass, and enveloping armchairs, are still good places to sit out a storm with a riveting book. Ask about lectures and story hours. ♦ Tu-W 9AM-1PM, 6-9PM; Th-Sa 9AM-1PM late June–early Sept; Tu-W noon-8PM; Th-F; Sa 10AM-2PM early Sept–late June. 1822 Main St (between Rtes 137 and 124), Brewster. 896.3913 &

14 Old Manse Inn $$ Built for Captain Winslow Lewis Knowles in the early 1800s, this imposing house enjoyed a checkered

career as an Underground Railroad stopover and a Lutheran chapel before becoming an inn in 1945. Chefs/owners David and Suzanne Plum have recently restored it to provide eight elegant guest rooms, with traditional decor and a superlative restaurant (see below).
♦ Closed January through March. 1861 Main St (at Lower Rd), Brewster. 896.3149

Within the Old Manse Inn:

Old Manse Inn Restaurant ★★★$$$
Enjoy a meal in either of the dining rooms or—even more appealing in good weather—on a screened sunporch surrounded by fragrant perennials. Indulge in the wonderful flavors of savory duck broth with a watercress spring roll, or try the fresh steamed lobster served over shellfish risotto and red wine sauce. Pastry chef Suzanne, a Culinary Institute of America graduate like her husband (who prepares the appetizers and entrées), makes all the delicious desserts. Sunday brunch is a treasure, but dinner is a must, even if you're not staying at the inn. ♦ Continental ♦ Th-Sa dinner; Su brunch and dinner Apr-Dec. 896.3149

15 Brewster Store This genial general store started out as an 1852 Universalist church, which was sold in 1858 because of declining membership. In 1866, proprietor W.W. Knowles removed the top of the tower and extended the front corners to make it look more storelike, but luckily he didn't touch the magnificent arched windows on the second floor. Today, the ambience is rather hokey but jolly; kids go nuts here (a lot of the touristy gewgaws fit their budgets), and thrown in among the Cape Cod mementos are some fairly useful kitchen gadgets and beach gear. Drop a dime in the "Nickelodeon," a piano-less player-piano machine, and peruse your reserved newspaper in one of the church pews arranged out front. ♦ Daily 6AM-10PM July-Aug; daily 7AM-5PM Sept-June. 1935 Main St (at Breakwater Rd), Brewster. 896.3744

15 Captain Freeman Inn
$$$ If you tend to associate bed-and-breakfasts with penury (no TV, minimal privacy), you owe it to yourself to try one of the three suites at this 12-bedroom, circa 1866 Victorian mansion.

Innkeeper Carol Edmondson, a former computer exec, has thought of everything: each suite comes with a canopied queen-size four-poster; a love seat; cable TV with a VCR and a long list of movies on videotape; a mini-fridge stocked with soda; and, on an enclosed balcony, a clover-shaped whirlpool bath. "People often come for a week or more," she says, and it's no wonder.

A serious cook, Edmondson attended the Grand Master Chefs program to prepare for her new vocation as innkeeper. The result is a lavish yet low fat breakfast—served in summer on a screened porch overlooking the pool—that runs from eggs Brewster (smoked salmon and poached eggs on a cranberry English muffin with orange hollandaise) to fresh corn pancakes and sausage-and-pepper quiche. During winter, guest chefs conduct cooking-school week-ends, where participants feast on their own handiwork. Captain William Freeman, a prosperous clipper shipmaster whose command included the *Kingfisher* (hence the inn's logo), designed the striking herringbone-pattern floors in the entrance way. The nine second-story bedrooms have the unusual feature of windows that start at the floor, which render the spaces wonder-fully cozy. On the third floor, you'll find three additional rooms tucked under the eaves—though they're small, they have a pared-down charm and beautiful views. Available only in summer, these rooms are very reasonably priced. Breakwater Beach, whence packet boats used to ply the bay to Boston, is a bucolic stroll away. ♦ 15 Breakwater Rd (at Rte 6A), Brewster. 896.7481, 800/843.4664 &

15 First Parish Church This 1834 white clapboard church, a mixture of Greek and Gothic Revival styles, is the second replace-ment for the 1700 original built for fiery preacher Nathaniel Stone. The pews are marked with prominent captains' names, and the burial ground out back contains many a notable headstone, including that of Captain David Nickerson and one "Rene Rousseau." Folklore has it that Nickerson was presented with an infant during the French Revolution and asked to raise him; it was rumored that the child was the lost *dauphin,* son of Louis XVI and Marie Antoinette. Rousseau became a captain himself and was lost at sea; his name is carved on the back of Nickerson's gravestone, as was the custom. Now a Unitarian Universalist church, it hosts two popular traditions in July and August: traditional chowder suppers Wednesday evenings at 6PM, and Mimsy puppet shows for children Thursday mornings at 10AM.
♦ Services: Su 9AM, 11AM. 1969 Main St (between Old North and Breakwater Rds), Brewster. 896.5577 &

16 Bramble Inn $$ Eight guest rooms and a suite are housed in two buildings dating from 1861 and 1849. The eight rooms come in "all shapes and sizes," says innkeeper Cliff Manchester, who opened this inn in 1985, following his parents' lead at the **Old Manse Inn**. The houses are decorated in a country mode, with brass canopy beds and wicker; honeymooners love the gardner's cottage out back with its private entrance, antique brass and iron bed, and secluded deck. All guests are the beneficiaries of Ruth Manchester's considerable skill in the kitchen: Morning repasts might include apple pancakes or chèvre-roquefort tart. ♦ Closed January through April. 2019 Main St (between Id North and Breakwater Rds), Brewster. 896.7644

Within the Bramble Inn:

Bramble Inn Restaurant
★★★$$$$ Every antique table setting is unique, as is the decor in each of five small dining rooms, from a pink-striped sunporch to a wood-paneled tack room and a formal parlor with pheasant motif. The personal attention that informs the setting also infuses the food. Chef/co-owner Ruth Manchester has an exploratory bent, and the menu has evolved over the years from inventive nouvelle to daring world-beat. The four-course prix-fixe menu, which changes monthly, typically offers a half-dozen appetizers and as many entrées, ranging from chilled white gazpacho to grilled Gulf shrimp with jalapeño glaze. The dessert selection is exquisite: make sure at least one person in your party orders the signature white chocolate *coeur à la crème* so you can all have a taste. ♦ New American ♦ Tu-Su dinner July-Oct; Th-Su dinner May-June, Nov-Dec. Reservations required. 896.7644

17 Bassett Wild Animal Farm Opened in the early 1960s and owned by Gail Smithson since 1978, this mini-zoo located in a 20-acre oak grove has the comfortable look and feel of a backyard enterprise. Peacocks (including some white ones, a rare sight) wander around in full display, and an African lion and a mountain cougar pace menacingly behind a chain-link fence. There's an enclosed petting area where goats roam free, looking for a handout, and patient ponies plod in a circle. Little kids will take it all in with wonder; slightly older kids might question whether these "natural surroundings" are really fair to the animals. ♦ Admission. Daily mid-May–mid-Sept. 620 Tubman Rd (at Desmor Rd), Brewster. 896.3224 &

18 Rail Trail Bike Shop One of the better-stocked shops along the trail, this store has all the basics for cycling, maintained at top condition, plus child carriers, trailers, and other handy accessories. The free parking is real plus. ♦ Daily Apr-Oct. 302 Underpass R (at Snow Rd), Brewster. 896.8200

18 Pizza & More ★$ The "more" in this case includes grinders and gyros, sandwich and spinach pie; there's even pasta for pre-marathon carbo-loading. And the honey-suffused baklava will bring that blood sugar right back up. ♦ International ♦ Daily lunch and dinner. 302 Underpass Rd (at Snow Rd) Brewster. 896.8600 &

19 Brewster Fish House ★★★$$$ It's roadside-ordinary on the outside, small and nautically neat on the inside, with a minuscul bar that seats five and a scattering of linen-topped tables encircled by burnished Windsc chairs. It's not until you get your hands on th menu that the restaurant's self-character-ization as "nonconforming" becomes clear. There aren't very many places on the Cape where you can sample fried artichokes with garlic-and-ginger marinade, say, or a mixed grill (swordfish, shrimp, scallops, and Andouille sausage) with a dipping sauce of soy, sesame, and molasses. For an uplifting dessert, try the lemon bavarian cake. ♦ New American ♦ Daily lunch and dinner late May–early Sept; Th-Su lunch and dinner early Apr–late May, early Sept–mid-Dec. 2208 Mai St (between Snow and Rd and Stonehenge Dr), Brewster. 896.7867 &

Chillingsworth

20 Chillingsworth $$ Three Ralph Lauren—accoutred rooms are available in this 1689 homestead reputedly built by a *Mayflower* passenger, but the main draw is indisputably the restaurant. If you're looking forward to being temporarily immobilized by the feast o a lifetime, these chambers, with their eclectic antiques, make a pleasant and convenient place to crash. ◆ Closed late November–mid-May. 2449 Main St (between Foster and Point of Rocks Rds), Brewster. 896.3640

Within the Chillingsworth:

Chillingsworth Restaurant

★★★★$$$$ Supremely elegant and agreeably eccentric, this establishment has long reigned as the Cape's premier dining spot. It is truly a "once in a lifetime" experience —although sometimes the excellent food comes seasoned with an arrogant attitude from the staff. Still, over the years patrons have been served very well by the seven-course table d'hôte dinner, which unfolds at two seatings in a warren of candlelit, salonlike dining rooms appointed with antiques (some dating as early as Louis XV). Chef/owner Robert Rabin revises the menu daily to make the most of market offerings, and he stands ready to produce any of a dozen appetizers and as many entrées, along with soup, salad, sorbet, and pre-dessert amusements. Narrowing down the menu can be torment: for starters, should you try the snails with tomatoes, hazelnuts, garlic, sage, and brandied green peppercorn sauce, or a foie gras, *haricots verts* (green beans), jicama, and arugula salad with warm truffle vinaigrette? Remember to pace yourself for the main course (veal loin with saffron risotto and garlic custard, perhaps, or venison with celery-root puree and sun-dried cranberries) and the assorted killer desserts, the deadliest of which is Chocolate Nemesis drizzled with *crème anglaise*. At lunch, lighter versions of similar dishes are offered à la carte. If eating were a competitive sport (one sometimes wonders), this would qualify as the Olympics, with all due pomp and circumstance. ◆ French ◆ Daily lunch and dinner mid-June–mid-Sept; call for off-season hours. Reservations required; jacket required at dinner. 896.3640 &

Le Bistrot ★★$$ For a lighter repast than the offerings at the **Chillingsworth Restaurant,** stop in at this place that also features a complete take-home meal at its retail counter (and an intriguing assortment of antiques). The desserts—raspberry crème brûlée, fresh plum cobbler, chocolate Bavarian cream pie—are all sublime. ◆ American ◆ Daily lunch and dinner mid-June–mid-Sept; call for off-season hours. Reservations recommended. 896.3640

Old Sea Pines Inn

21 Old Sea Pines Inn $$ This 1907 shingle-style mansion on 3.5 acres was originally the **Sea Pines School of Charm and Personality for Young Women,** and owners Michele and

Steve Rowan have hosted some nostalgic graduates. Mostly, though, the guests are urban residents seeking a respite from modern-day stress. The main house is preserved at its 1930s apogee, with green cane rockers set out on the wraparound porch; the rooms here range from spacious to rather small and are priced accordingly. The guest house annex is more contemporary in decor, featuring cheery floral prints and pink TV sets (well, why not?). With 21 rooms in all, for all budgets, the hotel tends to attract a lively and varied clientele. ◆ Closed January through March. 2553 Main St (between Ellis Landing and Foster Rds), Brewster. 896.6114; fax 896.7387 &

Within the Old Sea Pines Inn:

Old Sea Pines Inn Restaurant ★★$$$

No longer only a dinner destination, this spot also now rings with the sound of music. The Rowans, in conjunction with **Cape Cod Repertory Theatre,** have set up a prix-fixe menu of four courses to coincide with the four acts of musical reviews written for the occasion by director Robert Troie and others. It's a full evening's entertainment, helped by the simple but satisfying cuisine of chef Mark Ayala: cranberry glazed stuffed chicken breast or a melt-in-your-mouth prime rib. For dessert, the old-fashioned strawberry shortcake is tops. ◆ American ◆ Dinner/theater M, Su Aug; Su June-July, Sept. Reservations recommended. 896.6114 &

21 Tower House Restaurant
★★$$ The prices are reasonable, the staff pleasant, and the setting handsome, with dramatic wrought-iron chandeliers and pale napery. In summer, everyone competes for porch space. If you crave straightforward fish—baked, poached, sautéed, broiled, charbroiled, or blackened—that hankering will be well met here. The seafood casserole is also tops, combining shrimp, scallops, and cod in a lobster cream sauce. ◆ American ◆ Daily breakfast, lunch, and dinner mid-June–mid-Sept; call for off-season schedule. 2671 Main St (between Ellis Landing and Foster Rds), Brewster. 896.2671 &

22 Great Cape Cod Herb, Spice & Tea Co. Herbalist Stephan Brown's "natural apothecary" dates back only to 1991, but the native Cape dwellers of hundreds of years ago would recognize some of their favored natural remedies, such as burdock and sassafras. The store stocks more than 170 herbs, some incorporated in Brown's custom-blended teas, including Monomoy Morning. This rustic shed also serves, perforce, as a New Age nexus. Brown conducts regular classes as well as eye-opening "weed walks." ◆ Store: M-Sa; Su 11AM-5PM. Walks: Sa 9AM June-Oct. 2628

Main St (between Old Colony and Snow Rds), Brewster. 896.5900, 800/427.7144; fax 896.1972 ♿

23 Ocean Edge Resort and Golf Club $$$$
This 380-acre complex—plus the 1,955-acre **Nickerson State Park** to the east—is all that's left of the Roland C. Nickerson estate. Samuel Mayo Nickerson, a Chatham native, headed west in 1847 as a young man with no money to his name; within 16 years, he helped found the First National Bank of Chicago. In 1890, he built a magnificent shingle-and-stone mansion, **Fieldstone Hall,** for his only son, Roland. Boasting a nine-hole golf course, a game preserve, a windmill, and its own horse-powered electric plant, this grand summer "cottage" was a magnet for nobs throughout New England. The mansion burned to the ground in 1906 and Roland died two weeks later. In 1908, his widow, Addie, started rebuilding—this time with fireproof steel-reinforced concrete covered with stucco, in a mix of Renaissance Revival and Gothic styles.

The 400-foot-long house, with its overscale rooms and intricately carved oak trim, remained in the family until 1942, when it was sold to the LaSalette Fathers for use as a seminary. It was bought by Corcoran Jennison, Inc. in 1980 and converted to its present use as a conference center, complete with 321 guest rooms. While this Gilded Age treasure has been preserved, its surroundings have expanded to include all the advantages of a Caribbean resort: five Har-Tru tennis courts, a fitness center, and a 1,000-foot private ocean beach. Across Route 6A and west a bit is the rest of the complex: a championship 18-hole golf course, six all-weather tennis courts, an assortment of indoor and outdoor pools, and nearby villas. ♦ 2907 Main St (between Linnell and Ellis Landing Rds), Brewster. 896.9000, 800/343.6074

Within the Ocean Edge Resort and Golf Club:

Ocean Grille ★★★$$$ On a clear night you'll be able to see the **Pilgrim Monument** in Provincetown from the dining room of this historical mansion overlooking Cape Cod Bay. Chef Gile Haskins features a black angus beef fillet with wild mushroom sauce and a wood-grilled swordfish with tomato beurre blanc. The bourbon chocolate torte is notorious. ♦ American ♦ Daily breakfast, lunch, and dinner. 896.9000 ♿

Restaurants/Clubs: Red   Hotels: Blue
Shops/ 🌳 Outdoors: Green   Sights/Culture: Black

86

Mulligans Restaurant ★★$$$ The glassed-in architecture is light and airy, the green-and-rose chintz accents pretty, and the view of the surrounding golf course unimpeded. The restaurant operates independently of the resort, and chef/owner Jake Jacobus turns out interesting dishes: Start with the smoked duck spring roll or wild mushroom strudel; and move on to almond-crusted sole with grapefruit, scallions, and beurre blanc. The menu is always compelling and, if you want an even better view of the course, go for the summer outdoor patio buffet. ♦ New American ♦ M-Sa lunch and dinner, Su brunch and dinner late May–early Sept; call for off-season schedule. Reservations recommended. 832 Villages Dr (between Rtes 137 and 6A). 896.8251 ♿

24 Cobie's ★$ If this silver-shingled clam shack looks like a classic, that's because it is—it dates back to 1948. Regulars have been known to drive long distances for the fried clams, and **Rail Trail** cyclists hardly have to break stride to enjoy a snack at the picnic tables on the porch. ♦ American ♦ Daily lunch and dinner late May–mid-Sept. 3260 Main St (between Ober and Millstone Rds), East Brewster. 896.7021

25 Brewster Historical Society Museum This small but touching collection, housed in an 1840 homestead, features snippets of the past: an 1884 barbershop, the old **East Brewster Post Office,** an assortment of dolls and toys, and a doll-size reproduction of the town's oldest dwelling, the 1660 **Dillingham House.** It's worth a brief look around before you head off on the **Spruce Hill Trail,** a quarter-mile nature walk over the dunes to the bay. The wide grassy path was once a carriage road and, it is rumored, a conduit for bootleggers during Prohibition. ♦ Free. Museum: Tu-F 1-4PM July-Aug; Sa-Su 1-4PM May-June, early Sept. Trail: daily sunrise-sunset. 3341 Main St (between Linnell and Ellis Landing Rds), East Brewster. 896.9521

26 Cape Rep Outdoor Theatre Come summer, the peripatetic **Cape Rep** gets an outdoor home of its own—a rustic amphitheater on the old **Crosby Estate.** The summer fare is straight Shakespeare (typically, two plays performed alternating weeks). Don't forget to bring the bug spray. ♦ Admission. Tu-Sa 8:30PM early July–early Sept. 3379 Main St (between Crosby La and Linnell Rd), East Brewster. 896.1888 ♿

26 Monomoy Antiques This carriage-house shop offers antiques at starter prices: ship models commencing at $200 or so, beds for $500 and up. Also featured here is a wide variety of sterling silver, ranging in price from $10 to thousands, and fine glass and china. ◆ Daily late May–mid-Oct. 3425 Main St (at Crosby La), East Brewster. 896.6570 ♿

27 William M. Baxter Antiques Much of William Baxter's holdings belong by rights in a museum, and they'll probably get there eventually, but meanwhile private buyers can take advantage of his "gradual liquidation sale." After more than three decades in this spot (he moved here from Boston's anti-quarian alley, Charles Street), he ponders retirement but has barns full of goods to unload. Among the treasures recently up for grabs was an upholstered Federal sofa from Salem, Massachusetts (ca. 1810) and an 1820s collection of four miniature paintings of children with pets. ◆ M-Sa late May–late Nov. 3439 Main St (between Mitchell and Crosby Las), East Brewster. 896.3998

28 Nickerson State Park Donated by Addie Nickerson (widow of Roland) in 1934, this 1,955-acre retreat is Massachusetts's fourth-largest state park. It contains 88,000 white pine, hemlock, and spruce trees, eight miles of bike paths (which hook up to the **Rail Trail**), and eight kettle ponds, the largest of which, Cliff Pond, is surrounded by "glacial erratics," huge boulders transported from the mainland by advancing glaciers. The park offers 418 campsites (usually booked solid in summer) and, although it may seem overrun in parts, is doing its best to protect its natural resources. ◆ Free admission; fee for camping. Daily. Rte 6A (between Holly Ave and Ober Rd), East Brewster. 896.3491 ♿

Within Nickerson State Park:

Jack's Boat Rentals Choose from Hobie-cats, Sunfish, sailboards, kayaks, canoes, aquabikes, and even pedalboats at this shop on Flax Pond. ◆ Daily late June–early Sept. 896.8556. Also at: Gull Pond Rd (between Gross Hill Rd and Hwy 6), Wellfleet. 349.9808

29 Lion's Head Inn $$ Tucked away in a quiet neighborhood, this attractive bed-and-breakfast fashioned from an 1810 sea captain's house has it all: a comfortable living room with a fireplace and cable TV (none in rooms), six commodious bedrooms, plus two cottages that rent by the week, and a screened sunroom overlooking a 40-foot pool. It's here that bountiful continental breakfasts are served—home-baked pastries, fresh fruit, cereals, juice, and coffee. ◆ 186 Belmont Rd

(off Rte 28, between Riverside Dr and Silver St), West Harwich. 432.7766, 800/321.3155

30 Bishop's Terrace ★★$$$ This centuries-old captain's house has been a popular local spot since 1942. The same somewhat conservative fare is served in the terrace room with mint-green tablecloths as in the formal dining room with Queen Anne chairs and an impressive scrimshaw collection. At night there's dancing to jazz in the barn-turned-bar. ◆ American ◆ M-Sa lunch and dinner; Su brunch and dinner Apr–mid-Oct. Reservations required. 108 Main St (between North and Bells Neck Rds), West Harwich. 432.0253 ♿

THE COMMODORE INN "By The Beach"

31 Commodore Inn $$$ New owners have spiffed up what had been a very basic motel, outfitting the 27 rooms with cathedral ceilings, lots of wicker, and white cotton bedspreads. The rooms are tasteful and inviting, and only 100 pastoral yards from the beach, or steps from a large heated pool. There's also a good restaurant serving American and continental fare with a full breakfast buffet every day for inn guests. ◆ Closed January through February. 30 Earle Rd (south of Lower County Rd), West Harwich. 432.1180, 800/368.1180; fax 432.4643 ♿

32 Trampoline Center Only two rules apply: no shoes and no flips allowed. The 12 in-ground trampolines are in such constant motion throughout the summer, they could be harnessed as an alternative energy source. The sound track? "Mom, Dad, watch this!" ◆ Fee. Daily mid-June–early Sept; Sa-Su May–mid-June. 296 Main St (between Sisson Rd and Lothrop Ave), West Harwich. 432.8717

32 Seafood Sam's ★$ When the kids are through bouncing their brains out at the **Trampoline Center**, duck next door for some well-priced, no-frills seafood, from lobster bisque to deep-fried popcorn shrimp. ◆ American ◆ Daily lunch and dinner mid-Mar–Oct. 302 Main St (between Sisson Rd and Lothrop Ave), West Harwich. 432.1422. Also at: Coast Guard Rd (off Town Neck Rd), Sandwich. 888.4629; 350 Palmer Ave (between Ter Heun Dr and Rte 28A), Falmouth. 540.7877; 1006 Rte 28 (between Forest and Frank Baker Rds), South Yarmouth. 394.3504

33 Bud's Go-Karts Drivers as young as eight can solo at this busy track (maximum speed: 15 mph); younger speedsters can ride on their parents' laps. No helmets are provided, so you might want to bring your own for this not-exactly-cheap thrill. ◆ M-Sa 9AM-11PM; Su 1-11PM early May–mid-Sept. 364 Sisson Rd (at Rte 28), Harwichport. 432.4964

Brooks Academy Museum

34 Brooks Academy Museum This former navigation school (the first in the US, built by Sidney Brooks in 1844 and illustrated above) now houses the collections of the Harwich Historical Society commemorating high points in town history. An entire room is devoted to cranberry harvesting: Captain Alvin Cahoon of Harwich was the first commercial grower, starting his bogs in 1846. Other displays include Native American and maritime artifacts, such as a sample "Frosty," the bathtub-size sailboat that serves as a starter raft for many an amateur salt. Among the domestic goods are lace, wedding gowns, dolls, and games. There's also a display on local celeb Caleb Chase, who co-founded Chase & Sanborn coffee in 1878; volunteer historian Patricia Ellis Buck made headlines herself in 1993 when she pointed out that the founders' likenesses had been switched on the label—how many years back, even the 91-year-old company archivist couldn't say. The gents have at long last been restored to rights. Also on the grounds are a powderhouse used during the Revolutionary War and a restored 1872 outhouse. ♦ Free. Th-Su 1-4PM mid-June–mid-Oct. 80 Parallel St (between Sisson Rd and Forest St), Harwich Center. 432.8089 ⓖ

35 Goucho's Southwestern Hardwood Grill ★★$$ This suburban house, yellow with green shutters, doesn't look especially south-of-the-border, but step inside and you'll be sufficiently convinced: the walls are daubed in plaster, with archways crudely limned in blue, serapes are draped here and there, and way back on a stone mantelpiece hearth sits the requisite O'Keeffian cow skull. The menu blends classics with some curious hybrids: the "Mayan Pupu Platter" is an hors d'oeuvre sampler, the "Philly burrito" consists of steak, onions, and cheese enfolded in a flour tortilla, and "Margarita Pie" is a piquant variant on Key lime. If the lineup suggests more frivolity than serious cross-cultural exchange, that's the general idea. In July and August, there's live entertainment Wednesday through Sunday, culminating in a free midnight feast (since there's no cover charge or two-drink minimum, it's an especially good deal). ♦ Mexican/Southwestern ♦ Daily dinner Apr–mid-Oct. 403 Lower County Rd (between Rte 28 and Wahwahtaysee Rd), Harwichport. 432.7768

36 The Mews Antiques at Harwichport There's scarcely enough stuff in this small saltbox to furnish a room, but it's a good place to find decorative touches to finish one. The five dealers have complementary fortes, from stoneware and baskets to jugs and antique chocolate molds. ♦ M-Sa, Su noon-5PM May-Nov. 517 Main St (at Ayer La), Harwichport. 432.6397

36 Dunscroft by the Sea $$$ An old-fashioned gem of a beachside bed-and-breakfast, this classic gambrel-roof cedar-shake inn offers nine romantically decorated rooms, including four with their own private entrances and a honeymoon cottage with a fireplace. Innkeeper Alyce Cunningham's taste runs toward Laura Ashley fabrics, and just one of her welcoming touches is to leave some hand-dipped chocolates beside your sleigh bed or canopied four-poster every night. The inn's proximity to the seashore (the beach is only a few minutes' walk away) allows for plenty of soothing surf sounds in the background. Full country breakfasts include baked eggs supreme (with cream and cheddar cheese) and strawberry-banana or fresh blueberry yogurt pancakes. ♦ 24 Pilgrim Rd (off Rte 28, between Sea St and Ayer La), Harwichport. 432.0810, 800/432.4345

37 Monahan Michael O'Neill Monahan's great-great-great-grandfather founded this store in 1815, and there's never been a need to change the name. In addition to lots of old photographs, there's varied stock ranging from Cape Cod charms as low as $10 to $175,000 diamond necklaces. Monahan makes a lot of custom wedding rings—and since he's a justice of the peace, he can marry you as well. ♦ M-Sa. 540 Main St (between Cross and Forest Sts), Harwichport. 432.3302

38 Cape Sea Grille ★★★$$$ Beth Bryde and Jim Poitrast, the chefs/owners of this establishment, are shy about discussing their backgrounds. But they must have had at least some restaurant experience, judging from the finesse and stylish presentation of their delicious entrées. For instance, there's the mixed grill, featuring roast lobster, herb-crusted fish fillet, barbecued shrimp, and swordfish wrapped in applewood-smoked bacon. For dessert, try the imaginative "twin brûlée"—crème brûlée flavored with orange-ginger and espresso. The tariff for such a feast is surprisingly reasonable, and the atmosphere of the low-key, contemporary dining room is quiet, refined, and elegant. This youthful enterprise just steps from the sea has all the makings of a winner. ♦ New American ♦ Daily dinner mid-June–early Sept; M, W-Su dinner Apr–mid-June, early Sept–Nov. 31 Sea St (off Rte 28, between Bank St and Pilgrim Rd), Harwichport. 432.4745 &

38 Beach House Inn $$$ Gregg Winston and David Plunkett's inn is a perfect blend of nostalgia and modern comfort. The 10 original 1920s rooms have homey pine paneling and chenille bedspreads; the four spacious beachfront add-ons are more upscale and come with fireplaces and/or private decks. All are equipped with their own fridges, color TV sets, and air-conditioning—not that you'll much need the latter, since the place is right on Nantucket Sound, where cooling breezes accompany the gently pounding surf. ♦ 4 Braddock La (off Bank St), Harwichport. 432.4444, 800/870.4405 &

38 Sandpiper Beach Inn $$ Bill and Jayne Condon bought and revamped this 19-unit motel just as they did the **Commodore Inn** (see page 87), and what used to be a humdrum motel now sparkles. The layout is U-shaped, with a courtyard facing the beach, so the end rooms have the best views, but even with the lower-priced units you're guaranteed to get your fill of sun and sand. ♦ 16 Bank St (off Rte 28), Harwichport. 432.0485, 800/433.2234

39 Thompson's Clam Bar ★★★$$ In its move to the former locale of **Nick and Dick's** (see below), this traditional clam bar lost its famous waterfront views, but kept the great seafood dishes. The raw bar with fresh littlenecks and oysters can't be topped on price and quality, and the homemade clam chowder, accompanied by steamed lobster, remains a meal fit for a nautical king. On a sunny day, take a seat on the outdoor patio and enjoy the flavors in a cool summer breeze. ♦ American ♦ Daily lunch and dinner mid-June–early Sept. 594 Main St (at Bank St), Harwichport. 430.1239 &

39 Nick and Dick's Ice Cream Parlor Stop here for the best homemade ice cream and yogurt on Cape Cod. Cool down with a banana split, or try one of the house sundaes; you can also create your own with toppings ranging from crushed Oreos to rainbow jimmies, the latter being a Boston term for sweet chocolate bits. And the waffle cones, dipped in chocolate, are an extravagant frill to hold the ice cream . . . but why not? ♦ Daily mid-June–early Sept. 606 Main St (between Gorham Rd and Bank St), Harwichport. 430.2444 &

40 The Barn at Windsong It's a bit off the beaten track (which is to say, inland), but this antiques shop is worth seeking out. The five dealers are always well stocked with silver, wicker, prints, toys, and an exceptionally broad textile selection, from quilts to samplers to embroidered tablecloths and bed linens. Occasionally you might come across a nice piece of "primitive" furniture, dressed in its original, wonderfully worn paint. ♦ M-Sa; Su noon-5PM May-Oct. Sa-Su noon-5PM Apr, Nov-Dec. 245 Bank St (between Hoyt and Long Rds), Harwich. 432.8281

L'alouette Restaurant

41 L'alouette Restaurant ★★★$$$ You have only to smell the stock simmering to know this is *real* French food. Chef Louis Bastres, who came here from Biarritz in 1986, brings his native expertise to bear on sautéed frogs' legs *niçoise* (topped with chopped tomatoes), bouillabaisse, *filet mignon au poivre*, and Chateaubriand *bouquetière* (covered with béarnaise sauce). The delicious food is presented in two dining rooms decorated with muted blue-gray carpeting, paintings of Parisian street scenes, and fresh flowers. The atmosphere is elegant without being stuffy. ♦ French ♦ Tu-Sa dinner; Su brunch and dinner. 787 Main St (between Neel and Snow Inn Rds), Harwichport. 430.0405 &

41 Cape Cod Divers In addition to rentals and sales of related equipment, this shop offers swimming lessons for all ages and scuba instruction (for 12-year-olds and up) in a heated pool. They also conduct shipwreck dive charters out of Harwichport and Provincetown. ♦ Daily June-Sept; Th-Su Oct-May. 815 Main St (between Neel and Snow Inn Rds), Harwichport. 432.9035, 800/348.4641

Those "Danger, Keep Off!" signs on dunes are not there just to protect the beach grass; in the early 1970s, a 12-year-old boy who paid them no heed was smothered by a sand slide.

Chatham/Orleans

The coast of Chatham, known as "the First Stop of the East Wind," was visited by explorer Samuel de Champlain in 1606. But **Monomoyick,** as it was then called, did not attract a permanent colony until 1656, when William Nickerson of Yarmouth bought land from the sachem chief Mattaquason and built a house right next door to Mattaquason's wigwam on **Ryder's Cove.** Despite escalating tensions between the "First Comers" and the Native Americans, the two men remained lifelong friends. Upon incorporating in 1712, the town took the name of the English earl of Chatham. Perhaps because it's less accessible than the other communities on the Cape, Chatham has remained a cohesive village, with a main street that's chockablock with attractive shops. This is one of the few places on the Cape where you'll see throngs of people out on the street for an evening stroll, and the band concerts held on Friday nights in summer are legendary, drawing crowds in the thousands.

Orleans, the only town on the Cape that does not have an Indian or English name, was settled in 1644. When the hamlet separated from **Eastham** in 1797, the citizens named it for Louis-Philippe de Bourbon, Duke of Orleans, who had visited that year during his American exile; four decades later, he would become king of France. The town was targeted by the British during the War of 1812 and again in 1918 by a German sub; it's the only place in the continental United States to have suffered enemy fire in either world war. Today, the skirmishes are of a different sort. Because the area is so heavily traveled (it's here that **Highway 6** and **Routes 6A** and **28** meet), Orleans is half commercial hub and half bourgeois enclave, with no clear identity either way and plenty of pressure to topple into the former. Although there are charming restaurants and stores scattered about, they're hard to reach without getting trapped in seemingly inescapable traffic, where your chances of executing a left turn are about as good as spotting snow in July. The flow lightens somewhat to the east of town, until you hit **Nauset Beach,** along the southernmost part of the **Cape Cod National Seashore** (a 40-mile preserve that extends along the entire outer length of the Cape's "forearm"). There are other, less populated stretches of sand farther up the coast, but because Nauset is the closest, it is the most crowded, and as such the most appealing to those who want to mingle with their peers. You guessed it: teenagers and twentysomethings, as far as the eye can see, with just a few families and elders permitted to disport among them.

42 Cape Cod Cooperage The scent of sawdust is heady with possibilities. You can't imagine how many wooden things you really *need* until you start wandering around this rambling barn: window boxes, clothes racks, painted chests, Adirondack chairs, bookshelves, birdhouses . . . all for about half what you'd pay elsewhere, and the majority are made on the premises. Fish and cranberry barrels have been made here since the late 1800s, and now the company is the only remaining cooperage in Massachusetts. ◆ Daily. 1150 Old Queen Anne Rd (between Old Comers Rd and Rte 137), Chatham. 432.0788 ♿

43 Chatham Pottery Between them, Gill Wilson and Margaret Wilson-Grey have over a half-century's experience making pottery, and it shows in their line of thick, sturdy stoneware, mostly in deep blues against off-white. Motifs from floral to piscine are applied to the bowls and lamp bases, sinks and tiles, hanging planters and pitcher-shaped fountains. They use a white stoneware clay, fired two or three times per piece for strength and durability. Depending on the workload, they'll be happy to show you the studio out back. ◆ Daily. 2058 Main St (between Sam Ryders Rd and Rte 137), West Chatham. 430.2191

44 Marion's Pie Shop The Cape used to be loaded with these summertime larders, so handy when guests show up unannounced or when you'd rather bake in the sun than over a hot stove. The shop has been around since 1951, and the lemon meringue pies are as lofty as ever, the chicken and clam pie just as sustaining, and the cinnamon rolls and fruit breads (cranberry-nut, zucchini-pineapple) eternally yummy. ◆ M-Sa 7AM-6PM; Su 7AM 2PM. 2022 Main St (between Sam Ryders Rd and Rte 137), West Chatham. 432.9439

45 The Seafarer of Chatham $$ When is a motel not a motel? When you get the same pretty surroundings (fluffy coverlets, colonial-style wall stenciling, extensive garden) and concierge-quality referrals (from innkeeper John Houhoulis) as you would at a fancy bed-and-breakfast. The only "disadvantage" is that instead of having to tiptoe around and chat with other guests, you have no choice at the end of the day but to return to your spacious room—one of 20—and hit the voluminous bed with your travel companion and/or 44 channels of cable. There's no restaurant, but coffee and tea are provided in the rooms. ◆ 2079 Main St (between Ridgevale and Beach Plum Rds), West Chatham. 432.1739, 800/786.2772

46 1736 House Antiques John Miller's full Cape is packed with odd treasures, from mule-ear rockers to ancient hooked rugs. He also shows the landscapes of Chatham-based painter Linda George—definitely worth a lingering look. ◆ M-Tu, Th-Su May-Nov; by appointment only Dec-Apr. 1731 Main St (between George Ryder Rd and Colonial Dr), West Chatham. 945.5690

47 Cape Cod Flying Circus Ready to execute some rolls, loops, and inversions in an open-cockpit, 1927-model biplane? Pilot Jim McDevitt promises a smooth, graceful flight in his 1978 *Great Lakes 2T1A-2*, based at **Chatham Municipal Airport.** For the slightly less daring, for whom a faceful of wind is thrill enough, he's just as glad to offer straight sight-seeing in a *Piper Cub* seaplane or three-passenger *Cessna*. Go take a look at Chatham's famous "breach," where a cross-beach current that started as a trickle in 1987 became a full-scale breakthrough that turned several prime chunks of Chatham real estate into driftwood. ♦ Daily 8:30AM-8:30PM May–mid-Sept; daily 8:30AM-7PM mid-Sept–Apr. By appointment only. George Ryder Rd (between Rte 28 and Old Queen Anne Rd), West Chatham. 945.2363, 945.9000

48 Picnic Basket If you're not in the habit of buying your meals at a liquor store, make an exception and check out chef/owner Barbara Obrig's offerings. As a summer visitor some years ago, she couldn't understand why it was impossible to find high-quality food at good prices, so she decided to abandon her career in banking and provide it herself. The sandwiches on homemade bread are superb (don't miss the top-notch shrimp salad), as is the changing array of cold dishes, such as ripe plum tomatoes with slivered Spanish onion and fresh mozzarella. The refrigerator case is likely to yield the likes of peach cobbler or "mudballs"—mounds of chocolate mousse encased in drizzled chocolate. ♦ M-Sa 8:30AM-11PM late May–early Sept; M-Sa 8:30AM-5PM early Sept–late May. 1221 Main St (between Lime Hill and Barn Hill Rds), West Chatham. 945.0501 &

49 Munson Gallery In operation since 1955, this gallery numbers among Cape Cod's oldest; it is also one of the finest. Housed in a 1920s horse barn, the gallery shows a score of established artists, while regularly making room for promising newcomers. ♦ M-Sa mid-June–mid-Oct. 880 Main St (between Crowell and Old Queen Anne Rds), Chatham. 945.2888 &

50 Monomoy Theatre The Cape's second-oldest surviving stage (after the **Barnstable Comedy Club**), this former toy factory became an Equity theater in the 1930s. In 1957, it was taken over by the **Ohio University Players** (the university president was a longtime Chatham summerer), and now a mix of students from across the country and returning alums—some with impressive credits under their belts—put on a play a week every summer. The season starts with a musical and ends with Shakespeare, and usually manages to work in something provocative among the crowd-pleasers. They take one break in late July, when the critically acclaimed **Monomoy Chamber Ensemble** mounts a series of popular concerts, including a free morning performance for children. This charming theater seats only 276 patrons, all of whom enjoy excellent sight lines. ♦ Tu-W, F, Su 8:30PM; Th, Sa 2PM, 8:30PM late June–Sept. 776 Main St (between Old Harbor and Depot Rds), Chatham. 945.1589 &

50 Chatham Glass James Holmes blows the glass, and Deborah Doane helps design it, a collaborative effort that has earned many an award and a regular place in such upscale emporia as Barney's, Gump's, and Neiman Marcus. The line is constantly evolving, but one trademark is the unconventional use of color, or rather colors—some 70 in all, usually paired unpredictably. Their signature candlestick, for example, a clean-lined column transected by chubby rings, might stack up in lavender, lime, and aqua. Some of the pieces are more organic in shape, resembling strange gourds or warped fruit, and the latest line is *turbini,* platters and vessels aswirl in amazing hues. Observe all this and more in the making in their newly located studio/showroom. ♦ M-Sa. 758 Main St (between Old Harbor and Depot Rds), Chatham. 945.5547 &

50 Amazing Lace Donna Burns's selection of vintage clothing is excellent, with a special focus on cotton batiste (there's nothing lighter, or prettier, in summer) and ever-classic linen, including Scottish and French lace window treatments. Also thrown in here are such kitschy home accessories as chenille bedspreads and 1930s block-print tablecloths. ♦ Daily July-Aug. F-Sa; Su noon-5PM Apr-June, Sept-Dec. 726 Main St (between Old Harbor and Depot Rds), Chatham. 945.4023

51 Railroad Museum What a pleasure it must have been to ride the rails, with buildings like this 1887 Victorian beauty as a destination. This "Railroad Gothic" station, buttercup yellow with sepia trim, was decommissioned in 1937 and, fortunately, bought for the town by a generous donor in 1951 and restored as a museum in 1960. With its shingled "candle-snuffer" turret and Cheeriolike decorations spaced beneath the eave brackets, it's a welcome sight still, even if the trains beside it (including a 1918 **New York Central** caboose) are permanently parked—all the better to climb aboard. The station is full of models, relics, and photos, and the background tape of wheels and whistles helps conjure up aural memories. If you've got a young train buff along, leave plenty of free time for the **Play-a-round** park across the street. Built by townspeople in 1990, it's one of the largest **Robert Leathers**–designed playgrounds in the Northeast—a fantastical, vaguely medieval-looking conglomeration of chutes, slides, bridges, and parapets. ♦ Donation. Tu-Sa mid-June–mid-Sept. 153 Depot Rd (between Old Harbor and Crowell Rds), Chatham. No phone &

52 Old Atwood House and Museums This gambrel-roofed 1752 house has been a repository for the Chatham Historical Society since 1926, and the group has collected well. In addition to the usual colonial accoutrements and the memorabilia of prolific Cape writer Joseph C. Lincoln, it's saved portraits of sea captains and local characters captured in a straight-on yet painterly fashion by Frederick Stallknecht Wight (1901-86). However, it was his mother, Alice Stallknecht Wight (1880-1973), who received most of the attention during their shared lifetime, as well as after (there's an entire barn devoted to her murals). Although her work may have seemed fauve and bold in the 1930s, today it looks more cartoonish and crude, like overcalculated folk art; she worked local citizens into tableaux depicting a modern Last Supper and gained considerable notoriety for depicting Christ as a modern-day fisherman.

Among the museum's odder acquisitions is a 1947 fishing camp—a shanty that was nearly washed out to sea after the famous 1987 "breach" in Chatham's beach. It may seem a bit premature to preserve a type of cottage that's still quite common, but perhaps a half-century from now it will have proved a shrewd save. ♦ Admission. Tu-F 1-4PM mid-June–Sept. 347 Stage Harbor Rd (between Inlet Rd and Hardings La), Chatham. 945.2493

53 Monomoy National Wildlife Refuge

This stretch of land has been through quite a few changes since it was declared a refuge in 1944. First, a 1958 storm turned what had been Monomoy Point into Monomoy Island, and then a 1978 blizzard sliced that island in two. Monomoy, along with Provincetown, is the only area of the Cape that's actually growing, so perhaps in the future this currently 2,750-acre property, overseen by the US Fish and Wildlife Service, will shelter even more animal life. Right now it harbors about 80 percent of the bird species native to New England, some 285 in all, including

piping plovers, heron, and egrets; a prime resting spot along the Atlantic Flyway, it's frequented by birds from as far away as the Arctic and Brazil. Deer wander among the 175 species of plants, ranging from red cedar to orchids and sundews. Thousands of harbor and gray seals winter here; in fact, gray pups born here in 1990 heralded the establishment of the first gray seal colony in Massachusetts. The one species you won't see much of is Homo sapiens.

About 40 acres on Morris Island are accessible by car, then foot (there's a three-quarter-mile trail, closed during high tide), but the islands are uninhabited. You can visit them as part of a naturalist-guided tour conducted by either the **Cape Cod Museum of Natural History** (896.3867) or the **Wellfleet Bay Wildlife Sanctuary** (349.2615). ♦ Fee for tours. Park: daily. Tours: daily July-Aug; call for off-season schedule. Reservations required for tours. Wikis Way (off Tisquantum Rd), Chatham. 945.0594

54 Chatham Light & Coast Guard Station Two 43-foot wooden towers with oil lamps were first constructed here in 1808. They were replaced by brick towers in 1841, and then totally rebuilt in 1877. Today the modern 800,000-candlepower beacon is visible from 28 nautical miles at sea. The tower isn't open to the public, but the parking area is a popular spot from which to watch the sunrise or to observe the site of the 1987 "breach" that continues to alter Chatham's shoreline. Some take comfort in the fact that an 1846 breach patched itself up, and in fact South Island soon reattached itself to the mainland, adding a brand-new sandy peninsula to town. ♦ Main St (at Bridge St), Chatham. 945.3830

55 Port Fortune Inn $$ Renee and Michael Kahl, the new owners of the former **Inn Among Friends,** renamed the lodgings after the appellation that explorer Samuel de Champlain gave Chatham in the 1600s. It is perfectly situated near Chatham's beach, and within sight of seals cavorting in the sea in the colder months. The inn is a cluster of traditional gray-shingled houses with a surprisingly stylish common room. The 14 guest rooms were renovated with new baths, air-conditioning, and floral-patterned wallpaper, and are decorated with unstuffy antiques. It is as relaxing and welcoming here as the home of a good friend. The dining room of the former **Break-away Cafe** has been restyled as a breakfast room for inn guests. ♦ 201 Main St (at Hallet La), Chatham. 945.0792, 800/750.0792; fax 945.0792

56 **Odell's Studio Gallery** Carol and Tom Odell present their own fine art, jewelry, and metalwork in a historic Greek Revival house, with an adjoining studio in back where the larger works are made. Carol paints in a nonfigurative style, focusing on composition and color in oils and prints; she also makes decorative folding screens. Her husband, Tom, who apprenticed in Kyoto under Japanese master Shumei Tanaka, sculpts cast bronzes and creates original, contemporary jewelry designs. Even if you're not in the market to buy anything, this gallery is worth a wander through. ♦ M-Sa. 423 Main St (between Homestead La and Mill Pond Rd), Chatham. 945.3239

57 **Christian's Restaurant** ★★★$$$
Chef/owner Christian Schultz was quite young when he opened this restaurant in 1980, but clearly he knew what he was about: It was an immediate success, and remains one of the best restaurants in the region. The 1818 house lost many of its interior walls to create a bistrolike, see-and-be-seen ambience; the terrace room, with its brick floors, woven tablecloths, and striped shades, is especially inviting and, unlike the upstairs pub, is nonsmoking. Schultz's hybrids of the ever-popular Southwestern fare are inspired, like brie wrapped in a flour tortilla, served warm with fruit salsa. Fish, of course, is featured prominently, and well treated, but his rack of lamb is like no other: grilled in a crust of goat cheese, rosemary, and pumpernickel. ♦ New American ♦ M-Sa dinner; Su brunch and dinner mid-May–mid-Oct; F-Sa dinner mid-Oct–mid-May. Reservations recommended. 443 Main St (between Homestead La and Mill Pond Rd), Chatham. 945.3362

Within Christian's Restaurant:

Upstairs at Christian's ★★★$$$
Same kitchen, same menu, same prices as downstairs, but with instant nostalgia for a bygone cinematic era. Furnishings here include an oak bar, mahogany paneling, and scruffy leather couches and armchairs, with caricatures and movie posters dotting the walls. The drinks are all named for movies— a little gimmicky, perhaps, but it makes for

entertaining reading, and drinking. The South Pacific, for example, has the usual culprits— rum, coconut, orange, and pineapple juices— but with the added local flavor of cranberries. In summer, the deck is the place to be, in town but slightly above it all. ♦ New American ♦ Daily lunch and dinner June-Dec; M, Th-Su lunch and dinner Jan-May. 945.3362

57 **Mildred Georges Antiques** Georges has been in business since 1956, and her accumulated acquisitions make for rich and varied pickings. Poke through and you'll find just about everything you could possibly want. Personal adornments are especially strong, from tortoiseshell combs and painted porcelain buttons to jewelry of every era. ♦ Daily May-Oct. 447 Main St (between Homestead La and Mill Pond Rd), Chatham. 945.1939

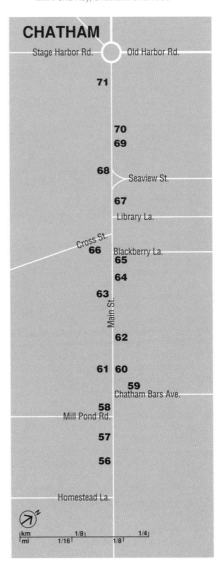

CHATHAM

Stage Harbor Rd.   Old Harbor Rd.

71

70
69

68

Seaview St.

67

Library La.

Cross St.
66

Blackberry La.
65

64

63

Main St.

62

61   60

59
Chatham Bars Ave.

58
Mill Pond Rd.

57

56

Homestead La.

km   1/8   1/4
mi   1/16   1/8

58 Midsummer Nights Here's a store to delight die-hard sensualists and even to convert the ascetically inclined. The stock spans extravagant body-care products (from natural sponges to antique manicure sets), modernist lingerie, and imaginative home accessories. ♦ M-Sa; Su noon-5PM June-Aug. M-Sa Sept-May. 471 Main St (between Mill Pond Rd and Cross St), Chatham. 945.5562

59 Impudent Oyster ★★$$$ Main Street strollers might overlook this popular spot, but not so the locals, who know to venture around the corner for outstanding local seafood prepared in a variety of international guises. Oysters Florentine, for instance, are baked on the half-shell with spinach, cheese, and an accent of Pernod; Hawaiian-style scallops Kaanapali are broiled in a casserole with a toasted macadamia nut breading, and topped with a lemon butter sauce. For dessert, try the homemade cranberry-apple pie. The decor is 1970s artsy-craftsy with a cathedral ceiling sporting exposed beams and skylights, plus a bit of stained glass. Even when jammed (which is often), it's a civilized place, with a bar fit for grownups and food that consistently surprises. ♦ International ♦ Daily lunch and dinner. Reservations recommended. 15 Chatham Bars Ave (between Main St and Kettle Drum La), Chatham. 945.3545 ⅏

60 Chatham Candy Manor Naomi Turner's mother started this business in the 1940s, and the quality hasn't slipped a bit, nor has the demand for premium, hand-dipped chocolates. Just walking in the door is a treat: take a deep whiff, then peruse the antique cases of molded chocolate scallop shells, cranberry cordials, dipped strawberries, and "turtles" of every stripe. The shop maintains an open kitchen policy, which means you're welcome to wander in and see what's cooking. During the holiday season, children and adults press their noses against the front window to watch candy canes evolve out of a big copper pot. Mail order is available for those who depart with appetites permanently whetted. ♦ Daily 9AM-10PM July–early Sept; daily early Sept–June. 484 Main St (between Chatham Bars Ave and Blackberry La), Chatham. 945.0825, 800/221.6497

Sand castles, observes Brewster architect Malcolm Wells in his charming self-published book on the subject, are "environmentally ideal. They create no pollution and they disappear with the next tide."

61 The Chatham Squire ★★$$$ This has been a family restaurant and year-round gathering spot since 1968. Although the decor remains from those years, the menu is eclectic, and the only raw bar in town is set in its own corner off the dining room— the freshest of shellfish from the most active fishing community left on Cape Cod is shucked right in front of you. You might also want to try Chatham cioppino—a stew of clams, mussels, scallops, and grilled fish; or fresh baked cod in a lemon beurre blanc. The pool tables and big screen TVs in the tavern past the raw bar are perfect for postprandial activity. ♦ American ♦ Daily lunch and dinner. 487 Main St (between Mill Pond Rd and Cross St), Chatham. 945.0945 ⅏

62 Kate Gould Park The brass-band concerts held here have long been a genteel summer tradition; today they draw crowds of 2,000 or more. Part of their popularity is no doubt attributable to the late conductor Whitney W. Tileston, who for nearly a half-century cheerfully coaxed, prodded, and cajoled the 40 local amateurs in the band to give their all. The baton now belongs to Ken Eldredge, the former assistant conductor, and the beat goes on. The repertoire ranges from the bunny hop to waltzes and big-band numbers, and spontaneous sing-alongs are common. If you've found yourself wondering whatever happened to family values, just take a look around and join in. ♦ F 8PM July–early Sept. Main St (between Chatham Bars Ave and Blackberry La), Chatham. 945.0342 ⅏

Next to Kate Gould Park:

The Chatham Wayside Inn

Chatham Wayside Inn $$$$ This 1860s landmark has played many roles through the years, from sea captain's home to stagecoach stop to a weathered local tavern. Now it's a 56-room luxury inn, beautifully furnished in an old-fashioned style. The spacious guest rooms are lavishly decorated with Waverly fabrics and wallpapers; within the faux-antique chests lurks cable TV. Some of the rooms in the extension out back have private patios overlooking the bandstand at **Kate Gould Park**. Ensconced in utter comfort, you can look down on the gaily teeming masses and pretend you're viewing a command performance. ♦ 512 Main St. 945.5550, 800/391.5734; fax 945.3407 ⅏

Within the Chatham Wayside Inn:

Chatham Wayside Inn Restaurant

★★★$$$ The decor is almost Shakerlike in its simplicity (Windsor chairs set at gleaming wood tables with forest-green napery), but the approach to food is far from plain. Chef Shane Coughlin shows his true mettle at breakfast, which features such indigenous treats as waffles with cranberry butter, or scrumptious cod cakes. The place is something of a social hub in off-season (local thespian Julie Harris comes here), and in summer an SRO haven—especially the shaded street-side deck. ♦ New American ♦ Daily breakfast, lunch, and dinner. 945.5550 &

63 Children's Shop Future fixtures on best-dressed lists will owe their start to Ginny Nickerson's excellent selection of kids' clothes. From sunhats to polar-fleece snowsuits, this stuff is the best, and for all its emphasis on traditional taste-fulness, there's plenty of room for playfulness, too—check out the hot-pink boas. ♦ M-F 9AM-9PM; Sa 9AM-5:30PM; Su noon-5PM July-Aug. M-Sa Sept-Jan, mid-Mar–June. 515 Main St (between Mill Pond Rd and Cross St), Chatham. 945.0234. Also at: 27 Wianno Ave (between W Bay Rd and Main St), Osterville. 428.9458

64 Chatham Cookware Opened by Vera Champlain in 1979, this shop features stylish and functional wares for the well-dressed kitchen, as well as the output from one very accomplished one: hers. From ready-to-heat hors d'oeuvres and entrées (such as smoked salmon-and-dill quiche) to coffee cakes, tortes, and sugar cookies, everything tastes as good as it looks. There's a tiny lunchroom in back, wallpapered a bright yellow, if you can't wait to get home to start snacking. ♦ Daily 7AM-6PM July-Aug; daily 7AM-5PM Sept-Dec, Feb-June. 524 Main St (between Chatham Bars Ave and Blackberry La), Chatham. 945.1550

65 Mayo House This diminutive yellow 1820 three-quarter Cape, maintained and occupied by the Chatham Conservation Foundation, has no outstanding historical significance, but it's right there, and gratis, so if it's open, why not look around? You might enjoy deciphering the homiletic sampler of Catherine Mayo, executed in 1829, or climbing the steep stairs to view the minuscule bedrooms. Friendly volunteers are on hand to field questions. ♦ Free. Tu-Th mid-June–Oct. 540 Main St (at Blackberry La), Chatham. 945.4084

66 Cyrus Kent House Inn $$$ If you're looking for truly grand accommodations, you'll find them in this fabulous restored 1877 Victorian, just a slight jog off Main Street (and therefore blessedly quiet). The 10 large bedrooms are tastefully furnished with four-posters, fireplaces, and English antiques—and innkeeper Sharon Mitchell-Swan's delectable homemade continental breakfast is another terrific plus. ♦ 63 Cross St (between Kent Pl and Main St), Chatham. 945.9104, 800/338.5368

67 Pentimento Great for browsing, even on a sunny day, this shop is packed with summery clothing ranging in style from neo-Victorian to minimalist contemporary. It also stocks some fun baby stuff, tasteful home decor, and not terribly tacky tourist gewgaws. ♦ M-Sa 9:30AM-9:30PM; Su noon-6PM July-Aug. M-Sa, Su noon-5PM Sept-June. 584 Main St (between Library La and Seaview St), Chatham. 945.0178

68 Vining's Bistro ★★★$$$ Housed on the upper floor of a well-camouflaged mini-mall, this grill proves that Chatham, though sedate, still has room for spice; indeed, there's plenty of it in the "pasta from hell" with banana-guava catsup, and in the Thai beef salad drenched in Panang vinaigrette with a satay dipping sauce. Gentler options are offered, too, including a vegetarian hazelnut and wild mushroom stroganoff. If you've had it with the same old same old, head to this loft, where Kurt Hedmark's murals hint at denizens with pastimes racier than chowder suppers. ♦ International ♦ Daily dinner Apr–mid-Jan. 595 Main St (between Cross St and Stage Harbor Rd), Chatham. 945.5033 &

Below Vining's Bistro:

Carmine's Pizza ★★$$ If you find yourself hankering for a pizza that's a bit out of the ordinary, try this cute little parlor where varieties include "white" (made without tomatoes or tomato sauce), "Greek" (topped with feta cheese and olives), or the pepper-packed "pizza from hell." The atmosphere may be a bit canned (despite the "Old Country" memorabilia scattered about the place), but the product certainly isn't. If the heat's stolen your appetite, settle for a superior cappuccino. ♦ Italian ♦ Daily lunch and dinner. 945.5300 &

69 Trading Company Somehow, the sculptural, earth-toned couture of Armani and Vestimenta seems at home in this rustic barnboard interior. Country living needn't mean giving up all the finer things, and city-sophisticated women will find appropriate crossover dressing here. ♦ Daily mid-Apr–Dec; Tu-Sa Jan–mid-Apr. 614 Main St (between Seaview St and Old Harbor Rd), Chatham. 945.9191

As late as 1982, seven Chatham "wreckers" worked for hours to remove a 1,000-pound bronze propeller, electronics, and fittings from the *Venture I* despite the threat of legal action by the ship's owner.

70 Spyglass New owner Brad Finch's main stock in trade is 18th- and 19th-century nautical antiques: telescopes, barometers, early maps, navigational instruments, sea captain portraits, and chests.
♦ M-Sa; Su 1-4PM June-Sept. M-Sa Oct-May. 618 Main St (between Seaview St and Old Harbor Rd), Chatham. 945.9686 ఈ

71 The Dead Zone This is the kind of shop you'd least expect in Chatham. Hidden in a basement space around back, its Grateful Dead merchandise and incense, tie-dyes, Native American prints, and beads are selling as if it were 1968. ♦ Daily. 647 Main St (between Cross St and Stage Harbor Rd), Chatham. 945.5853 ఈ

72 Chatham Bars Inn $$$$ Built as a hunting lodge in 1914, and designed by Boston architect **Harvey Bailey Alden,** this 41-room shingled inn, with 112 more rooms in cottages along the shore, is a living reminder of an opulent age. In fact, thanks to massive infusions of capital to refurbish several buildings and the grounds, the property is probably grander than ever now, yet it still retains its relaxed, gracious air. There are plenty of facilities to explore on its 22 acres (a nine-hole golf course, four tennis courts, shuffleboard, croquet, volleyball, fitness room, heated outdoor pool, and private beach) and along the surf of the Outer Bar (a complementary launch ride away), but it's tempting just to sit on one's private balcony—nearly all the rooms have one—and take in this lovely shore.

Choose between the breezy summerhouse decor of the original units (featuring cheery fabrics and prints) and the Neo-Victorian luxury of the newly refurbished rooms (with heavy brocades and antique reproductions). The vast lobby has added several cozy touches, including plump couches and masses of flowers; however, the hallways, in shades of beige, cream, and green, still seem to stretch on forever—staffers joke that it reminds them of *The Shining*. Malevolence is the last thing that comes to mind, though, as you sip cocktails on the veranda, reminiscing to the smooth riffs of live jazz piano music. Children are offered supervised daily recreation so that parents can enjoy some time by themselves.
♦ Shore Rd (at Seaview St), Chatham. 945.0096, 800/527.4884; fax 945.5491 ఈ

Within the Chatham Bars Inn:

Main Dining Room ★★★★$$$$ As the sea views deepen into dusk, copper lanterns cast a romantic glow over this spacious formal hall. Chef Al Hynes's cuisine, from fill of beef with foie gras to a hefty two-pound lobster, is mostly classically continental; however, there are some adventurous dishes on the menu as well, such as spicy Chatham lobster tail with *soba* noodles and warm sala of demi-cured bass with tarragon vinaigrette and a large polenta crouton. ♦ Continental/New American ♦ Daily breakfast and dinner. Reservations required; jacket required. 945.0096 ఈ

North Beach Tavern & Grille ★★$$$ Many of the same dishes that are served in the **Main Dining Room** turn up in this more casual setting, along with some decidedly proletarian (but kid-pleasing) fare such as sloppy Joes.
♦ New American ♦ M-Sa lunch and dinner; Su brunch and dinner. 945.0096 ఈ

Beach House Grill ★★$ Beach potatoes too sun-besotted to make the trek up to the main inn can sustain themselves on quahog fritters, lobster croissants, and the like. Or they can kick back, relax, and enjoy a knock-out drink such as the "Awesome Tropical Passion"—a concoction of bananas, strawberries, and Midori. On Monday nights, there's line dancing with live music, and Wednesday nights feature a classic clam-and lobster bake to the tunes of Dixieland jazz.
♦ American ♦ Daily breakfast, lunch, and dinner early July–early Sept. 945.0096 ఈ

73 Fish Pier From midafternoon on, you can watch Chatham's hard-working fleet bringing in the day's catch: mostly haddock, cod, and flounder (and some are pretty large). A wooden observation deck provides a good vantage point, and there's a postage-stamp park with an impressive sculpture by Sig Purwin called *The Provider*. Toward dusk, the sand fleas get vicious, so come fore-slathered with insect repellent. ♦ Shore Rd (between Claflin Landing and Barcliff Ave), Chatham. 945.5186 ఈ

The real-life model for James Fenimore Cooper's novel *The Spy* was a man named Enoch Crosby, born in Harwich in 1750. Crosby worked as a shoemaker, going from one Loyalist home to another. He then reported information he overheard to Revolutionary leaders. When Loyalists finally figured out why they were being arrested after getting their shoes fixed, they severely beat Crosby. He survived to enlist in the new American Army, and in 1827 was a guest of honor at a New York performance of a play based on *The Spy*.

At the Fish Pier:

Water Taxi John W. McGrath Jr., represents the third generation to run this family business, in operation since 1944. Its "cabs" will zip you to remote beaches or wherever you want to go—on a seal watch, perhaps, or a sunset cruise. "We run on demand," says McGrath. "You make the schedule." ♦ By appointment. 430.2346

4 Moses Nickerson House $$$ This 1839 captain's house exemplifies Jeffersonian classicism at its height, and innkeepers Linda and George Watts's interior decoration lives up to the exterior. The living room, with its impractical white sofa and needlepoint rug, hints at the extravagances in store: The seven rooms are decorated in a spectrum from ultrafeminine (lace, bouquets of flowers, and such) to ruggedly masculine (hunting prints, Ralph Lauren bedding). Breakfasts of homemade baked goods are served in a cheerful solarium surrounded by an exuberant garden. ♦ 364 Old Harbor Rd (between Barcliff Ave and Shore Rd), Chatham. 945.5859, 800/628.6972; fax 945.7087

5 Captain's House Inn of Chatham $$$ The house, an 1839 Greek Revival mansion, is grand, and the spacious rooms (there are 19, including those in the stables, cottage, and carriage house) are country-palatial. Expect four-posters with crochet canopies, lush Oriental rugs, wingbacks, a blazing fire (if you wish), and breakfast and tea served on fine linens in a glassed-in garden room. ♦ 371 Old Harbor Rd (between Barcliff Ave and Orleans Rd), Chatham. 945.0127, 800/315.0728; fax 945.0866 &

6 Pleasant Bay Village Resort Motel $$$ This 58-room property has something of a split personality: The guest rooms are nothing special (standard motel decor), but the breakfast room, with its kilims and antique cupboards, wants to belong to a China Trade–era bed-and-breakfast, and the six-acre grounds, intensively landscaped with Japanese plantings and a waterfall-fed koi pool, seem to be lifted from a botanical garden. All these extras have been added over the past quarter-century by owner/gardener Howard Gamsey, who admits to having spent $1 million on improvements in just the past decade. He obviously loves the place, as do his loyal guests. The motel, you might want to note, is not right *on* the bay but a short walk away. ♦ Closed November through April. 1191 Orleans Rd (at Training Field Rd), Chathamport. 945.1133, 800/547.1011; fax 945.9701

77 Wequassett Inn $$$$ The Native American name for this lovely setting cupped by Pleasant Bay means "crescent on the water." The inn started out in the early 1940s as a pair of transplanted 18th-century homesteads, but soon nearly a score of cottages sprouted up around it, covering 22 acres. So well assimilated are these outbuildings into the leafy landscape that you feel as if you've landed in a particularly nice village, not a full-scale resort. With 104 rooms, decorated in an elegant country motif, the property *is* large, though, with amenities to match. These include four all-weather "plexi-pave" tennis courts, with three pros in attendance, one new croquet court, and a fleet of sailboards, Sunfish, Daysailers, and Hobie Cats for rent—again, with instruction if needed. (Clinic packages are sometimes offered in both sports.) The 68-foot heated pool sits at the neck of Clam Point, a little promontory perfect for strolling or calm-water swimming. If you yearn for surf, the inn's launch can ferry you over to the unspoiled southerly stretches of Nauset Beach; sight-seers can hop a seaplane for a scenic tour or a quick jog to Boston or the Islands. It's awfully tempting, though, just to stay put, kick off your shoes, and feel your accumulated stresses subside. ♦ Closed December through March. 173 Orleans Rd (at Cove Landing Rd), Chatham. 432.5400, 800/225.7125; fax 432.5032

Within the Wequassett Inn:

Eben Ryder House ★★★★$$$$ Appended to a late 18th-century Brewster house once known to locals as **Square Top,** this elegant dining spot enjoys sweeping views and chef Frank McMullen's classic/contemporary artistry. To start, try the plump Wellfleet oysters with a cranberry mignonette sauce, or an unbeatable Nantucket scallop and saffron bisque. Follow with Gulf shrimp stuffed with provolone, ricotta, and spinach, baked in puff pastry, and served in a sea of sun-dried tomato beurre blanc. Desserts fully measure up, especially the toffee torte. ♦ New American ♦ Daily breakfast, lunch, and dinner Apr-Nov. Reservations recommended; jacket required. 432.5400, 800/225.7125 &

Henry David Thoreau wrote of Brewster, "This town has more mates and masters of vessels than any other town in the country."

Thar' She Blows: Whale Tales

Before the colonists came along, Native Americans had always killed whales while canoeing close to shore. Harpoons attached with vines to "drogues" (large chunks of wood) impeded the whales' progress until the hunters could catch up and lance their lungs. In the mid-17th century, the settlers of Southampton, New York, began sailing in search of whales; they would stay out for up to three weeks, camping along the shore and cutting whale blubber into "horse pieces" (large strips), then mincing it into "books" and rendering the books into oil in large iron "try-pots." The practice spread up the coast, and in 1690, **Nantucket** islanders hired Ichabod Paddock of **Truro** to teach them how to hunt whales.

Noting the profits to be gleaned from the "Royal Fish," the English crown established regulations under which the government received a portion of the spoils from any beached whales. Another elaborate set of rules was developed to divvy up whale meat and return harpoons to their rightful owners. As an incentive, whaling vessels were exempted from paying taxes for their first seven years at sea, and whalers were released from military service during the whaling season.

By the turn of the century, coastal whaling was so prevalent that the south side of Nantucket was divided into four half-mile stretches, each with its own lookout mast, a hut to house five or six men, and a "try works" to render the blubber on the spot. The preferred prey was the 50-foot, 50-ton right whale, so-called because it swam close to shore and remained afloat after it was killed. The "baleen"— with bony upper jaw slats—was fashioned into fishing rods, corset stays, umbrellas, and the like. By the early 18th century, however, the right whales had become wise to whalers' tactics and moved offshore; their numbers also were greatly depleted (some 300 are thought to survive today).

It happened that, in 1712, Captain Christopher Hussey was blown off-course into deep water, where he speared the first sperm whale, a feisty mammal with teeth in lieu of baleen. In its head cavity, whalers found spermaceti, an oil which was far superior to that rendered from blubber and which, when exposed to air, hardened into a waxy substance ideal for candlemaking. The hunting of sperm whales was perilous, often involving a death-defying "Nantucket sleigh ride" through rough seas; nevertheless, tiny Nantucket rapidly outflanked England's own whaling fleet, and maintained its ascendancy for more than a century.

With the need for bigger boats came backers willing to invest on a share basis for a shot at "greasy luck"—whaling profits. Soon, the economy

blossomed all along the coast: Shipwrights, coopers, and chandlers alike had their hands full. Gradually, **New Bedford,** a Massachusetts fishing town west of Cape Cod with an exceptionally deep harbor, nudged its way to the forefront of the whaling industry; between 1825 and 1860, its fleet ballooned to 735 ships. Whaling captains in search of marketable spermaceti braved the South Atlantic and ultimately ventured into the uncharted waters of the Pacific and Indian Oceans, where their voyages often lasted as long as seven years. As Herman Melville wrote in *Moby Dick,* "These Sea Hermits conquered the watery world like so many Alexanders." The challenges were daunting, indeed; not only did whalers brave the whims of the ocean, but they also had to contend with Spanish privateers, military French (at war with the Crown and the colonies until 1763), the British themselves (who made a practice of conscripting any crews they came across during the Revolution and the War of 1812), and run-of-the-mill island cannibals. Add the daily reality of on-board rats, roaches, moldy stores, and a high incidence of scurvy to an intrinsically dangerous and lonely profession, and it's no wonder crews became increasingly hard to round up. The discovery of petroleum-derived kerosene in Pennsylvania in 1836 and its introduction on the market in 1859 sounded a virtual death knell for the industry.

Still, a few whaling fleets persisted, employing Norwegian whaler Sven Foyn's late-1860s invention: a harpoon cannon capable of spearing the elusive blue whale (the world's largest mammal) and the finback. Within 20 years, big blues and finbacks nearly disappeared from the Northern

Hemisphere. In 1923, Norwegian Carl Larsen brought in factory ships capable of processing an entire whale within an hour—that is, as many as 39,000 animals a year. In 1946, 17 nations formed the International Whaling Commission (IWC) to regulate (and thereby preserve) the industry. Alarmed by the prospect of the species' extinction, the United States ceased all its whaling efforts in 1971. In 1986 the IWC called for a worldwide ban on whaling, but the call was resisted by Japan (which uses whale meat for food and animal feed), Iceland, Norway, and Russia (which use whale oil for such products as soap, cosmetics, paint, and machinery lubricant).

Not long after America's whaling activity stopped, Captain Al Avellar of **Provincetown**'s **Dolphin Fleet** hit upon the idea of enabling ordinary landlubbers to go "whaling" armed with cameras instead of harpoons. In 1975, with marine biologist Charles Mayo as a guide, Avellar offered whale-watching cruises to the **Stellwagen Bank,** a major marine feeding ground seven miles off Provincetown. Stellwagen Bank is an 840-square-mile, crescent-shaped undersea cliff some 80 to 100 feet high; here, ocean currents force cool, nutrient-rich water to the surface, attracting small fish and, in turn, whales. Avellar's innovation soon spawned imitators, whose numbers have increased so rapidly that on any given day you're apt to spot more boats than behemoths. Still, there's nothing quite like the thrill of coming upon a 50-ton

mammal playfully breaching on the surface of the water, or gliding by, huge and mysterious.

Although no charter company can guarantee sightings (at best they will let you go again for free), you can improve your odds by venturing out in spring or fall, when many whales make the 4,000-mile journey between their seasonal feeding grounds. The three species you're most likely to see are finbacks (typically 50 to 70 feet long), humpbacks (at 40 to 50 feet, they're the type known for their lovely, eerie "singing"), and pilots (averaging 13 feet). The tourist fleets all have on-board naturalists; some are expert researchers who can recognize distinctive patterns on the flukes and bodies and offer a life history of individual whales.

Whale-watching cruises generally cost under $20 per person, and last about three or four hours, depending on the distance covered. It makes more sense to depart from Provincetown, which is closest to the Bank, but if you don't mind whiling away a bit of extra time on the water, the particular port of call doesn't much matter. The following companies are all well regarded:

From Barnstable Harbor: Hyannis Whale Watcher Cruises. 362.6088, 800/287.0374.

From Plymouth: Capt. John Boats. 746.2643, 800/242.2469.

From Provincetown: Dolphin Fleet. 349.1900, 800/826.9300; **Portuguese Princess.** 800/442.3188; **Ranger V.** 800/992.9333.

If you come home feeling a special fondness for the whales you've met, you might consider contributing to the **Whale Adoption Project** (563.2843), a **Falmouth**-based fund-raising effort dedicated to whale research, rescue, and education, sponsored by the International Wildlife Coalition.

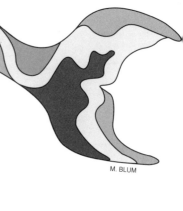

M. BLUM

hillbourne house

on Pleasant Bay

78 Hillbourne House $$ Located in a quiet pocket between Chatham and Orleans, this bed-and-breakfast inn with a motel extension has a superb view of Pleasant Bay and its own private beach and dock (you're welcome to bring your own boat). Built in 1798, it served as a stop on the Underground Railroad (escaped slaves hid in a stone pit beneath a trap door) and weathered the age when the bay was a favored rendezvous for pirates. The five in-house rooms have more character (one has a water view via a well-placed toile chaise), but the three motel units are quite nice, too—very unboxy, with beamed ceilings. Barbara Hayes, a schoolteacher, makes a scrumptious breakfast—Dutch oven pancakes, perhaps, with homemade cinnamon syrup. ♦ Closed in February. 654 Orleans Rd (at Tarkiln Rd), South Orleans. 255.0780

79 Pleasant Bay Antiques Although Steve Tyng's house and barn are far off the beaten path of Route 6A, the finest antiques on the Cape have a way of falling into his hands—perhaps because sellers know they'll be appreciated. Buyers flock here, too, looking for goods that are fresh on the market. As a result, some of his most coveted inventory—a $24,000 Queen Anne highboy, for instance—might enjoy a 15-minute turnaround. Because the prices aren't jacked up by serial trading, it's possible to find relative deals. It's also a very instructive place just to look. ♦ Daily. 540 S Orleans Rd (between Tarkiln Rd and Rte 39), South Orleans. 255.0930

80 Morgan's Way $$ Thanks to innkeeper Page McMahan's warm welcome, you won't feel like a stranger for long at this charming bed-and-breakfast, nestled up a quiet country lane. The handsome contemporary house was created by Page and her husband, engineer Will Joy. It features two beautifully decorated bedrooms (one with its own attached greenhouse), a wraparound deck with lovely woodland views, and a large, heated pool. There's also a one-bedroom cottage with a full kitchen and a cathedral ceiling, which rents by the week. Especially inviting is the loftlike library, where you'll find a TV set and VCR, as well as a wood-burning stove that will combat the chill of winter evenings. After graciously serving a customized breakfast of egg dishes, cereal, or grilled entrées (such as French toast or pancakes) on fine family china, Page can give you plenty of good advice about exploring this inviting area. ♦ 9 Morgan's Way (between Rte 28 and Old Timers Rd), Orleans. 255.0831

81 Meeting House Museum This 1833 Greek Revival Universalist church now houses the collections of the Orleans Historical Society: clothing, photographs, marine artifacts, farm implements, a cast-iron artillery shell from the War of 1812. The amalgam, alas, is less than riveting unless you have a special interest in town history. ♦ Free. M-F 1-4PM July-Aug. 3 River Rd (at Main St), Orleans. 240.1329

82 Fancy's Farm It may be rustic, with dried herbs and flowers slung from hand-hewn rafters, but this farmstand has city smarts. In addition to top-grade produce, exotic as well as domestic, you can buy fresh gazpacho, fruit smoothies, jellybeans by the scoop, and all sorts of home-baked treats from pies to tea cakes. ♦ Daily 7AM-7PM late June–early Sept; daily 7AM-6PM early Sept–Dec, Mar–late June. 199 Main St (between Cheny and River Rds), East Orleans. 255.1949 & Also at: The Cornfield, 1291 Main St (between Lime Hill and Barn Hill Rds), West Chatham. 945.1949 &

83 Countryside Antiques As you meander through this large shop, the eight rooms unfold like a maze; owner Deborah Rita jokes, "I offer people bread crumbs at the door." It's a good place to get lost in, with a great assortment of English, Irish, and Scandinavian antique pieces in pine, mahogany, and fruitwood, mixed in with reproductions and contemporary accessories. Rita has a knack for arranging the groupings so that each item singularity stands out, and for all the invest-ment-level furniture, there are plenty of affordable knickknacks, such as flattering silver-plate picture frames. If you find your way out, take a look at the barn—it's full of stuff waiting for a slot in the big house. ♦ M-Tu; W by appointment; Th-Sa; Su noon-4PM June-Aug. M-W by appointment; Th-Sa; Su noon-4PM Sept-May. 6 Lewis Rd (off Main St between Barley Neck and Cheny Rds), East Orleans. 240.0525

THE BARLEY NECK
INN
& LODGE

84 Barley Neck Inn ★★★$$$ This venerable old building was built in 1857 and renovated by ex–New Yorkers Joe and Kathi

Lewis. The former small, cozy parlors were turned into dining rooms that feature intimate feasts prepared by chef Franck Champely. His creations include yellowfin tuna wrapped in seaweed with a tomato-ginger coulis and lobster roasted in a Champagne butter sauce. The exquisite desserts, such as blueberry tart, lemon cheesecake tartlet, chocolate mousse with praline crust, and Italian custard, more than measure up to the entrées. Best of all, this is a lively spot with a cosmopolitan buzz, devoid of the portentous solemnity that sometimes mars other elegant dining places. Here, you can eat well *and* have a good time.
♦ New American ♦ M-Sa dinner; Su brunch and dinner. 5 Beach Rd (at Main St), East Orleans. 255.0212, 800/281.7505 &

Within the Barley Neck Inn:

Joe's Beach Road Bar ★★★$$ Like the **Barley Neck Inn**, this big barn of a place—complete with fieldstone fireplace, French WWI posters, and vintage menswear ads (harking back to the Lewises' former occupation in the garment trade)—has been a smash from the moment it opened. The atmosphere exudes bonhomie, and tourists feel as much at home as the locals who hang out here. The menu offers several hearty continental specialties, such as Normandy onion soup made with sparkling cider, baked mussels with almonds, and grilled chicken breast on focaccia with pesto, tomatoes, and fontina. Or you could opt for more casual fare, like the juicy sirloin burger. Rounding out the complex is an 18-unit motel (with pool). The reasonably priced rooms are nothing fancy, but come with a breakfast of freshly baked scones. ♦ New American ♦ Daily lunch and dinner. 255.0212 &

85 Nauset House Inn $$ This circa 1810 dormered farmhouse is full of lovely eccentricities, starting with a turn-of-the-century conservatory filled with intoxicating camellias and welcoming wicker settees. The brick-floored dining room features a rustic hearth and plank table where Diane Johnson's delectable breakfasts are laid out. The meal is optional, for a nominal charge, but who would want to sleep through ginger pancakes with lemon sauce, or oatmeal butterscotch muffins? The 14 rooms vary in size and splendor (those in the carriage house are the most spacious), but all partake of the bucolic grounds, and Nauset Beach is a breezy 10-minute walk away. ♦ Closed November through March. 143 Beach Rd (between Smith Neck and Brick Hill Rds), East Orleans. 255.2195

86 Nauset Beach Club ★★★$$$ This pint-size roadside restaurant (a former duck-hunting cottage) packs a surprisingly sophisticated punch. Chef Jack Salemi keeps tinkering with the menu and concocting specials that really are. Among the appetizers, you're likely to encounter *spiedini* (layers of bread and cheese, battered and fried, then served with a lemon butter sauce), as well as ultrarich *pasta puttanesca* (with olives, capers, peppers, and onions). One warning, though: You must order an entrée or they won't serve you at all, no matter how much you promise to spend. The terra-cotta–hued dining room is typically abustle, or you could sit out on the patio and watch the beachgoers buzz by. ♦ Italian ♦ Daily dinner late May–Nov; Tu-Sa dinner Nov–late May. 222 Main St (between Beach and Great Oak Rds), East Orleans. 255.8547 &

86 Kadee's Gray Elephant $$ Owner Chris Cavanaugh is not afraid of color; she loads it on, with hand-decorated furniture, layers of bright quilts, and purple-painted wicker. The six studio apartments, which rent by the night or by the week, and the three-bedroom Cape house, which rents by the week, are so busy and bright, you might not mind an occasional gray day. ♦ 212 Main St (between Beach and Great Oak Rds), East Orleans. 255.7608; fax 240.2976 &

On the grounds of Kadee's Gray Elephant:

Kadee's Lobster & Clam Bar ★★$$ The same bouncy energy extends to this dolled-up sea shack, with floral umbrellas for fine weather and tarps and a blue-striped awning when the sea air turns cold and wet. The creamy seafood stews—oyster, crab, lobster—are modeled after those served at the Oyster Bar in New York City's Grand Central Station. Try a "seabob" (marinated swordfish and shrimp skewered and grilled), or the "seafood simmer"—shrimp, scallops, and lobster sautéed with sherry, butter, lemon, parsley, and sweet basil. ♦ American/ Takeout ♦ Daily lunch and dinner late June–early Sept; Sa-Su lunch and dinner late May–late June. 255.6184 &

Apple Grove Mini Golf Perhaps not the world's most challenging course, it's certainly picturesque, with miniature houses and a lighthouse; in any case, it's a good way to pass the time while waiting for a take-out order. ♦ Daily 10:30AM-9PM late June–early Sept; Sa-Su late May–late June. 255.6184

86 East Orleans Art & Antiques Owner Katherine Fox does her best to keep prices low, and as a result, many of her customers are dealers themselves. Specialties include estate jewelry, majolica, china, pattern glass, kilims (new as well as old), unusual antiques, Victorian oil paintings, and whatever country pine furniture she can find. She also represents a few local artists. ◆ Tu-Sa June-Sept; Th-Sa Oct-Dec. 204 Main St (at Great Oak Rd), East Orleans. 255.7799

87 Parsonage Inn $$ English innkeepers lend a civilized lilt to this eight-bedroom bed-and-breakfast, fashioned from an extended 1770s-era full Cape. Elizabeth Brown, a piano teacher who grew up in Kenya, might play a little Liszt or Chopin during the evening in the moss-green living room, and breakfast might consist of scones with Devonshire cream. Among the more dramatic rooms is **The Barn,** with a daubed ceiling and fencepost bed. ◆ 202 Main St (at Great Oak Rd), East Orleans. 255.8217

88 Academy Playhouse Orleans outgrew its 1873 town hall in 1949, but the former forum for town meetings turned out to be an excellent setting for an arena stage. The **Academy of Performing Arts** mounts performances here year-round; typically, fluffy stuff (mostly musicals) in summer, and more substance for the locals during off-season, plus concerts, dance, and poetry readings. ◆ Call for schedule. 120 Main St (between Meetinghouse and Tonset Rds), Orleans. 255.1963

On 12 July 1918, a German submarine surfaced three miles off Nauset Inlet, sinking four barges and a tug before sending several shells toward town (one struck land). Though most of the Chatham Naval Air Station crew was engaged in a baseball game in Provincetown that particular day, two seaplanes managed to drop four retaliatory bombs that missed their mark but scared the sub away.

The first school of navigation in the United States originated in Harwich in a building that today houses the Harwich Historical Society.

That hulk of a boat visible from the bay sides of Brewster and Eastham is the USS *James Longstreet,* used for military target practice in the years 1943-70.

ORLEANS

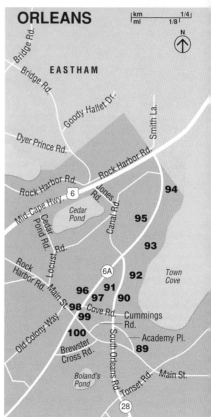

89 Wheel Haus Cafe ★$$ Like many a retired schooner captain before him, Uli Pruesse came to the Cape from his hometown (Hamburg) to set up a small business— several of them, in fact, including this tiny, stylish cafe. Whether in the dining room or out in the garden, you can lunch on light sandwiches like the Little Mermaid (crab salad with fresh shrimp), or sup on platters such as the October Fest: roast smoked pork with homemade cinnamon applesauce, barrel cured sauerkraut, and fried potatoes. The desserts are so elegant—bombes and tortes, imported from New York and the continent— that it's tempting to follow European tradition and make no pretense of eating anything wholesome at all. ◆ International ◆ Daily lunch and dinner Apr-Dec. 2 Academy Pl (at Main St), Orleans. 240.1585, 240.0022 &

On the grounds of the Wheel Haus Cafe:

Wheel Haus Guest House $$ The four rooms are pretty and neat, if not especially atmospheric; but the great location and reasonable prices make this hostelry a real find. ♦ Closed January through March. 240.1585

90 Addison Holmes Gallery Herb Holmes and Helen Addison recently opened the most exciting new gallery in Orleans. It is set in a red Cape with wide pine floors and classic beams, and has an outdoor sculpture garden and fish pond. Among the artists represented is Lois Griffel, whose impressionistic oils continue in the style pioneered by Charles Hawthorne at the Cape Cod School of Art. Another is Charles Kolnik, whose atmospheric oil paintings are among the best of recent regional work. Photography by Jane Booth Vollers, realistic watercolors by Garry Gilmartin, and paintings by colorist Charles Sovek round out a varied collection. ♦ Daily May-Jan; call for off-season schedule. 43 S Orleans Rd (between Cove Rd and Rte 6A), Orleans. 255.6200, 800/654.5888

90 French Cable Station Museum From 1891 to 1941, this office was a key communications link between America and Europe. Before the wireless and the radio rendered the practice obsolete, stock reports and news were transmitted daily across the ocean to Brest, France (originally via Newfoundland, and by 1898 direct) by means of a hefty cable. It was here that word of Lindbergh's successful 1927 New York–Paris flight first reached the United States, as well as the announcement of the German invasion of France. The station was decommissioned in 1959, and in 1971 nine local citizens incorporated and bought the building. The Smithsonian helped prepare the displays; the contents are rather complex and can be confusing to the uninitiated, so if you're interested, ask for the full tour, or just view it as a house-size fax machine. ♦ Donation. Tu-Sa 2-4PM July-Aug; call for appointment Sept-June. 41 S Orleans Rd (between Cove Rd and Rte 6A), Orleans. 240.1735

90 Peacock Alley Antiques Jerry Kibbe's funky shop is filled with Art Deco and 1950s artifacts, plus a case containing longtime Cape resident and antiques enthusiast Jane Merrill's collection of vintage fashion accessories and jewelry, from beaded bags to Bakelite bracelets. Part of the store extends into the 19th-century captain's house that was once the studio of artist Peter Hunt, who started a fad in the 1940s and 1950s for furniture painted with folk motifs. A few of his creations can usually be found here, along with some more traditional antiques. ♦ M-Sa; Su noon-4:30PM mid-May–early Sept. M, F-Sa; Su noon-4:30PM early Sept–mid-May. 35 S Orleans Rd (between Cove Rd and Rte 6A), Orleans. 240.1804

90 Yellow House Lucille Danneman's antiques are on the pricey side, but perfectly picked to dress up any setting. She's a designer, too, so the showroom is pleasingly laid out. Cupboards, bureaus, tables—it's all very practical stuff, just unusually good-looking. Stop in if only to see the exposed brick hearth, almost sculptural in its stark simplicity. ♦ Daily May-Oct; by appointment Nov-Apr. 21 S Orleans Rd (between Cove Rd and Rte 6A), Orleans. 255.9686 &

91 Arbor Restaurant ★★$$$ Who needs a floor show when you've got decor this entertaining? It looks as if a flea market hit the fan. You're greeted by a barber's chair and a crib converted into a settee. Every square inch is plastered with tchotchkes, and not a single plate matches another. The menu is on the quirky side, too: mussels baked in mushroom caps with Port and garlic butter, veal in a Harvey's Bristol Cream sauce with capers and leeks—there's even Cajun pasta. It's all rather rich, and you won't lack for conversation pieces. ♦ American/Continental ♦ Daily dinner. 20 S Orleans Rd (between Cove Rd and Rte 6A), Orleans. 255.4847 &

Within the Arbor Restaurant:

Binnacle Tavern ★★$ The fun-house atmosphere continues here, and the place is usually packed. The draw: family-friendly prices, and what some consider the best pizza on the Cape, in odd topping combos like chopped apples and shrimp, or currants and gorgonzola (but don't worry—they're not all so bizarre). ♦ International ♦ Daily dinner. 255.7901 &

92 The Cove $$ This is one very handsome motel, painted a greenish-blue and over-looking its namesake. The rooms have condo-style furnishings (not dazzling, but nice enough), and most have decks with views of the heated pool and waterside gazebo. Guests are offered a complimentary "FloteBote" ride around Town Cove. There's no restaurant. ♦ 13 S Orleans Rd (between Cove Rd and Rte 6A), Orleans. 343.2233, 800/343.2233 ♿

92 Continuum Old-house owners seeking just the right vintage lighting fixtures have a friend in Dan Johnson, who keeps more than 400 in stock, from Victorian to Art Deco. The selection's so good, you'll have to forgive the corny lightbulb jokes in his *Light Reading* newsletter. ♦ M-Sa mid-June–Dec; off-season by appointment. 7 S Orleans Rd (between Cove Rd and Rte 6A), Orleans. 255.8513

92 Cottage St. Bakery JoAnna Keeley's concoctions are outstanding, ranging from all sorts of healthy breads (dill-cheese, carrot-onion-oatmeal, and such) to insidiously delicious desserts. For a brunch party, take home one of her pizza-size mega-Danishes. ♦ Daily 7AM-9PM late May–early Sept; call for off-season schedule. 5 Cottage St (at Rte 6A), Orleans. 255.2821

93 Spindrift Pottery Mahala Bishop has been spinning her wheel here since 1980, and she's unflaggingly friendly, happy to chat as she throws. Her plates, bowls, and casseroles (all oven-, microwave-, and dishwasher-safe) are durable as well as beautiful. She favors glazes the color of sea and sand and imprints some pieces with scallop shells. ♦ Daily late May–mid-Oct; call for off-season schedule. 37 Rte 6A (between Rte 28 and Hwy 6), Orleans. 255.1404, recorded information 255.3184 ♿

KELY KNOWLES
Orleans, Massachusetts
JONATHAN YOUNG WINDMILL

93 Jonathan Young Windmill Built circa 1720 in Orleans, later moved here and there (millers typically took their tools along when relocating), and eventually returned to the town in 1938, this mill unfortunately is no longer in operation: when the Orleans Historical Society took it over, they had to choose between preserving its architectural integrity or functionality. You'll be glad that aesthetics won out when you peer up into the intricate wooden gears. The helpful docents are well versed in their milling lore, pointing out, for instance, that the phrase "keeping one's nose to the grindstone" was necessitated by the grain's tendency to go up in flames, and the mill along with it. ♦ Free. Daily late-May–Oct. Town Cove Park (between Rte 28 and Hwy 6), Orleans. 240.1329

94 Goose Hummock Shop This long-established shop spans two buildings. The or up by the road features every conceivable wrinkle in fishing and hunting gear, with advi thrown in for free. The **Outdoor Center,** behin it, stocks general sporting and camping good including bikes, canoes, tents, kayaks, and, fc the action-oriented, a ramp slanting out the back door to try the boats out in Town Cove. ♦ Daily. 15 Rte 6A (between Rte 28 and Hwy 6), Orleans. 255.0455. Also at: 2 Rte 28 (between Camp St and Yarmouth Rd), West Yarmouth. 778.0877 ♿

94 Kemp Pottery One of the Cape's most prominent potters, Steve Kemp is just as comfortable producing functional pieces as he is creating one-of-a-kind artworks. The former category includes affordable crockery mirrors, lamps, and sinks; the latter, well-crafted busts and torsos; and in between, some fanciful, elaborately decorated tureens and garden statuary. He doesn't mind being watched as he works, and, given a curious crowd, he'll expound entertainingly on the history of ceramics. ♦ M-Sa. 9 Rte 6A (between Rte 28 and Hwy 6), Orleans. 255.5853. Also at: 258 Main St (between A. Percie Newcomb and Stony Brook Rds), Brewster. 385.5782 (May-Dec only) ♿

94 Pump House Cape surfers are a small but hardy bunch. Even if you don't plan to join their ranks (Wellfleet's beaches are said to be the best for beginners, and you can start out, prone, on a bodyboard), stop here if only to update your wardrobe. The wetsuits and boards come used or new, and the baggy flannels and cool shades require no prior dud experience. ♦ Daily May-Sept; Sa-Su 2-6PM Apr, Oct-Dec. 9 Rte 6A (between Rte 28 and Hwy 6), Orleans. 240.2226

Bird Watcher's General Store

95 Bird Watcher's General Store It's no secret that Cape Codders are bird-crazy, but until hobbyist Mike O'Connor opened his shop in 1983, no one could have gauged thei numbers and fervor. After less than a decade in business, this store had to relocate to large quarters, and it now moves almost a ton of birdseed a day. Among the hundreds of avian items sold in the barn-size emporium is "the Avarium," a windowsill bird feeder with a one way mirror; elegant granite birdbaths; and spotting lenses. More mundane items include giftwrap, puzzles, socks, and so on, all decorated with our feathered friends. ♦ M-Sa 9AM-9PM; Su July-Aug; daily Sept-June. 36 Rte 6A (between Rte 28 and Hwy 6), Orleans. 255.6974, 800/562.1512 ♿

96 Oceana Carol Wright's small shop offers charming gift items (though you may want to keep a few for yourself)—including ocean-related books, tapes, and puzzles; silver and gold jewelry; and educational toys for children. It's a peaceful place, a pleasure to browse through, and a percentage of the sales goes to the Center for Coastal Studies. ♦ M-Sa; Su 11AM-5PM. 1 Main St Sq (off Main St, between Rte 6A and Locust Rd), Orleans. 240.1414 ♿

97 Hot Chocolate Sparrow ★$ This espresso bar/bakery isn't quite the hip enclave one might expect (it's a little too cheerful and squeaky-clean), but those seeking the likes of raspberry latte will not be deterred. If you're dieting, watch out—you'll be sorely tempted by the caloric goodies here, including cappuccino mousse torte, and the delectable homemade, hand-dipped chocolates. ♦ Cafe ♦ Daily 7AM-11PM mid-June-early Sept; call for off-season schedule. 85 Rte 6A (between Cove Rd and Rte 28), Orleans. 240.2230 ♿

98 Off-the-Bay Cafe ★★$$$$ Steve Hickock's place, in a rehabbed century-old Main Street shop, is the spiffiest eatery in town, with lots of gleaming brass and burnished pine wainscoting, a tin ceiling, revolving fans, and flowered tablecloths. The cuisine is as varied and skilled as you'll find in these parts, ranging from grilled crab cakes with red pepper and papaya hollandaise to spit-roasted duckling with beach plum and cranberry compote. Come back for brunch: lobster omelettes accompanied by jazz. ♦ New American ♦ M-Sa breakfast, lunch, and dinner, Su brunch and dinner July-Aug; M-Sa lunch and dinner, Su brunch and dinner Sept-June. 28 Main St (between Rte 6A and Locust Rd), Orleans. 255.5505 ♿

99 Land Ho! ★★$$ You'd have to be a local just to figure out that this nondescript white clapboard building harbors a restaurant. Owner John Murphy has been so busy keeping hordes of regulars happy for the past quarter-century that he certainly doesn't need to solicit the tourist trade. It's basically a pub, with wood walls plastered with business ads. The menu's pretty simple—just burgers, pizza, and some fish dishes—but you may want to try the more adventurous kale soup. ♦ American/International ♦ M-Sa lunch and dinner; Su brunch and dinner. 38 Main St (at Rte 6A), Orleans. 255.5165 ♿

99 Head & Foot Shop If you're escorting teenagers who insist on having the right labels (Esprit, Levi, Champion, et al.) before they'll consent to appear in public, stop here for a great selection, all of it slightly knocked down in price. If you're very inconspicuous, they might even suffer you to buy some for yourself. ♦ M-Sa 9AM-9PM; Su noon-5PM late May–early Sept. M-Sa; Su noon-5PM early Sept–late May. 42 Main St (between Cummings Rd and Rte 6A), Orleans. 255.1281 ♿ Also at: 578 Main St (between Library La and Seaview St), Chatham. 945.9019; 193 Commercial St (between the Coast Guard Station and the post office), Provincetown. 487.3683 ♿

In the summer of 1944, alarmed at the growing popularity of halter-tops and shorts in their town, Harwich police handed out several hundred cards requesting that, in future, the recipient stick to "conventional dress."

In 1860, a new teacher in the school at Monomoy Point in Chatham was surprised when all of his pupils suddenly bolted from his classroom and did not return that day. He later learned there was a "wreck ashore."

The Wreckers Prayer dates back to Old England: "We pray Thee, O Lord, not that wrecks shall happen, but that, if any shall happen, Thou wilt guide them onto our shores for the benefit of the inhabitants."

Restaurants/Clubs: Red   **Hotels:** Blue
Shops/ 🎋 Outdoors: Green   **Sights/Culture:** Black

Happy Trails: Scenic Cycling Routes

If theme-park developers ever wanted to come up with "Bikeworld," they'd do well to look to the Cape and the Islands. The terrain is just about perfect: predominantly flat—with a few mild hills for kicks—and unrelentingly scenic. For these very reasons, bike trails have branched out all over the area. You can bring your own bike, borrow a bed-and-breakfast loaner, or rent one from the many shops situated along the trails.

Among the longer paths is a 14-mile loop, spanning both banks of the **Cape Cod Canal,** maintained by the US Army Corps of Engineers (759.5991). The **Shining Sea Bikeway** (548.8500) runs 3.6 miles from **Woods Hole** to **Falmouth,** connecting with 24 miles of marked blacktop routes. A former **Penn-Central** right-of-way, the **Cape Cod Rail Trail** (896.3491) cuts a 26-mile swath that's eight feet wide, originating in **South Dennis** at **Route 134** and running parallel to **Route 6A** up to **Lecount Hollow Beach** in **Wellfleet.** Within the **Cape Cod National Seashore** (487.1256) are **Eastham**'s **Nauset Trail,** which covers the 1.6 miles between the **Salt Pond Visitor Center** and **Coast Guard Beach; Truro**'s two-mile **Head of the Meadow Trail,** which leads from the beach along the old 1850 overland route toward **Provincetown,** ending at **High Head Road;** and Provincetown's **Province Lands Trails,** a seven-mile roller coaster of loops and spurs that gyrates through forests and swooping dunes.

Both islands are also ideal for biking, either on or off a path. On **Martha's Vineyard,** a loose triangle of bike paths, about eight miles to a side, links **Vineyard Haven, Edgartown,** and **West Tisbury** (here, a loop through the state forest is especially peaceful); the most scenic trail by far is the six-mile path connecting **Oak Bluffs** with Edgartown, and continuing on from there three miles to **South Beach.** On **Nantucket,** bike paths radiate from town to the beaches at **Madaket** (about six miles west), **Surfside** (three miles south), **Sconset** (eight miles east), and **Polpis** (eight miles east).

The better bike stores will inquire as to your proficiency before suggesting a route and sending you off with a map; it's better to be honest than to end up gasping for breath in some remote cul-de-sac. Many also offer parking and easy access to trails, and stock such essentials as helmets, car racks, and child seats. Among the top bike shops are:

Brewster: Rail Trail Bike Shop, 302 Underpass Rd (at Snow Rd); 896.8200

Eastham: The Little Capistrano Bike Shop, Schoolhouse Rd (off Nauset Rd); 255.6515

Falmouth Heights: Holiday Cycles, 465 Grand Ave (off Falmouth Heights Rd); 540.3549

Martha's Vineyard: Anderson's Bike Rentals, 14 Saco Ave (between Seaview and Circuit Ave Extensions), Oak Bluffs; 693.9346

Nantucket: Young's Bicycle Shop, Broad St (between Easy and S Water Sts); 228.1151

Provincetown: Arnold's, 329 Commercial St (just north of MacMillan Wharf); 487.0844

100 Artful Hand Gallery Mary Pocari founded this crafts shop in the early 1980s and has since attracted some 500 artisans and opened branches in Chatham and in Boston's upscale Copley Place. Her guidelines, as far as can be deduced, are the lush and the offbeat, sometimes both. Glassware and glass jewelry are strong suits. A lot of the goods have a humorous touch (e.g., a da Vincian jellybean mill) but stop just short of the dreaded "whimsy." ◆ M-Sa 10AM-9PM; Su noon-5PM July–early Sept. M-Sa; Su noon-5PM early Sept–June. 47 Main St (between Brewster Cross Rd and Rte 6A), Orleans. 255.2969. Also at: 459 Main St (between Homestead La and Mill Pond Rd), Chatham. 945.4933

101 Charles Moore Arena Families can skate away the rainy- or snowy-day blues at this cavernous public rink, which offers rentals and space just to kick loose. Once combining public roller skating in summer and ice skating in winter, the rink is now open to the public only for ice skating. Friday is "Rock-Nite," a DJ'd, strobe-lit party reserved exclusively for kids 9 through 14 from 8 to 10PM. ◆ Tu-W, F 11AM-1PM; Th 3:30PM-5PM; Su 2-4PM Sept-Feb. O'Connor Rd (off Lots Hollow Rd), Orleans. 255.2971 ⅙

OLD JAILHOUSE TAVERN

92 Old Jailhouse Tavern ★$$ How many bars are housed in a hoosegow? This rubble-stone building was actually constable Henry Perry's home a century ago, but he did put up a few surplus miscreants from time to time, so owner Lynn Hirst and architect **Anthony E. Ferragamo** ran with the motif. A massive iron gate separates the bar from the dining room proper, which opens out into a greenhouse. The menu is nothing out of the ordinary, except for its prison-talk nomenclature, but there are some tasty snacks available at any time of day. The toast Nelson—French bread topped with bacon, onion, crabmeat, shrimp, scallops, hollandaise, and parmesan—sure beats bread and water. ♦ International ♦ M-Sa lunch and dinner; Su brunch and dinner. 28 West Rd (between Rte 6A and Skaket Beach Rd), Orleans. 255.5245 &

03 Captain Linnell House ★★★$$$ With its Neo-Classical Ionic columns, Captain Eben Linnell's 1840 mansion is often compared to the fictional Tara, but in fact he copied it from a seagoing colleague's Marseilles villa, planning to retire here with his wife and three daughters. Unfortunately his dream never became reality: His final voyage turned out to be a fatal one. At press time, long-term renovations were under way to upgrade the interior.

Chef/owner William Conway's work in the kitchen is beyond reproach. His bourbon-splashed lobster bisque is a front-runner for best of the Cape, and his innovative approach to fish is exemplified in a baked scrod wrapped in parchment with lemon-lime vermouth sauce. Of the three dining rooms, the prettiest is the one overlooking the garden with its mossy brick wall, gazebo, and voluminous catalpa. ♦ New American ♦ Daily dinner. Reservations required. 137 Skaket Beach Rd (between West Rd and Honeysuckle La), Orleans. 255.3400

104 Rock Harbor Charter Fishing Fleet Serious recreational fishers (no oxymoron there) make a beeline for this lineup of 16 boats, the Cape's largest for-hire fishing fleet. You can walk along the pier and see which appeals: perhaps the 39-foot *Empress,* whose captain, Stu Finlay, has had four decades of experience tracking down bluefish, bass, haddock, cod, flounder, and, with any luck in late summer, tuna. Each boat accommodates up to six people for half- or full-day excursions. ♦ By reservation mid-May–mid-Oct. Rock Harbor (Rock Harbor Rd, off Hwy 6), Orleans. 255.9757, 800/287.1771

104 Capt. Cass Rock Harbor Seafood ★★$$ This buoy-strewn, shingled cottage is picturesque to the hilt, and authentic, too—it hasn't changed a whit since the 1950s. The tables are covered with oilcloth, the menu is scrawled on posterboard, and the fare is simple but ample: all the usual bounty, plus she-crab stew, and, for a splurge (twice the price of most items on the menu), a shore dinner centered on a two-pound lobster. ♦ American ♦ Daily lunch and dinner late May–mid-Oct. 117 Rock Harbor Rd (off Hwy 6), Orleans. No phone

Orleans native son Isaac Snow, whose house—with a plaque—still stands on Brick Hill Road, was so keen to enlist for the War of Independence that he walked to Boston, wearing out his shoes en route. After participating in the siege of Dorchester Heights (where he filled barrels with clay and stone to roll down on British soldiers), he returned home "strongly in love with my country's cause" and promptly reenlisted.

Tony Stetzko, of Orleans, holds the world record for catching a giant striped bass, a 73-pounder landed off Nauset Beach in November 1981. The fish is mounted on the wall of his Cape Copy Shoppe.

Recent archaeological evidence suggests that the "People of the First Light" (that is, Native Americans of the Algonquin tribes) may have occupied the "Narrow Land" during the late Pleistocene, soon after the last glaciers receded some 10,000 to 12,000 years ago, leaving behind the "terminal moraine," or ridge of rubble, that now constitutes the Cape and Islands. The tribes subsisted as nomadic hunter-gatherers for about 10,000 years before settling into more permanent winter and summer sites. They had spent a few millennia developing a sustainable agriculture when the English showed up, bearing not only a very different agenda but devastating diseases; from an estimated population of 30,000 early in the 17th century, their numbers dwindled to the hundreds.

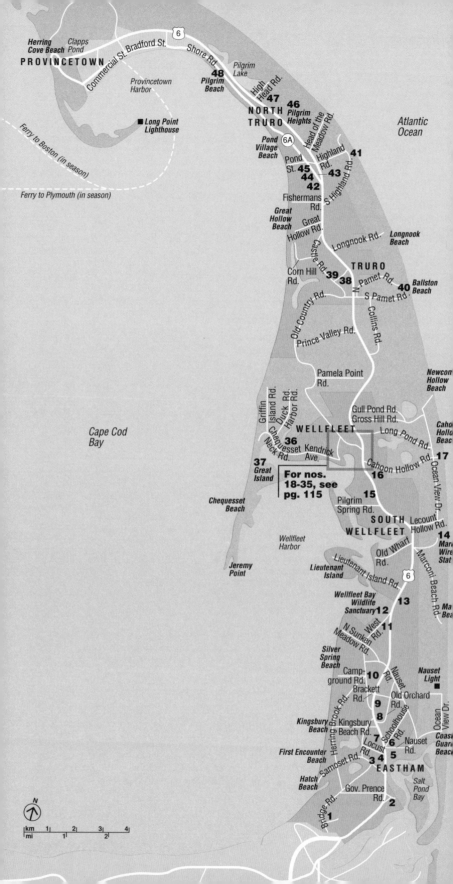

Eastham/Wellfleet/Truro

At Eastham in 1620, a *Mayflower* scouting party led by Myles Standish met the Nauset Indians at what is now called **First Encounter Beach**. The Indians attacked the would-be settlers with bows and arrows, scaring them off. Then in 1644 a group of Plymouth Colony malcontents came on the scene, seeking larger land grants and more fertile turf than they found in other places. They hit agricultural pay dirt; even as the colonists set about deforesting their new home, they extracted two bumper crops from the sandy soil: asparagus and turnips.

In the early 1800s, Eastham became a locus of revivalist fervor; thousands of devout Methodists gathered here each summer to hear sermons by as many as 150 ministers-in-residence. (The Methodists soon packed up their tents, however, and headed for more scenic Craigville and Oak Bluffs.) Today, Eastham fans like the town for what it's *not:* not too crowded, not very developed, and not offering a lot to do, except hit the beach and maybe grab a bite somewhere before heading back to your cottage or motel. The bay-side beaches are shallow and placid, with a broad intertidal zone that's great for shell-hunting and kite-flying. Invigorating surf churns at the base of the spectacular oceanside bluffs, a protectorate of the **Cape Cod National Seashore.**

Wellfleet is a classic New England town, most likely named for Wallfleet, England, which is equally renowned for its oysters. Cultural attractions that are absent in Eastham can be found in Wellfleet. The galleries are easily as lively as those in Provincetown (without the attendant commercialization), and several stores and restaurants warrant a leisurely visit. Women in search of affordable and au courant designer clothing will be particularly well served at shops such as **Karol Richardson** and **Hannah**. There's even challenging drama to take in at the **Wellfleet Harbor Actors' Theater (WHAT)**, and for those who prefer to play the philistine while on vacation, nothing beats a trashy double feature at the **Wellfleet Drive-In.**

In Truro there's really "no there, there"—just a general store (admittedly somewhat upscale), a post office, and a sign facetiously heralding "Downtown Truro." Originally part of Eastham (it separated in 1790), Truro started out as a Native American village called **Payomet**, or **Pamet**, named for the resident tribe. Its 18th-century settlers called it **Dangerfield**, alluding to the treacherous waters offshore (the region lost so many of its citizens at sea that it was known as "the town of empty graves"). Later, residents fearing bad PR rechristened it after an English town in Cornwall that it resembled. Truro once rivaled Provincetown as a fishing port, but in the 1800s, **Pamet Harbor** started filling up with sand. The fishing vessels went elsewhere, and the town dozed for a century or so.

With a year-round population of some 1,400 (spread over 42 square miles), Truro still qualifies as the Cape's sleepiest community. Years ago, Henry David Thoreau wrote in *Cape Cod*, "In the north part of town there is no house from shore to shore for several miles, and it is wild and solitary as the Western Prairies used to be." Today there are quite a few more houses tucked in the woods and along the shore, but the overall feeling of space and isolation remains. **Truro Center** is the favored summer retreat of writers and psychiatrists, while **North Truro** is more of a working-class suburb of Provincetown, its bay side plastered with cute, if rather crowded-together, cottages.

1 Mid-Cape American Youth Hostel $
Here's another great AYH deal. Eight tiny barn-red cabins sleeping six to eight apiece surround a common room with a screened-in porch. On the down side, you're locked out from 9:30AM to 5:30PM, there's hardly anyplace to go during those hours when the weather's nasty, and it's bring-your-own-grub. However, the place does have picnic tables and a pair of outdoor grills, as well as a communal kitchen. Those accustomed to hostel life will appreciate the setting, on three wooded acres just a brisk 15-minute walk from the bay and close to the 26-mile **Rail Trail.** ♦ Closed mid-September–mid-May. 75 Goody Hallet Dr (off Bridge Rd), Eastham. 255.2785 &

1 Whalewalk Inn $$$ This 1830s Greek Revival captain's house was converted to an inn in 1953, but it took the ministrations of Dick and Carolyn Smith, who bought it in 1990, to make it shine. The seven rooms and five suites, including a saltbox cottage, are decorated in a country mode: lots of honey-toned antiques, accented by crisp comforters and curtains in a color scheme of pale blue, peach, and pink. Breakfast, served on a terraced garden in summer, is well worth waking up for: Grand Marnier French toast, for instance, is a great way to start the day. ♦ Closed mid-December–March. 220 Bridge Rd (between Goody Hallet Dr and Charles Noble Way), Eastham. 255.0617; fax 240.0017

2 Captain Edward Penniman House A prosperous whaler, Edward Penniman, had this French Second Empire mansion constructed in 1868 while he and his wife and one of their three children were off to sea. Painted yellow, with a two-tone red mansard roof, it's a veritable dictionary of decorative detail, from its lantern cupola and upstairs windows sheltered by wedding-cake pediments down to the ground floor's faux masonry quoins and elaborate portico supported by Corinthian columns. There's not much to look at in terms of furnishings—a Victorian bedroom set and some turn-of-the-century photographs by daughter Bessie—but the **Cape Cod National Seashore (CCNS)** guides have interesting tales to tell. Mother Betsie's 1864-68 whaling journal, illustrated with sketches, is on display at the **CCNS's Salt Pond Visitor Center** just up the road. And a two-mile loop comprising two **CCNS** trails, the **Fort Hill** and **Red Maple Swamp Trails**, passes right by the yard, guard by a gate of lichen-encrusted whale jawbones. ♦ Free. Visitors' Center: daily mid-June–early Sept; call for off-season hours; closed January–mid-February. Penniman House: call for hours or appointment. Fort Hill Rd (off Governor Prence Rd), Eastham. 255.3421

3 First Encounter Concert Series at Chapel in the Pines Many folk music legends—including Wellfleet resident Patty Larkin and Vineyard import Livingston Taylor—have played for intimate crowds at this yellow clapboard 1889 chapel in a Unitarian-Universalist church. Concerts are held the second and fourth Saturday of every month year-round; there's an open mike the first Saturday of the month. Fewer than a hundred rapt listeners can crowd into the small room decorated with Gothic stained-glass windows. ♦ Admission. Call for concer schedule; closed in May. 220 Samoset Rd (between Hwy 6 and Great Pond Rd), Eastham. 255.5438 &

4 Beach Plum Motor Lodge $ Behind her house, Gloria Moll tends five cabin rooms—two are pine paneled, the other three are decorated with homey wallpaper. Each year the place turns into "a little United Nations" as word of mouth helps to bring in an international clientele—celebrated by the dozen flags that fly outside. Americans are attracted as well by the tiny kidney-shaped pool, the thousands of flowers Moll plants every year, the banana bread and lemon cake she bakes for breakfast, and some of the lowest rates on the Cape. There is no restaurant. ♦ Closed mid-October–mid-May. 2555 Hwy 6 (between Samoset and Locust Rds), Eastham. 255.7668

5 Salt Pond Visitor Center This modern complex, which overlooks a tidal pond and serves as an educational gateway to the 44,000-acre **Cape Cod National Seashore,** offers newcomers an excellent introduction to the ecology of the Cape. A 10-minute video screened every half hour provides an overview of the area's natural history, while other films go into more detail on a variety of related topics. A diorama illustrates the vagaries of the ocean floor, and the small museum has fascinating exhibits on local history, architecture, industry, and flora and fauna. Special events in summer include ban concerts, slide-show presentations, and classic movies such as *Moby Dick* and *Captains Courageous.* The center is a hub for several nature trails, including **Button Bush Trail for the Blind,** a quarter-mile path marked with descriptive plaques in large type and Braille. Other, longer hikes lead to Nauset Light Beach and Coast Guard Beach, popular with harbor seals in winter and human swimmers in summer.

The cottage where Henry Beston wrote *The Outermost House* was washed away in the Great Blizzard of 1978, but an informative sign marks its location. Further erosion in 1990 revealed to an amateur archaeologist what appeared to be an ancient hearth; rushing to excavate before more storms intervened, the US Park Service uncovered the oldest undisturbed archaeological site found in New England to date. It contains evidence of several eras of habitation. The oldest material dates as far back as the Early Archaic Culture 11,000 years ago, when the site was a good five miles from the sea. ♦ Daily, including occasional evenings; call for information. Nauset Rd (between Doane Rd and Hwy 6), Eastham. 255.3421 ൿ

6 1869 Schoolhouse Museum This yellow clapboard was the town's one-room schoolhouse from 1869 to 1936. It's now the headquarters of the Eastham Historical Society, and offers displays including Native American artifacts and farming and nautical implements, among other things. Of particular interest is the exhibit devoted to Henry Beston, who spent a year at nearby Coast Guard Beach writing the conservation classic *The Outermost House* (published in 1928 and still eagerly read). The Historical Society also maintains the 1741 **Swift-Daley House and Tool Museum** on Highway 6; in the mid–19th century it was home to future mega–meat packer Gustav Swift, but its contents are not especially distinguished. ♦ Free. M-F 1-4PM July-Aug. Nauset and Schoolhouse Rds, Eastham. 255.0788

7 Over Look Inn $$ This 1869 Queen Anne Victorian is as colorful inside as out—a tough act to follow when you're talking about a creamy yellow behemoth trimmed in avocado, rust, and lilac. The **Churchill Library** is dominated by a green leather couch, the mustard-and-emerald **Ernest Hemingway Billiard Room** by game trophies, and the **Sarah Chipman Parlor** by a life-size doll commemorating the original owner. If you venture to say that the place is unusual, Scottish innkeeper Nan Atchison will tell you, "Eccentric is more like it." The 10 bedrooms tend toward excess—there's one in mauve with a cathedral ceiling, fireplace, claw-foot tub, and brass bed—but amenable visitors revel in the subtlety of it all. You may be in for

an "eccentric" breakfast as well—kedgeree, which is smoked cod, rice, onion, chopped egg, and raisins, with mango chutney. ♦ 3085 Hwy 6 (between Locust and Kingsbury Beach Rds), Eastham. 255.1886; fax 240.0345

8 Arnold's ★$$ This casual eatery offers all the usual deep-fried treats (including its celebrated onion rings), plus mussels steamed in white wine and garlic that give white-tablecloth restaurants a run for their money. Eat in a beer garden decked out in the traditional nets and traps, or take your tray to picnic tables in the pine grove for a more quiet repast. The brews in tall plastic cups hit the spot. ♦ American/Takeout ♦ Daily lunch and dinner mid-May–mid-Sept. 3580 Hwy 6 (at Old Orchard Rd), Eastham. 255.2575 ൿ

9 Eastham Lobster Pool ★★$$$ With cement floors and seating at long tables, this restaurant is far from fancy. But it's a place to revel in fish—in so many permutations (fried, grilled, broiled, baked with crumbs, stuffed with lobster sauce, or poached in a fat-free, lemon-herb court bouillon) that the menu uses a chart to list them. The daily specials can be quite sophisticated—grilled halibut with Champagne-shallot butter, for instance, or lobster with tomato-basil cream over linguine. The fresh peach daiquiris hit the spot, and the ice-cream pies make a memorable dessert choice. Come straight from the beach, before the place is packed to its buoy-strewn rafters. ♦ American/Takeout ♦ Daily lunch and dinner Apr-Oct. 4380 Hwy 6 (between Old Orchard and Brackett Rds), North Eastham. 255.9706, takeout 255.3314 ൿ

Though Cape Cod's historic windmills may seem plentiful, they're but a tiny fraction of the original number. As Josef Berger wrote in *Cape Cod Pilot* (a 1937 WPA project): "Wealthy summer residents began to buy the old mills as adornments for their estates, and many of them had the machinery removed and junked, using the empty tower for storage of lawn mowers, bridge tables, children, and other impedimenta; so that now, with a large premium attaching to any mill that works, many an owner can stand in the hollow tower and regret the day he stripped her of her drive-shaft, her wheels and spindle, and followed the fashion of setting the millstone down for his doorstep."

Restaurants/Clubs: Red   **Hotels:** Blue

Shops/ 🌳 Outdoors: Green   **Sights/Culture:** Black

Lighthouses: On the Move

Over time, many of Cape Cod's seaside cliffs, roadways, and even buildings get washed away because of erosion caused by the mighty **Atlantic**. Lighthouses are particularly in peril since they must be near the shore to warn ships, and are often built on high points of land to gain the greatest distance for their lights. Unfortunately, the highest spots on the Cape are hills of sand, and like hourglasses emptying their contents, they are beaten away by time and tide and storm.

Cape Cod Light, also called **Highland Light**, was the Cape's first wooden lighthouse. It was erected in 1797 on a bluff in **North Truro** at the end of what later became **Lighthouse Road**. At that time it was 510 feet to the cliff. By the time Henry David Thoreau arrived here in 1855 and stayed overnight, the face of the cliff had noticeably retreated. The prophetic writer intoned, "Erelong the lighthouse must be moved."

By the summer of 1995, **Highland Light** was only 112 feet from the precipice. Several groups came to the rescue. The Truro Historical Society helped to form the Committee to Save Cape Cod Light, which enlisted the aid of the **Cape Cod National Seashore,** the US Coast Guard, the State of

Massachusetts, and private donors to come up with the 1.5 million dollars needed to make the move.

By May 1996, the cliff was only 100 feet away. The physical moving of the lighthouse took most of the month of July 1996, and when the task was completed, it was 553 feet from the precipice, situated between the seventh and eighth fairways of the **Highland Links,** one of the 10 oldest golf courses in America.

Coincidentally, **Nauset Light,** located farther south along the same shoreline in **Eastham,** was also moved in 1996. The Nauset Light Preservation Society organized financial support, and with the expertise of the International Chimney Company and Expert House Movers Inc. moved the lighthouse 300 feet back from its eroding cliff. This was **Nauset Light**'s second move: Originally standing side-by-side with **Chatham Light** in **Chatham**, the tower was moved to Eastham in 1923 and renamed **Nauset Light.** Historical records do not contain any details on exactly how the 1923 move was accomplished. As with **Highland,** the light continues its watch—while locals count on calmer seas.

10 The Penny House Bed & Breakfast $$
A full breakfast (featuring such delicious jump-starters as *strata*—baked layers of bread and cheese topped with egg mixture) is served in the beamed dining room of the circa 1751 main house. Eleven nicely appointed rooms, of varying sizes and prices, fill the more recent addition, and a spacious common room encourages conviviality. Margaret Keith, who hails from Australia, is a friendly, informative, but unobtrusive host. The inn is set back behind a high hedge, so you'll forget you're on teeming Highway 6. Restaurants are a short drive away. ◆ 4885 Hwy 6 (between Old State Hwy and N Sunken Meadow Rd), North Eastham. 255.6632, 800/554.1751; fax 255.6632

11 Tang Dynasty ★$$ You might not think to stop here if you're just driving by, but if you're driving *in*—to the drive-in, that is—nothing beats the Chinese pot stickers or scallion pancakes for a cinematic snack. Or go all out and order a "family dinner," a feast for three or four. ◆ Chinese ◆ Daily lunch and dinner. 49 Hwy 6 (between Maguire Ave and West Rd), South Wellfleet. 349.7521 &

11 Wellfleet Drive-In Built in 1957, this indispensable institution is the last of its breed. Loyal patrons fully appreciate the treasure, and many show up practically every time the program changes (typically, once a week). Long the province of teenagers on the make, drive-ins are also great family entertainment. Take along some pillows and blankets in case younger viewers conk out. Until they do, they'll enjoy the little tot lot behind the well-stocked concession stand, or perhaps the mini-golf just outside the gate. For your rainy-day or off-season pleasure, there's also a little miniplex on the grounds. ◆ Daily starting at dusk late May–mid-Sept. 51 Hwy 6 (between Maguire Ave and West Rd), South Wellfleet. 349.7176, 800/696.3532 &

Within the Wellfleet Drive-In:

Wellfleet Flea Market Seconds dealers and wholesalers pushing everything from vacuum cleaners to "designer" T-shirts proliferate here, but it's still worth a look around. Among the 300 or so booths, you might find something as useful as a pair of used in-line skates or a vintage brass Victrola. ♦ Nominal admission. M holidays, W-Th, Sa-Su July-Aug; M holidays, Sa-Su mid-Apr–June, Sept-Nov. 349.2520, 800/696.3532 ♿

12 Wellfleet Bay Wildlife Sanctuary
Wandering through the Massachusetts Audubon Society's 1,000-acre preserve, it's hard to imagine that 100 years ago this area was a virtually treeless turnip and asparagus farm. Now it's a lively patchwork of salt marsh, moors, and piney woods, laced with five miles of hiking trails and capped in 1993 by a $1.6 million visitor center designed by **Gerard Ives** of Boston. The low-slung, modestly shingled building suits its site environmentally as well as aesthetically. Its "green design" incorporates superinsulation, natural light combined with passive solar heating, and even composting toilets—a feature that's expected to conserve some 100,000 gallons of water a year. Swirls of wavelike blue-green walls demarcate exhibits, a gift shop, and a lecture hall. All sorts of workshops and guided walks are offered, along with special activities for children, plus canoeing, snorkeling, whale watching, and cruises along the bay, Nauset Marsh, and Monomoy Island. Audubon members may camp in the wooded groves; call for details. ♦ Trail fee for nonmembers. Trails: daily dawn-dusk. Building: daily July-Aug; Tu-Su Sept-June. 291 Hwy 6 (near West Rd), South Wellfleet. 349.2615; fax 349.2632 ♿

JP'S

13 Finely JP's ★★$$ It doesn't look like much from the road, and the pine-paneled interior is more suited to a rec room than a restaurant, but the beauty lies in chef/owner John Pontius's ambitious yet unaggressively priced menu. Choosing from the likes of warm spinach and scallop salad with balsamic vinegar, or sautéed medaillons of pork with green apples and goat cheese, diners get to feel they've made a real discovery. ♦ New American ♦ Daily dinner July-Aug; call for off-season schedule; closed mid-December–mid-January. Hwy 6 (between Gill and Marconi Park Site Rds), South Wellfleet. 349.7500 ♿

13 Even Tide Motel $$ This 32-room, mid-1970s motel is set back in the woods, just off Highway 6 and the bike path; behind it, hiking trails lead to the sea, about three-quarters of a mile away. If it's raining, or you're lazy, you can make do with the 60-foot heated indoor pool. Some of the smaller rooms are rather snug, but for not much more you can snag a two-room suite or kitchen-equipped studio apartment. The owners, Dick and Grace Filliman, don't care for standard-issue motel furniture; instead, in half the rooms everything's handmade of blond oak. There is no restaurant. ♦ 650 Hwy 6 (between Gill and Marconi Park Site Rds), South Wellfleet. 349.3410, 800/368.0007; fax 349.7804 ♿

14 Marconi Wireless Station Guglielmo Marconi started fooling around with wireless communication as a teenager in Italy; at 16, he fashioned a working model out of tin plates in his father's garden. Perusing the sketches of the station built here in 1902 (it was dismantled in 1920 as the surf encroached and successive inventions took the fore), it's clear that the project was the work of either a visionary or a maniac: 25,000 volts were required to activate the four 210-foot towers, secured with a cat's cradle of cables. Amazingly, this Rube Goldbergian device did the job. On 18 January 1903, King Edward VII received "most cordial greetings" in Poldhu, Wales, from President "Theadore" Roosevelt (the system still had a few bugs). Marconi's technology, leapfrogging on the work of Serbian-American inventor Nikola Tesla, suddenly shrank the world; the global communications now taken for granted began at this desolate outpost.

Virtually no traces remain beyond some concrete foundations and sand anchors, but the observation deck, with its interpretive plaques and dioramas, induces contemplation. Shore access has been closed off because of erosion, but nearby Marconi Beach is flanked by dramatic dunes. Also close at hand is the fascinating **Atlantic White Cedar Swamp Trail,** where the species so prized by the settlers for its light weight, workability, and pale color maintains a dwindling toehold (red maples are taking over). There are boardwalks to get you across the mucky peat bogs, but trekkers have to cross a half-mile of soft sand. If you take the trail in August, you can pick wild highbush blueberries along the way. ♦ Marconi Park Site Rd (off Hwy 6), Wellfleet. 349.3785 ♿

"It is a mistake to talk of the monotone of ocean," naturalist Henry Beston observed. "The sea has many voices. Listen to the surf, really lend it your ears, and you will hear in it a world of sounds: hollow boomings and heavy roarings, great watery tumblings and tramplings, long hissing seethes, sharp, rifle-shot reports, splashes, whispers, the grinding undertone of stone, and sometimes vocal sounds that might be the half-heard talk of people in the sea."

15 Oliver's Clay Tennis Courts Seven clay courts and one Truflex are hidden away in an oak grove. A clubhouse, only about the size of a kid's, is the place for arranging lessons and matches or getting your racquet restrung. It's a treat to play in so pastoral a setting. ♦ Fee. Daily 7AM-7:30PM May–mid-Oct. 2183 Hwy 6 (between Pilgrim Spring and Cahoon Hollow Rds), Wellfleet. 349.3330

16 Cahoon Hollow Bed & Breakfast $ It has only two suites, but they're beauties, as is this secluded 1842 house. Baily Ruckert has decided flair, and, lounging in her elegant ivory-hued living room or feasting on her gourmet breakfasts (sherried eggs and ham, perhaps, or Dutch babies with rhubarb-orange compote), you'll feel as if you've landed in the home of an especially stylish friend. Take off on a loaner bike, and you'll hit salt water two miles in either direction. ♦ 56 Cahoon Hollow Rd (between Old Kings Hwy and Hwy 6), Wellfleet. 349.6372 ⅑

17 The Beachcomber Raise a glass to the Surfmen who once lived at this 1897 Coast Guard station—they're said to have saved some 100,000 lives. But the twentysomethings who frequent the "Comber" (or, alternately, "Coma") clearly live for today, enjoying wild Cahoon Hollow Beach right at the doorstep and the best bands on the Cape. The Incredible Casuals have a lock on Sunday; the rest of the week usually fills up with stellar reggae and blues acts. ♦ Cover. M-F 8PM-closing; Sa-Su 4PM-closing late June–mid-Sept. F 8PM-closing; Sa-Su 4PM-closing late May–late June. 1220 Cahoon Hollow Rd (just east of Ocean View Dr), Wellfleet. 349.6055 ⅑

18 Painter's ★★★$$$ Having interned at such culinary hot spots as San Francisco's Stars and Boston's Biba, Kate Painter started small, with a funky lunchroom down on the waterfront (now run by her brother), and in 1995 acquired a "real" restaurant. Fortunately, she has retained her slapdash design panache (evident in the almost op-art—like checkered wainscoting) and her winning ways with fresh provender and often torrid spices. Some of her "low-rent" dishes—including a white bean soup with chipotle sour cream, and her luscious "Rockin' Lobster Roll"—made the move with scarcely a ripple in pricing. In fact, all the dishes are quite reasonable, even such exotic ones as Tanqueray juniper tuna with lime tomato chutney. Desserts are modestly billed as well as priced; be sure to try the cakey, custardy "Something Lemon." A light menu is served in the upstairs bar, and a changing roster of local musicians are called upon for entertainment. ♦ New American ♦ M, W-Su dinner mid-May–mid-Sept; call for off-season schedule; closed November–mid April. 50 Main St (between Hwy 6 and School St), Wellfleet. 349.3003

19 Inn at Duck Creeke $ Some of the 25 rooms in this 1810 captain's house, converted into an inn in the 1940s, can be a bit cramped—they're adequate, though, and a bargain for the location and price. The five wooded acres overlook a salt marsh, but traffic noise from Highway 6 can still be a problem if you're the sensitive sort. ♦ Closed mid-October–mid-May. 70 Main St (between Hwy 6 and School St), Wellfleet. 349.9333

Within the Inn at Duck Creeke:

Sweet Seasons ★★$$ The look is spare yet inviting, with splashes of floral prints, and you get the full benefit of the view. Chef/owner Judith Pihl has worked up some very appealing signature dishes, such as shrimp sautéed with tomatoes, garlic, ouzo, and feta, and chilled poached lobster with caviar mayonnaise. ♦ New American ♦ Daily dinner late June–mid-Sept. Reservations recommended. 349.6535 ⅑

Tavern Room Restaurant ★★$ Check out the bar, made from antique doors. The food here is simple (pizza, pasta, assorted fish) but comes with a musical accompaniment of jazz, folk, pop, and what-have-you. ♦ International ♦ Tu-Su dinner late May–early Oct. 349.7369

20 First Congregational Church of the United Church of Christ If the proportions look a little odd, it's because this 1850 Greek Revival lost its original tapering steeple to a storm in 1879. Someone thought a bell-shaped cupola on columns might prove more wind-resistant, and it has. The **Town Clock**, installed in 1952, is the only one in the world to strike ship's time, a complicated system of one to four bells. There has been a recent $75,000 restoration of the 738-pipe 1873 Hook and Hastings organ, so it's worthwhile to attend one of the occasional summer evening concerts to hear it resonate; be sure to take a look along the right wall at the church's rare stained-glass window showing a ship of the *Mayflower* era. ♦ Services: Su

9:30AM mid-June–mid-Sept; Su 10AM mid-Sept–mid-June. 200 Main St (at School St), Wellfleet. 349.6877 &

21 Cherry Stone Gallery This gallery is among the Cape's most distinguished, having shown such giants as Motherwell and Rauschenberg since opening in 1972. The former curator, Sally Nerber, remains as advisor while co-directors Michael Landis and David Mamo take the reins. Few works are on view at any given time (10 shows usually are put on over the span of the summer), but the gallery has the works of two dozen artists in stock. Among those represented are Janice Redman, Eugene Atget, and Jasper Johns. ♦ Tu-Sa noon-6PM late May–Sept. 70 E Commercial St (between Bank and Main Sts), Wellfleet. 349.3026 &

22 Swansborough Gallery The often-impressive artwork focuses largely on semiabstract landscapes, with a dash of mixed media—Ilse Johnson's neo-tribal sand castles, Laura Baksa's exquisite alabaster body parts. And the place itself is well worth the trip. Architect **Richard Hall** bought a crumbling 1830 barn in 1980 and essentially turned it inside out. Its worm-eaten beams are things of beauty, the pine-siding ceiling is a low-key Surrealist joke, and great bright spaces with polished floors spin out from a spiraling central staircase. ♦ M-Sa 10AM-6PM; Su 1-6PM late May–mid-Oct. 230 Main St (at School St), Wellfleet. 349.1883 &

22 Hannah Since 1982, Susan Hannah has been supplying women with a collection of extremely comfortable garments that inevitably become classics in their wardrobes. Three rooms in this 1820s former parsonage are filled with an assortment of clothing in all kinds of textured fabrics: linens, cottons, plush fibers, and more. Hannah carries both designers' works as well as her own line. ♦ M-Sa; Su 1-4:30PM late May–mid-Sept. 234 Main St (between School St and Briar La), Wellfleet. 349.9884 & Also at: 47 Main St (between Brewster Cross Rd and Rte 6A), Orleans (open year-round). 255.8234

Within Hannah:

234 Gallery at Hannah Look here for striking art in a small, well-lit setting. There are Carrara marble forms sculpted by Susan McDonald, graphics and sculpture by Chuck Holtzman, and paintings by Stephen Aiken. ♦ M-Sa; Su 1-4:30PM late May–mid-Sept. 349.9884

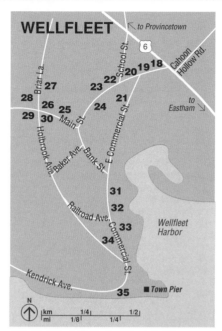

WELLFLEET

23 Wellfleet Historical Society Museum "Anything that 'might come in handy some day' found its way into the Cape Codder's attic," wrote Josef Berger in his personable guidebook *Cape Cod Pilot* (1937), "and for most of the gimcracks thus disposed of, 'some day' has not yet arrived." In the intervening decades, a lot of these things have found their way into historical collections of this sort, including almost anything that is even remotely town-related. The holdings have been roughly sorted into topics (e.g., Marconi, oystering), so it's possible to pursue a special interest. The atticlike upstairs is especially worthwhile for its toys (such as felt "ten pins") and two sketches by early Provincetown Arts Association member Ann Wells Munger, an artist apparently overdue for resurrection. ♦ Admission. ♦ Tu-Sa 2-5PM late June–early Sept. 266 Main St (between School St and Briar La), Wellfleet. 349.9157

STATIONERS

24 Jules Besch Stationers This is a stationery shop with a difference—its owner, Michael Tuck, creates most of the stock himself. He is a master calligrapher and examples of his art

115

abound in portfolios left for customers to browse through—personalized wedding invitations, business cards, and holiday cards. The tools of his trade are all about, as are pen sets, handmade journals, wrapping papers, and a terrific series of cards done by Cape Cod artists. ♦ Daily June–mid-Sept; Tu-Su Apr-May, mid-Sept–Dec; F-Su Feb-Mar. 275 Main St (between E Commercial and Bank Sts), Wellfleet. 349.1231

25 Hatch's Fish Market/Hatch's Produce A 1954 fish shack, this shingled cottage behind **Town Hall** is the local variant on Dean & DeLuca, serving nothing but the best. Rob McClellan stocks not only the freshest fish but tasty take-homes like smoked mussel pâté and sea-clam pie; Lauren McClellan's fruits, vegetables, herbs, and flowers are luscious. You could also cart off some homemade salsa, or enjoy a fresh fruit popsicle on the spot. ♦ Daily late May–late Sept. 310 Main St (between School St and Briar La), Wellfleet. Fish 349.2810, produce 349.6734 &

25 Aesop's Tables ★★★$$$$ Brian Dunne's festive restaurant is just the right mix of special occasion (this white-clapboard house was once the summer home of a Massachusetts governor) and come-as-you-are. Each intimate dining room has a slightly different feel; the unifying motif is playful yet elegant paper art by Dunne's wife, Kim Kettler. The extensive menu celebrates the bounty of the region: The exotic edible flowers that go into "Monet's Garden Salad," for instance, come from the restaurant's own farm, and the "Midsummer Night's Scallops"—sautéed whole with garlic, shallots, spinach, and basil, and served on saffron spaeztle—spend no more than three hours en route from bay to plate. Among the delectable desserts served here is "La Petite Isadora," a cheesecake topped with native raspberry-blueberry sauce. For many regular summer visitors to the Cape, no season would be complete without at least one meal here. ♦ New American ♦ M-Tu dinner; W-Su lunch and dinner late June–early Sept. W-Su dinner Apr–late June, early Sept–mid-Oct. Reservations recommended. 316 Main St (between School St and Briar La), Wellfleet. 349.6450

Within Aesop's Tables:

Upstairs Bar at Aesop's Tables This raftered attic boîte looms over Main Street like a glassed-in, life-size dollhouse. Inside, it's a sensual mix of rose velvet armchairs and Victorian divans, where, to the mellow accompaniment of local jazz musicians, one can enjoy a light snack or dessert, or settle down for a drink in style. The Tea Isadora, an Earl Grey/apricot blend steeped with apricot and Wild Turkey liqueurs, is a particularly bracing aperitif for a blustery da ♦ W-Su 5:30PM-1AM Apr–mid-Oct. 349.6450

26 Off Center Owner/buyer Gail MacGibbon favors the kind of clothes that could easily make the transition from sleepy beach town Soho—slinky rayons and ready-to-rumple cottons and linens in earth tones and muted colors. ♦ Daily May–mid-Oct; Sa-Su Apr, m Oct–Jan. 354 Main St (between School St a Briar La), Wellfleet. 349.3634

27 Box Lunch So popular are the "rollwiches"–rolled pita sandwiches—prepared here that franchises have sprung up all over the Cape; there's even one in Portland, Maine. Some of the combos are pretty clever (such as the "Humpty Dumpty," a deviled egg salad with bacon), but if you like things simple, there's always the "Boring"—three kinds of melted cheese. There's a kid's menu (the "Piglet" is a mini ham and cheese) and roll-up breakfasts t go at selected stores. ♦ Daily 7AM-7PM July-Aug; call for off-season hours. 50 Briar La (between Main St and Hwy 6), Wellfleet. 349.2178. Also at: 357 Main St (near Barnstal Rd), Hyannis. 790.5855; Underpass Rd (between Long Pond and Snow Rds), Brewst 896.6682; 353 Commercial St (between MacMillan Wharf and Pearl St), Provincetowr 487.6026

28 Flying Fish Cafe & Deli ★★$$$ The tourist throngs that mob Main Street have n yet discovered this quiet convivial cafe, whe you can have a leisurely conversation over a breakfast of "green eggs and ham" (vegetables provide coloration), a lunch of "risky pizza" (chef's choice), or a dinner of "penne from heaven" (with raisins, pine nuts, garlic and sun-dried tomatoes). The rustic breads and fine pastries are made in-house. ♦ New American ♦ Daily breakfast, lunch, and dinn mid-May–early Sept; call for off-season hours; closed mid-October–late April. 29 Br La (between W Main St and Hwy 6), Wellflee 349.3100 &

29 Left Bank Gallery, Small Works This shop specializes in exhibiting original small works (under 16-by-16 inches) in oil, watercolor, collage, and fiber, as well as photographs. It also shows work in silver, fine gemstones, and high karat gold of some 125 outstanding jewelers from around the country. Store manager Susan Blake, formerly gallery administrator of Boston's Society of Arts and Crafts, is clearly an artist in her own right: The themed jewelry displays are as interesting as the jewelry itself. ♦ Daily late May–early Sept; call for off-season hours. 3 W Main St (at Holbrook Ave), Wellfleet. 349.7939

29 Karol Richardson A London-trained clothing designer, Richardson gave up her thriving Tribeca-based business in 1977 to live in the country, where she quickly built an avid following. She seeks the finest fabrics for her line of women's attire—velours in jewel tones, nubby linens, and ribbed cotton knits. This whitewashed, barnlike shop, with its sidelines of comfortable/trendy shoes and statement jewelry, will satisfy style-conscious teenagers and dowagers alike. ♦ M-W; Th-Sa 10AM-9PM; Su noon-5PM May–mid-Oct. 3 W Main St (at Holbrook Ave), Wellfleet. 349.6378. Also at: 47 Main St (between Brewster Cross Rd and Rte 6A), Orleans. 255.3944 ＆

30 Eccentricity An offshoot of **Off Center** across the street, this shop showcases exotic fashions of its own, including magnificent antique kimonos (some remnants have been fashioned into patchwork vests). Creating an appropriately Zen-like atmosphere are lovely hand-carved slate fountains, ready for home installation. ♦ Daily May–mid-Oct; Sa-Su Apr, mid-Oct–Jan. 361 Main St (between Bank St and Holbrook Ave), Wellfleet. 349.7554 ＆

30 The Wellfleet Collection An appealing jumble of home decor, fine arts, and clothing, this lively shop reflects the tastes of owners Marty and Lorraine Rosenbaum, who winter in Mexico. Hence the colorfully embroidered cotton "wedding dresses" (hard to find this far north), and lace shirts and petticoats. Other items originate closer to home, such as the handmade quilts and Nancy Shieferstein's intense color photographs. ♦ Daily 9:30AM-9PM July-Aug; call for off-season hours; closed January–mid-April. 335 Main St (between Bank St and Holbrook Ave), Wellfleet. 349.9687

As you indulge in yet another bounteous bed-and-breakfast, consider the feast that confronted Henry David Thoreau when he took shelter with a Wellfleet farming family: eels, buttermilk cake, cold bread, green beans, doughnuts, and tea.

31 Cove Gallery Larry Biron's stable houses a lively bunch, including master engravers Leonard Baskin and Barry Moser, landscape painter Wolf Kahn, abstract painter Larry Grillo, children's illustrator Tomie de Paola, and two dozen other artists. The gallery, once a blacksmith's shop, also offers fine framing and has a sculpture garden set beside Duck Creek. ♦ Daily May-Aug; call for off-season hours; closed mid-October–April. 15 Commercial St (between Kendrick Ave and Bank St), Wellfleet. 349.2530 ＆

31 Left Bank Art Gallery This 1933 **American Legion Hall** has served splendidly as a gallery since 1970. The space itself is actually more impressive than what's on the walls—the art, much of it hyperrealistic, seems mainly commercially oriented. However, you'll find superb creations by Arthur Bauman, and one of the largest selections of crafts on the Cape. Toward the back is a "potter's room," which features all sorts of table-ready ware. ♦ Daily Apr-Dec; Sa-Su Jan-Mar. 25 Commercial St (between Kendrick Ave and Bank St), Wellfleet. 349.9451 ＆

32 On The Creek Cafe ★★$ Great harbor views combined with reasonable prices and an original menu make this spot a winner. Start the day with a breakfast of Cape Cod pancakes, slathered with fruit jam and orange sauce; at lunchtime sample a custom sandwich (including an eggplant caponata with pita points) and various home-baked treats. You can sit outside and enjoy the peaceful creek. ♦ International ♦ Daily breakfast and lunch Apr-Oct. 55 Commercial St (between Kendrick Ave and Bank St), Wellfleet. 349.9841 ＆

33 Bayside Lobster Hutt ★★$$ This 1857 oyster shack, its roof sporting a yellow-slickered fisherman in a dory hauling in a lobster twice his size, is so quintessential a lobster joint its praises have been sung in periodicals ranging from *Glamour* to *Outside*. What you get is self-service, picnic-style feasting at communal tables—and plenty of lobster. They also serve fresh oysters from their own approved oyster beds. You can bring your own bottle, but "no neckties, please." ♦ American ♦ Daily dinner late May–mid-Sept. 91 Commercial St (between Kendrick Ave and Bank St), Wellfleet. 349.6333 ♿

33 Just Dessert Like Chinese food, shore dinners don't usually rate much by way of sweet endings, but this patio overlooking the cove aims to make up for that lack. Stop here after dinner for a mile-high apple pie, marble cheesecake, "chocolate outrage," strawberry shortcake, or similar treat. ♦ American ♦ Daily 5PM-10:30PM late June–early Sept. 91 Commercial St (between Kendrick Ave and Bank St), Wellfleet. 349.6333 ♿

34 Holden Inn $ Captain Richard Freeman's 1840 manse was converted into an inn in 1924, and has been in the same family ever since. The 27 breezy rooms are timeless (braided rugs, iron bedsteads, flounced curtains), and the prices are a throwback as well; the monthly rates are especially tempting. It's a five-minute walk to restaurants. ♦ Closed mid-October–mid-April. 140 Commercial St (between Holbrook and Railroad Aves), Wellfleet. 349.3450

35 Zack's ★$ How about a turkey sandwich with thinly sliced green apple, red onion, lettuce, tomato, and melted cheddar on French bread for under $5—with harbor views included? Or you can splurge and have the fresh, locally caught lobster fashioned into a delectable lobster roll—the only thing on the menu over $5. ♦ American ♦ Daily 11:45AM-4PM May-Oct. 1 Kendrick Ave (at Commercial St), Wellfleet. 349.7343 ♿

35 Uncle Frank's ★$ In the same long room, just beside **Zack's**, is a coffee bar with stools and a few tables. Owner Frank Cain serves good coffee and donuts here, which is maybe why locals frequent this place when they need a jolt of caffeine. ♦ American ♦ Daily 5:30AM-4PM May-Oct. 1 Kendrick Ave (at Commercial St), Wellfleet. No phone ♿

In 1858, Captain Josiah Knowles of Eastham was bound from San Francisco to South America when he wrecked the *Wild Wave* on a coral reef. While the crew took shelter on a tiny island, he and a mate rowed to Pitcairn Island, presumed to be inhabited by mutineers from the *Bounty*. They'd departed, leaving some livestock behind, so Knowles killed and dressed the livestock, fashioned a boat from abandoned lumber, with clothes for sails, and set off for Tahiti, 1,500 miles away. The captain was lucky enough to run into a "sloop of war" somewhat short of there, and they returned to rescue the crew, who'd subsisted for six months on crabs and coconuts. Knowles finally made it home, to be surprised by a baby he hadn't known his wife had been expecting.

35 Wellfleet Harbor Actors' Theater (WHAT) This modest black-box theater, founded in 1985 by Jeff Zinn and Gip Hoppe, is the clearest heir apparent to the mantle of the **Provincetown Players.** The output can at times be jejune, but it's never dull, and the repertoire of six plays per summer usually includes some original works or other bold choices. ♦ Admission. Curtain: 8PM late May–mid-Oct; call for schedule. 1 Kendrick Ave (at Commercial St), Wellfleet. 349.6835 ♿

36 The Colony of Wellfleet $$$ Established as a private club in 1949 by architect and arts patron **Nat Saltonstall** (one of the founders of Boston's Institute for Contemporary Arts), this cluster of 10 cottages with outdoor terraces, set on 10 piney acres, is a rare and marvelous Bauhaus preserve. The smallish, squarish living-room/bedrooms (which have kitchen facilities, but no TVs) clearly serve their intended function of spilling occupants outdoors to enjoy the wooded setting. Many also have bay views. The original furnishings —designed by Charles and Ray Eames, among others—have counterparts in the collections of New York's Museum of Modern Art. For all its artfulness, and a guest roster that spans some notable names, the atmosphere is relaxed. Cottages usually rent by the week or more, but you might be lucky enough to find one for a two-night minimum stay. ♦ Closed late September–late May. 640 Chequesset Neck Rd (between Hiller St and Duck Harbor Rd), Wellfleet. 349.3761; fax 349.1182

37 Great Island Rated the most difficult among the **Cape Cod National Seashore**'s nine self-guided trails, this 8.4-mile loop consists primarily of soft sand, leading from woods through meadow to a remote beach at Chequesset Neck. This is where in 1970 archaeologists from the National Park Service and **Plimoth Plantation** excavated the remains of **Smith Tavern,** a 1690-1740 whalers' haunt. The finds included not only the usual shards but a 1724 farthing and a huge whale vertebra that had evidently been used as a chopping block. ♦ Daily dawn-dusk. Off Chequesset Neck and Griffin Island Rds, Wellfleet. 349.3785

38 Jams Vacationing New York psychiatrists get their deli fix at this gourmet grocery; in fact, they're honored with a namesake sandwich, "The Shrink"—nova and cream cheese with sliced onion. The pizzas are pretty special, made with fresh tomatoes and herbs and appearing in such exotic guises as *niçoise* and pupu. The French "wall of fire" rotisserie leaves chickens, ducks, and ribs coated with caramelized juices. And the pastry case displays such delectables as peach-strawberry cobbler and ricotta tart. Day in and out, there's the sumptuous aroma of baking, from baguettes to peanut butter chocolate-chip cookies. ◆ Daily 7AM-9PM late May–early Sept. 14 Truro Center Rd (at Castle Rd), Truro Center. 349.1616 &

38 The Blacksmith Shop ★★$$$ A local favorite (actually, it's the only restaurant "downtown"), this unassuming spot exhibits surprising charm; the interior is decorated with dollhouses and a folk-art rocking horse. The kitchen offers homey dishes like shepherd's pie, as well as fancier fare like roast duck with apricot, Amaretto, and almond sauce. The house specialty is haddock broiled in sour cream. ◆ International ◆ Daily dinner late May–early Sept; Th-Sa dinner early Sept–late May. 17 Truro Center Rd (between Hwy 6 and Town Hall Rd), Truro Center. 349.6554 &

39 Truro Center for the Arts at Castle Hill This converted 1880s horse barn (the windmill, once used to draw water for the animals, now houses administrative offices) is a hotbed of artistic activity all summer long, attracting distinguished instructors. For example, Penelope Jencks teaches figurative sculpture, Donald Beal teaches basic painting, and Daniel Mack leads a course in "Rustic Furnishings." In addition, Pamela Painter conducts fiction exercises based on her book *What If?*, Eleanor Munro teaches memoir writing, and Pulitzer Prize winner Alan Dugan leads an informal poetry group. In all, scores of absorbing classes, workshops, and lectures are offered for learners all ages. ◆ Office: daily July-Aug; closed September through June. 10 Meetinghouse Rd (at Castle Rd), Truro. 349.7511 &

40 Little America AYH-Hostel $ This beautifully bleak former Coast Guard station near Ballston Beach is straight out of an Edward Hopper painting. There are 42 beds, the ocean's a few hundred yards away, and the only major drawback—common to all American Youth Hostels—is a curfew (10:30PM). With such glorious countryside to explore, the 9:30AM-5PM lockout is really no problem at all. There is a well-equipped communal kitchen. ◆ Closed mid-September–mid-June. 111 N Pamet Rd (off S Pamet Rd), Truro. 349.3889

41 Truro Historical Museum The **Highland House,** a semi-decrepit turn-of-the-century inn, is the perfect home for the holdings of the Truro Historical Society, which run the gamut from a collection of shipwreck detritus (including a pirate's chest) to farming tools to old tourist postcards—and a whole lot more. The tiny rooms upstairs contain odd little period tableaux. ◆ Admission. Daily June-Oct. 6 Lighthouse Rd (off S Highland Rd), North Truro. 487.3397 &

41 Highland Links This public course is the oldest on the Cape (established in 1892), and with its straight-out-to-sea views, it's assured of maintaining its status as the most scenic. The nine holes skirt the bluffs like a restless sandpiper. ◆ Daily 7AM-7PM July-Aug; 7AM-5PM Apr-June, Sept-Oct. 10 Lighthouse Rd (off S Highland Rd), North Truro. 487.9201 &

To protect the productivity of the community's farms, unmarried Eastham men in 1695 had to kill six blackbirds or three crows before they were allowed to wed.

Thoreau made tallow for candles from bayberries in Truro by boiling a quart of the wild berries, then letting it cool. He then skimmed the tallow off the surface, melted it again and strained it. The broth smelled like a balm or herbal tea.

In his yearlong sojourn on the dunes of Eastham in the 1920s, Henry Beston, author of the classic *The Outermost House,* found a transcendental awareness thrust on him by the diurnal rhythms of the dunes: "In that hollow of space and brightness, in that ceaseless travail of wind and sand and ocean, the world one sees is still the world unharrassed of man, a place of the instancy and eternity of creation. . . ." He only meant to stay a fortnight but found himself lingering on: "As the year lengthened into autumn, the beauty and mystery of this earth and outer sea so possessed and held me that I could not go."

41 Highland Light The original—built in 1797 and powered by whale oil—was the first lighthouse on Cape Cod; during his celebrated travels, Henry David Thoreau boarded briefly at this 1853 replacement, capped by a 66-foot tower of whitewashed brick. The light was the last to be automated (in 1986) and remains the brightest beacon on the New England coast. When the light was built, it was 510 feet to the edge of the nearby cliff, but years of erosion pushed it back to 112 feet from the edge by 1995. For details on how the lighthouse was saved, see "Lighthouses: On the Move" on page 112. This working lighthouse is not open to the public.

The intriguing parapet visible to the south also received an eleventh-hour rescue; called the **Jenny Lind Tower**, it's part of Boston's old Fitchburg Railroad Depot. It was from this tower, in 1850, that the "Swedish nightingale" sang gratis for a mob of fans who'd been flimflammed by her overbooking promoter, P.T. Barnum. In 1927, when the station was slated for demolition, a Boston attorney moved it here for safekeeping. The tower is not open to the public (though plans for opening it have been bandied about), and it's surrounded by profuse poison ivy that helps reinforce its privacy. ♦ At the end of Lighthouse Rd (off S Highland Rd), North Truro.

 **ATLANTIC SPICE CO.**

42 Atlantic Spice Company This 25,000-square-foot building, a former boat shop, offers one-stop shopping for herbal preparations and fresh spices, from esoteric teas and fragrant oils to multi-colored peppercorns and rosebud pomanders. Although it's primarily a wholesale business, amateur chefs, herbalists, and hobbyists are welcome, and there's a wide array of normal-sized spice jars for those who have no need of, say, a pound of high-quality paprika, fiery cayenne, or minced garlic. Don't go there for the atmosphere but if you're interested, you're sure to come away with something you couldn't resist. ♦ M-F; Sa 10AM-2PM. Rte 6A (at Hwy 6), North Truro. 487.6100, 800/316.7965 &

The sea was an unwitting abettor in the War of Independence. Occasional small skirmishes broke out along Cape Cod's coast, but the most vivid action at sea occurred in November 1778, when the British man-of-war *Somerset* struck some shoals off North Truro and sank. The 480 survivors who washed ashore were promptly captured and marched to Boston.

 **SOUTH HOLLOW VINEYARDS**

43 South Hollow Vineyards $$ Oenophiles are in for a treat at this five-acre, five-bedroom 1836 Federal farmstead bed-and-breakfast. Innkeepers Kathy Gregrow and Judy Wimer, both horticulturalists, have launched the first winegrape vineyard on the Cape, and the striking decor reflects their passion. The common room is almost monastic, with wide, pine floorboards and massive beams. The rooms feature four-posters and sumptuous wine-dark decor, in shades ranging from Chardonnay to Cabernet (both of these varieties grow on the grounds). All but dwarfing the house is a massive 1830s mulberry tree, a carryover from another ambitious enterprise (silkworm farming), which unfortunately didn't take. Even given the finicky ways of the vineyard, this one seems an excellent bet. From May through September, breakfasts could include fresh fruit, French toast with Grand Marnier and homemade maple syrup, or tomato basil frittata. ♦ 11 Shore Rd (between Hwy 6 and Highland Rd), North Truro. 487.6200; fax 487.4248

44 Susan Baker Memorial Museum Cross *Mad* magazine with *Ms.* and you may have an inkling of what to expect at this gallery/store, run by the very much alive Susan Baker. The name, Ms. Baker explains, came about "because I always wanted my own museum and I figured I'd be dead before I got it." It's a good thing she didn't wait, because her graphic output is timely and interesting, if occasionally abrasive. One of her self-published travel books is titled *Fat Family in a Fiat*. The shop offers works from the estate of Provincetown's Mary Hackett, a self-taught artist. There are two other main strains in the inventory: colorful folk-art papier-mâché objects, from wall clocks to mermaids, and her latest craze, engagingly primitive landscapes, which she paints in her car at odd hours. Both the shop and its driving force are true Cape originals. Or, as Baker puts it in her Xeroxed catalog, "You couldn't get away with the place in Connecticut." ♦ Daily 11AM-6PM June-Aug; call for off-season hours. 46 Shore Rd (between Hwy 6 and Pond St), North Truro. 487.2557. Also at: 379A Commercial St (between MacMillan Wharf and Pearl St), Provincetown. 487.1063

45 Terra Luna ★★$$ This modest pine-paneled space has breakfasts fit for champions. You may start your day right with such exotica as a breakfast burrito (scrambled eggs wrapped in a whole-wheat tortilla, or South American pancakes (topped with bananas and sprayed with a thin chocolate syrup). An array of *nuova cucina* pizzas and pastas fill out the dinner menu, along with fish, chicken, steak, and—at the lighter end of the cholesterol spectrum—tofu strudel. ♦ New American/Italian ♦ Daily breakfast and dinner late May–mid-Oct. 104 Shore Rd (between Hwy 6 and Pond St), North Truro. 487.1019 ♿

46 Pilgrim Heights This easy-to-moderate hiking loop, part of the **Cape Cod National Seashore,** links two three-quarter-mile trails. The **Pilgrim Spring Trail** leads to where the newcomers found their first fresh water (wrote a witness: "We . . . sat us downe and drunke our first New England water with as much delight as ever we drunke drinke in all our lives"). The **Small Swamp Trail** is named not for its size but for farmer Thomas Small, who grew corn and asparagus here, and planted apple and plum trees, starting in 1860. So fruitless were the latter efforts, though, that the farm was left unclaimed after his death in 1922. ♦ Daily dawn-dusk. Off Hwy 6 (between Head of the Meadow and High Head Rds), North Truro. 349.3785

47 Outer Reach Motel $$ The bay views from atop the dunes are spectacular, but this 59-room complex is such a blight on the landscape that it's hard not to feel exploitative enjoying it. The rooms are nothing special, but a very good deal for the price. Guests have access to the facilities (pool, beach, and, most precious of all, parking) at the **Provincetown Inn,** a huge, sprawling resort that makes this barracks-like place look almost dainty. ♦ Closed mid-October–late May. 535 Hwy 6 (between Head of the Meadow and High Head Rds), North Truro. 487.9090, 800/942.5388; fax 942.5388

Within the Outer Reach Motel:

Adrian's ★★★$$ Independently operated by Adrian and Annette Salcedo Cyr, this restaurant shares vistas with the **Outer Reach,** but brought its own ambience along when it made the move in 1993 from less visible Route 6A. The motif is mellow house party, with jazz wafting through the barnlike space, potted herbs on the tables, and Peroni Italian beer to take the edge off. The various antipasti, *insalate* (salads), and pasta are inviting, but it's hard to hold off on the wood-fire pizza, in such irresistible renditions as "Greco" (with lamb and feta) or layered potatoes and pesto. Another unbeatable combo is *scampi e carciofi* (shrimp and artichokes) on a crunchy cornmeal crust. Breakfasts are just as adventurous, ranging from the delicate cranberry pancakes with orange butter to the robust frittata with zucchini, provolone, and romano. ♦ Italian/Takeout ♦ Daily breakfast and dinner July-Aug; W-Su breakfast and dinner mid-May–June, Sept–mid-Oct. 487.4360 ♿

48 Kalmar Village $$ Standing out from the boxy cottages that line the bay, these attractive, white-shingled, black-shuttered cottages are set amid green lawns along a 400-foot stretch of private beach. This oasis has been in Don Prelack's family since the early 1940s. You will find kids striking up friendships around the pool, relaxed parents tending the hibachi at dusk, and tuck-ins in the pine-paneled bedrooms promising more sun, sand, and salt tomorrow. Cottages go for the week in July and August, but if you book far ahead, you might be able to secure an efficiency or motel room (there are 42 units). This is not a place to get away from it all, but parents who appreciate plentiful playmates for the kids will find it congenial. Restaurants are a five-minute drive away. ♦ Closed mid-October–mid-May. 674 Shore Rd (between Knowles Heights Rd and Roosevelt Ave), North Truro. 487.0585; fax 487.0585

"The man who ventures a trip on a trawler," wrote George H. Proctor in *The Fisheries and Fishery Industries of the United States* (1887), "finds . . . little of romance. He must rise early and work late in order to visit his trawls, remove his fish, rebait and reset the lines, and take care of the day's catch. A moment of carelessness or inattention, or a slight miscalculation may cost him his life. And at any time fog could leave him afloat in a measureless void."

A single aquifer underlies the entire Cape, serving as its only source of drinking water.

Provincetown

In every sense, Provincetown is as far out as the Cape gets. Here the prim shingled cottages and sedate New England greens one associates with the traditional Cape have been transformed into an entirely different style, with carnival overtones. Surrounded by peaceful dunes under the protectorate of the **Cape Cod National Seashore**, this long, narrow, harbor-hugging port at the tip of the Cape is a three-mile stretch of lively restaurants, galleries, and shops. In summer the population swells tenfold, from about 4,000 to over 40,000, and it may seem that every last visitor is strolling **Commercial Street** from daybreak until sometime after midnight.

This onetime outpost of civilization abounds in historical significance. It is, after all, the spot where, in 1620, the Pilgrims first set foot in the New World—even if they soon moved on in search of more arable land. But the town's venerable roots have been all but obscured by the showy growth of tourism since the turn of the century. Presidents Theodore Roosevelt and William Howard Taft put this remote fishing village on the map in the early 1900s, when they sailed in to bless first the cornerstone, then the completion of the **Pilgrim Monument**. Curiosity-seekers soon followed, including, in the century's early decades, the Greenwich Village intelligentsia, who established an artistic enclave here. These writers and artists were favorably impressed not only by the low rents and cheap food (all that fish!), but by the town's seeming tolerance of nonconformity—a trait successive waves of gay and lesbian tourists have treasured as well.

Of course, friction does arise from time to time among the town's diverse factions—the Portuguese fishing families whose traditional ways go back to the whaling days, the artists, the gay and lesbian community, and—last but not least—the garden-variety tourists who flock to the tip of the Cape every

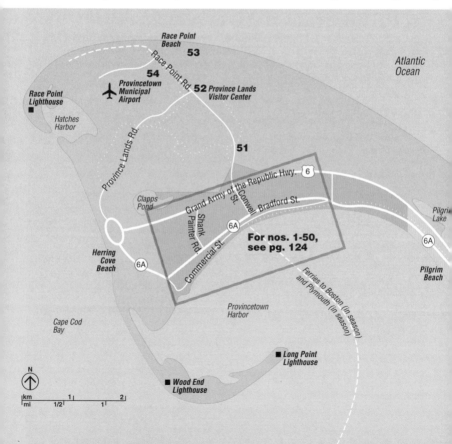

summer. Nevertheless the town enjoys a wonderfully liberating spirit overall. It's easy to see how the different elements of Provincetown society draw energy and inspiration from one another, and why, for many residents and repeat visitors, no other place quite compares.

Watermark Inn

1 Watermark Inn $$$ Harvard-educated architect **Kevin Shea** is responsible for the clean lines that characterize this light-filled contemporary inn in the quiet East End. And his wife and partner, graphic designer Judy Richland, deserves credit for the decor—bold splashes of color against whitewashed walls and sea-blue views. Ten suites, featuring (variously) sleeping lofts, mini-kitchens, fireplaces, and private decks, make the most of the hotel's little stretch of beach. While the aesthetics are perfect, the ambience is casual, and time spent here is relaxing. ♦ 603 Commercial St (a quarter mile west of Rte 6A). 487.0165, 800/734.0165

2 Provincetown Tennis Club This cluster of seven courts (five clay, two rubberized asphalt) looks so private, passersby would never suspect that they're welcome—but they are. Native players swear these are the best courts in the area; there's a pro if your backhand needs improving. ♦ Daily 8AM-7PM mid-May–mid-Oct. 286 Bradford St (between Thistlemore Rd and Duncan La). 487.9574 &

Within the Provincetown Tennis Club:

DNA Gallery The acronym stands for "definitive new art," and if it happens to suggest a certain life force as well, that's part of the symbolism. Among the exhibitors gathered here by owner/artist Nick Lawrence is notorious Provincetown local Jay Critchley, a conceptual artist who once fashioned a Statue of Liberty out of washed-up tampon applicators to protest ocean pollution, and parked a "sand car"—completely covered with sand, including the figures of two tourists clutching a sand-covered map—outside the Chamber of Commerce office on mobbed Macmillan Wharf. (It became a tourist attraction in its own right.) Other artists include native-born Conrad Malicoat, who makes intriguing Moebius-like metal sculptures, and premier Cape photographer Joel Meyerowitz. Lawrence himself grew up in the world of Boston publishing (his parents, Merloyd Lawrence and the late Sam Lawrence, shepherded some of the outstanding talents of the late 20th century), and the writers he draws for readings are usually of great interest. Other special events include films,

music, and performance art—all worth checking out when you're in town. ♦ Daily noon-8PM late May–mid-Oct. 487.7700

3 Windamar House $$ This grand 1840s guest house is peaceful and cheery. It contains six guest rooms and two apartments. The standout room is **The Studio,** with a cathedral ceiling and a glass wall overlooking the spacious garden. There's a common room conveniently equipped with TV, VCR, refrigerator, and microwave. A continental breakfast of fresh muffins and loaves is served. ♦ 568 Commercial St (between Conway St and Kendall La). 487.0599; fax 487.7505

4 Pucci's ★$$ A casual eatery right on the water, this place features good food, and best of all, customer parking. Chef and owner Mary Pucci serves such well-presented, simple fare as sandwiches, burgers, salads, and the usual local seafood dishes. Come for weekend brunch and try one of the omelettes. ♦ American ♦ Daily lunch and dinner mid-Apr–mid-Oct. 539 Commercial St (between Kendall La and Hancock St). 487.1964

5 White Horse Inn $ Frank Schaefer bought this rambling late–18th-century captain's house in 1963 and set about transforming it with the help of his artist friends. Their work not only adorns the walls but also informs the architecture; the six studios are artful assemblages of salvaged materials, including stained-glass windows said to have come from Eugene O'Neill's cottage. The 12 guest rooms are a bit plainer, with hooked rugs and heavily daubed plaster (a necessary measure when the house's original horsehair walls gave out); but Schaefer has equitably distributed his extensive art collection, so you're assured of something interesting to look at. ♦ 500 Commercial St (at Howland St). 487.1790

6 Rising Tide Gallery Downstairs from the **Long Point Gallery** (they share a rehabbed 1844 schoolhouse), this 18-artist co-op features emerging and mid-career artists— among them Elspeth Halvorsen, with her box constructions, and Sidney Hurwitz, known for his pastels. Members have a solo show every other year, and the season starts and ends with a group sampling. ♦ Daily noon-5PM, 8-

10PM mid-June–mid-Sept. 494 Commercial St (at Howland St). 487.4037

6 Long Point Gallery In light of its long association with such figures as Robert Motherwell and Paul Resika, this gallery is among Provincetown's most prestigious. Founded in 1977, it's one of the town's oldest co-ops. Shows may pair a painter with a sculptor, and a *Summer's Work* exhibit at the end of the season lets you see what everyone's been up to. Keep an eye out for Gilbert Franklin's faceless bronze figures, eloquent in pose and posture, and for new inductees like abstract sculptor Dimitri Hadzi and painter Michael Mazur. ♦ Daily 11AM-3PM, 8-10PM mid-June–mid-Sept. 492 Commercial St (at Howland St). 487.1795

7 Berta Walker Galleries This space, though off the beaten path on Provincetown's "back" street, is far from quiet. Walker has assembled an impressive collection of works appealing to varied tastes—from landscapes by Paul Resika to concrete and glass sculpture by the younger, up-and-coming Tom O'Connell, and the wonderful chrome animals of John Kearney. ♦ Daily 11AM-4PM, 8-10PM late

May–late Oct. 208 Bradford St (between Howland and Bangs Sts). 487.6411 &

8 Asheton House $$ A circa 1840 captain's residence fronted by a white Nantucket fence, this guest house has only three rooms, but they're good ones. The **Captain's Room,** with a four-poster bed and Queen Anne armchairs, looks out on an English garden and the **Pilgrim Monument;** the **Suite,** furnished with French antiques, boasts a dressing room, fireplace, and bay view; and the **Safari Room** features an assortment of bamboo and wicker. This is about as close as you can get to downtown without sacrificing peace and quiet. ♦ 3 Cook St (between Commercial St and Rte 6A). 487.9966

9 Provincetown Art Association & Museum (PAAM) Founded in 1914 by a handful of established artists and the local bank president, this organization continues to uphold its stated mission: "to promote education of the public in the arts, and social intercourse between artists and laymen." A notable benefit of its longevity is the extensive collection of works created in the region. Charles Hawthorne and four other co-founders brought in a painting apiece at the outset, and since then an impressive body of work has accrued from a Who's Who of 20th-century artists who've stopped off in Provincetown. The collection now stands at over 1,700 pieces. Some of the older works have lost their luster—hence the museum's innovative

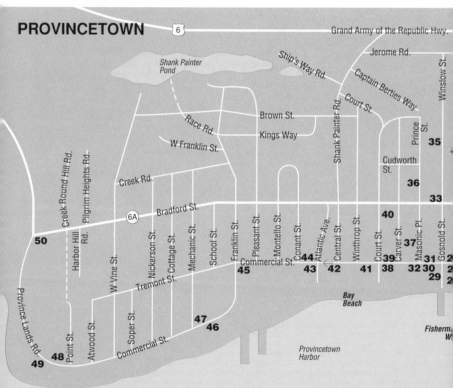

"Adopt a Painting" program, in which patrons select a favorite piece and underwrite its restoration. The juried shows of members' works usually include major names (with price tags to match), as well as fledgling artists amenable to patronage. Schoolchildren are also brought into the act; several winter shows consist of their picks from the permanent collection. A year-round array of classes (including dance and yoga), lectures, readings, and concerts rounds out the outreach program. ◆ Admission. Daily noon-5PM, 7-10PM late May–early Sept; call for off-season hours. 460 Commercial St (between Cook and Bangs Sts). 487.1750 ₺

10 The Dancing Lobster Cafe/Trattoria ★★★$$$ Formerly on Fisherman's Wharf, this popular restaurant is now located at the site of the former **Flagship** restaurant on recently renovated Flagship Wharf. The dory bar stays, but the dining room now has a Venetian decor, highlighted with tapestries and mirrors. Some of the restaurant's signature dishes include: mussel and saffron cream soup, crab-and-Cognac ravioli, and Sicilian *zuppa di pesce con el cucasu* (assorted seafood in a spicy broth with couscous). With superb cuisine, decent prices, and a spacious dining area, this is the place to go. ◆ Mediterranean ◆ Tu-Su dinner Apr-Oct. 463 Commercial St (opposite Bangs St). 487.0900 ₺

11 Cortland Jessup Gallery Genial gallery owner Cortland Jessup likes to mix it up; featured items have included Mary Rhinelander's manipulations of Elsa Dorfman's oversize Polaroid portraits, and Alan Petrulis's black-and-white etchings of Cape landscapes. Between the Saturday salons and Friday evening opening receptions, there's always something interesting going on. ◆ Daily 11AM-11PM, late May–early Sept; call for off-season hours; closed January–late May. 432 Commercial St (at Kiley Ct). 487.4479

TIFFANY LAMP STUDIO

REPRODUCTIONS   RESTORATIONS

11 Tiffany Lamp Studio In a small atelier on a tree-shaded alley, Stephen Donnelly pieces together Tiffany lamps—both authentic models and his own adaptations, some fetching as much as $5,000. Certainly not to be confused with cheap reproductions, these are singularly beautiful objects, and it's fascinating to see patterns emerge from vivid chunks of glass. ◆ Daily 9AM-10PM July-Sept; call for off-season hours. 432 Commercial St (at Kiley Ct). 487.1101

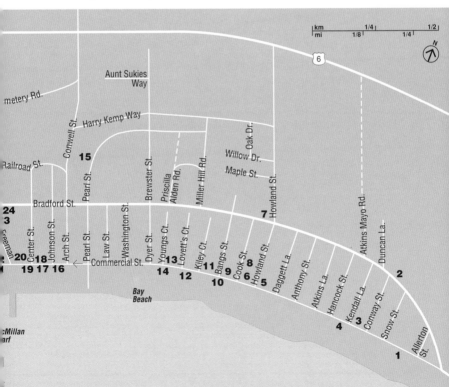

Cape Cod National Seashore

John F. Kennedy is remembered for many things, but those who admire vistas of unspoiled heathlands and scrub forests, sand dunes and wave-wracked beaches, consider the creation of the **Cape Cod National Seashore (CCNS)** in 1961 to be one of his greatest achievements. It encompasses 27,700 acres of federally protected land. New homes cannot be built within the Cape Cod National Seashore's boundaries, but those already standing when it was formed were allowed to remain.

Some of the first conservation laws in America were written to preserve headlands around **Provincetown** harbor. In 1670, only 50 years after the Pilgrims' first landing, the General Court of Plimoth County passed laws protecting the forests and beaches of The Province Lands. Colonists needing wood for building houses, boats, and saltworks had cut down many trees that had stabilized the sand dunes.

Difficult to enforce from across **Plymouth Bay,** the 1670 law was ineffective. By the 1790s, many Provincetown families were forced to move their homes to prevent them from being buried under shifting sands. Federal funds were made available in 1826 for beach grass planting. By the late 1800s, conservation efforts extended to planting evergreen trees and Scotch broom, building breakwaters and

jetties, and laying foundations for roads. By the 1930s, 1,200 acres near Provincetown had been reforested, and today beach grass planting continues over acres of dunes.

The quickest way to observe conservation efforts in today's **CCNS** is by taking one of **Art's Dune Tours** (487.1950), which depart from the center of Provincetown. As Art rises over the first series of the highest dunes, he'll point out waving fields of beach grass plantings. These "no go" areas are cordoned off to prevent more beach houses from being buried under mounds of sand.

Once you have a general lay of the land from Art's tour, rent a bike at one of several bike shops in Provincetown and explore on your own. There are seven miles of **Province Lands Trails** through the high dunes rising behind Provincetown. Try the **Race Point Beach Spur** that goes out in well-paved access to the **Ranger Station;** then return on **Herring Cove Spur** for the ascent of steeply rising dunes at **Snake Hills**. Visitors have been seen walking bikes uphill along this section. That's all right—the views are so stunning it would be a shame to keep peddling. From the highest peak, the **Pilgrim Monument** can be seen towering over pine forests.

12 William-Scott Gallery One of the newer additions to the Cape Cod scene, this gallery made an immediate impression with David Tomb's large gestural drawings. Others represented include popular landscape artist John Dowd, as well as Matthew Snow, whose "Stilt Walkers in Town" is a striking, eerie portrait of Provincetown at play. ♦ Daily 11AM–11PM July-Sept; call for off-season hours; closed November–late May. 439 Commercial St (between Kiley and Lovett's Cts). 487.4040 ♿

Driving into Provincetown on Highway 6, you pass Pilgrim Lake on the right. This magnificent stretch of water, with its backdrop of sand dunes, was actually joined to Provincetown Harbor in the 19th century and called East Harbor. Blowing sands and shifting tides finally silted up the mouth of the harbor and formed today's lake.

12 The Mews ★★★$$$

Step down to an understated, sand-hued restaurant that blends effortlessly into the beach. The menu includes some definite winners, such as blackened scallops with tequila lime butter. Elegant yet utterly relaxed, this is the perfect spot from which to watch night descend over the harbor. ♦ International ♦ Daily lunch and dinner mid-June–mid-Sept; call for off-season hours; closed mid-December–January. Reservations recommended. 429 Commercial St (between Kiley and Lovett's Cts). 487.1500 ♿

Upstairs from The Mews:

Café Mews ★★$$ Step upstairs from **The Mews** into a sea-blue, window-walled space decorated with masses of carved mahogany, where the pace is a bit brisker. But it's the same kitchen turning out the same salads and appetizers, plus pasta and pizza, gorgonzola or garden burgers, and assorted "plates," geared to any appetite. In the evening a jazz pianist provides music, and on Monday nights in the winter the place becomes a community coffeehouse. ♦ International ♦ Donation requested for coffeehouse. Daily brunch and dinner June-Sept; M-F dinner, Sa-Su brunch and dinner Oct-Thanksgiving; Su brunch mid-Feb–May; call for hours Thanksgiving–mid-February. 487.1500 ♿

AlbertMerola
gallery

13 Albert Merola Gallery A fascinating output of art is showcased here—from primitive face platters by established enfant terrible Todd McKie to the weighty, almost sculptural still lifes of local painter Richard Baker. The season is fairly short, but very intense. ♦ Daily 11AM-5PM, 7-11PM late May–mid-Oct. 424 Commercial St (between Lovett's and Youngs Cts). 487.4424

14 The Ironmongers Owner Leona Rust Egan, author of *Provincetown as a Stage*—a fascinating account of the intellectual ferment of the colony's teens and twenties—has amassed an extraordinary collection of first editions of Cape-related books. Besides these collectors' items you'll also find some "smalls" (antique dealer talk for little stuff) and vintage jewelry in this tiny shop. ♦ By chance or appointment Apr-Dec. 419 Commercial St (opposite Youngs Ct). 487.3365

14 Giardelli/Antonelli Studio Showroom Studio Showroom local designer Jerry Giardelli makes dramatic, sculptural clothing for women, with fabrics that change in response to the season: a rainbow of dolman-sleeved cotton jersey shirts, for instance, might give way to styles in sueded rayon for the fall. Diana Antonelli contributes the stylish silver jewelry. ♦ Daily 11AM-6PM, 8-10PM late May–early Sept; daily 11AM-6PM early Sept–Dec; Sa-Su 11AM-6PM Jan–late May. 417 Commercial St (opposite Youngs Ct). 487.3016 ♿

15 Fine Arts Work Center (FAWC) Housed in the former **Day's Lumber Yard,** a source of patron-subsidized lodging for artists since early in the century, this fellowship program hosts 10 writers and as many visual artists from fall through spring—a period long enough for them to forge strong bonds among themselves and with the community. That's what the founders (including influential figures like Robert Motherwell and Stanley Kunitz) had in mind when they initiated the program in 1968; they wanted their artistic successors to be inspired and supported by Provincetown as they had been. In addition, the **FAWC** sponsors seminars, workshops, exhibits, and readings year-round. There's also a program of summer workshops—both weeklong and weekend—in creative writing and the visual arts. ♦ Call for schedule. 24 Pearl St (between Rte 6A and Brewster St). 487.9960 ♿

SILK & FEATHERS

16 Silk & Feathers "Gourmet lingerie" describes this shop's collection of upscale underwear, some of it on the demure side of kinky. Floaty clothing, hats, and accessories round out the look, which is not strictly limited to the boudoir. ♦ Daily 10AM-11PM Apr-Sept; daily noon-6PM Oct-Mar. 377 Commercial St (between Arch and Johnson Sts). 487.2057 ♿

16 Pepe's Wharf ★★★★$$$$ This restaurant has a Mediterranean ambience, and with its waiters dressed in naval white, its blue-and-white awning, and its wide-open view of the bay, it gives many patrons the feeling of being on a cruise ship. The classically inclined chef, Astrid Berg (a graduate of the Culinary Institute of America), grew up in the place; her parents turned what was originally a run-down trap shed into a sandwich shop in 1967. Berg's own aspirations aim considerably higher, and there is an unmistakable elegance to her preparations, such as bouillabaisse au Pernod and grilled swordfish steak au poivre. For adventurous modern palates, much of the well-prepared fare may at first seem a bit tame—but it will perfectly suit anyone tired of trendiness. In summer the Top Deck offers light bites and a raw bar with a sweeping view. ♦ International ♦ Daily lunch and dinner July-Aug; call for off-season hours; closed mid-October–late May. 371-373 Commercial St (between Arch and Johnson Sts). 487.0670 ♿

The Provincetown Public Library, with its unique Second Empire–style architecture, was built by Nathan Freeman in 1873. Freeman had one stipulation: If the property was not used as a library, it would revert back to his heirs. The library sits close to the sidewalk at 330 Commercial Street.

Restaurants/Clubs: Red   Hotels: Blue
Shops/🍴 Outdoors: Green   Sights/Culture: Black

16 Halcyon Gallery This roundup of hand-crafted women's clothing and adornments melds practicality with fun at agreeable prices. Among the nicer items are Cynthia Krause's chenille tunics in graded hues, and Maralyce Ferree's fleece parkas and nylon raincoats. ♦ Daily 10AM-11PM mid-May–mid-Sept; Sa-Su noon-6PM mid-Sept–mid-May. 371 Commercial St (between Arch and Johnson Sts). 487.9415 ♿

17 Northern Lights Hammock Shop Every conceivable kind of suspended seating is available here, from cozy Mexican slings to a cypress-wood stand that resembles an abbreviated boat. Best of all, the staff encourages you to sample the wares. ♦ Daily 11AM-11PM June-Aug; 10AM-8PM May, Sept-Oct. 361 Commercial St (between Johnson and Center Sts). 487.2385 ♿

17 Small Pleasures After a quarter century of handling estate jewelry, Virginia McKenna doesn't have to shop around; the top dealers (many from England) come to her. Her stock is particularly strong on furnishings for gentlemen, but women are well served, too, with exquisite Victorian emeralds and opals, along with intricate clusters of garnets. ♦ Daily 11AM-11PM mid-May–Oct; call for off-season hours. 359 Commercial St (between Johnson and Center Sts). 487.3712 ♿

18 Mad as a Hatter Enhance your fantasy life with one of these instant identities. The stock ranges from velvet cloches to straw boaters and leather caps, with some fantastic creations that defy categorization. There's an in-depth selection of hats, some with feathers, and there are assorted jackets, vests, and shirts to go with the hat of your choice. ♦ Daily 10AM-11PM late June–Aug; Sa-Su Sept–late June. 360 Commercial St (between Johnson and Center Sts). 487.4063 ♿

18 Provincetown Heritage Museum Established by the community in 1976 and housed in a former church, this museum is a marvelous mix of eclectic elements. Dominating the collection is a half-scale model of the fishing schooner *Rose Dorothea*, which rises from the second floor right up into the rafters. The ground floor is given over to various period rooms inhabited by "lifelike" wax figures; the effect is somewhat hokey. One of the main reasons to visit is to see the artworks documenting the changing face of Provincetown. Here the homespun quality of the galleries detracts not in the least from the sprinkling of gems, among them a semi-abstract study of Truro's Back Beach by Edw Dickinson. ♦ Admission. Daily mid-June–mi Oct. 356 Commercial St (at Center St). 487.7098 ♿

19 Moda Fina Euro-rock wafts through the racks of au courant clothes, including linen skimmers and Sam & Libby footwear. The sunglasses selection is the best in town. ♦ M-F, Su 10AM-11PM; Sa 10AM-midnight late May–early Sept. Daily 10AM-8PM early Sept–Jan, Apr–late May. 349 Commercial S (between Center and Freeman Sts). 487.6632

19 East End Gallery Over the past decade, Bunny Pearlman's astute selections have made this a formidable gallery. Her front-runners include the team of Richard Selesnic and Nicholas Kahn who use a fresco technique to paint portraits. Also look for the work of Thomas Vinton, who paints on plywood with acrylics. Definitely worth a stop. ♦ Daily 11AM-11PM July-Aug; call for off-season hours; closed late November–mid-April. 349 Commercial St (between Center and Freeman Sts). 487.4745

20 Clem & Joe's If you're not in the mood (or financial bracket) for sit-down and would rather picnic by the wharf, try a slab of succulent barbecued ribs from this cheerful, efficient take-out joint. They've also got rotisserie chicken, as well as potpies, and tasty side dishes like corn bread and baked beans. Pick out a home-baked cake, pie, or pudding while you're at it. ♦ Daily noon-9PM May-Sept; call for off-season hours. 338 Commercial St (between Center and Freeman Sts). 487.8303

21 Cafe Edwige Restaurant/Gallery ★★★ $$$ Mornings, this cathedral-ceilinged space serves a bountiful, natural-foods breakfast: fresh orange juice, homemade granola, omelettes, pancakes, fritattas—the works, including broiled flounder and eggs. In the evening, tiny lights twinkle on the deck, and Art Deco lamps cast a romantic glow indoors. Chef Steve Frappolli's menu melds comfort with chic, in such dishes as grilled spring chicken marinated in virgin olive oil and herbs with porcini mashed potatoes. Here is one of the few places along this stretch of the strip where you can duck the tourist hordes—a fact not lost on the locals, so expect a wait. ♦ International ♦ Daily breakfast and dinner July-Aug; call for off-season schedule; closed late October–March. 333 Commercial St (just east of MacMillan Wharf). 487.2008

21 Lobster Pot ★★$$$ It may look a little corny, and you have to file in past the kitchen—after a long wait in line—but you'll know you've made a good choice once the seafood appears. Lobster is the main event—whether boiled, broiled, baked-stuffed, pan-roasted, scampi-style, or Alfredo. Keep an open mind, though, and consider alternatives such as blackened tuna sashimi or one of six different bouillabaisse-type fish stews. ♦ Daily lunch and dinner Feb-Dec. 321 Commercial St (just east of MacMillan Wharf). 487.0842 &

22 Café Blasé ★★$$ People watching is the main reason to frequent this highly visible cafe, a festive convocation of tasseled umbrellas and giant Japanese lanterns at the epicenter of the shopping/shmoozing quarter. The prices are gauged just right for grazing, and among the more inviting delectables are Terrine Oceanus (a shrimp pâté with roasted red pepper sauce) and a classic *salade niçoise*. Sandwiches, pizzas, quiches, quesadillas, and more fill out the bill. But you might just want to sip an arcane Italian aperitif, or perhaps a "Post-Modern Marguerita" (it's purple). ♦ International ♦ Daily breakfast, lunch, and dinner late May–mid-Sept. 328 Commercial St (between Freeman and Standish Sts). 487.9465 &

22 Governor Bradford This beer-steeped old bar has made no concessions to the yuppie crowd. Year-rounders play chess in the window tables, and blues-lovers flock here for headliners like Luther "Guitar Jr." Johnson, Roomful of Blues, and the homegrown Provincetown Jug Band. ♦ Cover. Daily 11AM-1AM. 312 Commercial St (at Standish St). 487.9618 &

22 Art's Dune Tours To get a look at the humble dune shacks that sheltered such luminaries as Eugene O'Neill, Jack Kerouac, Tennessee Williams, and Jackson Pollock, hop a ride in a GMC Suburban with Art Costa, who has been covering this territory since 1946. These driftwood hovels may not look like much (the Park Service wanted to raze them as eyesores), but after years of crusading they've been granted National Historic Landmark status, solely for the quality of the tenants they attracted. You could actually join their illustrious company by becoming a member of the nonprofit **Peaked Hill Trust** (PO Box 1705, Provincetown 02657); rentals are arranged by lottery. You may never get a chance to rough it (no plumbing, no electricity) in so lovely a place. ♦ Fee. Apr-Oct. By reservation only. Commercial and Standish Sts. 487.1950 &

23 Napi's ★★$$$ For decades now, Napi and Helen Van Dereck's 1970s arts-and-crafts–style restaurant has served as a haven for artists and others burned out on the hurly-burly of Commercial Street; in fact, a lot of local talents were roped in for the construction, which involved salvage elements and outtakes from the Van Derecks' antiques business. The kitchen covers the world; scallops Alfredo is available alongside Chinese pot stickers or falafel. Home-baked whole wheat bread accompanies every meal, and the dessert of choice is Double Fudge Madness, a chocolate-glazed rum-custard cake. ♦ International ♦ Daily dinner May–mid-Oct; daily lunch and dinner mid-Oct–May. 7 Freeman St (at Standish St). 487.1145, 800/571.6274 &

24 Iguana Grill ★★$$ The "Latin home cooking" here is authentic Mexican, with strong Dominican influences. Definitely try the *pica pollo* appetizer (shredded chicken and turkey marinated with citrus and chilies). A plus for health-conscious diners, *pavo* (lean, ground turkey) replaces beef in all the traditional recipes, from enchiladas to mole—the third-generation recipe of Dona Lucy. Another standout entrée is *salmón de la isla* (broiled salmon in a spiced coconut sauce). It's a cheery dining spot, with many windows, potted plants set among the tables, and wood-paneled walls displaying mirrors and pictures. ♦ Mexican ♦ Th-Su brunch buffet and dinner July-Sept; daily dinner Oct-June. 135 Bradford St (at Standish St). 487.8800

According to a Provincetown law of 1773 against the picking of cranberries before the 20th of September, the person who reported the offender could keep all confiscated berries.

Above the Iguana Grill:

Lizard Lounge As farouche as the Iguana is homey, this funky bar features "video entertainment" and live drag shows such as Boyz R Us. Did you know Bonnie Raitt is now part of the repertoire? ♦ Cover. Call for schedule. 487.8800

24 Austin's ★★$$$ The interior of this dining spot is almost lugubriously plain, especially painted a dull butternut shade, but the menu tries to make up for it. Try such festive platters as a "cabaret" of appetizers (including smoked seafoods and baked oysters) or the bountiful, colorful mixed grill: tilapia with beach-plum butter, prawns with crab-apple butter, chicken breast with roasted red-pepper butter, and beef tenderloin with green-peppercorn butter. ♦ Californian ♦ Daily dinner July-Aug; call for off-season hours; closed November through March. 133 Bradford St (between Standish and Ryder Sts). 487.3304

25 Provincetown Portuguese Bakery This venerable bakery has been turning out savories and sweets since the turn of the century. In summer, the demand is so high that they bake around the clock. The meat pies and *linguica* sausage rolls are on the heavy, greasy side; you might opt for an unusual pastry, such as an orange-soaked *torta* (cake) or a plain, refreshing flan. ♦ Daily 7:30AM-11PM late June–early Sept; call for off-season hours; closed November through March. 299 Commercial St (between MacMillan Wharf and Ryder St Extension). 487.1803

25 Whale and Dolphin Information Center & Shop This educational/commercial operation is the outreach arm of the nonprofit **Center for Coastal Studies** (59 Commercial St, near Soper St, 487.3622; open year-round), which not only studies whales but also rescues cetaceans in trouble. It represents one-stop shopping for whale-lovers (or the merely curious), offering everything from souvenirs to serious tomes. The **CCS** is headed by noted marine biologist Dr. Charles "Stormy" Mayo, whose work inspired the whole whale watching mania. "It seems likely," he has written, "that the future of the seas and of the earth system as a whole will be assured only if we can win a race with technical development, and know our environment before the system, the whales, and we ourselves are overcome." The education programs mounted by the **CCS**—nature walks, lectures, and research publicly conducted aboard the *Dolphin Fleet,* which operates out of MacMillan Wharf (255.3857, 800/826.9300)—are a step in that direction. ♦ Center: daily 10AM-9PM July-Aug; call for off-season hours; closed November–mid-April. Whale watching: mid-April–October, several departures daily, weather permitting. 2 Ryder St Extension (at Commercial St). 487.6115 &

26 The Whydah Museum The geographic isolation of Provincetown turned it into a magnet for outcasts, rebels, and pirates in the 17th and 18th centuries. This museum, with treasure from the pirate ship *Whydah,* lost off Wellfleet in 1717, gives ample proof of the riches rogue sailors could acquire through force of arms. You can learn the history of the ship itself, or walk through quickly while waiting for a whale watching boat and see what "pieces of eight" really looked like. ♦ Admission. Daily 10AM-7PM June-Sept; 10AM-5PM Apr-May, Oct–mid-Dec. 16 MacMillan Wharf (off Commercial St). 487.7955 &

27 Mario's Mediterraneaneo on the Beach ★★★$$ If you're hungry for Mediterranean food, try this place; you won't believe the quantities piled on your plate. For a good variety, try the *Pikilia,* a Greek sampler platter of *humus tiropita* and *spanakopita* (filo-crusted hummus and spinach pies, respectively), dolmas (rice-stuffed grape leaves), feta, olives artichokes, meatballs, marinated vegetables— all nicely arrayed on a regular salad. Other generous salads, pizzas, pastas, sandwiches, affordable entrées, and international tapas fill out the menu, and there are deli cases filled with inviting desserts. The streetside portion of the restaurant is a cafe, and the light, airy "back room" is on the waterfront; both are understandably popular. ♦ International ♦ Daily 7AM-2AM late Apr–mid-Oct. 265 Commercial St (between Ryder St Extension and Gosnold St). 487.0002 &

28 Rambling Rose Carriage Company Christine Lorenz offers elegant horse-and-buggy jaunts through town at surprisingly reasonable rates. Afterward, you can reward your conveyor with a carrot. And if you've got kids looking for more equine adventures, take them out to Lorenz's picturesque **Bayberry Hollow Farm** (27 W Vine St Extension, west of 6A, 487.6584) for a rollicking pony ride. ♦ Fee. Daily 11AM-11PM June-Aug; daily 10AM-4PM May, Sept-Oct. Commercial and Ryder Sts. 487.4246

28 Provincetown Trolley, Inc. For a brief, nontaxing local history lesson, try this 40-minute tour that meanders past the **Monument,** out to the **Province Lands Visitor Center** in the dunes, and back into town via the East End. There are five spots where you can hop off and look around for a half-hour or more before reboarding, and thus avoid the hassle of maneuvering a car through Provincetown's congested, virtually unparkable streets. ♦ Fee. Daily every half-hour 10AM-4PM and hourly 5-7PM May-Oct. Commercial and Ryder Sts. 487.9483

28 Provincetown Town Hall Built in 1878, this grand old antique still serves its original function, while doubling as a 600-seat performance space. Up a massive horseshoe staircase, the auditorium has seen such headliners as Odetta, Shawn Colvin, and the Klezmer Conservatory Band perform under the Muse Series banner since 1982. En route, don't miss Ross Moffett's Neo-Classical WPA-era murals—farming women on the right, fishing men on the left. Wander the halls to turn up *Fish Cleaners,* a portrait by Provincetown's pioneer painter Charles Hawthorne, and many other intriguing works, such as Henry Hensche's *His Breakfast.* The lighting is woefully inadequate—possibly a boon for the aging artwork but a real detriment for viewers. ♦ Building: daily. Concerts: call for schedule. 260 Commercial St (at Ryder St). 487.7000; concerts 487.0955 &

28 Euro Island Grill and Cafe ★★$$$$ A thatch tiki bar plunked on a deck above teeming Commercial Street, this place does a convincing job of lulling you into an island frame of mind. Quaff a Red Stripe beer, or perhaps a "Mermaid's Passion" (fortified with Midori, vodka, and Amaretto), while enjoying your conch chowder, then move on to grilled fish in red-hot Caribbean mumbo sauce, or go the Sicilian route and order pasta or a thin-crusted pizza. ♦ Caribbean/Italian ♦ Daily lunch and dinner May-Nov. 258 Commercial St (between Ryder and Gosnold Sts). 487.2505 &

Within the Euro Island Grill and Cafe:

Club Euro A cavernous space that was once an 1843 Congregational Church now sports an oceanic dreamscape mural (complete with 3-D mermaid) and welcomes world-music bands on summer weekends. The schedule is sporadic, so check newspaper listings or call for an update. ♦ Cover. 487.2505

29 Julie Heller Gallery As a child, Julie Heller was entranced by the works of early Provincetown artists, and she started acquiring examples as soon as she could. Today, she offers groundbreaking works by Charles Hawthorne, Milton Avery, and the like, plus contemporary works that she feels continue the tradition. This fishing shack–turned-gallery contains museum-quality pieces as well as prints and photos priced right for start-up collectors. Especially noteworthy are the white-line lithographs of Blanche Lazzell, who pioneered the style. ♦ Daily 10AM-11PM June-Sept; call for off-season hours. 2 Gosnold St (off Commercial St). 487.2169 &

30 Marine Specialties Since 1961, this hangar-size space has offered an Army-Navy type rummage sale, with the displays—virtually indistinguishable from the heaps of goods—getting ever more convoluted and bizarre. You'll find everything from dried starfish and plastic lobsters to grungewear and camping equipment, with all sorts of odd lots thrown in. Hung from the rafters are some handsome and highly coveted ships' bells. ♦ Daily 10AM-midnight July-Aug; call for hours Sept-Dec, mid-Feb–June; Sa-Su noon-5PM Jan–mid-Feb. 235 Commercial St (between Gosnold and Court Sts). 487.1730 &

31 Universalist Meetinghouse This handsome 1851 Greek Revival edifice, found on the National Register of Historic Places, has near-mythic origins; it's said that, in 1820, *Mayflower* descendants Sylvia and Elizabeth Freeman came across a waterlogged book on a beach, entitled *The Life of the Rev. John Murray: Preacher of Universal Salvation.*

The salvaged tome was passed around the community, and developed a following. The meetinghouse is a repository for all the architectural and decorative glories of its day. Its mahogany-trimmed pine pews are graced with scrimshaw medallions, the chandelier comes from the Sandwich Glass factory, and the Holbrook tracker organ, installed in 1854, is the oldest instrument of its kind still in use on Cape Cod. The trompe l'oeil murals are the work of Swiss artist Carl Wendte (who in 1844 had dressed up Nantucket's **Unitarian Universalist Church** in a similar manner). While the meetinghouse is badly in need of repainting, the church has its hands full with commitments to the community, including an AIDS Ministry (Provincetown has the second-highest number of people with AIDS per capita in the United States), a soup kitchen, and various twelve-step programs. It also hosts seasonal events, such as a "Blessing of the Animals," and makes space available to cultural groups such as the Flirtations (a gay a cappella quintet) and the Salt & Pepper Gospel Singers (a racially mixed choir). ♦ Service: Su 11AM. 236 Commercial St (between Gosnold St and Masonic Pl). 487.9344 &

31 Front Street ★★★$$$ One of the first restaurants to spark the culinary awakening of the late 1970s, this is still a delightful place. Located in the brick-walled cellar of a Victorian mansion, a few steps down from street level, it can be a bit cramped and noisy. But the hubbub just adds to the sense of excitement generated by such dishes as leek and lobster bisque, raspberry balsamic grilled salmon with capered mashed potatoes, and a fabulous coffee toffee pie. Chef Donna Aliperti's menu changes weekly, and keeps improving year after year. If you want a glimpse of the "real" Provincetown, come here. ♦ New American ♦ Daily dinner June-Oct; M, W-Su dinner May, Nov-Dec. Reservations recommended. 230 Commercial St (between Gosnold St and Masonic Pl). 487.9715

32 Lorraine's ★★★$$ Chef-owner Lorraine Najar's Guadalajaran grandmother made tortillas on a Pasadena street corner and eventually opened a restaurant; Najar started helping out at the age of seven and now has her own dining spot. She embroiders on tradition to great effect in such dishes as *pecosos* (shrimp wrapped in fresh jalapeños, rolled in cornmeal, and garnished with cilantro lime *ajo,* or mashed garlic), and *enchilades carnitas* (pork tenderloin with cheese and a mole sauce in corn tortillas). The decor is Art Deco–ish, with booths lifted from the 1950s. ♦ Mexican ♦ Daily dinner mid-April–Oct; call for off-season hours; closed January through March. 229½ Commercial St (between Gosnold and Court Sts). 487.6074 &

32 Clifford-Williams Antiques Though the reception can be brusque at times, this is the only antiques shop in Provincetown that demands a serious once-over. It's packed with English pine and oak, porcelains, and works by Provincetown artists, such as the late Pulitzer Prize-winning *Life* photographer John Gregory. ♦ Daily 11AM-11PM. 225 Commercial St (between Gosnold and Court Sts). 487.4174

33 Fairbanks Inn $$ Bradford Street's bed-and-breakfasts tend to be slightly less expensive than those right on Commercial Street, and this 1776 captain's house is surprisingly affordable, especially given that it's one of Provincetown's oldest buildings. (The very oldest, the **Seth Nickerson House,** a 1746 full Cape at 72 Commercial Street, is a private home.) All the expected niceties are accounted for—broad planked floors, Oriental rugs, four-posters, and wood-burning fireplaces in 10 of the 13 rooms. Continental breakfast is served in the recently restored dining room in winter and on a wicker-filled porch overlooking a patio in summer. There's also private parking (a rarity in town). ♦ 90 Bradford St (at Webster Pl). 487.0386, 800/324.7265; fax 487.3540

33 6 Webster Place $$$ Tucked behind the **Fairbanks Inn,** this 10-bedroom bed-and-breakfast is even older (circa 1750); indoor plumbing wasn't introduced here until 1986. Today, guests can enjoy all the modern amenities, plus the peace of a paneled library and a country-style decor that's tastefully restrained. The breakfasts feature fresh muffins or homemade quiche. ♦ Off Rte 6A (between Winslow and Prince Sts). 487.2266, 800/932.7837; fax 487.2266

Edward Hopper's Cape Cod

You've seen the famous paintings by Edward Hopper of solitary men or women brooding in apartment rooms as they gaze out on blank shop fronts below: City life seems to be crushing the people with loneliness and alienation. But Hopper didn't spend all his time in New York City. He summered in **Truro,** returning to New York by the first of November every year until his death in 1967.

His Cape Cod paintings are also about contemplation and solitary figures, but the landscapes are country vistas rather than diners or drab apartments. Some of the places he painted are still there. Drive the back roads and you may find a few. Opposite the former Truro railroad station is the solitary house Hopper painted in *House by the Railroad*; its atmosphere so struck Alfred Hitchcock that he used it as a model for the foreboding house in the movie *Psycho*. The gas station Hopper used for his painting *Gas* is located on **Highway 6** in Truro, where he filled his own tanks. It's on the west side of the highway going to **Provincetown.** Look for the only gas station on Highway 6 with 250 cords of wood stacked around it. (The station's owners have a side business selling wood.) Then imagine a man standing at a gas pump with an ominous backdrop of Cape Cod pine forest and you have the Hopper painting in real life right in front of you.

---

34 Pilgrim Monument & Provincetown Museum
The Pilgrims may have slighted Provincetown by moving on to greener pastures in Plymouth, but the Cape Cod Pilgrim Memorial Association, a civic group founded in 1892, was determined to remember them. Hence this 253-foot-high Neo-Renaissance memorial. Modeled after the Torre del Mangia in Siena, Italy, it's the tallest granite structure in America. A flight of 116 steps leads to the gargoyle-guarded heights, where on a clear day it's possible to scan all of the Cape's curving

Pilgrim Monument & Provincetown Museum

"arm" and even make out the Boston skyline 42 miles away. The museum, added in 1962, is a fascinating catch-all collection of maritime artifacts and artistic mementos, from a polar bear captured by Admiral Donald MacMillan to programs and photos from some of Eugene O'Neill's early plays. Give it at least an hour, leaving perhaps another half-hour (depending on your fitness level) to climb the gradual but seemingly endless steps. ♦ Admission. Daily 9AM-7PM July–early Sept; daily Apr-June, early Sept–Nov. High Pole Hill Rd (off Winslow St, between Rte 6A and Jerome Rd). 487.1310, 800/247.1620

35 Outermost Hostel $ The starving artists of O'Neill's day would be happy to find an honorable tradition upheld. This privately operated hostel offers 30 bunk beds in five cabins (one with a kitchen) at a rock-bottom price. Conditions may remind you of a documentary on the plight of migrant workers, but Provincetown still beckons outside. ♦ Closed November through late May. Registration: daily 8-9AM, 6-9:30PM at 30A Winslow St. 28 Winslow St (between Rte 6A and Jerome Rd). No phone

36 The Piaf $$ With only three guest rooms—four if you count a tiny dormer room entirely done up in red toile—innkeepers Christopher Sands and Vincent Coll have plenty of time to roll out the red carpet, which they do. Rooms in the 1820 main house include **La Vie en Rose** (featuring a hand-painted bed which once belonged to Mrs. William K. Vanderbilt) and **Hymne à l'Amour,** essentially a skylighted, spiral-staircased private wing with a cathedral living area and kitchen; both boast marble baths and cable TV, as does **Milord,** a little cottage decorated cheerily with *Provençale* prints. Among the many complimentary extras are airport pickup, a cocktail hour or afternoon tea on request, and a French continental breakfast—in the garden or dining room, or in bed. ♦ 3 Prince St (between Rte 6A and Mozart Ave). 487.7458, 800/340.7423; fax 487.8646

37 Atlantic House As you might judge from the leather-trussed contenders lounging outside, this is the place: the "A-House," Provincetown's premier gay bar, and one of the best known in the nation. Actually, everyone is welcome downstairs in the lively **Dance Bar,** decorated with nautical flotsam that conjures this hostelry's past as an 18th-century inn, or in the **Little Bar,** whose hearth attracts camaraderie-seeking locals off-season. As for the upstairs **Macho Bar,** it's a self-selected group. ♦ Cover. Daily 4PM-closing. 4-6 Masonic Pl (between Commercial St and Rte 6A). 487.3821 ♿

Provincetown's earliest schools were funded with a fishery tax. It is said that the least successful fisherman in town each year was assigned to schoolmaster duty.

38 Century Taste often resides in what you *don't* see—in the case of this personal adornment and home decor shop, gimmicky gewgaws or tacky souvenirs. Owner Rene Leblanc scours the world for dramatic accents, including fantastic frames and lamps, heirloom and handmade jewelry, and a smattering of select bath goods. ♦ Daily 10AM-11PM July–early Sept; call for off-season hours; closed November through April. 205 Commercial St (opposite Carver St). 487.2332 ♿

38 Cafe Heaven ★$ A plain and boxy storefront enlivened with splashy paintings, this stylish cafe dishes out custom omelettes until 3PM. The home fries are state of the art, and you can wash them down with fresh-squeezed juice (orange or grapefruit) by the pitcher. Chilled salads and sandwiches on **Provincetown Portuguese Bakery** bread fill out the lunchtime slot, and at night, patrons can go to hamburger heaven—choices include a brie-topped French burger, and even a vegetarian garden burger. Pasta dishes are also on tap. Don't overlook the inspired desserts, such as a fresh plum *clafoutis* (tart). ♦ American ♦ Daily breakfast, lunch, and dinner June–early Sept; daily lunch and dinner May, early Sept–Oct. 199 Commercial St (just east of Court St). 487.9639

38 Pied Piper There's not much to it—a triangular dance space with a bayside deck for cooling off—but no less an authority than *Time* magazine called it the best women's bar in the country. Actually, it's gay co-ed. Things get cooking right after Tea Dance at the **Boatslip** (see page 135) and heat up again after 10PM. Check out "local talent night" for an early chance at catching tomorrow's headliners. ♦ Cover. Daily 1PM-1AM June-Aug; call for off-season hours; closed November–mid-April. 193A Commercial St (at Court St). 487.1527 ♿

39 Spiritus ★$ Between 1AM, when the bars close, and 2AM, when this glorified pizza parlor locks its doors, as many as 1,000 people have been known to crowd around, still cruising. If all you want is a pizza, you can get a good one here, with various toppings, including garlic and *linguica*. Or come back for a morning pastry when things have quieted down. You can always gaze at the cherubs and gargoyles frolicking in a mural above the massive stoves. ♦ Pizza ♦ Daily breakfast, lunch, and dinner Apr-Nov. 190 Commercial St (between Carver and Court Sts). 487.2808. Also at: 500 Main St (at High School Rd), Hyannis. 775.2955

40 Brass Key Guesthouse $$$ A historic restoration and expansion by innkeepers Michael MacIntyre and Bob Anderson has enlarged this hostelry to include seven buildings and a dramatic outdoor heated pool with a waterfall. They've kept the smaller outdoor hot tub and moved the inn's entrance to the block behind the former entry gate. All 3 rooms have been upgraded and furnished in different decors, from high Victorian to cottage style. One room tucked under the eaves features a remote-control gas fireplace, harbor view, and massive marble whirlpool. Higher still, via a spiral staircase, is a deck where sunning au naturel is encouraged. All rooms have VCRs (the inn maintains an extensive video library), but the innkeepers, who winter at their Key West bed-and-breakfast, also encourage sociability. Continental breakfast is served, and restaurants are a short stroll away. The inn also hosts special weekends and events year-round, including a wine maker's dinner at which an actual wine maker, often from California, serves wine samples with the different courses of the meal, which is catered by a top chef, either local or imported. ♦ 67 Bradford St (between Carver and Court Sts). 487.9005, 800/842.9858; fax 487.9020 ♿

41 Bubala's By The Bay ★★$$ This eatery has it all—it's in the heart of the action, with outdoor and indoor dining, its own parking lot, and tasty food that's reasonably priced. There's even a big, quirky mural by New York City artist James Hansen, who summers in Provincetown. This spot has become a popular meeting place for lunch, and the seafood dishes—like Caribbean fish cakes with lime cilantro mayonnaise, or baked Cuban cod in a spicy citrus marinade with mango chutney, black beans, and rice—are the rave. The fish is freshly caught and, unlike at many restaurants, it is cleaned and filleted on the premises. ♦ International ♦ Daily breakfast, lunch, and dinner mid-Apr–Nov. 183 Commercial St (at Court St). 487.0773 ♿

41 Sebastian's Waterfront Restaurant ★★$$ Owners Scott Belding and Larry Wale are willing to leave culinary innovations to the more trendily inclined. They offer a bank of water-view windows, nongouging prices, and generous portions of good home cooking. You can enjoy a slab of prime ribs or salmon, or a homey dish such as "chicken Sebastian" —baked chicken breasts stuffed with apples, walnuts, and Ritz crackers, and topped with apricot glaze. Evenings, for those inclined, Larry presides over a small bar that's essentially a stage for his nonstop, X-rated stand-up comedy. For decor, Larry gave his sister in Indiana $150 to buy paint-by-numbers "masterpieces" at yard sales. "She still has change," he says, and every square inch of wall space is covered with imagery not to be taken seriously. ♦ American ♦ Daily lunch and dinner mid-May–Sept; call for off-season hours; closed late October–mid-April. 177 Commercial St (just west of Court St). 487.3286 ௯

42 Boatslip Beach Club $$ This modern 45-room hotel is more of a permanent party than a mere place to stay. The waterfront footage and views, as well as the sundeck and pool, are pluses, but the main reasons to hang around are the social events, if you're interested. It's here that Provincetown's gay summer season is officially launched in late June with a drag "debutante ball," and guests stay in the social swim by attending afternoon "tea dances" or nightly DJ'd sessions alternating two-step with disco. Although the clientele is mostly male, females will not be made to feel de trop; in fact, a special Women's Week is an annual event. ♦ Closed December through March. 161 Commercial St (between Court St and Atlantic Ave). 487.1669, 800/451.7547; fax 487.6021

Within the Boatslip Beach Club:

Years after Charles Webster Hawthorne had taught classes at Provincetown's Cape Cod School of Art in the early 1900s, some of his students' paintings were found stuffed in the walls as insulation. The paintings were called "mudheads" because Hawthorne's students were taught to concentrate on shapes, and so they left facial features blank. People still collect mudheads today.

Before the 1870s, shipwreck victims had virtually no chance of survival unless they happened upon a "charity house"—a crude shed with fireplace—erected along the shore by the Massachusetts Humane Society. In 1872, Congress approved the building of nine lifesaving stations on Cape Cod; four more were added in 1902 (one survives as a Life-Saving Museum at Race Point in Provincetown).

By the 1890s the population of Provincetown was nearly 50 percent Portuguese. In contrast, 90 percent of the residents on the rest of Cape Cod were of English descent.

The Boatslip Restaurant ★★$$$ Long a Provincetown "in" spot, its reputation is in good hands with chef Polly Hemstock, formerly of **The Flagship**, offering such specials as seared sesame tuna with ginger tamari aioli and baked lobster stuffed with corn bread and fresh corn. There's an open atmosphere with a nautical flavor, and works of local artists hang on the walls. ♦ New American ♦ Daily breakfast, lunch, and dinner June-Sept; call for off-season hours. Reservations recommended. 487.2509, 487.4200

MARTIN HOUSE
FOOD & DRINK

43 Martin House ★★★★$$$ Run by a trio of energetic siblings, this charming restaurant—a 1740 captain's house with a warren of low-slung, firelit dining rooms, a beamed loft daubed a cheery Van Gogh yellow, and a garden terrace—has a reputation as one of the most innovative and consistently excellent eateries in town. While relying on local delicacies, such as organic greens grown at Narrowland Farms, chef Glen Martin roams the world for inspiration. The raw oysters— as large and succulent as Wellfleets get—are offered with *ponzu* dipping sauce, wasabi, and pickled ginger. Freshly caught lobster turns up sautéed with shallots and sugar snap pears over gingered *soba* noodles; the roast duck gets a Moroccan spice rub, date chutney, and saffron couscous. And the bread pudding with apricots, pine nuts, and warm whiskey sauce makes the perfect ending. ♦ International ♦ Daily dinner Apr-Dec; M, Th-Su dinner Jan-Mar. 157 Commercial St (at Atlantic Ave). 487.1327 ௯

43 Walker's Wonders Not content with her fine art gallery at the east end of town, Bertha Walker has created a shop at the busy west end featuring art for the house. Here you can buy furniture, pottery, clocks built by Jim Manning from weathered wood, folk paintings, and birdhouses crafted by Richard Hagen. ♦ Daily 11AM-5PM late May–late Oct. 153 Commercial St (just west of Atlantic Ave). 487.8794

44 West End Antiques The stock consists principally of ephemera—lots of elixirs, advertising art, commemorative plates, and the like. There's even a packet of bobby pins from the 1950s, still intact in its cellophane wrapping. Children's books and dolls are among the other subspecialties; it's a great place to revisit your childhood past. ♦ Daily 10AM-11PM June–early Sept; call for off-season hours; closed January through March. 146 Commercial St (at Conant St). 487.6723

45 Gallerani's Café ★★$$$ This bistro-style restaurant, with three walls of windows surrounding a grid of booths, buzzes with a hum of well-being. Entrées range from a straightforward swordfish marinated in rasp-berry vinaigrette to "Southern Decadence," a rich shrimp dish stuffed with crawfish, pecans, and lime. One of the few restaurants to remain open year-round, and also offer parking in the boatyard behind, it's appreciated by residents and visitors alike. ♦ International ♦ Daily dinner June–mid-Sept; W-Su dinner mid-Sept–May. 133 Commercial St (between Pleasant and Franklin Sts). 487.4433

45 Flyer's Boat Rental Provincetown is ringed with splendid beaches, but those in the know take **Flyer's Long Point Shuttle** straight across the harbor to bask on the outermost finger of sand curling Capeward (a.k.a. "the end of the Earth"). What would be a four-mile semi-Saharan trudge from the center of town is reduced to a brief, scenic ride to a place where privacy is plentiful. This boatyard, in business since 1945, also offers boat rentals, sailing lessons, and fishing expeditions. Rates are surprisingly reasonable, and one of the best ways to take in the town is to get out of it and onto the water. Shuttle service is also available from MacMillan Wharf, Float Space No. 8. ♦ Fee. Daily 8AM-6PM mid-May–Sept; off-season by appointment. 131A Commercial St (between Pleasant and Franklin Sts). 487.0898, 800/750.0898

SAL'S PLACE

46 Sal's Place ★★★$$$ If it's a timeless quality you're seeking, you'll want to put in a relaxed evening here. This wharfside trattoria is strewn with Chianti bottles and serenaded with opera. It includes an expansive vine-covered deck that transports you straight to Sorrento. The strictly traditional menu abounds in inimitable staples, from *spaghettini puttanesca* (with tomatoes, capers, and olives) to *vitello saltimbocca* (veal cutlet with prosciutto and cheese). The Friday

piatto di giorno is squid stuffed with pignoli, and the tiramisù is a superlative dessert. ♦ Italian ♦ Daily dinner mid-June–mid-Sept; call for off-season schedule; closed Novemb through April. Reservations recommended. 99 Commercial St (between Tremont and Mechanic Sts). 487.1279

47 Captain Lysander Inn $$ This 1840s captain's house, with fancy fanlight, stands at the end of an inviting walkway lined with flowers. The 13 handsome traditional rooms and an apartment enjoy the advantage of a quiet West End setting with on-site parking, and the modest price includes a continental breakfast. ♦ 96 Commercial St (between Tremont and Mechanic Sts). 487.2253; fax 487.7579

48 Lands End Inn $$$ After spending two decades decking out his 1904 Gull Hill bungalow with Art Deco and Art Nouveau furnishings, clinical psychologist David Schoolman placed his creation in a trust so that it could operate forever in all its unique glory. Set amid two terraced acres of formal and indigenous plantings panoramic, this one-of-a-kind bed-and-breakfast consists of 17 rooms, each full of collectors' items that will strike some visitors as exquisite, others as oppressive (Bauhaus buffs beware). Whatever your taste, it's hard to resist the view of town and the dunes beyond, best seer from the octagon-shaped tower rooms of this unabashedly outré dwelling. ♦ 22 Commercia St (between Province Lands Rd and Point St) 487.0706, 800/276.7088; fax 896.9130

49 Red Inn $$ When this 1805 Federal house first opened as an inn in 1905, guests delighted in diving into the sea from the front porch at high tide. A more proper decorum prevails now, as befits a historic dwelling said to be located at the very spot where the Pilgrims landed. Innkeepers Bob Kulesza and Mike Clifford, who took over the inn in 1992, have rejuvenated the restaurant and played up the inn's homespun charms. The sitting room is dominated by a crazy-quilt of a chimney created by local artist Conrad Malicoat. The four double rooms, plus a two-room apartment, feature antiques, original oils, and enviable bay views. ◆ 15 Commercial St (between Point St and Province Lands Rd). 487.0050, 888/473.3466; fax 487.6253 ₺

Within the Red Inn:

Red Inn Restaurant ★★★$$$ Each of the three intimate dining rooms holds fewer than two dozen people, so everyone's assured of a peaceful atmosphere as well as a water view. The fare is mostly traditional New England, with a few twists—rice-stuffed duck, for instance, with an orange–litchi-nut glaze (the treatment varies nightly). There's ample opportunity to go overboard—ordering a 1.5-pound stuffed lobster for brunch, for instance, or enjoying clam and corn chowder, giant native sea scallops in orange cream sauce, and cappuccino cheesecake for dinner, amid the glow of oil lamps on linen tablecloths. ◆ New England ◆ M-Sa dinner; Su brunch and dinner late May–early Nov; call for off-season schedule; closed in March. Reservations recommended. 487.0050 ₺

50 The Moors ★★$$ Maline Costa built his atmospheric restaurant out of nautical wreckage in 1939. It looks like the kind of place Long John Silver would have favored; real clients have included literary figures such as Tennessee Williams and Norman Mailer, but no famous pirates. Pianist/comedian Lenny Grandchamps holds forth in the briglike bar, and the bustling, dimly lit restaurant serves classic Azorean cuisine, including tasty kale soup, *porco empau* (marinated pork cubes), and Portuguese wedding cake. ◆ Portuguese/American ◆ Daily lunch and dinner mid-May–mid-Oct; F-Su lunch and dinner Apr–mid-May, mid-Oct–late Nov. Reservations recommended. 5 Bradford St Extension (at Province Lands Rd). 487.0840 ₺

51 Nelson's Riding Stable What could be more relaxing than exploring the dunes by horseback? Guided Western-style tours are offered along three **National Seashore** trails, each lasting about an hour; for experienced riders there's a two-hour beach trek where you'll get up some speed. The minimum age is 13, and riding helmets are provided. ◆ Fee. Daily 10AM-dusk Apr-Oct. 43 Race Point Rd (off Hwy 6). 487.1112 ₺

52 Province Lands Visitor Center If you plan to bike the swooping dune trails, you might want to stop here first to get your bearings: The 360° observation deck can be very helpful in that regard, and it's beautiful besides. The trails, which include a one-mile self-guided nature walk, can be accessed at five points; here, the parking is free. There's a worthwhile exhibit of local flora in the lobby, and the rangers arrange activities, such as a children's discovery hour and sunset

campfires with storytelling. ◆ Daily 9AM-6PM July-Aug; call for off-season hours; closed December through March. Race Point Rd (off Hwy 6). 487.1256 ₺

53 Life Saving Museum Now operated by the **Cape Cod National Seashore,** this shingled building was once the Chatham outpost of the short-lived but valiant United States Life Saving Service (established in 1872, it was folded into the US Coast Guard in 1915, after the Cape Cod Canal was completed). Hoping to stem the tide of shipwrecks along the Cape's Atlantic shore, Congress funded nine lifesaving stations, each manned by a crew of six "Surfmen." They patrolled the beaches in all kinds of weather (holding wooden shingles in front of their faces during sandstorms), on the lookout for ships in distress. Spotting one, they'd light a flare, and the team would launch a surfboat. Or, if the surf was unnavigable, they'd shoot a Lyle gun (a small cannon) and rig up a "breeches buoy"—like a pair of roomy canvas shorts attached to a ring buoy. In this laborious way they'd haul the victims in, one at a time.

The museum not only houses the original equipment but also mounts dramatic demonstrations every Thursday at 10AM. This is the very beach, incidentally, of which Thoreau wrote: "Here a man can stand and put all America behind him." Stellwagen Bank is straight out, and if you take along binoculars, you might spot a whale. With its western orientation, this is also a popular spot to catch a psychedelic sunset; dazzled audiences have been known to break out in spontaneous applause. ◆ Beach entrance fee. Daily 10AM-4PM July-Aug; call for off-season hours; closed November through April. Race Point Beach (off Race Point Rd). 487.1256 ₺

54 Willie Air Tour Before you head back to the mainland, consider a barnstormer flight aboard *Willie,* a buttercup-yellow 1930 *Stinson,* for one last thrilling overview. ◆ Fee; two-person minimum. By appointment. Daily 10AM-6PM July-Aug; call for off-season hours; closed November through April. Provincetown Municipal Airport (off Race Point Rd). 487.0241

The commercialism that grips Cape Cod is nothing new, judging from Henry David Thoreau's discovery, in mid–19th century Provincetown, of a sign advertising "fine sand for sale." Thoreau chalked up the gambit as "a good instance of the fact that a man confers value on the most worthless thing by mixing himself with it."

From January to April, right whales move inside Provincetown Harbor and at times can be seen close to shore from several restaurants that have windows overlooking the beach.

Martha's Vineyard

Native American legend held that the giant god Maushop, discomfited by sand in his moccasins, flung them out to sea, where they formed the islands of Martha's Vineyard (the "Vineyard") and Nantucket. Geologically, both were once connected to the Cape; they're all part of the same terminal moraine. While some scholars hold that the 100-square-mile Martha's Vineyard (New England's largest island) was named for a 17th-century Dutch seaman, Martin Wyngaard, credit is more commonly accorded to explorer Bartholomew Gosnold, who named it either for his young daughter (the romantic version of the story) or for his mother-in-law, who financed his trip. The "vineyard" part was apt—the land once was overrun with wild grapes, and remains remarkably fertile to this day. Great chunks of the westward "up-island" (longitudinally speaking) are still farmland; wander far enough from the lively towns down-island and you'll swear you've somehow ended up in Vermont.

Blessed with protected harbors, and only seven miles from the mainland (a 45-minute ferry ride), the Vineyard's down-island attracted the first droves of settlers in 1642—starting with Thomas Mayhew Jr., who converted 1,600 natives to Christianity within a few years of his arrival. His father, a

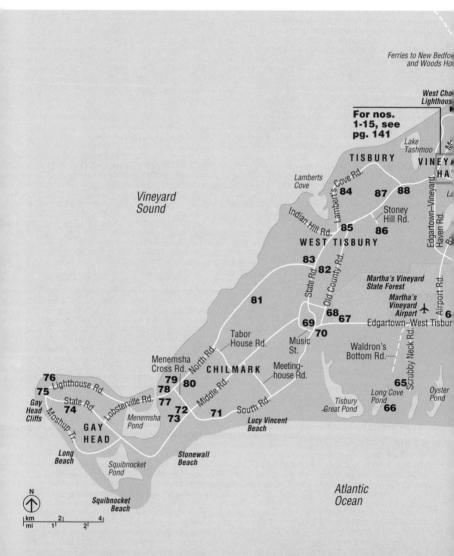

For nos. 1-15, see pg. 141

Watertown, Massachusetts, entrepreneur, had bought Martha's Vineyard, Nantucket, and the Elizabeth Islands from an English nobleman who had no use for them. The purchase price: 40 pounds.

The younger Mayhew established **Edgartown,** naming it for England's heir apparent, the young son of the Duke of York (who had died a month before his honor was conferred, unbeknownst to the colonists). The town, which benefited from the great whaling boom, remains an extraordinary repository of black-trimmed, white clapboard Greek Revival captain's houses; it's remarkably elegant, as summer colonies go. Since it doesn't get the heaviest of summer ferry service, Edgartown has managed to retain the ambience of an upscale enclave. You'll find plenty of expensive boutiques for browsing, but nary a T-shirt shop in sight.

Vineyard Haven, the island's second-oldest town, is its primary port and year-round commercial center. (If it doesn't look very old, that's because an 1883 fire virtually leveled it.) Vineyard Haven's residents, who tend to be more liberal counterparts of Edgartown's landed gentry, take pride in the town's proletarian image. As resident William Styron wrote in *On the Vineyard II,* a collection of essays edited by photographer Peter Simon, Vineyard Haven "thrives on a kind of forthright frowsiness." It has pockets of beauty, though, such as **William Street**, lined with National Register houses, or pretty little **Owen Park**, overlooking the harbor.

Oak Bluffs is an outgrowth of Methodist camp meetings that began here in 1835 and gained popularity as the century advanced. The town survives today as a vast grid of elaborately decorated and painted gingerbread cottages, whose basic shape resembles that of the canvas tents they replaced. The original structures clustered around the **Trinity Park Tabernacle**, which itself started out as a tent. Subsequent spokes of what was then called "Cottage City" represent one of the earliest examples of urban planning in the United States. With its atmosphere of religious fervor and refreshing sea air, Oak Bluffs was an enormously popular beach resort in Victorian times. One of the few vacation communities to welcome visitors of color in those days, it has reigned for generations as a "black Newport," attracting such high-profile summer sojourners as Adam Clayton Powell and, more recently, Spike Lee. The interracial ease that prevails here enhances the pleasure of strolling down the town's lanes, lined with infinite variations on a charming form of folk art.

Ferries to
Woods Hole (in season)
and Falmouth (in season)

Ferry to Hyannis
(in season)

East Chop
Lighthouse

Ferry to Nantucket
(in season)

OAK BLUFFS

For nos.
17-34, see
pg. 144

35

Nantucket
Sound

Beach Rd.

ngekontacket
nd

Joseph Sylvia
State Beach
Park

Cape Pogue
Lighthouse

elix Neck
Wildlife
anctuary

Cape
Pogue
Bay

EDGARTOWN

Edgartown
Harbor

62

For nos.
37-60, see
pg. 149

Meeting House Way

Herring Creek Rd.

Katama Rd.

Chappaquiddick
Island

Dike Rd.

61

Wasque Rd.

gartown
eat Pond

Poucha
Pond

63

Katama
Bay

62

Wasque
Point

South
Beach

The up-island towns are mere villages by comparison: **West Tisbury**, with its landmark **Alley's General Store** and Saturday-morning farmers' market (the social event of the summer season); the Wampanoag settlement of **Gay Head** (at press time the state legislature was set to approve changing Gay Head back to its former Native American name, Aquinnah); the picturesque fishing port of **Menemsha**, with its legendary sunsets; and the agrarian community of **Chilmark**—where the "downtown" consists of the **Beetlebung Crossing** (so named for its grove of tupelo trees, which provided the makings of both beetles and bungs—that is, mallets and cask stoppers).

So diverse is this landscape, and so entrancing, it's little wonder that residents of Martha's Vineyard begrudge any business that calls them to the mainland—a journey they refer to, sighing, as "going to America."

1 Black Dog Tavern ★★★$$$ For many (possibly too many), this shingled saltbox overlooking the harbor represents the essence of the Vineyard. The tavern's once-secret charm became common knowledge long ago; in fact, now there's an entire mail-order catalog (offering everything from boxer shorts to biscotti) emblazoned with the familiar logo of a "Martha's Vineyard whitefoot lab," a mixed breed. The enterprise was sparked in 1971, when Robert Douglas sailed into Vineyard Haven harbor and wondered why no one had thought to open a restaurant there.

Though the staff has since ballooned into a cast of hundreds, the tavern has preserved its quiet simplicity and personal scale; with its bare plank floors and close-packed tables it looks like the kind of place Herman Melville might have frequented. But he's unlikely to have had the chance to enjoy grilled swordfish with banana, basil, and lime, or bluefish with mustard soufflé sauce. He certainly wouldn't have encountered the likes of fudge-bottom pie or "blackout cake." Though the lines grow ever longer, nothing much has changed at this beloved restaurant, and as long as the crowds from the tour buses flock instead to the nearby bakery, and a spacious cafe at the edge of town, chances are good that not much will. ♦ New England ♦ M-Sa breakfast, lunch, and dinner; Su brunch and dinner. Beach St Extension (off Beach Rd), Vineyard Haven. 693.9223 ♿ Bakery: Water St (between Beach and Union Sts), Vineyard Haven. 693.4786, 800/626.1991. Bakery/Cafe: 162 State Rd (between Edgartown–Vineyard Haven Rd and Huckleberry Hill Dr), Vineyard Haven. 696.8190 ♿

2 Shenandoah Robert Douglas sailed into Vineyard Haven harbor on a 108-foot square-topsail schooner just like this 1964 reproduction of an 1849 revenue cutter. It's the only one of its kind in the US, a throwback to the days of the seafaring trade. An excursion on the *Shenandoah* is real adventure; with 7,000 square feet of sails, the ship makes speeds in excess of 12 knots. Ten cabins house up to 29 passengers, who bond quickly over hearty meals cooked on the coal stove. The roomy main saloon, decorated with Civil War cutlasses and marine oil paintings, is lit by kerosene lamps; a chanteyman and pump organ provide entertainment. The six-day cruises have no set route; ports of call might encircle the islands or extend to New London, Connecticut. Children's cruises and educational group excursions are offered, and the newly acquired, 92-foot sister ship, *Alabama*, makes day sails. ♦ M-Sa mid-June–mid-Sept. Reservations required. Coastwise Wharf (at the end of Beach St Extension), Vineyard Haven. 693.1699

3 Wintertide Coffeehouse ★★$$ Don't expect much in the way of decor at this nonprofit, performing arts center and cafe, volunteer-run since its founding in 1978; bohemian improv is about the extent of it, with plenty of folding chairs (capacity: 80) on standby for folk/jazz/blues headliners such as Tom Paxton, Dave Van Ronk, Patty Larkin, Robin Batteau, Ellis Paul, and islander Kate Taylor (James's talented sister). Free jazz jam sessions are held on Sunday afternoons. In addition to music, you might catch some provocative dinner theater or the ad-libbed comedy of **WIMP (Wintertide Improv Troop)**. For a token fee, you could even reserve an open-mike slot and try performing yourself. The club's high-season actually peaks in late September, after the tourist influx has abated somewhat; it's then that the **Wintertide** mounts its Singer/Songwriter's Retreat and Concert Series. The players get to stay and hang out together and participate in a series of workshops; audiences get to enjoy a parade of

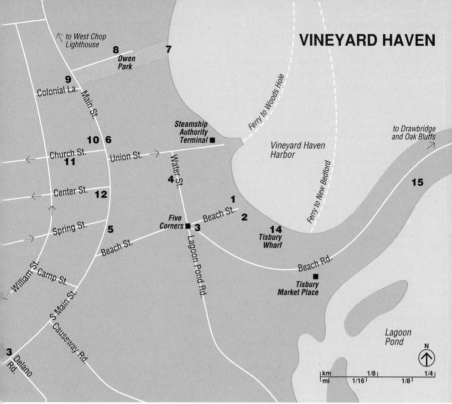

VINEYARD HAVEN

top names at their playing-for-the-fun-of-it peak. Though the cafe is smoke- and alcohol-free, it still offers coffee, of course, including cappuccino, as well as pizza, soups, sandwiches, burritos, and a selection of pies and ice cream. ♦ Cover for live entertainment nights. M-Tu, Th-Su noon-7PM; call for performance schedule. Beach St (at Beach Rd), Vineyard Haven. 693.8830, 693.8832 ♿

4 Midnight Farm This shop stands out— from its exterior window displays to the well-designed stone-wall counters inside. Tamara Weiss, an independent film producer who fled Manhattan, and business partner Carly Simon, singer and author of the children's book *Midnight Farm,* have created an attractive spot to browse. They carry clothing, quality leather goods, table settings, jewelry, furniture made of reclaimed wood (from old New England barn boards), and high-quality paperback and hardcover books. ♦ Daily 9AM-10PM July-early Sept. Daily early Sept-June. 18 Water St (at Cromwell La), Vineyard Haven. 693.1997 ♿

5 Bramhall & Dunn Dedicated to decorating people as well as homes, this stylish store features not only English country pine furniture, hooked and woven rugs, and all sorts of handsome accessories, but hand-knit sweaters, fabulous hats, delicate cotton lingerie, and smocked clothing for children. The stock, handpicked by owners Emily Bramhall and Tharon Dunn, will remind you of everybody you've been meaning to buy presents for, including yourself. ♦ Daily 9:30AM-10PM July-Aug. Daily Sept-June. 19 Main St (between Beach Rd and Union St), Vineyard Haven. 693.6437 ♿ Also at: 16 Federal St (between India and Chestnut Sts), Nantucket. 228.4688 ♿

5 Summer Solstice Jennifer Gardner collects colorful textiles from all over the world and turns them into comfortable clothing for women and children. The same splashy patterns that make a great summer shift, for instance, might also turn up as a toddler's romper suit. Heavily beaded batiks become vests, jackets, and elegant evening slippers. ♦ Daily 9:30AM-9:30PM late May-early Sept; 10:30AM-6:30PM early Sept-late May. 57 Main St (between Beach Rd and Union St), Vineyard Haven. 693.6665 ♿

Noman's Land, three miles south of Martha's Vineyard, was once home to 40 English settler families. In 1952 the US Government bought it for a practice target for bombers. Currently the island is being considered for wildlife refuge status.

6 Travis Tuck Sculptor Travis Tuck—who can usually be observed at work, wearing a leather apron and wielding an acetylene torch—employs the pre-Industrial Revolution repoussé method, whereby copper is warmed and then "pushed out" (hammered) from within. All work is by commission, and his specialty—copper weather vanes—start at around $7,000, or a good deal more for 23-karat gold leaf. His first project, in 1973, was a great white shark for *Jaws,* which now guards the art director's Los Angeles home. For the roof of a Menemsha summer home, he created a seven-foot figure of Mercury in the Superman mid-glide position, holding aloft a cellular phone (the business in which the client made his fortune). Tuck has also made a few things besides weather vanes over the years, too—such as a copper mask for James Taylor and a copper clock for Beverly Sills. ♦ M-Sa. 71 Main St (between Union St and Owen Park), Vineyard Haven. 693.3914 ♿

6 LeRoux This shop fills a niche by providing everyday clothes for both sexes, with labels ranging from Urban Outfitters to Patagonia. The look is neither staid nor trendy. ♦ M-Sa 9:30AM-9:30PM; Su June–early Sept. Daily early Sept–June. 89 Main St (between Union St and Owen Park), Vineyard Haven. 693.6463 ♿ Also at: Winter St (at Nevin Sq), Edgartown. 627.7766 ♿

6 Compass Bank If you're intrigued by the outside of this 1905 fieldstone building, designed by Boston architect **J. William Beals** in the form of a Greek cross, don't hesitate to step inside, where friendly tellers will coach you in how to use the bank lobby's acoustic "sweet spot" to effect an eerie echo. The interior is magnificent, with milky stained glass, decorative plaster in a fleur-de-lis pattern, and acanthus side supports. This tile-roofed, vaguely Mediterranean anomaly, an architectural jewel in the reconstructed town, was commissioned by gramophone magnate William Barry Owen. Owen's business interests took off when he paid a French artist $250 for the image of a dog, head cocked, listening to a record player; "Nipper" went on to become one of the best-known logos in advertising history. Retiring to enjoy the fruits of his labors, Owen became a director of the bank founded in Edgartown in 1855 by prominent whaling merchant Dr. Daniel Fisher, and he decided to move the operation closer to his Lambert's Cove home. This personal style of management served islanders well during the panic following the Crash of October 1929. When ordered by President Roosevelt to close the bank vault to stem withdrawals, Owen's successor, Stephen Carey Luce, complied under protest, but announced he would offer anyone who so desired a personal checking account with his own backing, so that the island's economy would not suffer. Despite federal disapproval the strategy was not illegal, and "Lucebucks" saw the islanders through the crisis. ♦ M-F; Sa 8:30AM-noon June-Aug. M-F Sept-May. 91 Main St (between Union St and Owen Park), Vineyard Haven. 696.4400, 800/322.9313 ♿

7 M.V. Parasail and M.V. Ski Coast Guard–licensed captain Mark Clark offers two thrilling ways to tour the harbor: either up in the air, tethered to a parachute towed by a 25-foot Paracraft turbo diesel winchboat, or in the water, via water skis, a kneeboard, a "Bump & Ride" inner tube, or just barefoot. He gives lessons in the aquatic category, but promises an easy and literally dry run by parasail: "If you can sit," he insists, "you can fly." ♦ Fee. Daily by appointment 9AM-sunset mid-May–mid-Oct. Owen Park Pier (off Main St), Vineyard Haven. 693.2838 ♿

8 Lothrop Merry House $$ This rambling 1790 bed-and-breakfast, with a broad lawn sloping down to a sliver of placid beach, has that sea-washed feel that will loose a flood of memories of summers past. The seven bedrooms, some with fireplaces, are on the plain side, but far from austere. The implicit message is that sleeping is but a prelude to the pleasures at hand—such as knocking about in a loaner canoe or Sunfish, or just lounging in an Adirondack chair with a view of the harbor. Innkeepers John and Merry Clark actually live out there in summer, aboard their 54-foot Alden Ketch; they offer half-day and daylong cruises. Continental breakfast is served, and restaurants are a five-minute walk away. ♦ Owen Park (off Main St), Vineyard Haven. 693.1646

9 Martha's Place $$$$ This 1840 Greek Revival bed-and-breakfast has an appealing simplicity. There's a subdued tan parlor, with floor-to-ceiling windows and a pair of wingback chairs. The four bedrooms, each with a fireplace and some with harbor views, are equally dramatic with half-canopy beds, Egyptian cotton linens, and newly refinished floors. The dining room, with its 1855 Baccarat chandelier, is an elegant place to greet the day over fresh pastries and muffins. French doors lead from the dining room to an open porch. ♦ 114 Main St (at Colonial La), Vineyard Haven. 693.0253 &

10 Le Grenier ★★★$$$$ With the ascendancy of the nouvelle school, it has grown increasingly difficult to track down traditional French cuisine. Chef-owner Jean Dupon hails from Lyons, France's gastronomic capital, and has the moves down, as evidenced in such classics as calf's brains *Grenobloise* with *beurre noir* and capers or lobster *Normande* flambéed with Calvados, apples, and cream. For an "attic" (the literal translation, and the actual location), this place is rather romantic, especially when aglow with hurricane lamps. ♦ French ♦ Daily dinner mid-Mar–Jan. Reservations recommended. 96 Main St (between Church St and Colonial La), Vineyard Haven. 693.4906

11 Vineyard Playhouse Having started out as a Methodist church in 1833, this boxy building served as a Masonic lodge for nearly a century before it was claimed for amateur theatrics in 1982. Now the nonprofit output is very definitely professional, with Equity actors cast in New York and such luminaries as Spalding Gray turning up to try out new work. The physical plant is in good shape as well, with 120 comfortable seats in the black-box theater and a smartly renovated lobby. While putting on a summer season of some five plays, artistic director M.J. Munafo also manages to oversee a pair of classics performed outdoors at the **Tisbury Amphitheater,** several benefit performances, various late-night shows, and an arts-and-theater camp for kids. ♦ Call for schedule. 24 Church St (between Main and William Sts), Vineyard Haven. 696.6300, 693.6450 &

12 The Dry Town Cafe ★★★$$$$ The name refers to Vineyard Haven's legal status vis-à-vis alcohol—the only places you can buy a drink on the island are Oak Bluffs and

Edgartown. You're welcome to bring your own, though, and this very stylish bistro can supply dishes that would warrant fine wine. Dinner might run to sautéed soft-shell crab (in season) with spicy coleslaw and blackberry vinegar or seared rare yellowfin tuna over creamy polenta and peas with lime-*hijiki* (Japanese seaweed) sauce. With its elegant arched ceiling and sleek woodwork, this place looks as if it could have been lifted wholesale from Soho, rather than rehabbed out of a former barbershop. ♦ New American ♦ Daily dinner. Reservations recommended. 70 Main St (at Center St), Vineyard Haven. 693.0033

12 Alley Cat This tiny shop, with its flame-painted walls, is a great place to stock up on up-to-the-minute women's fashions—which might be 1940s-like dresses in silks and velvets or Arche shoes made in France. Definitely not the usual thing. ♦ Daily 10AM-9PM July-Aug; call for off-season hours; closed February through March. 66 Main St (between Spring and Center Sts), Vineyard Haven. 693.6970 &

13 Lorraine Parish If this gifted designer of women's clothing has yet to become a household name, that's by design, too. Having seceded from Manhattan's Garment District to the Vineyard in 1980, for a long time Parish marketed her line—ranging from understated "investment dressing" to playful summer frocks—primarily though subscription-only catalogs and invitation-only trunk shows. Her local coterie includes Carly Simon, who commissioned a wedding dress. For outfits with that Vineyard look of free-flowing, effortless chic, this is the first place to look. ♦ Daily June–mid-Oct; call for off-season hours. 18 S Main St (between Look and Camp Sts), Vineyard Haven. 693.9044 &

14 Stripers ★★★$$$$ An intimate, plain and pretty restaurant plunked amid a posh marina aromatic with *rosa rugosa,* this place offers a view of the bustling harbor from indoor and outdoor seating. Enjoy superbly handled seafood: swordfish in a grilled pineapple salsa, for instance, or Cajun ravioli with grilled sea scallops in brandied lobster cream. And there's no closer seat on the island to where the action is. ♦ Fusion ♦ Daily dinner Apr-Oct. Reservations recommended. 52 Beach Rd (at Tisbury Wharf), Vineyard Haven. 693.8383 &

C.W. MORGAN MARINE ANTIQUES

14 C.W. Morgan Marine Antiques Frank Rapoza, a nautical expert, has amassed an extraordinary collection of museum-quality marine antiques: ship models, paintings, instruments, chests, scrimshaw, and telescopes. Anyone with the faintest interest in the field will be well rewarded by a visit. ♦ M-Tu, Th-Sa 10AM-noon, 1PM-5PM Apr-Oct. Tisbury Wharf (off Beach Rd), Vineyard Haven. 693.3622 ᓬ

15 Wind's Up! Set on protected Lagoon Pond, this windsurfing/sailing school and rental shop is ideally situated for beginners. Lessons and boards are available for those as young as four, as well as for wary adults. Those with experience can gear up and head out, using the establishment's handy map. An eight-hour certification course adhering to the Mistral International system starts with a dry-land lesson on a simulator, moves out onto the water (wet suits are included), and concludes with a three-hour stint of supervised practice. ♦ Daily late June–early Sept; call for off-

season hours; closed January–mid-March. 95 Beach Rd (between the drawbridge and Tisbury Market Place), Vineyard Haven. 693.4252. Store annex: Tisbury Market Place, Beach Rd (between the drawbridge an Lagoon Pond Rd), Vineyard Haven. 693.434€

16 Admiral Benbow Inn $$ Built for a minister at the turn of the century, this seven bedroom house, topped by a cupola and encircled by a shady porch, has the dark, ornate woodwork typical of that time. Yet the bed-and-breakfast has a young, energetic fee to it, and it's owned by the Black Dog Tavern Company—which means for breakfast you can enjoy a few of those pastries that look so inviting in the display cases. There's no ocean view, and the inn is set on a busy road somewhat removed from town; but it's still only a short bike to shopping or to the Sound beaches. There is no restaurant. ♦ Closed November–mid-May. 81 New York Ave (at Munroe Ave), Oak Bluffs. 693.6825

17 Wesley Hotel $$$ Though not as grand as when it started out in 1879, this 62-room behemoth has been thoroughly spruced up, though it could use a good cook, not to mention a full-scale dining room. But the lobby and guest rooms are spacious and nicely furnished with Victorian reproductions The unusual first-come, first-served policy fc giving out rooms with harbor views (they're priced the same as those without) means it

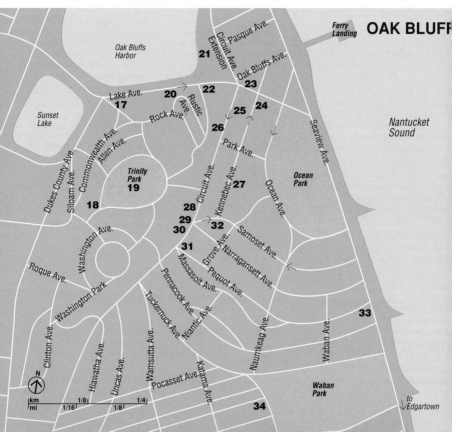

pays to reserve early. Should you end up at the back of the building, or in the 20-room Wesley Arms annex (where the rates, with shared bath, are half the norm), you can always commandeer a rocker on the vast front porch. No meals are served, but many fine restaurants are only a short distance away. ♦ Closed mid-October–April. 1 Lake Ave (at Dukes County Ave), Oak Bluffs. 693.6611, 800/638.9027; fax 693.5389 ♿

18 Cottage Museum You'll see them the minute you pull into town: winding rows of colorful, cheek-to-jowl cottages ornamented with intricate Carpenter's Gothic woodwork. The first such structure was erected in 1859 to replace one of the Methodist revivalists' 500-odd canvas tents, and within the next two decades more than 300 cottages sprouted in Wesleyan Grove, each vying with its neighbors for the most elaborate trim and garish color combinations. The museum, a cream-and-orange 1867 cottage, is fairly typical; its tiny veranda is topped by a small balcony (off the peaked front bedroom) with French doors shaped like church windows. A look at what's inside, from the portable organ to an ancient bathing suit, will give you a feel for those heady early days, when campers tried to squeeze in a few recreational activities such as "bluffing" (strolling along the sand with a sweetheart, then considered a scandalous act) into a schedule dominated by thrice-daily prayer services. To this day, following a tradition that began in 1869, one evening every August (the date is kept secret to discourage crowds) is designated "Illumination Night," and the entire campground is lit with Japanese lanterns. ♦ Nominal admission. M-Sa mid-June–mid-Sept. 1 Trinity Park (within the Camp Meeting Grounds), Oak Bluffs. 693.0525 ♿

19 Trinity Park Tabernacle When crowds for the Methodist revivals surpassed 16,000 in the late 1860s, it was clear that something more solid—and permanent—than a circus-size tent was required to shelter worshipers from the elements. Designed by architect **J.W. Hoyt** of Springfield, Massachusetts, and built in 1879 for just over $7,000, this open-air church, now on the National Register of Historic Places, is the largest wrought-iron and wood structure in America. Its conical crown is ringed with a geometric pattern of amber, carmine, and midnight blue stained glass. Old-fashioned community sings take place Wednesday at 8PM, and concerts are scheduled irregularly on weekends. James Taylor and Bonnie Raitt

have regaled the faithful here, but usually the acts are more homespun—e.g., the Parson's Plunkers, a local banjo band. The Martha's Vineyard Camp Meeting Association publishes a schedule of events open to the public, including interdenominational services and flea markets. ♦ Service: Su 9:30AM July-Aug. Trinity Park (within the Camp Meeting Grounds), Oak Bluffs. 693.0525 ♿

20 Attleboro House $ As old-fashioned as the afghans that proprietor Estelle Reagan crochets for every bed, this harborside guest house—serving Camp Meeting visitors since 1874—epitomizes the simple, timeless joys of summer. None of the 11 rooms is graced with a private bath, but the rates are so retro, you may not mind. What was good enough for 19th-century tourists more than suffices today. ♦ Closed November–late May. 11 Lake Ave (between Central and Dukes County Aves), Oak Bluffs. 693.4346

21 Café Luna ★★$ Mellower than some of the other nightlife options in town, this gingerbread house offers a choice of comestibles: designer pizzas, focaccia sandwiches, salads, and so forth, at the boardwalk level; upstairs there's a tapas, wine, and coffee bar with occasional jazz and microbrewery specials of the week. Try the "Old Peculiar," a traditional Yorkshire ale. ♦ Italian ♦ No Cover. Daily 11AM-midnight late May–mid-Oct. Circuit Ave Extension (between Lake Ave and Seaview Ave Extension), Oak Bluffs. 693.8078 ♿

22 Dee's Harbor Café ★★$ This tiny restaurant keeps busy serving up gourmet breakfasts until midafternoon, at extremely reasonable prices (when's the last time you scored eggs florentine for under $5?). The sandwiches, quesadillas, and salads are

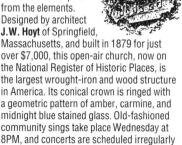

appealing, too, as are refreshing drinks such as the "southern fruit tea" (iced tea splashed with pineapple juice). ♦ International ♦ Daily 6:30AM-3PM May–mid-Oct. Lake Ave (between Circuit and Central Aves), Oak Bluffs. 693.6506 &

COURTESY OF MARTHA'S
VINEYARD HISTORICAL SOCIETY

23 Flying Horses Carousel Declared a National Historic Landmark and operated by the Martha's Vineyard Preservation Trust, this 1876 carousel hails from Coney Island and is purportedly the oldest in the country that's still in operation. The rigging is fairly primitive, and the ride is tame—the horses just go round and round, not up and down. But the 22 hand-carved steeds, with their genuine horsehair manes and soulful glass eyes, are fascinating to look at, even if most riders are too busy grabbing rings in hopes of winning a free spin. ♦ Nominal fee. Daily 10AM-10PM late May–early Sept; call for off-season hours; closed mid-October–mid-April. 33 Circuit Ave (at Lake Ave), Oak Bluffs. 693.9481

24 Zapotec Cafe ★★$$ This cottage cafe, bedecked in Christmas colors and festooned with chili-pepper lights, serves gourmet Mexican dishes, ranging from enchiladas, quesadillas, fajitas, and burritos to such specialties as chicken mole or *suiza*. Everything's fresh, and the chilies go down well with the Mexican beer, available in many varieties. ♦ Mexican ♦ Daily lunch and dinner May–mid-Oct. 10 Kennebec Ave (between Park and Lake Aves), Oak Bluffs. 693.6800 &

25 Ritz Cafe ★$ Circuit Avenue is Oak Bluff's version of Bourbon Street, and this funky bar, popular with locals, is where the blues rule. There's live music six nights a week and beer on tap. Food is not the draw here, but what's offered—burgers, turkey sandwiches, burritos, and Portuguese *linguica* (sausage)—is hearty and reasonably priced. ♦ American/Continental ♦ Nominal cover on weekends. Daily dinner. Circuit Ave (between Park and Lake Aves), Oak Bluffs. 693.9851 &

25 Lampost/Rare Duck The huge and boisterous **Lampost** features live music alternating with DJ dancing. The nautically decorated **Rare Duck** is calmer, though not much. ♦ Cover. Daily Apr-Oct; call for schedule. 111 Circuit Ave (between Park and Lake Aves), Oak Bluffs. Hotline: 696.9352

25 Mad Martha's This hands-down island favorite features homemade ice cream in exotic flavors like mango sorbet (Bill Clinton' choice). The Wurlitzer is stocked with oldies, encouraging one to linger. ♦ Daily 11AM-midnight early July–early Sept; noon-9PM May–early July, early Sept–mid-Oct. 117 Circuit Ave (between Park and Lake Aves), Oak Bluffs. 693.9151 & Also at: 8 Union St (between Water and Main Sts), Vineyard Haven. 863.5883 &; 4 Main St (at S Water St) Edgartown. 627.8761 &

26 David's Island House $ The hotel's 17 rooms are eminently affordable although rather dreary. If all you need is a place to lay your head after the exhausting Oak Bluffs nightlife, they'll do just fine. The restaurant features American fare. ♦ Closed early September–late May. 120 Circuit Ave (between Tabernacle and Lake Aves), Oak Bluffs. 693.4516

26 The Atlantic Connection DJs alternate with live performers at this popular club, where you might encounter hotshot summerers like Spike Lee or Ted Danson. Comedy night attracts a more settled, sedentary crowd, while the homegrown roots/reggae band Entrain does a weekly gig guaranteed to get everyone dancing. ♦ Cover. Daily 8:30PM-closing; call for details. 124 Circuit Ave (between Tabernacle and Lake Aves), Oak Bluffs. 693.7129

27 Jimmy Seas Pan Pasta Restaurant ★★$$$$ It's not much to look at (basic luncheonette decor), but regulars swear by the generous pasta dishes, served in the pan they were cooked in. Everything's fair game fc toppings, from chicken and shrimp with fresh pesto to swordfish in a balsamic vinaigrette. Rare is the customer who manages to lick the plate/pan clean. ♦ Italian ♦ M-Th dinner, F-Su breakfast and dinner May–mid-Oct; call for of season hours; closed January through March 32 Kennebec Ave (between Samoset and Park Aves), Oak Bluffs. 696.8550

28 Jamaikan Jam Of all the great ethnic shops along Circuit Avenue, this one's a certified winner. The clothes are colorful and comfortable, and the soundtrack a trip in itself. In addition to selling artifacts from that other entrancing island, the shop sells and rents in-line skates—a great way to take in the sights. ♦ Daily 9AM-11PM June–mid-Sept; call for off-season hours; closed January through April. 154 Circuit Ave (between Trinity and Tabernacle Aves), Oak Bluffs. 693.5003

9 Hilliard's Kitch-in-vue Painted pink, blue, and white, and trimmed with heart cutouts, this old-fashioned cottage/candy store is so beguiling you half expect to find a witch inside, making sweets for unsuspecting children. Instead it's David Hilliard, scion of a line of confectioners, carrying on a tradition of handmade chocolates that dates back a half-century. ♦ Daily 9AM-10PM late May–early Sept; call for off-season hours. 158 Circuit Ave (between Trinity and Tabernacle Aves), Oak Bluffs. 693.2191

29 Papa's Pizza ★★$ Along with a slice of good pizza, enjoy a slice of the past. Long wooden tables line this old-fashioned storefront, which has a marble counter, brass lamps, and tin ceiling and walls. Check out the vintage photographs of "campers" past, including one group posed so meticulously in front of their cottage, it looks like a stage set. ♦ Italian/Takeout ♦ Daily lunch and dinner. 158 Circuit Ave (between Trinity and Tabernacle Aves), Oak Bluffs. 693.1400 ♿

29 Brasserie 162 ★★★$$$$ At the site of the former **Oyster Bar,** this new, Mediterranean-looking restaurant has a café au lait–colored exterior with washed-out blue Grecian doors; inside, on the long back wall, is a mosaic fresco done by artists Jen Strachen and Steve Lohman. Chef Perry Ambulos, who cooked at **Savoir Fare** in Edgartown, has a menu that changes every three weeks and offers such entrées as a sautéed spice-rubbed shrimp with carrot-ginger juice served in an oversized martini glass with roast-garlic seasoned mashed sweet potato, or a house cioppino that includes lobster and fresh shellfish in a rich fresh broth. There's also a 30-foot mahogany raw bar featuring sushi, shellfish, and lobster tails. Owners Larry Johnson and Perry Ambulos have purchased the catering company that operated out of the **Truly Scrumptious Cafe** in Edgartown and offer the same gourmet menu for off-premises parties. ♦ International/Eclectic ♦ Daily dinner July-Aug; call for off-season hours; restaurant closed November through April; catering available year-round. 162 Circuit Ave (between Trinity and Tabernacle Aves), Oak Bluffs. 696.6336 ♿

30 Two Fabulus Guys, One Swell Buritow ★★$$ These days just one guy—moonlighting artist Johnathan Derry—can't spell for beans, but he does know how to run a lively little restaurant: Take over a cottage and fill it with mismatched tables and chairs, turn the lilac arbor into a shaded garden cafe, and sign up some local talent for jazz and Jamaican nights. The Mexican staples are cheap and delicious, and the guy's mom, Carol Derry Corso, makes a really mean mole for the chicken enchiladas, as well as old-fashioned lattice pies and double fudge cakes—all from scratch. ♦ Mexican ♦ Daily breakfast, lunch, and dinner July-Aug; call for off-season hours; closed December through February. No credit cards accepted. 164 Circuit Ave (between Trinity and Tabernacle Aves), Oak Bluffs. 696.6494 ♿

31 The Oak Bluffs Inn $$ Winsomely painted in a patchwork of mission rose, blue, green, and fuchsia, this cupola-topped Victorian bed-and-breakfast has all sorts of cozy spaces, with eight rooms and a suite, all with baths, and some handsome Mission furniture and private balconies. All guests are encouraged to enjoy the octagonal "viewing tower," up some steep nautical stairs, where the view takes in all of Oak Bluffs. Equally pleasant is the chance to while away the hours on one of the wicker rockers that grace the wraparound porch. ♦ Closed November through April. 167 Circuit Ave (at Pequot Ave), Oak Bluffs. 693.7171, 800/955.6235

The Native Americans of Cape Cod, Martha's Vineyard, and Nantucket never joined the uprising of 1675-76 that devastated the rest of the Indian population in New England. Only disease limited their numbers.

32 Union Chapel Built in 1870 as a monument to the hard-won Civil War, Boston architect **Samuel Freeman Pratt**'s octagonal wooden building (now on the National Register of Historic Places) is a beauty to behold, inside and out. Triangular windows with diamond panes set high in the three-tiered roof cast a summery glow on the woodwork, painted robin's-egg blue and dark green. Superb acoustics intensify the warm rumblings of the "organ prelude" and the ensuing eloquence of an interdenominational roster of ministers convened from around the country. ♦ Service: Su 10AM July–early Sept. Samoset Ave (between Grove and Circuit Aves), Oak Bluffs. No phone &

33 The Oak House $$$ When Massachusetts Governor William Claflin bought this Queen Anne house (designed, like the Union Chapel and many a Newport "cottage," by **Samuel Freeman Pratt**), he jacked up the roof to add another floor of bedrooms, all paneled in the manner of ship cabins. The rooms toward the back are quieter; then again, the front ones have Nantucket Sound views. The common rooms, like the 10 bedrooms (two are suites), are furnished in an opulent Victorian mode. Complementing the mood is the aroma of fresh pastry wafting from innkeeper Betsi Convery-Luce's kitchen. A Cordon Bleu chef, she enjoys baking peach or pecan-pear cake for breakfast, and perhaps caramel cookie tarts to go with tea or lemonade served on the glass-enclosed porch. ♦ Closed mid-October–mid-May. Seaview and Pequot Aves, Oak Bluffs. 693.4187; fax 696.7385

34 Sea Spray Inn $$ Separated from the water by a grassy field, this comfortable seven-bedroom bed-and-breakfast reflects the personality of its owner, artist Rayeanne King. Her work—oversize pastels of flowers —adorns the peach walls of the dining room/ parlor. She knows the island well and is happy to steer guests to its many pleasures. ♦ Closed December through March. 2 Nashawena Park (between Naumkeag and Katama Aves), Oak Bluffs. 693.9388 &

35 Island Inn $$$ Set amid seven wooded acres adjoining the public **Farm Neck Golf Club** (rendered famous by Bill Clinton's many forays), this 51-unit complex has all the bonuses of a full-scale resort—pool, three Har-Tru tennis courts, conference facilities— but the feel of a family compound. The placid bay and lovely Sengekontacket Pond are both within a short walk. There is no restaurant. ♦ Closed mid-December–mid-March. Beach Rd (between Joseph Sylvia State Beach Park and S Circuit Ave), Oak Bluffs. 693.2002, 800/462.0269; fax 693.7911 &

35 Lola's Southern Seafood ★★$$$ Adjacent to the **Island Inn** but independently operated, this pretty restaurant lures with sound as well as savor. Live jazz and DJ dancing occupy the late evenings; the Sunday brunch gets a gospel accompaniment. With a fixed-price entrée—everything from blackened catfish to Detroit-style barbecue baby back ribs—that comes with creole Caesar salad, corn bread and buttermilk biscuits, collard greens and potatoes, diners are sufficiently fueled to dance the night away. ♦ Southern ♦ M-Sa dinner; Su brunch and dinner. Reservations recommended. Beach Rd (between Joseph Sylvia State Beach Park and S Circuit Ave), Oak Bluffs. 693.5007 &

36 Felix Neck Wildlife Sanctuary Nearly wiped out by DDT in the 1960s, the osprey, a hawk with a five-and-a-half-foot wingspan, is making a promising comeback at this 350-acre Massachusetts Audubon Society preserve, where nesting platforms have elevated these fish-eating birds out of the endangered list. Six miles of trails transecting woods, fields, marshes, and beaches can afford glimpses of many other species; should they elude you, look to the aquariums, turtle tanks, and majestic raptors at the visitors' center. Various interpretive exhibits are on view, and nature programs are scheduled throughout the year. ♦ Admission. Trails: daily dawn-7PM. Visitors' center: daily June–mid-Sept; Tu-Su mid-Sept–May. Off Edgartown-Vineyard Haven Rd (between Edgartown-Oak Bluffs Rd and Allen St), Edgartown. 627.4850 &

37 The Arbor $$ It may look modest from the outside, but innkeeper Peggy Hall treated her 1880 farmhouse to a dramatic addition: a house-size sitting room with a cathedral ceiling. Crocheted bedspreads and eclectic antiques adorn the 10 pretty rooms. However, this is one bed-and-breakfast where you'll definitely want to emerge to socialize—not only because the chintz sofas in the living room are so inviting, but because Hall is a charming and knowledgeable hostess, and you'll want to solicit her advice over the elegant continental breakfast, if not sooner. The inn is about a five-minute walk from the

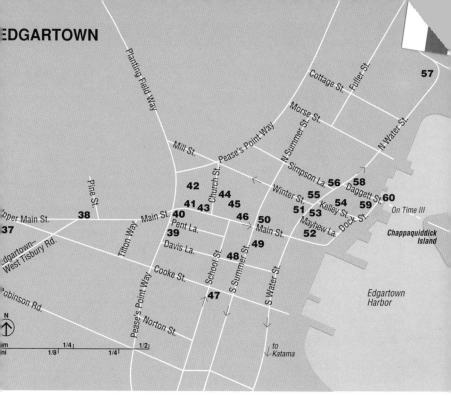

57

Cottage St.

Fuller St.

Planting Field Way

Morse St.

N. Water St.

Mill St.

Pease's Point Way

N. Summer St.

N. Simpson La.

Winter St.

56

58

Daggett St.

60

42

Church St.

44

55

54

59

On Time III

Pine St.

41

43

45

Kelley St.

51

53

Dock St.

38

Main St.

Tilton Way

Pent La.

46

50

Mayhew La.

52

Chappaquiddick Island

Upper Main St.

37

39

Davis La.

Main St.

49

Edgartown–West Tisbury Rd.

School St.

48

S. Summer St.

Robinson Rd.

Cooke St.

Pease's Point Way

47

Norton St.

S. Water St.

Edgartown Harbor

N

to Katama

m 1/4 1/2
mi 1/8 1/4

---

center of town or a minute of pedaling via the bike path right out front. ♦ Closed November through April. 222 Upper Main St (between Edgartown–West Tisbury and Chase Rds), Edgartown. 627.8137

38 O'Brien's ★★$$$$ The rose garden, set with Roman parasols, is a lovely spot for partaking of serious seafood—straight-forwardly pan-seared or grilled, plumped atop pasta, or blanketed with various sauces and stuffings. The indoor dining room, in a house that dates from the 1890s, is appealing, too, with raspberry sponge-painted walls and trompe l'oeil ivy trailing along the cross beams. Downstairs, the dimly lit, brick-walled bistro offers a piano bar where there is often a singer and guitarist. ♦ Continental ♦ M, W-Su dinner May-Dec. 137 Upper Main St (between Pine St and Curtis La), Edgartown. 627.5850

38 Ashley Inn $$$ As sweet as grandmother's house but probably a lot spiffier, this 1860s captain's manse offers eight standard rooms and two grander-sized rooms, all charmingly done up with quilts and country accents, some with fireplaces or whirlpool baths.

There's a spacious yard with a hammock awaiting you and a summer-weight book. Continental breakfast is served; there is no restaurant. ♦ 129 Main St (between Pine St and Curtis La), Edgartown. 627.9655, 800/477.9655; fax 627.6629

39 Shiverick Inn $$$ One of the more imposing mansions in town, this mansard-roofed 1840 Victorian, built for the town physician, remains unstintingly formal, from its mahogany front doors, up the black walnut staircase (lit with crystal chandeliers), and straight up to the square cupola. The 10 high-ceilinged bedrooms (six with fireplaces) are distinctively decorated with antiques, Oriental rugs, patterned wallpapers, and, typically, a four-poster or canopy bed. Some will find the atmosphere of this bed-and-breakfast romantic, as intended; others may find it too fussy. Waffles and homemade breads are served for breakfast, and it's a two-minute walk to the restaurants in town. ♦ 5 Pent La (at Pease's Point Way), Edgartown. 627.3797, 800/723.4292; fax 627.8441

Joseph Daggett of Martha's Vineyard married an island Indian princess in 1667. The descendants on the island were known as "the bow and arrow Daggetts" to distinguish them from other Vineyard Daggetts.

The first English name for Oak Bluffs, in 1646, was "Easternmost Chop of Holmes' Hole."

40 Point Way Inn $$$$ In 1979, Linda and Ben Smith concluded an 18-month, 4,000-mile cruise on their ketch by settling into this 1840 sea captain's house and turning it into a 15-room bed-and-breakfast. It's clear that a real family lives here. Happy mementos (charts, flags, trophies, photos) crop up everywhere, and visitors are given the impression that they're house guests who just happen to be paying. Among the more hospitable cues are the honor bar (with chip-in kitty), the use of a loaner compact car, and invitations to go clamming or play croquet with Ben. Better brush up beforehand: He's among the top-ranked players in the country. In fact, the inn's arbor vitae–bordered lawn is official headquarters of the Edgartown Mallet Club, where every July celebrities such as Art Buchwald participate in the charity Croquet Classic. Linda sees to breakfast (fresh juice, homemade granola, breads, and popovers) in the 1930s-style farmhouse kitchen. Few guests can resist the urge to tinker with the 500-piece custom-made Stave puzzle perennially awaiting completion in the comfortable living room. ♦ 104 Main St (at Pease's Point Way), Edgartown. 627.8633; fax 627.8579

COURTESY OF MARTHA'S VINEYARD HISTORICAL SOCIETY

41 Dr. Daniel Fisher House Fisher (1799-1876) was not just a physician, but a whaling magnate and merchant (his spermaceti candle factory was said to be the largest in the world) and founder of the Martha's Vineyard National Bank. Naturally, his house, built in 1840, was the biggest and grandest in town. It's headquarters for the Martha's Vineyard Preservation Trust, and the beautifully proportioned rooms can be viewed on a guided tour. Even if you're just passing by, you'll want to stop long enough to take in the front portico, with its fluted columns crowned by acanthus capitals; a complementary motif is echoed in the decorative roofwalk, and more columns appear in the semicircular side porch.

During his lifetime, Fisher garnered more admiration than envy. "His continuous efforts for the good of his fellow-men," read his *Vineyard Gazette* obituary, "will ever be remembered by his townsmen, who have saved thousands upon thousands of dollars by purchasing flour, corn, meal, coal, wood, etc., from him at a very small advance from first cost. . . . He leaves behind him a respectable fortune, not one mill of which was dishonestly obtained." ♦ Admission. Hourly tours starting from the Vincent House daily 10AM-4PM (last tour at 3PM) June-Oct; by appointment off-season. 99 Main St (between Church St and Pease's Point Way), Edgartown. 627.8017

42 Vincent House One of the oldest houses on the island, this 1672 shingled full Cape was moved here from Mashacket Cove in 1977 and restored by the Martha's Vineyard Preservation Trust to illustrate three centuries of island life. The house has been filled with period furnishings and it offers a unique opportunity to observe architectural details, from the wide white-pine floorboards to a central chimney made of island-fired brick. Plexiglas panels permit a view of the various layers that went into wattle-and-daub insulation. ♦ Admission. Daily 10:30AM-3PM June-Oct; by appointment off-season. Off Main St (between Church St and Pease's Point Way), Edgartown. 627.8619

43 Old Whaling Church The magnum opus of local architect **Frederick Baylies Jr.** (he also designed the 1828 Federated Church and the 1839 Baptist Church, now a private residence), this 1843 Greek Revival church (at upper right) was built with the same methods used for whaling ships; the infrastructure consists of 50-foot hand-hewn red pine beams barged down from Maine and assembled with wooden pegs and square joinings. Everything is on a grand scale—the portico with its six massive columns, the 92-foot spiked square tower (visible far out to sea), and the 27-foot, three-sash windows arranged four to a side so that the whole space

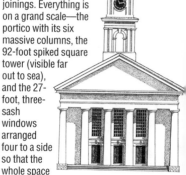

is awash with light. Elegant whale-oil lamps (since electrified) were used to illuminate the short, gloomy days of winter. Originally, the churchgoers owned their pews and furnished them as they saw fit, with carpets, footstools, and foot warmers; now the cushions are a uniform burgundy. In 1980, the Methodist congregation asked the Martha's Vineyard Preservation Trust to take charge of the building. Services are still held, but the church functions primarily as a 500-seat performing arts center offering lectures and symposia, films, plays, and music and dance concerts. Such island luminaries as actress Patricia Neal and composer Andre Previn have edified the populace from the stage. ◆ Hourly tours: daily 11AM-3PM June-Oct; by appointment off-season. Service: Su 9AM. Call for events schedule. 89 Main St (at Church St), Edgartown. 627.4442 &

44 Savoir Fare ★★★$$$$ One of the best restaurants in Edgartown is set back from the water, next to a not-exactly-scenic parking lot. But the immediate surroundings will fade once you settle in beneath a dainty pergola, where a raw bar shares its bed of ice with a bottle of Moet. Indoors there's a view of the open kitchen, where owner Scott Caskey attends to the garde-manger (salads, desserts, and other cold preparations), and chef Mike Presnal to the stove. Their collaboration yields beautifully balanced meals: exquisite bitter greens with pear, gorgonzola, and toasted walnuts, for instance, followed by herb-crusted wild boar chops with garlicky broccoli rabe and sweet potato polenta. The menu changes constantly, but you can always count on thoughtful—and delightful—presentations. ◆ New American ◆ Daily dinner Apr-Oct. Reservations recommended. 14 Church St (between Main and Winter Sts), Edgartown. 627.9864 &

45 Latanzi's ★★$$$$ With its pale pink walls and trendy faux-granite bar, this restaurant—dedicated to "traditional Italian" cuisine—looks urbane enough, but the fare may not always live up to the cost. Stick with the hickory-grilled house specials, like veal chop with porcini-mushroom cream or fillet of beef with prosciutto, tomatoes, and veal reduction; accompany these with choices from the antipasti list, like lemon-marinated baby octopus salad or littleneck clams steamed with garlic and tomatoes. ◆ Italian ◆ Daily dinner. Old Post Office Sq (off Main St, between N Summer and Church Sts), Edgartown. 627.8854 &

45 Main Street Diner ★★$ This retro diner displays items the owner collected over 20 years—original Coke signs, gumball machines, roadside art, and an Orange Crush machine. The jukebox promises 1950s tunes, and though inflation rules out 1950s prices, they're not bad for the 1990s. A one-egg breakfast with home fries and a buttermilk biscuit will set you back only three dollars; the burgers and sandwiches (including a classic open-face hot turkey with gravy, potatoes, and cranberry sauce) less than seven. At these prices, you can afford to bring the kids, and it's located right under the new 400-seat, two-screen **Edgartown Cinema**. ◆ American ◆ Daily breakfast, lunch, and dinner. Old Post Office Sq (off Main St, between N Summer and Church Sts), Edgartown. 627.9337 &

46 CJ's on Main Street ★★$$$ Operated by chef/owners Cindy and Jeff Madeiros, this centrally located dining room with red-brick walls, large mirrors, and banquette seating is a welcoming, unpretentious spot for locals and tourists alike. The steamed mussels in wine with artichoke hearts, garlic, and basil are a tasty prelude to fresh swordfish brushed with mustard, diced red onion, and orange sauce. ◆ American ◆ Daily dinner Apr-Dec; F-Su Jan-Mar. 71 Main St (between N Summer St and Old Post Office Sq), Edgartown. 627.8446

Upstairs from CJ's on Main Street:

The Sand Bar ★$$ This upstairs sports bar and grill is set in two rooms: one with a bar, working fireplace, and TVs showing the latest games; the other a plant-filled dining room with entry to a porch offering dining at seven tables overlooking Edgartown's historic Main Street. This spot specializes in tropical frozen drinks and reasonably priced appetizers like fresh littlenecks and oysters, chicken fingers with salsa, and mini-pizzas. ◆ American ◆ Daily lunch and dinner. 627.9027

Once a recondite symbol recognized only by fellow cognoscenti, the Black Dog's trademark T-shirt has become popular enough to attract imitators, or rather parodists. In 1993, when Black Dog restaurateur Robert Douglas sought an injunction against an islander cranking out "black hog" T-shirts in his basement, US District Court judge Joseph L. Tauro opined that no copyright infringement had occurred, since there was no mistaking the two: "Unlike plaintiff's somewhat noble depiction of man's best friend," he wrote, "defendant's swine strikes a less inspiring pose."

47 Vineyard Museum This block-square complex houses the intriguing collections of the Martha's Vineyard Historical Society. Changing displays in the 1765 **Thomas Cooke House**—a full Cape constructed by shipbuilders for the customs collector—concern island history; keep an eye out for the mammy bench in the pantry, the inlaid boxes made on whaling ships, the homely portrait of early resident Ephraim Pease (oil paint on mattress ticking, and remarkably well-preserved). The **Francis Foster Museum,** accessed through the **Gale Huntington Library of History,** is devoted to the maritime trade and exhibits some exceptional scrimshaw (including a pie crimp shaped like a two-headed serpent), an 1840 ship's log with primitive watercolors by Richard Norton, and a captain's portrait by Thomas Hart Benton. The **Captain Francis Pease House,** an 1845 Greek Revival structure, contains prehistoric, pre-Columbian, and Native American artifacts, including Wampanoag pottery made of multicolored Gay Head clay. Also on the grounds is a carriage shed housing an 1830 hearse, a fire engine from 1855, a 19th-century peddler's cart and whaleboat, and tombstones for Nancy Luce's pet chickens (a West Tisbury eccentric of the late 19th century, Miss Luce supported herself by selling postcards and poems about her beloved bantams). Outside, the transplanted **Gay Head Light Tower,** a 1,008-prism red-and-white Fresnel lens in use from 1856 to 1952, shines forth for a few hours every summer evening. ♦ Admission. Daily 10AM-4:30PM July-Aug; call for off-season hours. 59 School St (at Cooke St), Edgartown. 627.4441

48 Vineyard Gazette The circulation may be a modest 14,000 or so, but this influential little paper—now edited by Richard Reston—goes out to all 50 states and at least a dozen foreign countries; its far-flung readers don't want to miss any news of "their" island. You're welcome to wander in and look around, but for a full tour of the presses (including the original Seth Adams press), it's best to make arrangements in advance. The operation is housed in the shingled **Benjamin Smith House,** built by a Revolutionary War captain around 1760.

The very first issue of the *Gazette,* dated 14 May 1846, is preserved under glass. The paper's banner summed up its mission: "a family newspaper—neutral in politics, devoted to general news, literature, morality, agriculture and amusement." In the old days subscriptions cost $2 a year, and front-page news consisted of poetry and columns on such topics as "covetousness" and "married life." ♦ M-F. 34 S Summer St (at Davis La), Edgartown. 627.4311

49 Charlotte Inn $$$$
Since 1971, Gery and Paula Conover have been expanding and polishing up this exquisite

compound connected by English gardens and brick walkways. They're now up to five houses containing 23 lavish rooms and two dazzling suites. Each guest room is distinctively decorated, and four-posters and fireplaces abound. The white-clapboard 1860 main house (former home of merchant Samuel Osborne, whose daughter Charlotte turned it into an inn in the 1920s) tends to be more formal; the downstairs sitting rooms double as the **Edgartown Art Gallery,** showcasing English and American antiques, as well as 19th- and 20th-century paintings and prints. The 1705 **Garden House** across the street is done up in French country furnishings. The **Coach House Suite,** perched above the inn's collection of antique cars, features English antiques, a walk-in dressing room ornamented with hats and fans, and a Palladian window offering a sliver of harbor view. In the 1840 **Summer House,** which once belonged to a sea captain, one room boasts both a fireplace and a baby grand. The **Carriage House** (which Gery built without blueprints in 1980) is in some ways the most evocative of all. Tucked away amid wisteria vines, it shelters a cathedral-ceilinged suite done up in an English hunting motif, with a brass bed, striped wallpaper, vintage riding paraphernalia, and a prototypical tripod camera. What you make of this fantasy environment is your own affair. ♦ 27 S Summer St (between Davis La and Main St), Edgartown. 627.4751; fax 627.4652 &

Within the Charlotte Inn:

l'étoile

l'étoile ★★★$$$$ The dining room doubles as a conservatory—with its healthy collection of ferns and tropical trees. Brass hurricane lamps cast their flickering light across the glass canopy and the gold-edged Villeroy & Boch china. Equally delightful is the cuisine: Chef Michael Brisson, formerly of Boston's famed L'Espalier, has a deft, light touch and a gift for pairing complementary ingredients—warm Mission figs, for instance, to offset seared pheasant breast in an Armagnac-sage sauce, accompanied by sautéed summer greens and quinoa. Every flavor is played to its full effect, whether it be foie gras zapped with a confit of Vidalia onions and bing cherries, or the caramelized macadamia nuts that become the basis for an ice cream topped with Bailey's crème anglaise. When dinner with a decent wine runs to $100 or so a head, you expect perfection, and you are very likely to find it here. ◆ Contemporary French ◆ Daily dinner May–early Sept; call for off-season hours; closed late December–April. Reservations recommended; jacket requested. 627.5187 ♿

50 In the Woods Toward the front of this warehouse-size store are predictable little wooden gewgaws meant to tempt tourists. Press on and things get curiouser (as well as bigger and pricier): handsome Oriental rugs; antique sandalwood chests, cupboards, and ceremonial doorways from Pakistan; a sleek white spruce canoe with sail (priced at $4,200). If you're an "impulse" shopper you may have to restrain yourself. ◆ Daily 9AM–11PM June–mid-Oct; call for off-season schedule. 55 Main St (at N Summer St), Edgartown. 627.8989 ♿

51 Tuscany Inn $$$$ Rusty and Laura Scheuer (she's from Florence and a formidable chef) took a derelict captain's house and turned it into the most dazzling little inn in town. The interior comes as a total surprise; instead of Yankee austerity, it's a look transported straight from sunny Italy, with warm colors and an abundance of fine old paintings. Past a little library lined with leather-backed books is Laura's open kitchen, where she gives cooking classes off-season; lavish breakfasts (blueberry buttermilk pancakes, frittata with focaccia) are served here when the weather precludes a feast on the patio. Each of the eight rooms is a gem, with hand-painted antique armoires and fanciful beds—and, in some cases, skylights, marble whirlpools, and harbor views. ◆ Closed January–mid-March. 22 N Water St (at Winter St), Edgartown. 627.5999; fax 627.6605

Within the Tuscany Inn:

La Cucina ★★★$$$$ One of the best new dining spots in Edgartown, and no wonder: The chef/owner, Marco Canora, son of the aforementioned cooking school teacher, trained at Gramercy Tavern in New York City and studies cooking off-season in Florence. There are three dining areas—a formal candlelit room, an informal open kitchen with tables where diners can watch the chef, and eight tables outside overlooking extensive gardens. For starters, try shrimp wrapped in prosciutto. Then enjoy Chilean sea bass with asparagus tips and red wine or the house specialty, *pappardelle* (homemade thick pasta) with wild mushrooms, shallots, truffle oil, and *reggiano* parmesan. ◆ Italian/Eclectic ◆ Tu-Su dinner mid-Oct–Nov. Reservations recommended. 627.8161

52 The Great Put On If the name sounds like a flashback to the mod era, that's because this clothing shop dates back that far (to 1969). The stock, though, is absolutely up to the minute, and then some. Owner Ken Bilzerian is the brother of Alan Bilzerian, Boston's cutting-edge couturier, and their tastes are not dissimilar. Designers include such avant-gardists as BCBG, Norma Kamali, and Vivienne Tam. There's also a fine selection of men's fashions in casual Italian tweeds and silks. The small but select shoe collection ranges from understated chic to bold and bizarre. ◆ Daily 10AM–11PM May–early Sept; daily 10AM–7PM early Sept–Dec. Mayhew La (between Dock and N Water Sts), Edgartown. 627.5495 ♿

53 Among the Flowers Cafe ★$ Most of the seating is under an awning outdoors, where you'll just catch a glimpse of the harbor. This is one of the few spots in town where—assuming you can get in, not so easy a feat in summer—you can grab a pleasant meal without taking out a second mortgage. The omelettes, crepes, waffles, and quiches, all prettily garnished with fresh fruit, are available at lunch as well as breakfast. The dinners aren't elaborate (e.g., lemon chicken, lobster Newburg crepe), but they're very painlessly priced. ◆ American/Continental ◆ Daily breakfast, lunch, and dinner July-Aug; daily breakfast and lunch May-June, Sept–mid-Oct. Mayhew La (between Dock and N Water Sts), Edgartown. 627.3233 ♿

"The Vineyard is not a way station, it is a destination," wrote Henry Beetle Hough, revered editor of the *Vineyard Gazette* for 65 years. "It is not a place of rush and hurry, it is a state of rest."

53 The Fligors of Edgartown For year-rounders, this tasteful emporium, run by Carol and Dick Fligor since 1960, has long served as an all-purpose department store; for mere visitors, it's a handy concentration of preppie essentials. Grownups' clothes are conservative, but the traditionalist kids' clothing is terrific. Adults fare well in terms of gifts, and children perhaps even better, with both up-to-date toys and such classics as Steiff stuffed animals and Madame Alexander dolls. ◆ Daily 9AM-11PM late May–early Sept; daily early Sept–late May. 27 N Water St (at Kelley St), Edgartown. 627.4722 &

54 Kelley House $$$$ The only evidence of the building's origins as a rough-hewn tavern is the resurrected pub. This 55-room white-clapboard inn is instead thoroughly modern, with a light country veneer. If you place a premium on fresh decor and luxurious amenities (e.g., a heated outdoor pool), you might prefer it to a more intimate bed-and-breakfast—and the management does provide some nice personal touches, such as milk and cookies at bedtime. ◆ Closed December through May. 23 Kelley St (between Dock and N Water Sts). 627.7900, 800/225.6005; fax 627.8142

available
r 235/n
2 Dbl beds

Within the Kelley House:

Good Newes ★★$ When renovators started clearing out this basement space, they found the original rubble and ballast-brick walls and hand-hewn timbers of the 1742 tavern still intact. The added etched-glass partitions and captain's chairs padded with green leather don't exactly fit the era, but you'll have no complaints by candlelight, especially once you've imbibed a "Rack of Beers"—any five "shorts" from a selection of 10 outstanding international brews. The food is also fairly inventive: Sandwiches run the gamut from Brazilian chicken salad to grilled eggplant and a wood-smoked oyster poorboy with *linguica* relish. ◆ American ◆ Daily lunch and dinner. 627.4397 &

Bubble netting is a term for describing how a whale dives beneath a school of fish and blows columns of bubbles. As the whale circles back up to the water's surface, the bubble columns join to form a bubble net 100 feet across through which the whale swims with its mouth wide open to scoop up fish.

55 Colonial Inn $$$

Since 1911, this hotel has served as the unofficial center of town. Because the lobby also serves as a conduit to the Nevins Square shops beyond, it's a somewhat impersonal space, but also uninhibiting—you feel free to wander in and out. The complimentary continental breakfast is a casual, self-service affair in the atrium. The 43 rooms, however, are true havens, prettily appointed with pine furniture, pastel fabrics, and brass beds. Some rooms boast water views, and all guests have access to the roof veranda, where the waterfront vista is unsurpassed. ◆ Closed mid-December–mid-April. 38 N Water St (between Winter St and Simpson La), Edgartown. 627.4711, 800/627.4701; fax 627.5904 &   *booked*

Within the Colonial Inn:

Chesca's ★$$$ Joanne Maxwell, former chef at the **Daggett House**, has quite a following for her breakfasts in this redesigned restaurant with a porch dining option, and it's not surprising given dishes like the "egg bowl"—a hollowed-out bread loaf filled with baked scrambled eggs with assorted fillings. The focaccia sandwiches for lunch, from shrimp salad to seared swordfish, are appealing, and dinner consists primarily of pastas, along with some grilled fish and classic Italian entrées. ◆ Italian ◆ Daily breakfast, lunch, and dinner Apr-Dec. 627.1234 &

56 Edgartown Inn $$$ Nathaniel Hawthorne spent the better part of a year at this 1798 Federal inn, writing *Twice Told Tales*. Other notable guests have included Daniel Webster and John F. Kennedy, while still a senator. The 18 rooms in the main building are a bit stodgy, though perfectly nice. The knockouts are the two large, modern cathedral-ceilinged rooms in the **Garden House**, which enjoy a Monet-like light and complete privacy. The full breakfast served (for an additional charge) in the kitchen wing has its aficionados; unless you like cutesy country decor, however, you may find it oppressively quaint. There is no restaurant. ◆ Closed November through March. 56 N Water St (at Simpson La), Edgartown. 627.4794

the HARBOR VIEW RESORT

57 Harbor View Hotel $$$$ In 1891, this sprawling shingled grand hotel was actually two hotels, which were later linked by a 300-foot veranda. Since its $2 million centennial renovation, the amalgam has reclaimed the showplace status it enjoyed long ago. A palette of off-whites and neutral tones has been used to restful effect everywhere from the lobby, with its massive stone fireplace, to the 124 spacious rooms. Behind the hotel (away from the waterfront), a heated pool is flanked by eight cottages and the **Mayhew** building, a more motel-like arrangement, with porches. The topflight rooms overlook Lighthouse Beach, accessible down a grass-lined path. ♦ 131 N Water St (at Starbuck's Neck Rd), Edgartown. 627.4333, 800/225.6005; fax 627.8417 &

Within the Harbor View Hotel:

Starbuck's ★★★$$$$ Making no concessions to the barefoot mores of beachside living, this restaurant is unabashedly formal, with lute-back chairs and tasseled curtains; children (adults, too) will instinctively adopt their best restaurant behavior. The rewards are ample, from an elaborate breakfast menu featuring Yankee red flannel hash and choose-your-own-combo griddle cakes to dinners that offer intriguingly prepared "land food" as well as spectacular seafood. ♦ New American ♦ M-Sa breakfast, lunch, and dinner; Su brunch and dinner. Reservations recommended. 627.7000, ext 7560 &

Breezes ★★$ A boon for nibblers, the hotel's vintage bar offers nonstop snacks that can also be enjoyed on the veranda. Breakfast, with fresh juice and home-baked pastries, starts at 6:30AM, and "grazing hours" continue late into the night, offering such delectables as smoked breast of duck with lettuce, walnuts, and a cranberry Cassis vinaigrette, or a littleneck stew with potatoes and cream for under $10. There's also a vast selection of microbrewed and imported beers. ♦ American ♦ Daily breakfast, lunch, and dinner. 627.7000, ext 7580 &

★ *The* ★
Daggett
House
CIRCA 1660
★ *The Inn On* ★
Edgartown Harbor

58 The Daggett House $$$$ This inn was built in 1750 around the core of a 1660 tavern—where owner John Daggett was once fined five shillings for "selling strong liquor"

in addition to the sanctioned ale and beer. The tavern's old beehive fireplace has been incorporated into the dining room; beside it, a revolving bookcase hides a secret stairway leading to a bedroom with a harbor view. For all its colorful history (the house later became a sailors' boardinghouse, then a private school), the interior is rather bland. The paper place mats and piped-in music that accompany breakfast in that historic keeping room are distracting. Still, some of the 26 rooms are impressive—for instance, the **Widow's Walk Suite,** in the **Warren House** across the street, which has a skylight opening onto a rooftop deck with a hot tub. The lower-priced rooms are disconcertingly drab. But the central location is a plus, as is the secluded lawn that stretches down to a private swimming dock. ♦ 59 N Water St (at Daggett St), Edgartown. 627.4600, 800/946.3400; fax 627.4611 &

Within The Daggett House:

Daggett House Restaurant ★$$$$ Both conceptualized and priced like some of the more ambitious establishments in town, this venture never quite measures up. At least it tries, with appetizers like spinach strudel (phyllo-wrapped, with mascarpone and pine nuts), and by sconce light, the tavern is certainly atmospheric. But you might want to place your dinner bet elsewhere. Breakfasts (not included in the room rates) are hearty; a specialty is French toast made with the inn's signature Grapenut bread. ♦ American ♦ Daily breakfast and dinner July-Aug; call for off-season hours. 627.4600, 800/946.3400

59 Old Sculpin Gallery Would that this beautiful old building sheltered more consistently worthy work. It was originally a grain storage house belonging to Dr. Daniel Fisher, and in the first half of the century noted boatbuilder Manuel Swartz Roberts used it as his workshop. Now the nonprofit Martha's Vineyard Art Association mounts exhibitions and holds classes here, but the output shows more enthusiasm than skill. Of course, some pieces may take you by surprise, and the wood-beamed structure itself merits a look. ♦ M-Sa 10AM-5PM, 8-10PM; Su 2-5PM, 7-10PM June through Sept. 58 Dock St (at Daggett St), Edgartown. 627.4881 &

60 On Time III The original ferry to Chappaquiddick (Wampanoag for "the separated island") got its name because the builder promised to have it ready on time for the 1920 summer season. Most users figure it's a meaningless honorific because, with no schedule, how could the flatboat be late? It takes about five minutes to cross the 200-yard divide, carrying three cars and however many passengers want to crowd on. The ride is fun, but, other than taking a hike or looking around, there's not much to do here if you don't belong to the beach club. ♦ Fee. Daily 7:30AM-midnight June-Oct; call for hours Nov-May. Dock and Daggett Sts, Edgartown. 627.9794 ♿

61 Mytoi Less than three miles from the ferry landing is a 14-acre Japanese garden, created in 1958 by Hugh Jones. Badly damaged by Hurricane Bob, it's still mending. The azaleas once again bloom in spring, the Japanese iris in summer, and the goldfish glide in their picturesque pool beneath an ornamental bridge. ♦ Free. Daily sunrise-sunset. Off Dike Rd, Chappaquiddick. 693.7662

62 Wasque Reservation and Cape Pogue Wildlife Refuge Both protectorates of the Trustees of Reservations (TOR), these unspoiled tracts—some 200 and 500 acres respectively—cover most of the island's eastern barrier beach and shelter a great variety of shorebirds, including kestrels, ospreys, oystercatchers, snowy egrets, great blue herons, and such rare and endangered species as least terns and piping plovers. Humans and their off-road vehicles are admitted for a fee, and under strict regulations. TOR offers guided natural history tours by truck or canoe.

At the land's northernmost tip sits the **Cape Pogue Lighthouse,** built in 1893 after the first two lighthouses here succumbed to the sea. Automated in 1964, this 40-foot tower originally stood 500 feet farther out, 150 feet from what was then the coast; in 1987, when its foundation had been undercut to a 25-foot margin, the Coast Guard had to "sky-crane" it inland by helicopter. During the fall, look for small boats scalloping offshore. Well-protected Cape Pogue produces half of the state's scallop harvest. ♦ Admission. Closed mid-September–mid-June. Wasque Reservation: Wasque Rd (off Chappaquiddick Rd), Chappaquiddick. 693.7662; Cape Pogue Wildlife Refuge: At the end of Dike Rd, Chappaquiddick. 693.7662

63 Katama Shores Inn $$$ It may lack charm, but it's come a long way: This 68-room motel started out as an army barracks. Continental breakfast is served; there is no restaurant. The inn's major attraction is its proximity to South Beach (a five-minute walk past an unsightly aggregation of condos). Since this is basically the only oceanside beach accessible to the public (most beaches on Martha's Vineyard are privately owned), it can get pretty mobbed in July and August. It's accessible by car, bike, and shuttle bus from Edgartown, so only dedicated beach bums need to stay this close. ♦ Closed mid-

October–mid-May. Katama Rd (at South Beach Rd), Edgartown. 627.4747; fax 627.3252 ♿

64 Hot Tin Roof Carly Simon is one of the owners of this recently renovated hangar-turned-nightclub, where offerings span DJ mixes and live comedy, country, blues, R&B, and funk. ♦ Cover. M-Sa 7PM-closing, Su 4PM-closing May–mid-Sept; closed mid-September–April. Airport Rd (off Edgartown–West Tisbury Rd), West Tisbury. 693.1137

65 South Shore Stables Lessons are offered whatever the weather, in an indoor ring at this large, well-tended horse barn. Beginners and old hands alike, English or Western, can head out on forest trail rides from dawn to sunset —and even by moonlight. ♦ Fee. By appointment. Scrubby Neck Rd (off Edgartown–West Tisbury Rd), West Tisbury. 693.3770

66 Long Point Wildlife Refuge Nature lovers must brave some bumpy roads to reach this 633-acre Trustees of Reservations preserve, where a mile long loop trail passes through a pine-oak forest, then sandy plain, grassland, and heath, to reach Long Cove Pond, home to songbirds, blue-claw crabs, and river otters. Another milelong path leads to a secluded stretch of South Beach; it's a popular spot in summer, so get to the parking area very early in the day. ♦ Parking fee. Daily mid-June–mid-Sept. Off Waldron's Bottom Rd, West Tisbury. 693.7662

67 Manter Memorial AYH-Hostel $ The first "purpose-built" youth hostel in the United States, this homey cedar shake saltbox set at the edge of a vast state forest is still a front-runner. It hums with wholesome energy, from the huge group kitchen with recycling bins and two communal fridges to the five dorms accommodating 78 beds. The hallways are plastered with notices of local attractions (some stores offer discounts to hostelers), and the check-in desk also serves as info central. Outside, there's a volleyball court, a chicken coop, and a sheltered bike rack. The hostel is a little more than seven miles from the Vineyard Haven ferry by bike path; shuttle buses also make the rounds in summer. You'll have no trouble at all finding enjoyable ways to spend the 10AM-5PM lockout; just don't forget the 11PM curfew. ♦ Closed mid-November–March. Edgartown–West Tisbury Rd (between Airport and Old County Rds), West Tisbury. 693.2665; fax 693.2699 ♿

If you think modern bureaucracy is bad, consider the official name of Dukes County (which covers Martha's Vineyard and the Elizabeth Islands). The correct nomenclature, if you please, is the County of Dukes County.

African American Heritage Trail

It took the simple question of a second-grade student from **Oak Bluffs Elementary School** to plant the idea for a trail that would acknowledge the role African-Americans played in the Vineyard's history. While the class was reading a textbook on local history, the boy asked, "But what about the black people?" The teacher answered, "They weren't here then." But she hesitated. Why weren't they on the island then? They were in the rest of the United States, why not on Martha's Vineyard? Did the fact that African-Americans were not in the history books mean that they weren't on the island, that they didn't contribute to its early settlement, that they didn't appear in **Oak Bluffs** until forming the first black resort in the US, or was it a blatant omission?

One of the school's teachers, Elaine Cawley Weintraub, along with the vice president of the local chapter of the NAACP, Carrie B. Tankard, decided to delve more deeply into island history. While Tankard worked with the memories of African-American residents she had come to know in her 25 years on the island, Weintraub researched the wills of early island settlers and found enslaved Africans named in the estates as far back as 1703. She found many mentions of African-Americans in wills, whaling logs, diaries, and old editions of the *Vineyard Gazette*. Blacks were seamen, farmers, preachers, musicians, and conjurers—in the old African tradition, wise women—who could put a hex on a sailing trip or wish it luck. Weintraub and Tankard decided to commemorate the tradition of Vineyard blacks by loosely organizing the African-American Heritage Trail.

The following places are current stops on the trail, and it is expected that more will be added in the future. Most are in **Oak Bluffs**, but two locations outside town are included—one in **Chilmark**, the other on the island of **Chappaquiddick**. Elaine Cawley Weintraub and Carrie B. Tankard's booklet, the *African-American Heritage Trail of Martha's Vineyard*, offers details on the trail; it's available at several stores on the island. At press time an updated, more comprehensive edition was being prepared.

Although the earliest record of slave ownership on the Vineyard dates from 1703, the history of formerly enslaved African-Americans begins with the 1787 arrival of John Saunders and his wife. Saunders brought Methodism to the island, and preached it to African-Americans and Native Americans from **Pulpit Rock** at the end of **Pulpit Rock Way** in **Farm Neck,** south of Oak Bluffs.

The **Wesleyan Grove** in Oak Bluffs was the site of a revivalist camp founded by Jeremiah Pease in 1835, and the African-American preacher John F. Wright, spoke here. The tents of the campgrounds evolved into small summer cottages, and the area became known as "Cottage City." Wander among them today, and marvel at the intricate Carpenter's Gothic woodwork along the roofs, porches, and windows.

Shearer Cottage in the **Highlands** neighborhood of Oak Bluffs was the first African-American–owned boardinghouse on the island that took in black guests. Today people of all races stay here when it is open in the summer. Charles Shearer, a freed slave from Virginia, built the structure to house a laundry that he and his wife operated; his daughters turned it into an inn after their mother died. Notable guests have included Paul Robeson, Ethel Waters, Dr. Martin Luther King, and New York congressman Adam Clayton Powell, Jr. Powell liked Martha's Vineyard so much that he purchased a summer home minutes away on **Maple Avenue.** Today the house is still in the Powell family and is just two doors down from the home of writer Dorothy West, the last surviving member of the Harlem Renaissance. Her novel, *The Wedding* (Doubleday & Co., Inc., 1995), describes an African-American's view of life in Oak Bluffs.

Across from the Catholic church on **Pequot Avenue** in downtown Oak Bluffs is the **Cottagers Corner** building. The former town hall was taken over in 1955 by a hundred African-American women (mostly from New York) who owned summer cottages on the island. They started an organization to raise money for island charities, including the hospital, NAACP, and a college scholarship. Just off **Seaview Avenue** is **Inkwell Beach,** where black families have gathered for years.

Today a private home, the **Bradley Memorial Church** on **Masonic Avenue** was where Reverend Denniston preached after his arrival here from Jamaica in 1900. He stayed until 1946 and there are a few island people who remember his sermons—many written for local black sailors—with affection. Denniston's grandson now uses the house as a summer residence.

An inn in Chilmark, **Captain R. Flanders House** (see page 161), is on the site of a farm where an African slave named Rebecca lived. She married a Native American, and their children were subsequently sold away from them. One daughter, Nancy, died a free woman in 1857, and one of her daughters—also named Rebecca—was the mother of Captain William A. Martin, Martha's Vineyard's only African-American whaling captain (see below). Stroll around the grounds that are set in one of the island's most beautiful rolling-hilled areas.

Take the Chappaquiddick ferry, *On Time,* from **Edgartown,** and walk to the **Captain Martin House**, just past the Jeffers Auto Yard on the left. The whaling ship captain married a Native American woman, Sarah Brown, who lived on her family land on what was then the **Chappaquiddick Plantation.** Martin shared Sarah's house on the reservation, and they raised a family in a place where they wouldn't be bothered by racist sentiments. His gravestone in the **Chappaquiddick Cemetery** faces in the opposite direction from the other markers.

68 The Granary Gallery at the Red Barn Emporium At the core of this gallery, like a standing museum, are the prints of the late photographer Alfred Eisenstaedt, who first came to Martha's Vineyard in 1937 on assignment for *Life* magazine. Portraits run the gamut from scoundrels to stars (such as a radiant young Katharine Hepburn); among the more memorable images is the famous *Children at Puppet Theatre, Paris, 1963: The Moment the Evil Dragon Was Slain* (selling for about $17,000). Other rooms showcase an array of rising stars, such as *Vineyard Gazette* photographer Alison Shaw, whose color still lifes are studies in pure, vivid pattern, and David Potts Wallis, whose powerful water-colors of ships approach them from odd angles, so that the result is more geometric than representational. Assorted antiques are scattered among the artworks, and of special note are the McAdoo family's hooked wool rugs, an island enterprise for four generations. These CIBA-dyed wool scenes (some archetypal Vineyard, some simply playful, like a constellation of shoes) may indeed be "instant heirlooms," as the gallery manager describes them. ♦ Daily May–Oct; call for off-season hours. Old County Rd (near Elia's La), West Tisbury. 693.0455, 800/472.6279 ⑤

COURTESY OF MARTHA'S VINEYARD HISTORICAL SOCIETY

69 Alley's General Store "Dealers in almost everything" since 1858, this country store/news hub/social nexus was struggling to stay afloat when, in 1993, Martha's Vineyard Preservation Trust stepped in, fixed it (with the aid of the architectural firm of **Moore II** in West Tisbury), and gave it a new lease on life. Regulars such as Pulitzer Prize–winning historian David McCullough, who lives nearby, contributed to the fund-raising efforts, and the store—or, more specifically, its welcoming front porch—is once again a pulse point of this rural community. For a quick bite or a take-out picnic, visit **Back Alley's Bakery & Deli** at the rear of the building. ♦ Store: daily 7AM-7PM June-Aug; daily 7AM-6PM Sept-May. Bakery:

M-F 7:30AM-4:30PM; Su 8AM-2PM June-Aug; call for off-season hours. South Rd (between Edgartown–West Tisbury Rd and Music St), West Tisbury. 693.0088, bakery 693.7366

70 The Field Gallery & Sculpture Garden Tom Maley's frolicking white statues, a cross between Moore and Picasso in his more humorous moments, have been island emblems since the early 1960s, when Maley erected his first larger-than-life dancing lady out in an open field. Many more have followed, and visitors are welcome to wander among them, any time of year. The gallery itself, designed in 1971 by artist and architect **Robert Schwartz,** shows a changing roster of local and regional artists in summer, from collagist Lucy Mitchell to cartoonist Jules Feiffer, who summers on the Vineyard. The Sunday evening openings (5-7PM) are a lively "insider's" tradition open to all. ♦ M-Sa; Su 2-7PM. State Rd (between Edgartown–West Tisbury and South Rds), West Tisbury. 693.5595

71 Allen Farm As you round this hilly corner, with the ocean visible on one side and ancient stone fences lining the other, you'd swear you were in the Hebrides—or perhaps New Zealand, the homeland of the 150-odd sheep in residence at this 1730 farm. Clarissa Allen transforms their fine coats into the sweaters, scarves, hats, and shawls showcased in the tiny whitewashed shop. If you've heard this corner of the island is really rural, here's a concrete example. ♦ Odd hours (call ahead). South Rd (between Meetinghouse and Middle Rds), Chilmark. 645.9064

72 Chilmark Store There's a good reason this 1941 general store's porch is usually as well populated as **Alley's**: proprietor Primo Lombardi's excellent, puffy-crusted pizza, generously topped with spicy *linguica* or homemade pesto. To complete your repast, try another kind of pie in stock: fresh apple, blueberry, raspberry, or strawberry-rhubarb from the **Menemsha Bakeshop.** ♦ Daily 6:30AM-8PM May–mid-Oct. State Rd (at Menemsha Cross Rd), Chilmark. 645.3739 ⑤

72 **The Feast of Chilmark** ★★★$$$$
This plain clapboard house hides a two-level restaurant that ascends to surprising heights, in terms of both interior space and culinary sophistication. The main dining room extends into a mezzanine with vaulted ceilings and plenty of room for bright Vineyard landscapes by island photographers. Artistry on the plate includes lobster turnovers with shrimp and lemon cream, and roasted rack of domestic lamb with a spinach and Cognac glaze. Despite the latter, remember that Chilmark is dry, so bring your own. ♦ New American/Takeout ♦ Daily dinner July-Aug; call for off-season hours; closed November through April. State Rd (at Menemsha Cross Rd), Chilmark. 645.3553 &

Within The Feast of Chilmark:

Peter Simon Photography Gallery
Peter Simon not only has a great ear—he's produced three albums of local talent, called Vineyard Sound—he also has a great eye. He has been chronicling island life since its great hippie heyday in the 1960s and 1970s and continues to capture its special charms. **The Feast of Chilmark** restaurant (see above) serves as a permanent gallery for his work, some of it hand-tinted by his wife, Ronni. ♦ Daily 6-10PM June-Oct; call for off-season appointments. 645.9575 &

73 **Chilmark Chocolates** The chocolate lollipops are luscious, the truffles out of this world. Watch them being made, at what founders Mary Beth Grady and Alison Burger call an "unsheltered workshop" (most of the employees are mentally challenged), and your appetite will be whetted. ♦ W-Su 11:30AM-5:30PM Apr-Dec. State Rd (south of Menemsha Cross Rd), Chilmark. 645.3013 &

74 **Duck Inn** $$ Elise LeBovitt knows that some prospective guests might find her farmhouse bed-and-breakfast "too much," and that's fine with her. Others will take to its personality and to the glorious ocean views at every turn. Set on a meadow above the Gay Head Cliffs, the place is like a post-hippie pension, complete with hot tub. The five rooms, including one tucked into the 200-year-old stone foundation, are fancifully decorated, if not fancy, and the pink stucco living room is agreeably cluttered and comfortable. As another plus, Glenwood LeBovitt dishes out "gourmet organic" breakfasts, such as pear couscous muffins and chocolate-raspberry crepes. ♦ Closed November–late May. Off State Rd (near Moshup Trail), Gay Head. 645.9018

75 **Gay Head Cliffs** At the height of summer, you'll have to fight your way amid belching tour buses and snack-and-souvenir stands to get a look at these 150-foot-tall clay cliffs formed by glaciers some 100 million years ago. It's worth it—not just for the sight of the colorful striated layers ranging from white, gray, black, and brown to yellow, orange, pink, and red, but for the dramatic views of Noman's Land, directly south, and the Elizabeth Islands, stretching toward the mainland. These cliffs started out as coastal hills along the mainland. The exposed strata represent various geological epochs and contain related fossils, from the grays at the base, the remains of prehistoric forests, to the gravel at the top, which has yielded the remains of whales and sharks, plus the partial skeleton of a camel (extinct in North America for the last 12,000 years).

Most of the Gay Head area is now owned by the Wampanoag tribe, who have occupied it for at least 5,000 years; their rights to Aquinnah ("high land") were established definitively in a 1987 government settlement granting them $4.5 million with which to buy back approximately 475 acres. Wampanoag legend holds that the gargantuan deity Moshup once lived at Gay Head in "Devil's Den" and used to roast whole whales in fires made with trees he ripped from the ground; the cliffs were said to be his garbage heaps, their gray layers ashes from his fire. This natural wonder was exploited by the colonists, who used its colorful clay to paint houses, make bricks, and even build roads. Fossil hunters of the past two centuries tore up huge chunks, and in the 1970s naked hippies used to splash about in mud baths at the cliffs' base. Such disruptions are unthinkable now, when every effort is being made to stem the erosion that could ultimately destroy this millennial landmark. ♦ At the end of State Rd, Gay Head

75 **Gay Head Lighthouse** Closed to the public for decades, this 1856 lighthouse can now be visited weekend evenings in summer; proceeds benefit the Martha's Vineyard Historical Society. The views, not to mention the sunsets, are nonpareil. ♦ Admission. F-Su 7-9PM July-Aug. At the end of State Rd, Gay Head. 627.4441

76 **The Outermost Inn** $$$$ Named for Henry Beston's classic account of his seaside year in Eastham, this gray-shingled house with wraparound water views (see above) was built in 1971 by Jean and Hugh Taylor, of the musically gifted clan, and converted into a seven-room inn in 1990. The living room is packed with instruments ("We encourage guests to play if they know how—and not to, if they don't," says Jean with a laugh), and the bedrooms are beautifully sparse, the better to show off the rich woodwork in beech, ash, cherry, and hickory. Outside, 35 acres of grassy dunes slope toward the sea. The porch makes a splendid bring-your-own bar, and a hammock beckons in a tree beyond. ◆ Closed October–mid-April. Lighthouse Rd (between Lobsterville and State Rds), Gay Head. 645.3511; fax 645.3514

Within The Outermost Inn:

Outermost Inn Restaurant ★★★$$$$
Simple country-style elegance also rules in the seaview dining room, with its wicker place mats and linen tablecloths. Chef Barbara Fenner, who trained at the Culinary Institute of America, prepares a straightforward prix-fixe menu for the two seatings. The main course might be a slab of grilled Menemsha swordfish or charbroiled sirloin fillet, accompanied by homemade oatmeal rolls, a fresh garden salad, and steamed vegetables, followed by desserts like "brownies ecstasy" (with hazelnut ice cream), fruit shortcake, or white chocolate mousse. Done right, there's nothing tastier than basically plain food, as Fenner proves every night. ◆ New American ◆ M, Th-Su dinner 6PM, 8PM late May–Sept; call for schedule Oct, mid-May–late May. Reservations required. 645.3511

77 Arabella Hugh Taylor and two other captains sail his 50-foot catamaran on day trips to Cuttyhunk and sunset cruises of the harbor and Vineyard Sound. He also operates a pontoon that serves as a low-cost bike ferry, saving cyclists about 10 miles of steep and narrow backtracking to circum-vent Menemsha Pond. ◆ Fee. Sailing: by appointment. Ferry: daily July-Aug; call for off-season schedule; closed mid-September–mid-June. Menemsha Harbor (at North Rd), Menemsha. 645.3511

77 Home Port ★★$$$$ Fresh-off-the-boat fish has been the selling point of this harbor-side restaurant since 1931. Many of the more impressive specimens have ended up on the walls over the years, but they just keep coming. If mounted fish, paper place mats, and clamorous crowds aren't your idea of the ideal shore dinner, you could always do as the locals do and call (or fax) in a take-out order,

to be picked up at the kitchen door and taken to the scenic waterside locale of your choice for a sunset feast. ◆ New England/Takeout ◆ Daily dinner June-Sept; call for off-season hours; closed October–mid-April. Reservations recommended. North Rd (at Menemsha Harbor), Menemsha. 645.2679; fax 645.3119 ♿

78 Pandora's Box This tiny, seasonal store is packed with ready-to-wear women's clothes perfectly suited to the island's laid-back lifestyle. Some make a style statement, some are just comfortable, but all have a certain flair and are affordably priced—especially at the phenomenal close-of-summer sale. ◆ Daily mid-June–mid-Sept. Basin Rd (off North Rd), Menemsha. 645.9696

78 The Menemsha Bite ★★$$ "The Bite" is your quintessential seafood snack shack, flanked by picnic tables. Staples like chowder and fried fish come in graduated containers, with a jumbo portion of shrimp topping out at around $25. ◆ American ◆ Daily lunch and dinner July–mid-Sept. Basin Rd (off North Rd), Menemsha. 645.9239 ♿

78 Poole's Fish Owned by Everett H. Poole since 1944, this is *the* place to get seafood right at the source. The store does its own smoking, and one refrigerated case serves as a makeshift raw bar: staffers shuck the crustaceans while you wait, and provide cocktail sauce. ◆ Daily July-Aug; call for off-season hours; closed January through April. Dutcher's Dock (off Basin Rd), Menemsha. 645.2282 ♿

79 Beach Plum Inn $$$$ It's picture-perfect: a rambling white farmhouse surrounded by boisterous perennials, with a broad lawn overlooking the harbor. With its lovely grounds, comfortable living room/library, and 13 airy rooms (some in surrounding cottages), this is a wonderful place to stay put and unwind. You'll have company—high-placed and well-heeled. ◆ Closed mid-October–mid-May. Off North Rd (between Prospect Hill and Basin Rds), Menemsha. 645.9454, 800/528.6616; fax 645.9461

Within the Beach Plum Inn:

Beach Plum Inn Restaurant ★★★$$$$
With windows on three sides, this simple white room captures the full glory of Menemsha's famed sunsets. The prix-fixe menu changes nightly, but among the Cordon Bleu standard-bearers are *brie en croûte* (in puff pastry), beef Wellington, and a classic crème brûlée. ◆ Continental ◆ Daily breakfast and dinner mid-May–mid-Oct. Reservations required. 645.9454, 800/528.6616

79 Menemsha Inn and Cottages $$ A dozen cottages (rented by the week), nine rooms, and six suites share a secluded setting on 10-plus verdant acres, with westerly views of the water. Alfred Eisenstaedt was a regular guest for four decades, and the interior aesthetics would please any artist. Just as important as what you see is what you don't see: needless frills. There's no restaurant—just a restful breakfast room. The most luxurious suites are located in the **Carriage House,** which has a spacious common room with a fieldstone fireplace and inviting rattan-and-chintz couches. These rooms have private decks, so you can sit and gaze out to sea. ♦ Closed December through April. Off North Rd (between Prospect Hill and Basin Rds), Menemsha. 645.2521

80 Captain R. Flanders House $$$ Set amid 60 acres of rolling meadows crisscrossed by stone walls, this late 18th-century farmhouse, built by a whaling captain, has remained much the same over two centuries. It was transformed into a bed-and-breakfast with five guest rooms and two cottages, and has its own historic windmill, now used for storage. The living room, with its broad plank floors, is full of astonishing antiques that look right at home. This is also a working farm, so there's no time for posing (even if it was featured in Martha Stewart's *Wedding Book*). After fortifying yourself with homemade muffins, honey, and jam at breakfast, there are passes available to nearby Lucy Vincent Beach—or you might prefer to take a long country walk. Whatever your choice, you're apt to find yourself echoing the sentiments of one regular visitor: "I hope this place never changes." ♦ Closed December through March. North Rd (between Tabor House and Menemsha Cross Rds), Chilmark. 645.3123

81 The Inn at Blueberry Hill $$$$ This is a wave-of-the-future resort in terms of environmental awareness. Built around the core of a crumbling inn, which began as a farmhouse in the 1790s, the main house and added cottages fit the spruce-shaded grounds (56 acres, surrounded by thousands more of conservation land) as if they'd always been there. Owners Bob and Carolyn Burgess have done everything possible to minimize the impact on the land, without stinting in the least on luxuries. The 25-yard heated lap pool is lined with sleek black rubber so that essentially it heats itself; it's flanked by a hot tub and lots of inviting wooden chaises. Past the croquet lawn and beyond the model vegetable garden is a tennis court; and the large poolhouse, a former barn, contains a full-scale Cybex fitness center. This is Carolyn's domain (she's a personal trainer). She also attended to the decor. Almost Zen-like in their stripped-down simplicity, the 25 spacious rooms (some connect and can be booked as a cluster or private cottage) all contain hand-crafted objects worthy of contemplation. The interiors were designed so as not to compete with nature, and they're

almost transparent in that respect—while remaining cozy and relaxing. ♦ Closed January through March. North Rd (between State and Tabor House Rds), Chilmark. 645.3322, 800/356.3322; fax 645.3799 &

Within The Inn at Blueberry Hill:

Theo's ★★★★$$$$ Invent your dream restaurant, and it might look something like this: bustling yet intimate, subtly lit by candles flickering in colored glass goblets, with "ragged" walls in warm tones, and all sorts of interesting music, from Baroque to blues, uninsistently piped in. Chef Robin Ledoux Forte's health-friendly cuisine has its (literal) roots in the island—she's a longtime resident—but can stand up to the decadent cosmopolitan competition. The prix-fixe menu changes nightly to take advantage of local provisions, but you can expect the likes of seared swordfish, caught the same day off Menemsha, accompanied by mango beurre blanc, black sesame seed timbales, and a spicy Asian coleslaw. For dessert there's a wide array of pastries, and she'll usually throw in a special wild card, such as jalapeño-coconut sorbet or fallen chocolate cake with warm fudge sauce and cinnamon coffee cream. Prepare to be swept away. ♦ New American ♦ Daily breakfast and dinner Apr-Dec. Reservations required. 645.3322, 800/356.3322

82 Red Cat Restaurant ★★★$$$$ It may look like an ordinary roadhouse, but connoisseurs have faithfully followed chef Benjamin deForest (formerly of Vineyard Haven's **Dry Town Cafe,** Oak Bluff's **Oyster Bar,** and before that, Boston's Four Seasons) to this unprepossessing spot. Adorned with local artwork, the plain-looking interior, plus screened porch, scarcely hints at sophistication, but wait till the dishes arrive. DeForest favors showy presentations—like a "vertical cuisine" pyramid of fried sweet-potato curls topping a pork chop braised with pears, golden raisins, and Calvados, on a bed of bitter greens. If you're feeling extravagant, treat yourself to his five-course tasting menu. ♦ New American ♦ Daily lunch and dinner. State Rd (between Scotchman's La and Old Courthouse Rd), West Tisbury. 693.9599 &

Rosa rugosa, those raggedy roses you see everywhere along Cape beaches, arrived on these shores from Asia as stowaways on trade ships. They've flourished here, providing not only summerlong beauty but also a fall harvest of plump rose hips, which make a tangy tea that's rich in vitamin C, as well as a tasty jelly.

If you get pitch on your hands from the Cape's pinewoods, rub bayberries on the sticky substance and it will start coming off.

83 Martha's Vineyard Glass Works It's always fun (and a little scary) to watch glassblowers at work. Susan Shapiro and Mark Weiner's multicolored artistry is especially tricky, and you'll marvel at how those gobs of molten glass ever became the elaborate vessels showcased in the gallery side of this studio. ♦ Daily May-Oct. State Rd (at North Rd), West Tisbury. 693.6026 &

84 Lambert's Cove Country Inn $$$ The newly paved road meanders on so long through pine forest, you think you'll never arrive, but there it is at last, a 1790s farmhouse, expanded by an author and amateur horticulturist into a seven-acre estate in the 1920s. His most endearing legacy is a commodious library, with shelves on all four walls and a set of French doors to beguile bookish types into the English garden. Everything about the house invites relaxation. The decor doesn't look like decor per se, but more the aftereffect of comfortable affluence. Adding to the charm, many of the 15 rooms have decks overlooking the gardens, and in spring the air is perfumed with lilac and wisteria. ♦ Lambert's Cove Rd (off State Rd), West Tisbury. 693.2298; fax 693.7890

Within Lambert's Cove Country Inn:

Lambert's Cove Country Inn Restaurant ★★★$$$$ In fine weather dessert is served on an outdoor deck with a view of the apple orchards; the indoor dining room is pretty, too, with tables covered with peach and white linen cloths. The constantly changing menu might include such items as cheese and walnut ravioli with asparagus, roasted red pepper, and fresh basil in a gorgonzola cream sauce; veal piccata with truffle sauce; or Grand Marnier–glazed breast of duck. Sunday brunch here is a beloved tradition, where the usual egg dishes are supplemented by such treats as French toast made of home-baked oatmeal raisin bread. ♦ New American ♦ M-Sa

dinner, Su brunch and dinner July–mid-Sept; call for off-season hours. Reservations recommended. 693.2298

85 The Chilmark Pottery Geoffrey Borr has been hard at work in this rural studio, a former barn, since 1982, producing a sturdy assortment of useful ceramics—including porringers and oversize coffee cups—in a range of rich, multihued glazes. In addition to the functional, the gallery also displays purely artistic pieces: sculptures, decorative crystal, and raku pottery. ♦ Daily. Off State Rd (between Old County and Island Farms Rds), West Tisbury. 693.6476

86 Chicama Vineyards On a hunch that the soil here might prove hospitable to cultivate grapes (an experiment not attempted since Colonial days), former San Franciscans George and Catherine Matheisen planted 75 vinifera vines in 1971. They now produce thousands of cases of wine a year—over a dozen varieties in all, including Chardonnay, Cabernet, Riesling, Pinot Noir, and the island's first appellation Merlot. A tasty offshoot of the viticulture is a superb line of herb vinegars, plus salad dressings, mustards, jams, jellies, chutneys, and ice-cream toppings. Several handsome gift pack can be purchased in the shop or by mail order. Visitors are welcome throughout the year and treated to a tasting (given a choice, opt for the very creditable Chenin Blanc). In high season, you can take part in a lively, informative 20-minute tour. ♦ M-Sa; Su 1-5PM late May–mid-Oct; call for off-season hours. Stoney Hill Rd (off State Rd), West Tisbury. 693.0309 &

86 Thimble Farm Continue on this rutted dirt road from the vineyards just a bit farther, and—provided you're 12 or older—you can pick your own strawberries and raspberries in season. Also for sale are vegetables, flowers, melons, and pumpkins. Much of this prime produce is grown in vast computerized greenhouses that look like a set from a science-fiction film. ♦ Tu-Su mid-June–early Oct. Stoney Hill Rd (off State Rd), West Tisbury. 693.6396

87 Scottish Bakehouse Isabelle White of Peebles, Scotland, opened this homey bakeshop in the early 1960s, and islanders have come to depend on her high-calorie handiwork. In addition to 12 signature breads (including Portuguese, sourdough, Irish soda and one called "Scotch Crusty"), the bakery produces sausage rolls, Cornish pastries, "Forfer Bridies" (pork and onion turnovers), and plain, fresh, delicious shortbread. ♦ Daily 8AM-8PM June–mid-Sept; daily mid-Sept–June. State Rd (between Lambert's Cove and Shubael Weeks Rds), Vineyard Haven. 693.1873

38 Vineyard Studio/Gallery In 1978 Doug Parker, art director of Boston University's *Bostonia* magazine, turned the barn of his summertime home into an artists' co-op, more or less as "a philanthropic gesture." As an artist and art lover himself, he couldn't see the justice in high gallery commissions, so he charges none at all; artists pay only a nominal fee to cover overhead costs. The shows here are ambitious and sophisticated ("No lighthouses or jetties," Parker promises), and well worth a deliberate detour. ♦ Sa-Su noon-6PM May-Oct; call for appointment weekdays. 860 State Rd (between William Norton and Stoney Hill Rds), Vineyard Haven. 693.1338 &

ests

Carrie B. Tankard
Dental Assistant

Sunrise or sunset at the **Gay Head Cliffs,** depending on your sleep habits!

The children must go for a ride at the **Flying Horses Carousel**—the oldest in the country.

Watching the swans or ducks crossing the street, stopping all traffic until safely on the other side.

You never know who you'll meet at the **Inkwell Beach.**

The newly developed **African-American Heritage Trail on Martha's Vineyard.**

Elaine Cawley Weintraub
Writer/Historian, African American Heritage Trail of Martha's Vineyard

The **African-American Heritage Trail of Martha's Vineyard** takes you from **Chappaquiddick** to **Oak Bluffs.** It includes the home of the island's only African-American whaling captain, an ancient rock where people gathered to hear the preacher, and a farm in **Chilmark** where an African woman resided.

Chilmark Chocolates, Chilmark. The best handmade chocolates in the world. You can try some while you wait, but no one leaves without buying more.

Beach Road between Oak Bluffs and **Edgartown.** Drive or walk down this road. Its calm beauty soothes your soul.

Lola's Southern Seafood, Oak Bluffs. Wonderful Creole food served by friendly staff; great music and a wonderful mural.

Polly Mascott Nadler
Writer/Historic Walking Tour Guide

See whatever's showcasing at the **Vineyard Playhouse** in **Vineyard Haven.** The artistic direction is first-rate, and whatever production the company mounts is usually up to off-Broadway snuff (not off-off- but off, singular; it's that good).

Close your eyes and imagine a little girl's Victorian dollhouse. Expand that vision to a garden filled with 312 of these dollhouses. Now pretend you've shrunk down to an 8" height and you're strolling through this maze of gingerbread cottages. That's what it feels like to explore the **Oak Bluffs Camp Meeting Grounds.** Plunge in anywhere, prepare to get lost as you wander in a euphoric trance, your senses feasting on flowers, jigsaw scrollwork, knickknacks galore, and a toy maker's palette of pastels. You'll re-emerge hours, days, or even years later, your faith in magic restored.

Make friends with a **Chilmark** resident so you can visit the famous nudist 'hood of **Lucy Vincent Beach.**

On a trek Up Island, stop at the **Chilmark Store** for "Pizza on the Porch." Buy your slice inside, then sit in any of the dozen emerald green rocking chairs and wait for Ted Danson, Mary Steenbergen, and Dan Akroyd to come along and do porch pizza. Afterwards, invite your new friends, Teddy, Mare, and Danny, to amble up the road with you to sample some **Chilmark Chocolates,** arguably one of America's finest confections.

Toby Wilson
Actor/Director, Vineyard Playhouse/Taxi Driver

Sunset dinners at **Menemsha Harbor**—Grab a back-door dinner at the **Home Port** restaurant. It's popular, so get there early.

The **Boston Pops** at the **Trinity Park Tabernacle** in **Oak Bluffs.** Keith Lockwood and one of New England's greatest institutions play in August at the 120-year-old wrought-iron tabernacle.

Entrain, *the* dance band on Martha's Vineyard. Playing every Thursday at **The Atlantic Connection** in **Oak Bluffs.** Buy their CDs, their bumper stickers, T-shirts, join their fan club, visit their web site, and pester your hometown radio station to play their music. World beat dance music and an indelible part of "the Vineyard Sound."

Take an island tour with **Adam Cab.** A *Vineyard Gazette* readers' poll award winner. You get a personalized tour of the entire island. Historical background, photo ops, advice on places to go, and things to do. A great way to familiarize yourself with all the things that are here.

Wintertide Improv Troop at the **Wintertide Coffeehouse** in **Vineyard Haven.** One of the "top ten coffeehouses in the country" *(Billboard Magazine).* Every Monday night the folk singers go away and **WIMP** is in the house. Zany comedy improv skits based on audience suggestions.

A natural outdoor amphitheater is the setting for the **Vineyard Playhouse**'s annual productions of the Bard. Bring a beach chair and picnic lunch and enjoy a late afternoon of theater by the best playwright ever.

Nantucket

The Wampanoag natives—6,000 strong before the advent of colonists—called the island *Nanaticut* ("the faraway land"), and whaling captains nicknamed it "the Gray Lady," because of its frequent shroud of fog. The shape of this 14-by–3.5-mile landmass has been variously described as a pork chop, a whale flipping its tail, and a strutting swan; perhaps it really resembles nothing so much as a jellyfish sliding out as fast as it can to get away from the mainland.

A good 30 miles out to sea, Nantucket is a truly retrograde destination, preserved from the incursions of modernity first by a postwhaling economic depression, then by concerted community effort. Tourists undaunted by a ferry ride that lasts an hour or even two (depending on the vessel) are greeted by weathered wharves linked by cobblestone streets to a town that is quintessentially quaint. The square-mile **National Landmark Historic District** encompasses no fewer than 800 structures going back before 1850—the largest such concentration in the United States.

Compared to Martha's Vineyard and Cape Cod itself, Nantucket was settled late. Early explorer Bartholomew Gosnold didn't even bother to debark, and Thomas Mayhew, having bought the whole chain of islands for £40 in 1642, sold Nantucket, sight unseen, in 1659 to a group of would-be settlers for £30 and "two Beaver Hatts, one for myself and one for my wife." One of the nine "original purchasers," and the first to settle in, was sheep farmer Thomas

For nos. 1-64, see pg. 168

acy of Salisbury, Massachusetts, who, on the mainland, had been threatened with hanging for sheltering Quakers during a thunderstorm. Over the next few years, the nine original purchasers sold "half-shares," thereby enlarging the number of shareholders to 27. The bitter dissension that soon grew up between the two "classes" was assuaged when proprietor Tristram Coffin's grandson Jethro married newcomer John Gardner's daughter Mary in 1686—à la Romeo and Juliet, only with a happy ending. The couple moved into a house built on Gardner land of lumber from the Coffin sawmill; their saltbox abode survives as Nantucket's oldest house.

At the start of the 18th century, some 300 settlers and 800 natives (their numbers already decimated by disease) were peacefully coexisting, cultivating maize, beans, squash, and tobacco, raising sheep, and catching cod off **Siasconset** at the island's eastern end. The Native Americans also taught their new neighbors how to spear the slow-moving "right" whales that passed within striking distance of shore—a practice that in the coming centuries would turn the tiny island into a world power. When, in 1712, Captain Christopher Hussey was blown off-course into deep water and happened to spear the first sperm whale, a mighty industry was set in motion that would illumine the capitals of Europe while creating many a homegrown millionaire. Nantucketers built **Straight Wharf** in 1723; within 50 years the island became the biggest whaling seaport in the world. Though its fleet was largely destroyed in the War of Independence (Nantucket was actually invaded by the British), the islanders bounced back. They did so again for a few decades after the War of 1812, aided in part by the opening of the Pacific trade.

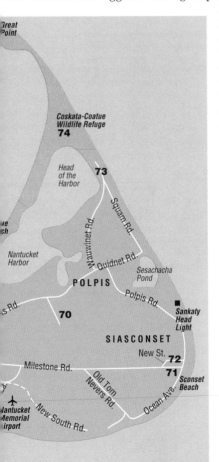

The boom years went bust, however, with a series of blows. First, the Great Fire of 1846 (which started in a milliner's shop) swept through the town's wooden buildings and oil- and tar-soaked docks, razing the port and destroying a third of the town. In 1849, the Gold Rush lured entrepreneurs west, and in the 1850s, petroleum-derived kerosene supplanted whale oil. By 1861, the island's population of 10,000 had plummeted to 2,000. The town did get discovered by the leisure class after the Civil War, and had sufficient visitors to support more than 50 boardinghouses by the last quarter of the 19th century— about the same number of bed-and-breakfasts as there are today. A narrow-gauge railway (later dismantled for use in World War I) was built in 1884 to carry tourists to the rose-covered fishing shanties of Siasconset (fondly abbreviated to "Sconset" by the locals). Among those drawn to the rustic charms and bracing waters of the remote village were actors Joseph Jefferson and Lillian Russell.

Still, island life remained relatively sleepy until the tourist boom of the early 1970s, which was prompted in part by the late-1950s restoration efforts of businessman Walter Beinecke Jr. (benefactor of Yale's Beinecke Library of Rare Books). Beinecke ruffled a few feathers by revamping the fishing shacks along the town wharves, turning them into boutiques and restaurants attractive to tourists. Fortunately, he also helped initiate extremely strict zoning and building codes that protected the community from the ensuing onslaught.

As a result of Beinecke's foresight, there's not so much as a traffic light today to jar you from the contemplation of a centuries-old aggregate of glorious architecture—much of which you can shop in, eat in, and even sleep in. Where other towns might boast a handful of historic bed-and-breakfasts, Nantucket has dozens; you can pick a good one at random, or with the guidance of the **Nantucket Information Bureau** (228.0925; open daily 9AM-9PM late May–early September; 9AM-6PM off-season) or the **Chamber of Commerce** (228.1700; open Monday through Friday 9AM-5PM, Saturday 10AM-2PM late May–early September; Monday through Friday off-season). Similarly, intriguing shops—many specializing in rarefied home decor and women's clothing—are packed along **Main Street** and **Centre Street** (once known as "Petticoat Row" for all the whalers' wives who maintained dry goods businesses there). The rare rainy day is a good excuse for an energetic buying spree here, with rest stops at the many winning restaurants in the area.

Perhaps the most remarkable aspect of Nantucket is its miles upon miles of beach open to all comers, unlike the mostly private shores of Martha's Vineyard. Although it can be a strain on property owners, the great majority are committed to maintaining public access. And thanks in large part to the early efforts of the Nantucket Conservation Foundation, about a third of the island's 30,000 acres are already under protective stewardship. A network of beautiful bike paths wind outward from the clustered houses in town, past rolling meadows carpeted with scrub oak, blueberry bushes, and heather to broad beaches where the capricious surf can be challenging one day and calm the next. Though peaceful and protected, Nantucket is never dull. There's a popular superstition that if, when departing, you throw a penny off the ferry as you pass **Brant Point**, you're sure to return. Almost everyone does.

THE ROPE WALK

1 The Rope Walk ★★$$$$ Open to the bay breezes and with a front-row seat at the waterfront, this is a wonderful place to eat intelligently treated seafood while getting acclimated to island time. Stop for a snack at the raw bar (in the evenings, you might find some sushi), or go all out and feast on grilled swordfish with sweet peas. The cuisine is more ambitious than the casual setting and service would suggest. ◆ American ◆ Daily lunch and dinner late June–early Sept; call for off-season hours; closed mid-October–mid-May. Straight Wharf (off Candle St). 228.8886 &

Restaurants/Clubs: Red
Shops/ ♥ Outdoors: Green
Hotels: Blue
Sights/Culture: Black

1 The Endeavor/Nantucket Whaleboat Adventures Boat by boat, Susan and James Genthner are working to restore Straight Wharf's colorful history. On board *The Endeavor*, a replica of a Friendship sloop used at the turn-of-the-century for fishing, modern-day passengers can experience a sail in Nantucket Sound with a captain who can tell whaling-era tales and answer nautical questions. Special sails geared for children have pirate and sea chantey themes, complete with cannon fire and treasure maps. There's also a replica of a mid–19th-century whaleboat, the *Wanderer* (named for the last whaleship to be launched from New Bedford); the six passengers who sign up for a cruise are expected to row, sail, and land, getting a firsthand experience of the rigors of nautical life in years past. ◆ Fee. Closed November through April; call for schedule. Slip 15, Straight Wharf (off Candle St). 228.5585

1 Nantucket Harbor Cruises The lobstering done aboard the canopied and cushioned launch *Anna W II* is quite a bit more genteel than the real thing, but kids especially will enjoy the opportunity to examine the haul, which may get to go home with you. Captain Bruce Cowan also offers sight-seeing, sunset, and nighttime cruises, and can accommodate private parties. In the winter you can head out to admire the many seals lolling on the jetty. ♦ Fee. Call for schedule. Slip 12, Straight Wharf (off Candle St). 228.1444

1 The Toy Boat If you're traveling with deserving children, and even if not, don't miss this exceptional toy shop, where proprietor Loren E. Brock offers "creative toys for creative people" of any age. Much of her stock is handmade, a good deal of it on-island—such as the working wooden sailboats. Nautical motifs are plentiful, and playfully presented; the educational aspect is a bonus. ♦ Daily 10AM-10PM June-Sept; call for off-season hours. Straight Wharf (off Candle St). 228.4552 ᵭ

2 Straight Wharf Restaurant ★★★$$$$ In 1982, Marion Morash of PBS's "Victory Garden" founded this handsome restaurant, a loft-type space with sailcloth panels ribboned through the rafters. In 1996, Steve and Kate Cavanero took over, with Steve as chef and Kate as manager. The menu changes weekly; the fare, served at two or three seatings, is straightforward in concept and superb in its simplicity (e.g., sautéed soft-shell crabs with pesto meunière, or a dessert of melon, kiwi, and berries with lemon crème fraîche and biscotti). The adjoining bar-with-patio serves a lower-priced, smaller-portion grill menu and is often packed until closing. ♦ New American ♦ Tu-Su dinner late May–mid-Oct. Reservations recommended. Straight Wharf (off Candle St) 228.4499

3 Leslie Linsley Nantucket Not only does Leslie Linsley have an eye for beauty (she's the author of *Nantucket Style*); she's handy as well. Her decoupage boxes sell at Tiffany's, and now here, in a little cottage shop that overflows with homey accessories crafted on-island, from baby quilts to hand-painted furniture. She also sells a variety of lavish craft and decor books, in case you get the

urge to do it yourself. ♦ Daily 10AM-5PM, 7-10PM July-Aug; daily late May–June, Sept–mid-Oct. 15 Old South Wharf (off New Whale St). 325.4900 ᵭ

3 The Café on Old South Wharf ★★$$$ Formerly **The Morning Glory Cafe,** this newly renovated eatery offers tables on an open patio or in a cozy dining room inside with walls decorated in trompe l'oeil. In a prime cafe location, away from the crowds, this is the place to meet friends on a sunny day for a lunch that might consist of chef's salad, grilled seafood, fresh vegetable platter, or a hearty burger. ♦ American ♦ Daily breakfast, lunch, and dinner July–early Sept; call for off-season schedule; closed November through May. 15 Old South Wharf (off New Whale St). 228.2212 ᵭ

3 Wharf Cottages $$$$ These 25 proper-ties, sprinkled through Old South and Swain's Wharves, are nautically compact and charm-ing, with crisp navy-and-white decor and a sitting area and small garden. The cottages have cooking facilities and sleep from two to eight. Bring your own boat if you have one; docking facilities are offered. ♦ Closed mid-October–mid-May. New Whale St (between Commercial St and Straight Wharf). 228.4620, 800/475.2637; fax 228.7197 ᵭ

Folk Art · Fine Art

Sailor's Valentine Gallery

4 Sailor's Valentine Gallery From naturally colored seashell artworks to Peruvian paintings, Russian icons, and folk art, the selection at this gallery is the most diverse on the island. Tickets for local theater and concert performances are also sold at the shop through a branch of **Box Office Nantucket** (228.8118). The gallery is situated in the sturdy brick **Thomas Macy Warehouse,** which formerly was used to outfit ships, and was one of the first buildings erected after the Great Fire of 1846. Walk in the front door and look at the ceiling—the boarded-up opening is where barrels of whale oil were hoisted upstairs during the 19th century. ♦ Daily 8AM-9PM June-Oct; call for off-season hours. Straight Wharf (east of Easy St). 228.2011

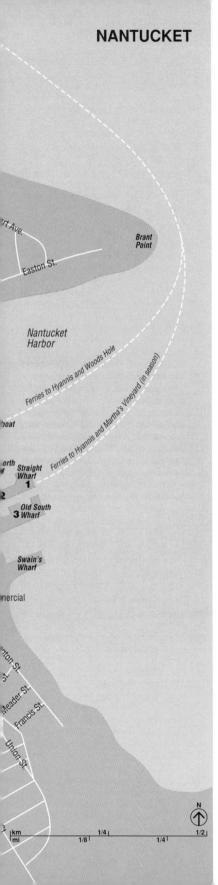

5 The Club Car ★★★$$$$ The piano bar part is a real train car, salvaged from the narrow-gauge that used to run to Sconset. The adjoining dining room is much more haute. Chef Michael Shannon keeps in mind that, even on Nantucket, fine diners appreciate an occasional break from seafood, so the menu also features premium veal, sweet-breads, sirloin, lamb, and rabbit, all inventively accoutred, in addition to salmon, soft-shells, swordfish, scampi, and so forth. ♦ Continental ♦ Daily dinner July–mid-Sept; call for off-season schedule; closed early December–mid-May. Reservations recommended. 1 Main St (at Easy St). 228.1101

6 Pacific Club This three-story brick building was built as a counting house and warehouse in 1772 by shipowner William Rotch, whose *Beaver* and *Dartmouth* carried the English tea that was dumped during the Boston Tea Party. The *Beaver* later became one of the first whalers to round Cape Horn. Rotch himself achieved notoriety by defending the case of a slave named Boston, who demanded pay for a whaling voyage he worked on, and won his freedom. (Quaker disapproval of slavery led to its abolition on the island in 1770, 13 years ahead of the Commonwealth as a whole.) In 1789, the building became one of the first US Customs Service houses, and in the mid-1800s it was turned into a club exclusively for captains of the Pacific whaling fleet. The interior of the club was completely renovated in 1996, and **The Robert Wilson Gallery** (228.2096), featuring maritime paintings, is open to the public from June to September on the first floor. (The other floors are not open to the public.) ♦ Main and S Water Sts. 228.0121

7 Main Street Gallery Like many a seaside resort community, Nantucket tends to foster pretty imagery more than serious art. Reggie Levine is willing to take an occasional risk and hang somewhat more challenging works in the score of shows he mounts each summer. Look for Will Berry's inchoate colorist landscapes and figures, which invite the viewer to fill in from memory or imagination. ♦ Daily June-Sept; call for hours Oct-May. 2 S Water St (at Main St). 228.2252

8 White Dog Cafe ★★$$$ No relation to Martha's Vineyard's **Black Dog** (and a fraction of the size), this minuscule patio with a

169

smattering of tables turns into a lively outdoor bar late in the evening. While warming up it serves refreshing lunches and somewhat more ambitious dinners—such as seared yellowtail tuna with *hoisin* glaze, toasted sesame seeds, and black bean vinaigrette, or swordfish with corn and avocado salsa. ◆ American/Takeout ◆ Daily lunch and dinner late May–Oct. 1 N Union St (between Main and Cambridge Sts). 228.4479 ♿

8 The Gaslight Theatre The island's only year-round cinema, this little shoebox is more like a private screening room, with only 100 quite comfortable seats and a changing array of first-run movies that favors the foreign and the experimental. ◆ Call for schedule. 1 N Union St (between Main and Cambridge Sts). 228.4435 ♿

9 Erica Wilson Needle Works When designer Erica Wilson, author of more than a dozen books and star of both a PBS and a BBC series, came to Nantucket in 1958, within a few years of graduating from London's Royal School of Needlework, the Historical Association commissioned her to provide period textiles for the **Jared Coffin House.** She stayed on, opening this casual counterpart to her Madison Avenue boutique and offering hands-on guidance to those interested. The shop spills over with her latest enthusiasms: not just the needlepoint kits one would expect (although these are abundant, and feature designers she admires as well as her own handiwork), but richly textured sweaters, smocked baby clothes, home accessories both silly and recherché, needlepoint shoes, and hand-crafted jewelry. Nantucket has many other, more high-concept shops focusing on home design, but this one is especially inviting. ◆ Daily 9AM-10PM mid-June–mid-Sept; call for off-season hours. 25-27 Main St (between N Union and Federal Sts). 228.9881 ♿

10 Stephen Swift Although certain influences are evident (from Queen Anne to Shaker), Stephen Swift's fine hand-fashioned furniture is far too individualized to pass as a repro-duction. At the same time, it could blend in the most traditional of homes, or easily adapt to a modern setting. Among Swift's signature pieces are wavy-backed Windsor chairs and benches (as sturdy as the original but more comfortable) and delicate, pared-down four-posters that would dress up any bedroom. At the top of the line (over $4,000) is a "scallop" bed with hand-carved headboard. Also appealing are his dressers with graduated drawers, and "huntboards" that conjure visions of lavish breakfast buffets. You can enjoy yourself buying or dreaming, as you wander about this roomy second-floor space ◆ M-Sa. 34 Main St (between Union and Orange Sts). 228.0255

10 Espresso Cafe ★★$ This counter-servic restaurant resembles an old-fashioned ice-cream parlor, with tin ceilings, black-and-white tile floor, and small marble tables. But the European photo posters hint at a differen menu, featuring some of the tastiest and mos affordably priced food on the island, from impromptu frittatas, quiches, and pizzas to a ever-changing array of hearty international dishes posted on the blackboard. The pastries, starting with morning croissants an culminating in an outstanding lemon-almond *torta*, are superb. Regulars snap up the "day olds," reduced to half-price and just as delicious. They also treasure the secluded patio behind the restaurant, where it's acceptable to linger as long as you like, shielded from the hurly-burly of Main Street. ◆ International/Takeout ◆ Daily breakfast, lunch, and dinner. 40 Main St (between Unio and Orange Sts). 228.6930. Take-out store: Fast Forward, 117 Orange St (between Cherr and Williams Sts). 228.5807

10 Golden Basket Glenaan Elliott originated the miniature golden lightship basket in 1977, and although the concept has since been copied, her designs are still the most delicately proportioned and exquisitely made each has working handles and hinges, and comes with a tiny gold penny tucked inside. Basic baskets in gold run from around $200 to close to $2,000; they're also available in al sorts of variations, including pavé diamond. Be sure to check out the other local charms, such as a golden whelk shell lined in delicate pink porcelain. ◆ Daily 9AM-10PM July–early Sept; daily early Sept–June. 44 Main St (between Union and Orange Sts). 228.4344, 800/582.8205 ♿ Also at: Straight Wharf (off Main St), Nantucket. 228.1019; Kelley and Dock Sts, Edgartown, Martha's Vineyard. 627.4459

11 Tonkin of Nantucket Brass and silver objects, ship models, and marine paintings are a forte of this perennially well-stocked antiques store, an island fixture since 1971. Many of the rarefied trappings, like a 16th-century carved English oak coffer, derive fron overseas, but there are also native artifacts o hand, including a choice selection of antique lightship baskets. In summer, the shop offers a free shuttle over to Tonkin's warehouse, where all the big items are stored. ◆ M-Sa. 33 Main St (between Federal and Centre Sts). 228.9697

11 Force 5 Water Sports Christopher and Francie Bovers' shop rides the surfer mystique, with up-to-the-minute music to browse by and a full line of wet suits, Windsurfers, Boogieboards, and surfboards for sale or rent; kayaks, Sunfish, and Daysailers are also available, as are lessons in these sports. The bathing suit selection is the best in town, and for off-water wintertime wandering there are plenty of Patagonia cover-ups. Kids are catered to, with minuscule Aqua Socks starting at size 3 and polar-fleece bunting for brisk days at the beach. ♦ Daily 9AM-10PM. 37 Main St (between Federal and Centre Sts). 228.0700 ♿ Also at: Jetties Beach (at the end of Bathing Beach Rd). 228.5358 ♿

11 Arno's at Main Street ★★$$$ Long a reliable if uninspired choice for an in-town meal, this place has been invigorated since Jeanne and Richard Diamond took over as owners and spiffed it up. Molly Dee's overscale paintings of bathers and tennis buffs, like sepia-toned blowups of vintage photos, enliven the brick walls, and a tall, spiky flower adds style to each glass-topped table. The menu looks livelier, too, starting with lobster-boursin omelettes for breakfast and culminating in a "Nantucket Mixed Grill"—grilled swordfish, scallops, shrimp, and *linguica* (sausage)—with a cranberry barbecue sauce. The windowed storefront right on Main Street still creates a slight fishbowl effect—but now onlookers are enviously peering in. ♦ American/Takeout ♦ Daily breakfast, lunch, and dinner Apr–mid-Jan. 41 Main St (between Federal and Centre Sts). 228.7001 ♿

12 Mitchell's Book Corner The "hand selling" of books is an endangered art, but Mimi Beman (who took over this bookstore from her parents in 1978) is an avid practitioner, matchmaking for regular customers and steering drop-ins straight to the appropriate shelf: "I don't have to look on a computer," she says, "to know what we have in the store." If you're hoping to get to know the island in depth, head for the **Nantucket Room** here, where you'll find every conceivable title on island lore (including some out-of-print gems), plus books on whaling, yachting, and the sea in general. ♦ Daily 9:30AM-10PM mid-June–mid-Sept; M-Sa 9:30AM-5PM mid-Sept–mid-June. 54 Main St (at Orange St). 228.1080 ♿

13 The Fragrance Bar A colorful fellow who goes by the single name of Harpo (there's a definite resemblance) is behind this unusual store. He's assembled some 400 essential oils with which he can duplicate designer scents or customize blends; uncut by alcohol (unlike their commercial counterparts, which typically are 94 percent alcohol), these perfumes purportedly do not cause associated problems such as allergies and headaches—and instead of rapidly vaporizing, they linger on the skin. The "elixirs" can also be mixed with various bases to create moisturizers, soaps, shampoos, conditioners, and massage oils; there's even a Kama Sutra line, which you can sample in the Weekender package. The shop, which looks like an ancient pharmacy, is actually a new creation fashioned from recycled mantelpieces and doors. The clientele is said to include a megastar who, like Harpo, goes by one name—this one starting with an M. ♦ Daily 10AM-6PM mid-Apr–Dec; Sa 10AM-5PM Jan–mid-Apr. 5 Centre St (between Main and India Sts). 325.4740, 800/223.8660 ♿

DeMarco
Restaurant

14 DeMarco ★★★$$$$ Downstairs, with its dark wood paneling, is too tavernlike a space to do justice to the haute Italian cuisine; see if you can get a table on the lofty second floor. Once ensconced, you can enjoy exquisite antipasti and bracing *secondi* (entrées), such as a seared salmon and potato pancake lasagna, or grilled veal chop with aged balsamic vinegar, roast shallots, rosemary, grilled radicchio, and polenta *crostini* (toasts). The entrées are among the pricier around town, but the clientele is not exactly pinching pennies. ♦ Northern Italian ♦ Daily dinner late Apr–Dec. Reservations recommended. 9 India St (between Federal and Centre Sts). 228.1836

Nautical expressions that have crept into common English usage since the whaling days of yore include "knowing the ropes" and "seeing if the coast is clear."

14 Company of the Cauldron ★★★$$$$
If atmosphere is what you seek, look for this vest-pocket restaurant lit by sconces and tin lanterns. Lavish flowers and a few apt antique decorative elements impart an elegant mood. The prix-fixe menu—there's only one—changes daily, and is set a week ahead, so you can call to pick the optimal night (you might also consider when the harpist is playing). One typical meal starts with crab and shrimp gumbo, and also includes a salad with locally grown tomatoes and basil-buttermilk dressing, hazelnut-crusted salmon, a vegetable and starch on the side, and chocolate-caramel mousse for dessert. Whatever night you pick, the cuisine is consistently excellent. ◆ New American ◆ Tu-Su dinner late May–early Oct; call for off-season schedule; closed November–late May. Reservations recommended. 7 India St (between Federal and Centre Sts). 228.4016

14 Boarding House ★★★$$$$ This is one terrific restaurant, topped only by its own bar and sidewalk cafe, a magnet for low-key socializing late into summer evenings. The restaurant is set slightly below ground and, with its arched walls, feels like a sanctum. That sense is reinforced by the creations of chef Seth Raynor (a graduate of the New England Culinary Institute), who straddles the fine line between stark, bold flavors and "comfort" foods—e.g., grilled quail with crisp-fried onion rings, or lobster tail with mashed new potatoes and beurre blanc. Several of the restaurant's greatest hits, including a sublime lobster bisque, reappear on the bistro menu for stylish off-hours snacking. ◆ New American ◆ Daily dinner Jan-Oct, Dec. 12 Federal St (at India St). 228.9622 ♿

The
Gallery

15 The Gallery at Four India Street The work displayed in this bright second-story space is quite traditional; even the 15 contemporary artists shown (such as landscape painter John Osborne) visibly demonstrate their allegiance to 19th-century schools of painting. Many of the pieces are not homages but the genuine artifact, with

prices in the tens of thousands. There's also a smattering of antiques: a few decoys, silver cigarette cases, Bakelite bracelets—whatever happens to catch gallery director Kathleen Knight's eye. ◆ M-Sa Feb-Dec. 4 India St (between Federal and Centre Sts). 228.8509

15 Obadiah's ★★$$$ Andrew and Lynda Willauer, who turned this 1840s captain's house into a restaurant in 1978, started out with modest but admirable ambitions: to serve good seafood at good prices. They've succeeded all these years. Eat outdoors, on an awning-covered brick patio with punched-tin lanterns and hanging baskets, or indoors, in an atmospheric brick-walled cellar. "No pretense" is the unspoken code; servers are friendly and responsive, and you can choose from about 20 traditionally derived entrées (one specialty is pan-cooked, cornmeal-coated yellowtail sole). Dinners come with native-grown accompaniments (perhaps homey mashed red potatoes) and a regularly replenished bread basket sparked with cranberry bread. That same concoction turns up in a delectable bread pudding; other desserts include strawberry shortcake and "Obadiah's Bad Bad Dessert"—a dark chocolate cake with mocha frosting, topped with walnuts, coconut, and whipped cream. You'll feel very good even after the check arrives. ◆ New England/Takeout ◆ Daily lunch and dinner mid-June–late Sept. 2 India St (between Federal and Centre Sts). 228.4430 ♿

15 Lynda Willauer Antiques You'd have to look far and wide for a better selection of American and English furniture, all painstakingly tagged as to provenance and state of repair. Slant-front desks are a particular interest; these might range from a mahogany Chippendale (around $4,800) to an 18th-century North Shore example (for something like $15,000). Other specialties include Chinese export porcelain, majolica, paintings, samplers, quilts, and brass and tortoiseshell accessories. Take your time and browse at length; it will be worthwhile, if only in terms of aesthetic pleasure. ◆ M-Sa July-Aug; call for off-season hours; closed mid-October–mid-May. 2 India St (between Federal and Centre Sts). 228.3631

16 Nantucket Atheneum In 1836, two small library associations, motivated by "the desire we have to promote the Cultivation of Literature, the Sciences and Arts and thereby advance the best interests of our Native town," formed a "proprietorship" to create a temple of learning. Local savant Maria Mitchell, then only 18, was appointed the first librarian. When the first building and its contents were lost to the Great Fire, the proprietors rebuilt within six months, aided by donations that poured in from across the country. Local architect **Frederick Brown Coleman** (whose previous credits included the "Two Greeks," a pair of showplace houses on upper Main Street), designed this exemplary 1847 Greek Revival building, fronted by fluted Ionic columns. Ralph Waldo Emerson gave a series of lectures here, followed by visits—at Mitchell's instigation—by such luminaries as Henry David Thoreau, Horace Greeley, Louis Agassiz, John James Audubon, Lucretia Coffin Mott, and Frederick Douglass (in his first address to a racially mixed audience). All the vital topics of the day, from abolitionism to suffrage, were heatedly discussed upstairs in the **Great Hall,** which also hosted concerts and "theatricals." The tradition of lectures and readings continues to this day in the recently restored hall and, in summer, in the adjoining garden. The newly reopened children's wing includes fantasy animal chairs created by popular local artist Claire Urbahn. The library itself (which, though privately funded in part, doubles as the town's public library) holds some 40,000 volumes, including many rare 19th-century books and manuscripts; venerable portraits and cases displaying a collection of whaling and shipping artifacts are on hand to remind visitors of the community's illustrious history. ♦ Call for hours and schedule of events. India St (between S Water and Federal Sts). 228.1110

21 FEDERAL

17 21 Federal ★★★$$$$ A sensation ever since it opened in 1985, this austere yet handsome restaurant is still going strong after several changes of chefs. Paneled dining rooms, illumined by pewter sconces, fill the 1847 Greek Revival house, and in summer the feasting overflows onto a flowery courtyard. Chef Russell Jaenig's menu changes weekly, but you might encounter the likes of warm confit of lobster with smoked bacon, leeks, and white beans. The flavors are robust and uncomplicated, and desserts are equally inspired—try the apple pancake soufflé with pecans and crème anglaise. ♦ New American ♦ Daily lunch and dinner, Su brunch Apr–mid-Dec. Reservations recommended. 21 Federal St (at Oak St). 228.2121 &

18 Sushi by Yoshi ★★$$ The kitchen is bigger than the four-table dining room, but what could be better than these compact little packages of rice-enrobed, seaweed-wrapped morsels of super-fresh local fish? Chef Yoshihisa Mabuchi also offers such healthy, affordable staples as miso or *udon* (noodle) soup, but it's tempting to splurge and order a raft of Rhoda rolls (with tuna, avocado, and caviar). ♦ Japanese/Takeout ♦ Daily lunch and dinner mid-Mar–mid-Dec. 2 E Chestnut St (between S Water and Federal Sts). 228.1801

19 Dreamland Theatre This much-moved building started out in 1829 at 76 Main Street as the **Atlantic Hall,** a Quaker meetinghouse that was the largest building in the rebuilt town; it then became the **Atlantic Straw Company** (a hat factory), was transported to Brant Point to serve as the central building of the **Nantucket Hotel,** and, after being floated across the harbor by barge, ended up here in 1905. The drab interior gives no hint of the structure's colorful former lives, but the steady stream of first-run movies, changing every other day or so, are a summertime staple. ♦ June-Sept; call for schedule. 19 S Water St (at Oak St). 228.5356 &

20 Claire Murray As a New York transplant running a Nantucket bed-and-breakfast in the late 1970s, Claire Murray took up the traditional art of hooking rugs to see her through the slow season. She proved so well suited to the task, especially the design element, that she now runs a retail company grossing millions a year. While she is always busy creating new collections (Winterthur, Colonial Williamsburg, and the Museum of American Folk Art have all inspired special lines), she has hundreds of "hookers" working for her around the world. Customers can also hook their own; kits costing about two-thirds the price of finished rugs (a few hundred dollars to over $1,000) come with complimentary lessons. In addition to needle arts supplies, this pretty store (the first of seven so far, coast to coast) stocks ready-made quilts and sweaters, hand-painted furniture, flowery tableware, and Nantucket Wildflowers toiletries and scented stationery. ♦ M-Sa 10AM-9PM; Su 10AM-4PM June-Sept. Call for hours Oct-May. 11 S Water St (between Cambridge and Oak Sts). 228.1913, 800/252.4733 ♿ Also at: 867 Main St (at Parker Rd), Osterville. 420.3562 ♿

21 Vincent's Restaurant ★★$$$ It would be a shame to overlook this 1954 establishment just because it looks run-of-the-mill, with its red-and-white-checkered tablecloths and the obligatory Chianti bottles strung from the rafters. Plenty of restaurants offer more polished Italian food, but you'd be hard-pressed to come up with dishes this all-out good. Vincent's has kept up with the times, offering, for example, a white pizza loaded with ricotta and roast garlic, and some very tasty neo-pastas, such as scallops pesto primavera and grilled swordfish *puttanesca* (with tomatoes, capers, and olives). The traditional dishes (seafood Cahoon, risotto *pescatore*—with seafood—and many more) are just as mouthwatering. There's a good reason why you'll see so many young couples and families packed in here; it's one of the few places in town where you can eat your fill for under $20. ♦ Italian/Takeout ♦ Daily breakfast, lunch, and dinner Apr–mid-Dec. 21 S Water St (at Oak St). 228.0189 ♿

22 Juice Bar You can indeed get juice here, from lemonade to fresh carrot—and pastries, too. But most people come for the homemade ice cream, in such tantalizing flavors as mocha macadamia nut brittle. Particularly popular are the "minisundaes," which are cloaked in homemade hot fudge and really quite substantial. You may keep coming back again and again! ♦ Daily 7AM-11PM Apr–mid-Oct. 12 Broad St (at S Water St). 228.5799

During the whaling era, there were strong links between Nantucket and Martha's Vineyard. Many Nantucket whaling ships had to off-load oil barrels on the Vineyard just to get back over the shallow entrance to Nantucket Harbor. The two islands shared crews and captains. After the whaling era and the end of the ferry line from New Bedford that stopped in the Vineyard before continuing to Nantucket, the connections withered. Today, the inhabitants of both islands deal more with the mainland than with each other.

Nantucket is an island, a county, and a town. It's the only place in America with the same name for all three.

23 Young's Bicycle Shop Since 1931, transients right off the boat have been coming here to outfit themselves with the quintessential Nantucket accessory: a bike. Three-speed clunkers with "baskets 'n' bells" may suit the merely curious; serious bikers might spring for the purple Cannondale mountain bikes (rates are quite reasonable). Young's also rents scooters, cars, and Jeeps, but keep in mind that Nantucket is a small island, best seen up close and quietly. If you're not planning to rent, you might still enjoy a look at the collection of antique two-wheelers. ♦ Daily 8AM-8PM early July–early Sept; daily early Sept–early July. Broad St (between Easy and S Water Sts). 228.1151

24 Nantucket House Antiques When many of the *antiquaires* along the main drag have added mass-produced "country" accessories to cater to the tourists, it's nice to find this shop still full of genuine treasures—including, for instance, a 1740 oak chest on stand for $12,500 or a late–18th-century burled maple slant-front desk for under $10,000. From the asparagus-patterned majolica to the farmhouse tables, everything's so well chosen, you can't help picturing the rooms these items were meant to grace. To help with the visualization, owners Sandy and Hudson Holland Jr. also offer an interior design service. ♦ M-Sa 9:30AM-noon, 2-5:30PM; Su 10:30AM-12:30PM, 3:30-5:30PM June–early Sept; call for off-season hours. 1 S Beach St (between Broad St and Whalers La). 228.4604

25 Peter Foulger Museum While researchers toil in the archives upstairs, on the ground floor of this brick building the Nantucket Historical Association (NHA) mounts temporary exhibits—they recently had one entitled "Away Off Shore" and are planning one on Nantucket paintings. Peter Foulger was an early settler who served as an interpreter when settlers were negotiating to purchase land from the natives in 1659; his daughter Abiah gave birth to Benjamin Franklin. Other members of his distinguished line include astronomer Maria Mitchell, abolitionist Lucretia Mott, and coffee mogul James Folger, all born on Nantucket. ♦ Admission. Daily mid-June–early Sept; daily 11AM-3PM late May–mid-June, early Sept–mid-Oct. 15 Broad St (at N Water St). 228.1894

Restaurants/Clubs: Red   Hotels: Blue

Shops/   Outdoors: Green   Sights/Culture: Black

25 Whaling Museum Housed in a former spermaceti-candle factory, this museum is a must-visit, if not for the awe-inspiring skeleton of a 43-foot finback whale (stranded in the 1960s) then for the exceptional collections of scrimshaw and nautical art (check out the action painting *Ship Spermo of Nantucket in a Heavy Thunder-Squall on the Coast of California 1876*, executed by a captain who survived). A map occupying one entire wall depicts the round-the-world journeys of the *Alpha*, accompanied by related log entries. The price of admission includes several lectures, scheduled throughout the day; they give a brief and colorful history of the industry, starting with the beachside "whalebecue" feasts natives and settlers enjoyed when a whale happened to ground. There's also a worthwhile gift shop. ♦ Admission. Daily late May–mid-Oct; call for off-season hours; closed early December–mid-April. 13 Broad St (between S Beach and N Water Sts). 228.1736

26 Cioppino's ★★★$$$$ This stylish and popular restaurant has a pretty side patio, and a houseful of handsome dining rooms painted the faintest of mauves; the lofty upstairs is especially nice. Owner Tracy Root, formerly the longtime maître d' at Nantucket's fabled **Chanticleer,** has a way of making every customer feel like a millionaire (many, of course, are, several times over). Aside from the namesake dish (a spicy San Franciscan shellfish stew), chef Andrew Tratel's approach is mostly evolved continental: For example, he'll place foie gras on a bed of crispy shredded potatoes, with a shallot confit and Port wine sauce, or roll a salmon fillet in crushed hazelnuts and top it with a raspberry vinaigrette. The trellised garden is great for lunch or late-night drinks and desserts, such as an exotic sorbet or a warm pecan pie with bourbon ice cream. ♦ New American ♦ M-Sa lunch and dinner; Su brunch and dinner mid-May–Oct. Call for off-season hours. 20 Broad St (between Federal and Centre Sts). 228.4622

26 Le Languedoc Restaurant ★★★$$$$ At street level there's a pleasant patio; upstairs, a cluster of small formal dining rooms (some painted a deep tomato red); and downstairs a casual bistro with Breuer chairs and blue-and-white-checkered tablecloths. The cuisine is ambitious and contemporary (e.g., porcini-dusted rack of lamb with quinoa pudding), and accordingly priced. But the cafe menu lends itself to low-capital ventures— for instance, the lobster scallion hash with saffron aioli—and some very impressive

wines are available by the glass. ♦ New American ♦ Tu-Sa lunch May–late June; daily dinner July-Oct; call for off-season schedule; closed mid-December–mid-April. Reservations recommended for dining room. 24 Broad St (between Federal and Centre Sts). 228.2552, 800/244.4298 ♿

27 Brotherhood of Thieves ★★$$ Look for the lines invariably loitering outside. This low-beamed, semi-subterranean 1840 whaling bar (its name derives from an 1844 antislavery pamphlet) is so popular that patrons willingly wait an hour or more to work their way inside, where it's so dark that candles are required in full daylight. What you'll be eating (though it may be hard to see) are great burgers, sandwiches, and blackboard specials served with curly fries on pewter plates at plank tables. Folksingers hold forth every weekend (plus a few weekdays in summer), but not so stridently that you can't talk over them. There are mostly tourists here in summer, but in winter it's a fraternity of long-term Nantucketers. ♦ American ♦ Daily lunch and dinner Jan, Mar-Dec. 23 Broad St (between N Water and Centre Sts). No phone ♿

27 Nantucket Bookworks The giant orange orangutan—with a mandrill on either side— that sits above the doorway is a preview of the playful ambience of this eclectic bookstore. Elvis Presley angels and sculptures adorn the shelves, and masks and puppets decorate the walls. A children's room in the rear features educational and fun books, as well as drawing supplies and bizarre, yet wonderful, toys. Another back room is stocked with stationery and the two front rooms specialize in serious literature, biography, and poetry. A browser's delight, this shop also offers a fascinating mix of titles not normally found in commercial bookstores. ♦ Daily 10AM-10:30PM Apr-Dec; M-Th, Su; F-Sa 10AM-10:30PM Jan-Mar. 25 Broad St (between N Water and Centre Sts). 228.4000 ♿

Although the plover is a protected bird today, that wasn't always so. On 29 August 1863, both curlew and plover appeared over Nantucket in such numbers as to "almost darken the sun." By the time islanders ran out of powder and shot, seven or eight thousand had been destroyed.

27 Jared Coffin House $$ If there were posthumous awards for trying to please one's spouse, Jared Coffin would surely qualify. A wealthy shipowner, in 1845 he built this grand three-story brick house, the largest in town, because his wife decided their original home, **Moor's End** (built in 1834 on Pleasant Street, a few blocks off Main, and now privately owned), was too "remote" to suit her social aspirations. After living in their new mansion only two years, the Coffins decamped for the more civilized pleasures of Boston, leaving their showplace—with its impressive Ionic portico and lofty cupola—to become an inn. Meanwhile, after a century-plus, the historic property has indeed become the social center of town—not just because it's a popular place to go, but because innkeeper Phil Read, who leased the inn from the Nantucket Historical Trust in 1963 and bought it in 1976, has been such an active force in promoting tourism and ensuring that visitors get a warm welcome as soon as they step into the antiques-filled lobby.

The house itself has 11 gracious rooms; 49 more are distributed among five surrounding houses, the most elegant of which is the 1841 Greek Revival **Harrison Gray House,** named for the owner of the whaleship *Nantucket.* queen-size canopy beds are the norm, but some very reasonably priced singles are scattered about. ♦ 29 Broad St (at Centre St). 228.2405, 800/248.2405; fax 228.8549

Within the Jared Coffin House:

Jared's ★★$$$$ Decorated with nautical paintings and a 19th-century portrait of the Coffin grandchildren, its salmon walls aglow with candlelight, this formal dining room is ideal for a dressy night out—even if the food can be a bit uneven. You might encounter a celestial lobster bisque, followed by an undressed salad garnish or lamb that's more charred than grilled. But the hits outnumber the misses, and there's plenty of originality—consider, for example, the Nantucket blue salad, with spinach and blue cheese in a blueberry vinaigrette. The breakfasts manage to maintain tradition (eggs Benedict, prime rib hash) while introducing such tasty innovations as lemon blueberry bread French toast with pecan honey butter. ♦ New

American ♦ Daily breakfast and dinner Apr-Oct; daily breakfast Nov-Mar. Reservations recommended. 228.2400 &

Tap Room ★★$$ If you miss the old standards, you have only to head downstairs to this dark-paneled pub for chowder, steaks, burgers, fried fish, Welsh rarebit, and the "Pride of New England" combo: fish cakes, baked beans, brown bread, and coleslaw. In summer the same menu is served outdoors c a patio overflowing with flowers. ♦ American ♦ Daily lunch and dinner. 228.2400

28 The Quaker House $$ New owners Kendrick Anderson and Stephanie Silva run this pretty eight-room bed-and-breakfast righ in the center of town—a plus for those who like to be centrally located. The continental breakfast is superior, with egg dishes like quiche or frittata. The rooms, especially in the renovated attic, offer intriguing views of the old town. ♦ 5 Chestnut St (at Centre St). 228.0400; fax 228.2967

Within The Quaker House:

Kendrick's at The Quaker House Restaurant ★★★$$$ This newly named restaurant has been enlarged, from two room to three, and spruced up—the traditional woo floors have been preserved and a small six-seat bar has been added in the brightly lit from room with its oversized windows. Chef/owner Rick Anderson trained at the New England Culinary Institute and worked locally at **The Club Car** and **Chanticleer.** His specialties include seared striped bass in a Key lime beurre blanc and Maine halibut in a reduction sauce that includes strips of fresh lobster meat. A separate, less expensive bar menu is offered noon through evening with delicacies like soft-shell crab with lemon aioli and quesadilla with rock shrimp and goat cheese. ♦ International ♦ Daily lunch and dinner June–mid-Sept. M, Th-Su lunch and dinner Apr-May, mid-Sept–Dec. M, Th-Su dinner Jan-Mar. 228.9156

29 Paul LaPaglia Antique Prints The prints—mostly maritime, botanical, and regional—are companionable, the framing beautifully selected and executed in burled woods and simple gilt. This is an excellent place to pick up a memento of lasting value. ♦ M-Sa late May–mid-Oct; call for off-season hours. 38 Centre St (between Hussey and Quince Sts). 228.8760

30 Off Centre Café ★★$$ This tiny restaurant, tucked away in a former meetinghouse turned mini-mall, is loved for its ornate breakfasts and creative dinners. Chef/owner Liz Holland started out at Boston

chic 29 Newbury Street, and what her eatery lacks in space it makes up for in panache. The breakfasts—featuring such blackboard specials as "blueberry popover with blackberry sauce" or "whole wheat plum pancakes"—are invigorating. Dinners include such dishes as fresh cod in parchment with lemon sections, white wine, and fresh herbs; or Renaissance lamb with mint couscous and spring vegetables. ♦ New American ♦ M-Sa breakfast and dinner. Su brunch and dinner June–mid-Sept. Sa-Su breakfast mid-Sept–Dec, Apr-May. 29 Centre St (between India and Chestnut Sts). 228.8470 ♿

31 Roberts House Inn $$$ Romantic touches like lace-covered canopies and colorful quilts grace the 26 rooms, of varying sizes, in this centrally located mid–19th-century inn. With over a quarter-century in the business, owners Sara and Michael O'Reilly are bed-and-breakfast pioneers–turned modest moguls. Continental breakfast is served in the parlor. If there's no room available here, you may be able to find accommodations at one of their other properties: the **Manor House Inn, Meeting House, Linden House,** or **Periwinkle Guest House and Cottage.** ♦ 11 India St (at Centre St). 228.9009, 800/673.4559; fax 325.4046

32 Black-Eyed Susan's ★★★$$ From the moment it opens, this tiny shoebox of a restaurant—a spiffed-up luncheonette whose grill makes a trendy "open kitchen" —is mobbed, with customers waiting an hour or more to get a seat. What's the deal? Intelligent, adventurous food, reasonably priced. The menu changes biweekly; among the treats you might come across are wreck grouper on a Tunisian-style omelette with lemon-dressed watercress, followed by chocolate-filled ravioli arrayed on prickly pear coulis. Though the physical setup is nothing fancy, the cuisine provides excitement enough. ♦ International ♦ M-Sa breakfast and dinner; Su brunch Apr-Oct. 10 India St (at Centre St). 325.0308

33 United Methodist Church This endangered but still magnificent 1823 building, with its imposing Doric-columned 1840 facade, is not only an active place of worship but also a haven for the island's performing arts. The basement houses the professional-caliber **Actor's Theatre of Nantucket** (228.6325), founded by islander Richard Cary in 1985; upstairs, in a space carved out of the church's back balcony, a tiny proscenium showcases various enterprises, including photographer Cary Hazlegrove's long-playing slide presentation, "On Island" (228.3783). ♦ Service: Su 10AM. 2 Centre St (between Liberty St and Rose La). 228.1882

34 Pacific National Bank It's business as usual at this elegant 1818 brick bank, spared by the Great Fire. Above the original teller

cages are rather vapid murals of the whaling days executed by Robert Charles Haun in 1954. Perhaps the most exciting thing ever to have happened here was Maria Mitchell's rooftop discovery of a comet in October 1847 (further information on her extraordinary career can be found at the **Maria Mitchell Science Center;** see below). ♦ M-F; Sa 8:30AM-noon. 61 Main St (between Centre St and Walnut La). 228.1917 ♿

35 Murray's Toggery Shop A town landmark since the early 1900s, this mini-department store (featured in *The Preppy Handbook*) specializes in "Nantucket Reds"—cotton pants, shorts, and skirts guaranteed to fade to a ruddy pink recognized in some circles as a badge of belonging. The stuff even comes in baseball caps now, as well as toddlers' overalls. For the most part, the rest of the stock is pretty conservative, with a few nods to junior preps in the form of Birkenstocks and Doc Martens. Part of this building was the early 1800s shop of John Macy, whose son Roland worked here before leaving to try whaling and gold prospecting; failing in both, he fell back on his sales skills and, in 1858, opened the New York shop that would soon balloon into the world's largest retail giant. ♦ Daily 8:30AM-7PM July-Aug; call for off-season hours. 62 Main St (between Orange and Fair Sts). 228.0437, 800/368.2134 ♿ Bargain outlet: 7 New St (between Orange and Pleasant Sts). 228.3584. Also at: 71 Main St (between Beach Rd and Union St), Vineyard Haven, Martha's Vineyard. 693.2640 ♿; 150 Circuit Ave (between Trinity and Lake Aves), Oak Bluffs, Martha's Vineyard. 693.3743 ♿

36 Unitarian Universalist Church A familiar part of the Nantucket "skyline," this 1809 church (listed in the National Register of Historic Places) didn't get its clock until 1823 and its bell (smuggled from Portugal during the War of 1812) until 1815; the 109-foot wooden tower had to be rebuilt to support the bell's ton-plus weight. In 1844, the congregation commissioned Swiss artist Carl Wendte, who had recently decorated the original Treasury Building in Washington, DC, to create a trompe l'oeil wall painting; newly rich from the whaling trade, the members wanted a continental look for their place of worship. The skylight, which casts a heavenly glow upon the pulpit, was brought back to life during a recent renovation. The organ is an 1831 William Marcellus Goodrich, one of the most valuable American-built organs. In summer the church mounts a series of "Noonday Concerts," ranging from classical to children's folk music. ♦ Interior: M-Sa July–mid-Sept. Concerts: Th noon-1PM July-Aug. Service: Su 10:45AM. 11 Orange St (between Martins La and Main St). 228.2730

37 Four Chimneys $$$$ The plain facade of this 1835 bed-and-breakfast gives no hint of the lovely proportions inside, much less of the Japanese garden hidden in back. Ten large and beautifully appointed rooms boast canopy beds with down comforters; half have fireplaces as well. The elegant yellow parlor, with crystal chandelier, is flanked by twin fireplaces that add a warming glow to the evening. It's here that you'll be treated to hors d'oeuvres, accompanied by innkeeper Bernadette Mannix's recommendations for things to do in Nantucket. ♦ Closed November through April. 38 Orange St (at Gorham Ct). 228.1912; fax 325.4864

38 The Woodbox Inn $$$ Built in 1709, this shingled house is the oldest inn on the island, and easily the most evocative. The sleeping quarters include six suites with fireplaces and three regular rooms, all with queen-sized beds. Breakfasts in the keeping room feature delicious egg dishes and popovers. ♦ Closed January–late May. 29 Fair St (between Darling and Hiller Sts). 228.0587

Within The Woodbox Inn:

The Woodbox Restaurant ★★★$$$$ The four small dining rooms, including a colonial kitchen, are so low-beamed that you'll probably have to duck to get through the doorways. It's hard to imagine anything further from dinner theater, yet more dramatic; the two seatings are staged as carefully as a show. Host Dexter Tutein ushers

guests into dark-paneled candlelit rooms set with pewter. The dinner menu features delicately jazzed-up classics, from chowder o perhaps grilled foie gras with apple chutney and roasted fennel powder, to beef Wellingto (the restaurant's signature dish), to Black Angus fillet with an Armagnac–black cherry reduction. These are just a few of the mouthwatering choices. And though they aren't cooked over an open hearth, as would have been the case in times past, they're all the more succulent done the modern way. ♦ Continental ♦ Tu-Su breakfast and dinner late May–mid-Oct; call for off-season schedule; closed January–late May. Reservations required for dinner. 228.0587

39 Ships Inn $$ Whaling captain Obed Starbuck built this handsome three-story home in 1831 at the site of the birthplace of abolitionist and women's rights activist Lucretia Coffin Mott. The exterior is Quaker-plain, the only decoration being the square-paned sidelights surrounding the door. The 12 rooms, all named for Starbuck's ships, are decorated like summerhouse guest rooms—they're not too fancy but quite comfortable. ♦ Closed December through March. 13 Fair S (between School St and Lucretia Mott La). 228.0040; fax 228.6524

Within the Ships Inn:

Ships Inn Restaurant ★★★$$$$ This peach-hued restaurant is halfway below street level, but so opened up, with small-paned windows lining two sides, that it feels roomy; the gentle lighting enhances the convivial mood. By constantly tinkering with his menu, chef/owner Mark Gottwald has come up with many appealing and healthy dishes, such as a creamless chilled tomato-basil soup garnished with a wedge of avocado, and grilled lamb and sea scallops with gazpacho ragout and eggplant napoleon And pastry chef Paul Benedict's soufflé du jour comes in exotic combinations—for example, tiramisù soufflé with chocolate sauce, or praline with sour cherry. ♦ New American ♦ M, W-Su dinner June–early Oct. Reservations recommended. 228.0040

40 Quaker Meetinghouse Built as a Friends' school in 1838, this building is simplicity itself, the only decorative element to speak of being the 12-over-12 antique glass windows. Visitors are always welcome at Friends' meetings; Sitting in may give you a feel for th high-minded forces that shaped this island during its two most formative centuries.

♦ Service: Su 10AM mid-June–mid-Sept. 7 Fair St (between Moors La and Rays Ct). 228.0136

40 Fair Street Museum This 1904 annex to the **Meetinghouse,** owned by the Nantucket Historical Association, is a two-floor gallery for changing exhibits on subjects of local interest such as Nantucket needlework and textiles. It's the second-oldest poured concrete structure in the United States (Harvard Stadium is the oldest). The unattractive exterior was actually state-of-the-art fireproofing for its day, much desired in Nantucket after the town's damage from previous fires. There are no guarantees as to what will be on view at any one time, but it's worth a look. ♦ Admission. Daily July-Aug; call for off-season schedule; closed mid-October–April. 1 Fair St (between Moors La and Rays Ct). 228.0722

41 Macy-Christian House Dry-goods merchant Thomas Macy built this lean-to saltbox in 1740 and it stayed in the family until 1827; the Reverend George P. Christian and his wife bought it in 1934 and spent years renovating it in the Colonial Revival style. Thus, all is not strictly authentic, but the Christians' collections exert an interest all their own, especially as explicated by knowledge-able guides. They'll point out the lustreware (which in the dim light of an old keeping room could pass for silver), the Nantucket-made Windsor chairs, and the curious lighting devices, including a cylindrical skater's lantern with mica windows. The upstairs bedrooms are more pure in appearance, but even the overdone kitchen renovation is worth seeing for all the fascinating gadgets it contains—including a "beebox," a trap that helped plunderers track wild bees to their hives. ♦ Admission. Daily June-Aug; call for off-season schedule; closed mid-October–April. 12 Liberty St (at Walnut La). 228.1894

42 Coffin School/Egan Institute of Maritime Studies Among the original purchasers, Tristram Coffin and his wife, Dionis, were unusually prolific, producing 9 children and 74 grandchildren. When Admiral Sir Isaac Coffin, a British Loyalist, decided to resettle in Nantucket in the early 19th century, he established a school providing "a good English education" for Coffin descendants, who included almost every child on the island. This 1854 brick temple, which replaced the original Fair Street building, is worth visiting for its grand Greek Revival architecture,

complete with white columns and steps. Today, the school is home to the **Egan Institute of Maritime Studies.** In the main hall is a fine collection of 19th-century portraits of prominent Nantucketers and works by accomplished island artist Elizabeth Rebecca Coffin, who studied with Thomas Eakins. (Notable among her works is a remarkably retiring self-portrait, in a three-quarters pose, as seen from the back.) The first-floor rear galleries house a collection of paintings of historic Nantucket events by British marine artist Rodney Charman. ♦ Admission. Daily late May–mid-Oct. 4 Winter St (between Main and Liberty Sts). 228.2505

43 Hadwen House One Starbuck sister married candle merchant William Hadwen (whose former factory is now the **Whaling Museum;** see page 175) and wound up living across the street from her three brothers in this house. Built in 1845, it was one of two nicknamed the "Two Greeks"—neighboring Greek Revival houses designed by local architect **Frederick Brown Coleman.** The mansion, with its imposing Ionic portico and rooftop cupola, now belongs to the Nantucket Historical Association and is open for guided tours. The interior decoration has been restored to the appropriate period, 1840-60, with the last owners' more recent belongings sequestered in a back room. Experts will point out such features as the sterling doorknobs, the Italian marble mantels, and the whalebone "mortgage button" installed in the newel post, a traditional way of celebrating a paid-off mortgage (the document itself, or its ashes, would be stored within). To the rear of the house is a period garden. Next door, under private ownership and not open to the public, is the other "Greek," this one with Corinthian capitals purportedly modeled after Athens' Temple of the Winds; built for Hadwen's adopted daughter, Mary Swain Wright, it features a second-story domed ballroom with a sprung dance floor and an oculus opening to the sky. ♦ Admission. Daily July-Aug; call for off-season schedule; closed mid-October–April. 96 Main St (between Traders La and Pleasant St). 228.1894

Nantucket is usually 10 percent cooler than the mainland in summer and 10 percent warmer in winter because of proximity to the Gulf Stream.

44 The Three Bricks Whaling mogul Joseph Starbuck, who owned 23 ships, commissioned these three identical (but for their iron fences) Georgian mansions for his sons, George, Matthew, and William. Built by Cape Cod house carpenter James Child and mason Christopher Capen in 1840, they cost a grand total of $40,124 and set a new standard for in-town elegance (certain details are echoed in the **Jared Coffin House,** built five years later). Starbuck handed over the keys to his sons but prudently held title for another decade, until they were full partners in the business. The family ties have held to this day; one house is still owned by a descendant. The houses are not open to the public. ♦ 93-97 Main St (between Winter and Gardner Sts)

45 African Meeting House on Nantucket Nantucket's newest cultural destination was built by free Africans in the 1820s. It is the nation's second-oldest community building, and was purchased by the Museum of Afro-American History in Boston in 1989. The meetinghouse is located in the Five Corners neighborhood, an area populated by the island's early African-American settlers. Included in this community of about 500 liberated slaves, offshore fishermen, and whalers was Absalom Boston, captain of the all-black whaling ship, *Industry*. African-Americans were members of the integrated naval crews during the War of 1812, and often served as harbor pilots up and down the East Coast. By the 1830s about 20 percent of the seamen shipping out of such northern ports as Boston and New York were black. After the Civil War the maritime unions confined African-Americans to service positions—cooks, stewards, etc.—and the sailing jobs went to whites only.

A restoration of the exterior was completed in the spring of 1997; at press time the inside was scheduled to be restored as well. The meeting house, with its paneled double front doors and wood-shingled roof, was first used as a school, and subsequently for church services (floor and wall outlines of its pews have been uncovered). Future plans for the building include using it for lectures and concerts, and opening it to the public on special occasions. ♦ Call for hours and information. York St (at Pleasant St). 228.4058

46 Old Mill Adapting his design from mills he'd seen in Holland, sailor Nathan Wilbur built th windmill out of shipwreck wood in 1746. Originally one of four that stood on the hills west of town, it's the only one remaining, and the only mill on the Cape and islands still in it original location. A 50-foot Douglas fir pole (the original was a mast) turns the 30-by-6-foot sailcloth-covered arms into the wind, setting in motion a wooden gear train that grinds corn between millstones weighing more than a ton apiece. You can buy some fresh meal after watching it (wind permitting) being made. ♦ Admission. Daily July-Aug; ca for off-season schedule; closed mid-October through April. S Mill and W York Sts. 228.1894

47 Maria Mitchell Science Center Born on the island on 1 August 1818, the third of 10 children, Maria (pronounced "mar-EYE-a") Mitchell was lucky enough to have, in Pacific National Bank head teller and amateur astronomer William Mitchell, a father who believed in equal educational opportunities for girls. By the time she was 12, she was helping him chart a solar eclipse; within the next year, whaling captains were bringing her their navigational devices to be set according to astronomical calculations. At 18, she was appointed the librarian of the **Nantucket Atheneum;** in her 20-year tenure, she would attract a phenomenal roster of speakers, including Emerson, Thoreau, and Melville. At age 29 she discovered a comet while skygazing from the roof of her family's quarters in the bank. The feat brought her international fame; she was feted throughout the US and in Europe, and was the first woman to be admitted to the American Academy of Arts and Sciences. Setting another precedent, Mitchell became the first female college professor of astronomy in the US, teaching at Vassar from 1865 until 1888, a year before her death.

In 1902, three of her cousins founded the Maria Mitchell Association to commemorate her remarkable life and continue her work. The nonprofit organization is dedicated primarily to study of the island's environment, with a special focus on passing along Mitchell's love of science to local children: "We especially need imagination in science," she once wrote. "It is not all mathematics, not all logic, but it is somewhat beauty and poetry."

Five of the Association's six facilities are open to the public (the exception is the **Maria Mitchell Observatory,** used for undergraduate research). The **Science Library** (2 Vestal St,

228.9219) is located in a former schoolhouse where William Mitchell taught celestial navigation; nearby is the **Hinchman House** (7 Milk St, 228.0898), a natural history museum that houses specimens and hosts lectures and walks. Across the street is the **Mitchell House** (1 Vestal St, 228.2896), Mitchell's birthplace, built in 1790, which contains extensive memorabilia, including the telescope she used to spot the comet. Some distance away is the **Loines Observatory** (Milk St, between Winn St and Hawthorne La, 228.9273), which has viewings on some summer nights (weather permitting), but is not regularly open to the public. And in town, on the water, is a tiny shack housing the Association's **Aquarium** (28 Washington St, 228.5387), which holds fresh- and saltwater tanks, a touch tank, and shark pool, with science interns on tap to field questions. ♦ Fee. Library free. Library: Tu-Sa mid-June–mid-Sept; W-Sa mid-Sept–mid-June. Other facilities: Tu-Sa mid-June–late Aug. 2 Vestal St (at Milk St). 228.9198

48 **Old Gaol** Sturdier than it looks, the building has a shingled facade that conceals a frame built of massive timbers bolted with iron; the petty thieves, embezzlers, and murderers who did time here, from 1805 right up until 1933, were securely ensconced. They had plank bunks, open privies, and iron grates for windows; but, lest you accuse the islanders of cruel and unusual punishment, keep in mind that most prisoners were allowed to go home at night, the risk of flight being slim. The Nantucket Historical Association keeps the building open, but there's rarely anyone to guide you; you can poke about at will, imagining what it might be like to spend lots of time there. ♦ Free. Daily July-Aug; call for off-season schedule; closed mid-October–April. Vestal St (between Bloom St and Quaker Rd). 228.1894

49 **Fire Hose Cart House** Little neighborhood fire stations sprang up all over town after the devastating conflagration of 1846. This one, built in 1886, is the only one remaining; it houses the late 19th-century fire pumper *Siasconset,* an elaborate beauty. ♦ Free. Daily July-Aug; call for off-season schedule; closed mid-October–April. 8 Gardner St (at Howard St). 228.1893

50 **India House** $$ The circa 1803 home of ropemaker Charles Hussey makes a splendidly spare nine-room bed-and-breakfast, with wide plank floors and plenty of canopied four-posters.

Guests are treated to one of the best breakfasts around, featuring such treats as blueberry-stuffed French toast, homemade breads, and muffins. The private garden out back is a lovely spot to sip a cocktail while recapping the pleasures of the day. ♦ Closed December through April. 37 India St (between Centre and Gardner Sts). 228.9043

Within the India House:

India House Restaurant ★★★$$$$
Three small dining rooms, with listing floors and low-slung ceilings, make a lovely, intimate setting for superb candlelit dinners. A favorite dish of many years' standing is lamb India House, with rosemary-studded breading and béarnaise sauce. But new influences have also surfaced of late, from Asian (12-spice salmon sashimi with garlic and mint soy oil) to Southwestern (Texas wild boar ribs with grilled pineapple barbecue sauce). The menu changes weekly, so you can be sure that this wonderful restaurant won't be resting on its laurels. ♦ New American ♦ M-Sa dinner; Su brunch and dinner May-Nov. Reservations recommended. 228.9043

51 **Jethro Coffin House** This circa 1686 saltbox, the oldest surviving structure on the island and a National Historical Landmark, is also known as the **Horseshoe House** for the brick design on its central chimney. It was built for Jethro and Mary Gardner Coffin, offspring of two of the island's earliest settlers; their marriage helped to quell a simmering feud between the "original purchasers" (the Coffin side) and mere shareholders (the Gardner's status). Lightning struck and severely damaged the house in 1987 (in fact, nearly cut it in two), prompting a long-overdue restoration. Dimly illumined by leaded glass diamond-pane windows, it's filled with period furniture such as ladder-back chairs and a clever trundle bed on wooden wheels. Docents from the Nantucket Historical Association can fill you in on all the related lore. ♦ Admission. Daily July-Aug; call for off-season schedule; closed mid-October through April. Sunset Hill Rd (between W Chester Rd and N Liberty St). 228.1894

52 **American Seasons** ★★★$$$$ Dinner here is fancy but fun, thanks to a playful yet sophisticated folk-arts decor featuring high-backed wooden benches, tables with painted-on game boards, and an exuberant harvest mural by Kevin Paulsen. Chef/owner Everett G. Reid III makes the most of domestic multiculturalism with a menu divided into four quarters: New England, Down South, Wild

West, and Pacific Coast. You get a continent's worth of options, from peppered native skate wings with a sauce of lobster, beets, and orange, and an apple-arugula salad, to crispy fried whole bass with a sauce of ginger and black beans and soy-marinated vegetables. Novelty-seekers will be in multiple-choice heaven. All dishes, including the elaborate desserts, are delivered on plates as large as platters, and are beautifully arrayed. ♦ New American ♦ Daily dinner May–late Dec. Reservations recommended. 80 Centre St (at Gull Island St). 228.7111

53 Centerboard $$$ There are not that many Victorian houses in town, and none has been as luxuriously updated as this 1890s example, replete with parquet floors, Oriental rugs, lavish fabrics, and lace-trimmed linens. The overall look is lighter and less cluttered than the original mode, and thus more in line with modern tastes. Of the six bedrooms, the first-floor suite is perhaps the most romantic, with a green-marble Jacuzzi and a private living room with fireplace. A large continental breakfast is served. ♦ 8 Chester St (between Easton and Centre Sts). 228.9696

54 Martin House Inn $$ Of the many historic bed-and-breakfasts in town, Ceci and Channing Moore's place—an 1803 mariner's home with 13 bedrooms—has the most congenial atmosphere, combined with reasonable prices. All guests, from budget-minded attic dwellers to the high rollers ensconced in the more opulent rooms boasting four-posters and fireplaces, enjoy equal access to the large, impeccably decorated living room, with its own roaring fire (in season). Beyond the window seats is a porch with conversational groupings of wicker settees, plus a hammock. Breakfast—a buffet affair featuring tasty homemade breads and coffee cakes—is served at a long gleaming table where strangers fast get to know one another as they trade tips for exploring the vicinity. ♦ 61 Centre St (between Step La and Chester St). 228.0678; fax 325.4798

At the height of the whaling era, Nantucket had the third-largest population in Massachusetts, after Boston and Salem. From 1840, when Nantucket numbered nearly 10,000 souls, until 1870, when 4,123 people counted the island home, the population had dropped by nearly 60 percent.

55 Anchor Inn $$ This comfortable 11-room bed-and-breakfast (pictured above), with period furnishings, was built in 1806 by Archaelus Hammond, the first captain to harpoon a whale in the Pacific. Visitors today are likely to have lesser pursuits in mind, such as heading off to the beach after a breakfast of homemade bran-and-fruit muffins on the enclosed sunporch; innkeepers Ann and Charles Balas are happy to provide beach towels as well as directions. The brick patio out back offers an inspiring view of the **First Congregational Church.** ♦ 66 Centre St (between Academy La and Lily St). 228.0072

55 First Congregational Church Built in 1834 by Boston housewright Samuel Waldon this spiky Gothic Revival church lost its steeple in 1849 (it was judged too precarious to withstand the island's high winds, and removed). A better-engineered replacement was installed via helicopter in 1968; photos documenting the feat are on display en route to the viewing platform 120 feet up. This aerie allows a staggering 360° perspective of the island. On the way out, have a look at the Neo Classical trompe l'oeil painting behind the altar, executed by E.H. Whitaker of Boston in 1852. The circa 1730 vestry behind the church has been moved from its original site but remains Nantucket's oldest house of worship ♦ Tower: nominal fee. Service: Su 10AM. Tower: M-Sa mid-June–mid-Oct. 62 Centre S (between Academy La and Lily St). 228.0950

56 Point Breeze Hotel $$ The Gonnella family took over the former **Folger Hotel** and at press time was completing a major restoration, including a return to its original 1891 name. The 60 old rooms have been converted into 14 suites and 4 single rooms, each with private bath, cable TV, and subdued wall and trim colors. Paintings by Nantucket artists such as William Welch and Marshall Dubock are featured in the lobby, now completely remodeled with white walls and Oriental rugs. The lobby is full of life; often there's an auction brewing that you can preview, and the front desk sells sodas and candy bars, a tradition kids appreciate. The best feature remains: the lengthy wraparound porch, complete with swings, leading to a secluded garden with a lily pond and three rental cottages. ◆ Closed mid-October–mid-May. 71 Easton St (at North Ave). 228.0313, 800/365.4371; fax 325.6044 ⑤

Within the Point Breeze Hotel:

Chancellor's on Easton Street ★★$$$
Some effort has been made to dress up this big, boxy dining room with hanging plants, wine racks, nightly piano music, and Victorian touches such as kerosene lamps. In any event, if you've had your fill of jicama and porcini, here's a place where you can find a good square meal. ◆ New American ◆ Daily breakfast and dinner mid-May–mid-Oct. 228.0313

57 Harbor House $$$$
A virtual village has grown up around this 1886 summer hotel: 112 rooms in all, the larger, more luxurious

(with country-pine furniture and private patios and decks) located in six town houses linked to one another and to an outdoor heated pool by nicely landscaped brick walkways. Just as some find the entire complex overbuilt, others consider it just the right mix of privacy and communality. Either way, the service and amenities are all a guest could wish for. ◆ Closed January through April. 7 S Beach St (between Sea and Easton Sts). 228.1500, 800/475.2637; fax 228.7639 ⑤

Within the Harbor House:

The Hearth ★★$$$$ With summery teal paneling offsetting a snowy field of white tablecloths, this is one of the larger dining rooms in town, and a traditional spot for a lavish Sunday brunch. While taking a firm meat-and-potatoes stance, the restaurant is not oblivious to culinary trends; the pan-roasted crab cakes come on a bed of corn salsa with pepper jelly; the Atlantic salmon comes on couscous with a mandarin orange cream sauce. This is one of the few island restaurants to offer an early-bird discount (what it calls "sunset dinner specials"), and the prix-fixe menu is a very good deal. Local musicians, such as the engaging songster team of Phil and Elizabeth, hold forth evenings in the adjoining **Hearth Lounge,** a barnlike space with a carved whale hanging over the fireplace and a huge chandelier sporting brass weather vanes hung amid the massive beams. ◆ New England ◆ M-Sa breakfast and dinner; Su breakfast, brunch, and dinner late May–Dec. Call for off-season schedule. Closed January through March. Reservations recommended. 228.1500, 800/475.2637 ⑤

58 Downy Flake ★★$ This beloved institution of several decades' standing is just a modest cottage fronting the **Children's Beach** playground and flanked by a stage where free concerts are held on summer afternoons. Let the kids run wild while you breakfast on blueberry pancakes or the justly renowned homemade doughnuts. ◆ American/Takeout ◆ Daily breakfast and lunch May–mid-Sept. 6 Harbor View Way (between Easton and S Beach Sts). 228.4533 ⑤ Also at: 18 Sparks Ave (between Hooper Farm Rd and Atlantic Ave). 228.4533 ⑤

THE White Elephant RESORT

59 White Elephant $$$$ Despite the name, this ultraluxurious resort seems to be a thriving concern. A mere lawn's width from the picturesque harbor, it embraces a shingled L-shaped building having 22 large rooms with decks, plus scattered cottages containing 34 more rooms, and the **Breakers** addition, with 26 concierge-attended rooms, even more opulently appointed than the English country norm (floral fabrics, stenciled pine armoires, sponge-painted walls). Every space is fresh and breezy, and none more so than the outdoor heated pool and hot tub surrounded by tasteful gray arbors. The hotel's location allows it to welcome "sail-in" guests. ◆ Closed mid-October–April. Easton St (between Brant Point and S Beach St). 228.2500, 800/475.2637; fax 325.1195 ⑤

Within the White Elephant:

The Regatta ★★★$$$$ If the weather's fine, you'll probably want to sit out on the terrace, under a crisp white Roman parasol, to watch the boats come and go. But the indoor dining room also has its allure, with celery-and-white-striped walls topped by pink latticework. Lunches feature such clever innovations as a "lobster Reuben," while dinners take a more elegant tack—for example (the menu changes weekly), a Maine lobster pan-roasted and served in a sauce of lemon beurre blanc and late harvest Riesling. Among the delightful desserts are *pizzelle* with cappuccino mousse, and a mille-feuille of fresh berries and minted ricotta. The only distraction is the glimmering view. ◆ New England ◆ M-Sa breakfast, lunch, and dinner; Su brunch and dinner May–mid-September. Reservations recommended. 228.2500, 800/626.2628 ⑤

Lower Main Street on Nantucket was laid with cobblestones in 1837 to enable heavy oil carts to move up from the wharves without sinking in mud.

THE BEACHSIDE AT NANTUCKET

60 **The Beachside at Nantucket** $$$ You'll see right away that this is no ordinary motel. The lobby, as well as the 90 air-conditioned bedrooms, have been lavished with *Provençale* prints and handsome rattan and wicker furniture; the patios and decks overlooking the central courtyard with its heated pool have been prettified with French doors and latticework. A complimentary continental breakfast is offered. If you enjoy the laissez-faire lifestyle of a motel, you might find this the ideal base. ♦ Closed mid-October–mid-April. 30 N Beach St (between Easton St and Cobblestone Hill). 228.2241, 800/322.4433; fax 228.8901 ♿

61 **Fair Winds** $$$ Just far enough from town that you feel you've found the "real" Nantucket, yet close enough that you can stroll in for dinner, this eight-bedroom bed-and-breakfast offers the peace many visitors are seeking. In fact, says innkeeper Kathy Hughes, a lot of first-time guests spotted the house while out cycling and, after coming in for a look, decided to make it their "second visit" destination. The light-drenched common rooms lead to a 50-foot deck with a panoramic view of the Sound; it's here that guests tend to bring their breakfast of fresh-baked breads and muffins. Four of the prettily decorated bedrooms enjoy that same priceless view. ♦ Closed mid-October–mid-May. 29 Cliff Rd (between Folgers La and N Liberty St). 228.1998; fax 617/244.8182

62 **Something Natural** This sandwich/bakery shop's large, shady picnic area makes it the perfect place to stop for a hearty midday repast. Call ahead with your order—especially in the busy midsummer months—or line up for huge custom-made sandwiches on seven kinds of freshly baked breads. Choose from such fillings as smoked turkey, tomato, and swiss; avocado, cheddar, and chutney; or vegetables, hummus, and sprouts. The prices are reasonable for the quantity offered—you probably won't be able to finish the whole sandwich in one sitting—and the carrot cake and oatmeal raisin cookies are bound to delay entry into the nearby waters. ♦ Daily late-May–mid-Oct. 50 Cliff Rd (between Folgers La and N Liberty St). 228.0504 ♿

63 **Cliffside Beach Club** $$$$ The nucleus of this luxury hotel, the only one on the island located right on the dunes, was a 1920s bathing club that went private in 1949, thus setting a troublesome precedent for ownership of this four-acre chunk of Jetties Beach. Here, as the club's brochure brags, "the beach was divided into sections and members waited years to secure one of the more prestigious spots." This scrambling for position seems comical—and somewhat pernicious—inasmuch as the rest of Nantucket's shoreline has been kept open to the public all these years. If you don't mind the questionable heritage, there's a lovely stretch of gentle bay beach here, and you can walk right out of your contemporary room (decorated with diagonal wooden wainscoting and island-made modern furniture) down a wooden deck to your own colorful beach umbrella. The 27-room hotel's low-profile, shingled exterior gives no hint of the modern amenities concealed within. The cathedral-ceilinged lobby is especially striking, its rafters hung with boldly patterned quilts to set off the white wicker furniture. ♦ Closed mid-October–late May. Jefferson Ave (off Spring St). 228.0618, 800/932.9645; fax 325.4735

Within the Cliffside Beach Club:

The Galley on Cliffside Beach ★★★$$$$ You couldn't pick a prettier place to settle down in, surrounded by flower boxes and the sound of the surf. And the cuisine is truly world-class, from the lobster cake, with roasted corn avocado relish and blood orange butter sauce, to the grilled Nantucket striped bass with lobster risotto and mango salsa. ♦ French ♦ Daily breakfast, lunch, and dinner mid-June–mid-Sept. Reservations recommended for dinner. 228.9641

64 **The Jetties Cafe** $$ Plunked right on a spacious bay beach and now under new management, this cafe features an array of summertime favorites—from burgers to sandwiches. With a porchful of picnic tables, it's nothing fancy, but a great place to retreat from the hot sun for lunch or a quick snack. Evenings are reserved for wedding parties and catered events. ♦ American ♦ Daily 10AM-5PM early June–mid-Sept. Jetties Beach (at the end of Bathing Beach Rd). 228.7094 ♿

65 **Westmoor Inn** $$$$ Longtime summerer W.H.N. Voss had this yellow Federal-style mansion, designed by New York architect **Frederick P. Hill,** built in 1917 for his new bride, née Alice Vanderbilt. During the transformation from summer home to luxury country inn, all the delightful detailing—from the grand portico to the widow's walk—was retained, but the interior design maximizes the effect of the mansion's light-suffused hilltop setting. The spacious living room is full of thoughtful touches, such as the vase of gladiolus on the baby grand and the 1,000-piece puzzle of Nantucket arrayed as a work in progress. There's also a cozy little TV room (anathema at most bed-and-breakfasts) with wicker couches and framed architectural blueprints. The 14 bedrooms, including a ground-floor suite with a full-size Jacuzzi and French doors leading to the lawn, are as romantic as you might expect. After breakfasting to classical music in the conservatory, you can head off down a sandy lane to a quiet stretch of bay beach or take one of the bikes provided for guests and explore the island. There is no restaurant. ◆ Closed early December through March. Westmoor La (at Cliff Rd). 228.0877

THE WESTENDER RESTAURANT

66 The Westender ★★★$$$$ After a refreshing swim at nearby Madaket Beach and a change of clothes, stop in for a reviving drink—perhaps a fruity "Madaket Mystery"—at the small but convivial downstairs bar and cafe. The restaurant upstairs is a handsome loftlike space, with windows all around to catch the ocean view. Owners Cary and Timothy Quish hired a well-known island chef, Carl Keller, and a guest chef, David Toole, to give the menu an international flavor. They have done so, in dishes that are prepared with local fish and soft-shell crabs. Another hit is the smoked duck. Prime time here is sunset, when a golden light floods this sandy point. You might also stop in the general store next door on your way to the beach for beach supplies. ◆ American ◆ Daily lunch and dinner May-Oct. Reservations recommended upstairs. 326 Madaket Rd (at Madaket Beach), Madaket. 228.5100 &

67 West Creek Cafe ★★★$$$ A bit of a jog from town, though not far from the Sconset bike trail, this charming little restaurant is definitely off the beaten path, and delightfully off-beat. Owner Pat Tyler, who started out at the **Boarding House** in 1975, has decked out the small bar, painted a smoky gray, with zebra-stripe pillows; the fireplace room, painted a mellow yellow, is further jazzed up with plaid tablecloths. The menu is moderately priced, with items such as a tuna burger with ginger mustard glaze and Asian slaw or a subtle *pizzetta* with mascarpone and white truffle oil. Chef Dan Ferrare changes the menu, from start to finish, every six days. ◆ New American ◆ M, W-Su dinner. 11 W Creek Rd (between Orange and Pleasant Sts). 228.4943 &

67 The Muse If you're young and have the urge to dance, it's easy enough to find this roadhouse/rock club on the way to Surfside Beach. This is where name bands appear when they leave the mainland—Hootie and the Blowfish and The Dave Matthews Band have played here. The interior is newly renovated with state-of-the-art loudspeakers and a side room with pool tables; decent pizza is produced on the premises to take out or eat at the bar. ◆ Cover. Daily noon-1AM. 44 Atlantic Ave (between Miacomet and Bartlett Rds). 228.6873 &

68 Robert B. Johnson AYH-Hostel $ Of all five hostels on the Cape and islands, this one takes the cake for location—as well as local color. Set right beside Surfside Beach, the former "Star of the Sea" is an authentic 1874 lifesaving station, Nantucket's first. Where seven surfmen once stood ready to fish out shipwreck victims, 49 backpackers now enjoy sex-segregated bunk rooms. (The women's quarters, upstairs, still contain a climb-up lookout post.) Typical lockout (9:30AM-5PM) and curfew (10:30PM) rules prevail. There is a well-equipped communal kitchen. ◆ Closed mid-October–mid-April. 43 Western Ave (off Surfside Rd). 228.0433

CLASSIC 20TH CENTURY DECOR

69 Modern Arts Nantucket abounds in interior design shops promoting the lavish country look. Designer Bill Ferrell, however, likes the clean lines and comparatively decadent tone of 1950s decor. Enter the redbrick 1960s ranch-style house and you'll find chenille bedspreads, McCoy vases, and Art Deco cocktail shakers. Retro jazz and blues play in the background. ◆ Daily 10AM-5PM late May–early Sept; call for off-season hours; closed January–mid-April. 67 Old South Road (between Macy's and Nancy Ann's Las). 228.6711

70 Altar Rock The winding dirt road to this elevated spot (108 feet high)—where boulders overlook moors, harbor inlets, and three sides of the island—slices through as rural an area as you can find on Nantucket. From here you can see the island's amazing variety of foliage, including wildflowers native to the region—red baneberry, dwarf jack-in-the-pulpit, grass pink, sweet everlasting—and those introduced to the area—dusty miller, Queen Anne's lace, Oriental bittersweet. Other flora includes heath and broom plants from Scotland, ivy from England, and *rosa rugosa* from Japan.

A plaque on one of the boulders states: "This reservation is given to the town of Nantucket as a memorial to Henry Coffin—a lifelong and much-beloved resident of the island—1807-1900." Although there is no proof, speculation is that Native Americans used this place as an altar. ♦ Altar Rock Rd (off Polpis Rd)

71 The Summer House $$$$ It seems straight out of a dream, this cluster of eight rose-covered cottages, built of salvaged wood in the 1840s on a bluff overlooking the sea. Tiny to begin with, they're all but dwarfed by the enveloping greenery: Fragrant honeysuckle aswarm with bees tumbles over the low, shingled roofs, and the ivy is so avid it climbs right into the rooms, probing the skylights and window frames. The 10 bedrooms are furnished, but not overdecorated, with English country antiques. The bathrooms (all but one) have marble Jacuzzis, and the beds are draped in fine linens and lace. Owners Danielle deBenedictus and Peter Karlson have tried to keep this a special place where time stands still; Adirondack chairs are scattered casually across the lush, shady lawn encircled by the cottages. The view is due east, where you can watch the sun rise—and sometimes the moon. Wooden steps lead down to a jewel-like pool set in the dunes and surrounded by the inn's kitchen gardens; you can order a poolside lunch on the blue-stone patio, or take a refreshing dip. From here, a short walk through the compass grass brings you to a quiet beach. ♦ Closed November–mid-May. Ocean Ave (at Magnolia Ave), Siasconset. 257.4577; fax 257.6816

Within The Summer House:

The Summer House Restaurant
★★★★$$$$ A blissful summery mood descends as Sal Gioe, a seasoned pianist, riffs his way gently through Gershwin and Porter. The rambling dining room, a comforting jumble of white wicker, pastel linens, and abundant informal flowers, is free of pomp and pretense. At the same time, chef Ruth Pitts offers highly distinguished cuisine. One course after another delights, from the macadamia nut–crusted foie gras with Anjou pears and pear relish, on through jalapeño-glazed baby quail with a shoe-peg corn and wild mushroom ragout, to a three-pound lobster steamed with orange beurre blanc. Abundance—of pleasurable sensations, and the time that makes them possible—is the impression you'll come away with. ♦ New American ♦ Daily lunch (at the pool) and dinner late May–mid-Oct. 257.9976 ♿

"Chatham Bend" was not on Cape Cod. It was a rural corner of Coskata on Nantucket where Chatham fishermen found the scalloping so good they would camp out and scour the sea bottom. To keep the scallops for themselves, Nantucketers then declared a yearlong residency requirement for anyone taking shellfish.

71 Sconset Café ★★★$$$$ This plain and tiny restaurant looks like somebody's oversiz kitchen. Actually, it's the working lab of chef Rolf Nelson, who has succeeded in conjuring a sophisticated international menu for a steady clientele of admirers. Menus change every few weeks, but a midsummer night's feast here might meander through crab cakes remoulade or carpaccio drizzled with truffle-and-olive oil; "veal Portofino" grilled with a parmesan-basil crust; or confit of duck with lemon caramel sauce and nectarine chutney. Breakfasts are just as enticing, with such specialties as waffles made with oatmeal and oranges. At lunch, try the succulent *melanzane* sandwich: grilled eggplant with pesto and fresh mozzarella on a baguette. ♦ New American ♦ Daily breakfast, lunch, and dinner mid-May–Oct. Post Office Sq (at Main St), Siasconset. 257.4008 ♿

71 Claudette's ★★$ You can eat on the little wooden deck, but if you're beach-bound, just pick up a reasonably priced box lunch: a meat loaf or seafood salad sandwich, for instance, with a brownie or lemon cake for dessert. ♦ American ♦ Daily breakfast and lunch mid-May–mid-Oct. Post Office Sq (at Main St), Siasconset. 257.6622

72 Chanticleer Inn ★★★★$$$$ Chef Jean Charles Berruet's glorious country inn has enjoyed a long reign as Nantucket's premier restaurant. One enters through a bower, past a courtyard full of white flowers. To the right is a clubby dining room with dark wood-paneled walls and fireplace; upstairs is a peach-hued, arched hall with private alcoves overlooking the garden. Either of these settings would suit a particular mood (chummy or romantic), but there's no mistaking the power room: the formal ell straight ahead, with decorative paneling in muted tones setting off massive sprays of cut flowers. The unifying theme is very serious French cuisine, of the sort you might expect only on the continent. To highlight just a few options on the prix-fixe menu (the dishes sound all the more glamorous in French): *gâteau de grenouilles aux pommes de terre* (a frogs' legs "cake" in a potato crust), *tournedos de lotte marinée au gingembre, sauce au rhum, croquettes d'ail* (a gingered monkfish scallopini with a lemon-rum sauce and sweet garlic fritters), and *pain perdu, glace au chocolat blanc, coulis d'abricots secs* (a bread pudding with white-chocolate ice cream and apricot sauce). Don't even look at the à la carte listings unless money is no object. But you'll rarely hear of anyone who comes away complaining. ♦ French ♦ M-Tu, Th-Su lunch and dinner mid-May–Nov. Reservations recommended; jacket required. 9 New St (between Park and Chapel Sts), Siasconset. 257.6231. Take-out outlet: 15 S Beach St (between Sea and Easton Sts), Nantucket. 325.5625

72 Siasconset Casino This magnificent Shingle-style private tennis club, built in 1899 by New York architect **Stanford White,** might on rare occasion have a court available for rent by nonmembers at 1 or 2PM; give a call. Evenings in summer, the delightful lattice-raftered theater—once used for productions in the community's heyday as an actors' colony—shows first-run movies. Junior members take the tickets and dole out paper bags of buttered popcorn. ♦ New St (between Park and Chapel Sts), Siasconset. 257.6661

THE WAUWINET
AN INN BY THE SEA

73 The Wauwinet $$$$ This ultradeluxe retreat, renovated by summerers Stephen and Jill Karp in 1988 for roughly $3 million, has earned several nicknames, including "The Ultimate," or, as the staff has been known to joke, the "We Want It." With 25 rooms in the main building (which started out as a restaurant in 1850) and 10 more in five modest-looking shingled cottages, the capacity is only about 80 spoiled guests, tended to by about 100 staffers. They'll look after you assiduously—even perhaps jitneying you into town in a 1936 "Woody" or dispatching you on a 21-foot launch across the bay to your own private strip of beach.

But why leave the grounds (unless you go broke—the cottage suites run up to $1,200 a night). Everything is thoroughly delightful. The inn, located on the last stop en route to a wildlife sanctuary, is perched between the ocean and the vast harbor (both nearby); the spot used to be called the "haulover," because fishers would drag their boats across it to avoid circumnavigating **Great Point.** On the premises are several clay tennis courts with a pro shop and pro, a croquet lawn, a platform for nearly life-size "beach chess," and plenty of boats and bikes to borrow.

The rooms themselves—all provided with a cozy nook from which to gaze out across the water—are so pleasant you may just want to stay indoors. New York interior designer Martin Kuckley created individualized decors

featuring pine armoires, plenty of wicker, exquisite Audubon prints, handsome fabrics, and antique accessories. A playful style is demonstrated in the lobby, where bleached pine floors have been painted with trompe l'oeil throw rugs and marble trim. There's a warm and colorful library where everyone convenes for sherry and Port at day's end. ♦ Closed November–mid-April. 120 Wauwinet Rd (north of Squam Rd), Wauwinet. 228.0145, 800/426.8718; fax 228.6712 &

Within The Wauwinet:

Toppers ★★★★$$$$ Named not for the banker who saw mischievous ghosts but for the family terrier (whose portrait enjoys a place of honor), this accomplished restaurant offers deluxe "shore dinners." You can debark from Straight Wharf on the *Wauwinet Lady* for a round-trip luncheon or dinner cruise. The high prix-fixe tariff makes this an exclusive outing—and there's a dress code to match. Those who come for dinner in the restaurant proper (which, for an additional fee, can culminate in an optional "sunset dessert" cruise) are in for a ritual of surpassing peacefulness. The seating consists of wicker armchairs with pale-blue plaid pillows, or comfortable chintz-covered banquettes with fringed linen antimacassars. A double-tailed gilt mermaid gazes down on a flickering fire, and brass-shaded candles warmly light each luxuriously set table.

The menu is a careful study of seasonal peaks; in September, for instance (an especially beautiful time to go), you might encounter Champagne risotto with golden chanterelle mushrooms and pancetta cracklings, or pan-seared tenderloin of beef with potato-leek *rösti* (cake) and Moroccan cherry tomato jam. Desserts are generous and fanciful, and the homemade ice creams and sorbets will be unlike any you've ever encountered. ♦ New American ♦ M-Sa lunch and dinner; Su brunch and dinner mid-June–mid-Sept. Call for off-season schedule. Closed late October–mid-May. Reservations recommended; jacket required. 228.8768 &

74 Coskata-Coatue Wildlife Refuge
 Shaped like a fishhook, Great Point reaches toward the Cape as if hoping to snag it. The entire point is a 1,100-acre preserve maintained by the Trustees of the Reservations, who offer three-hour tours guided by a naturalist. Rumbling along in a pickup truck, you can expect to see all sorts of shorebirds, including, possibly, piping plovers, egrets, and blue herons. You'll also get a close-up look at the **Great Point Lighthouse**—not the 1818 original, demolished by a storm in 1984, but a rubblestone replica erected in 1986, which relies partly on solar energy. ♦ Fee. Call for schedule. Leaves from **The Wauwinet**'s parking lot (see above). 228.6799

Bests

Jim Patrick
Artistic Director, Nantucket Short Play Festival/
Author

Seasonal whimsy determines Nantucket charms.
My favorite whimsies:

The **Brotherhood of Thieves** on a late fall afternoon.
Get a shoe's-eye view table by the fire, order a
memorably topped coffee drink, and compose envy-
inducing postcards to friends.

Then browse at **Nantucket Bookworks** next door.

The **Madaket Bike Path** is a stunning meander
toward a summer sunset over Mr. Rogers's
neighborhood.

The red clay tennis courts at the **Siasconset Casino**
in fall—the sport of kings at its most genteel.

And while in **Sconset**—the best fancy dinner is at
The Summer House Restaurant because of Sal
Gioe at the piano. The Gatsbyesque elegance and
unobstructed moonlit view toward Spain for your
after-dinner walk doesn't hurt.

Black-Eyed Susan's is a great mix of fine dining
with a diner atmosphere, where the locals go to
catch up after Labor Day.

The **Whaling Museum** is a treasure any season.

The Gaslight Theatre in mid-winter. A hundred or
so seats, postage stamp screen, one movie a week,
scratchy print guaranteed to break, keep your coat
on. My favorite theater anywhere.

And you haven't skated until you've skated on a
cranberry bog in January.

It's not spring until the **Juice Bar** opens. And that
means **Something Natural** sandwiches can be had
out of **Cliff Road.**

The **Nantucket Atheneum** is lovely framed by sand
cherry blossoms.

The best sand-in-your-shoes breakfast joint is the
Downy Flake at **Children's Beach.**

Unitarian Universalist Church—you can see or
hear the clock from almost anywhere in town—so
you can leave your watch home.

Charlotte Louisa Maison
Library Director, Nantucket Atheneum

Biking, running, or walking the **Madaket Bike Path**
in June with the mingled scents of *rosa rugosa,*
Scotch broom, and warm salty air.

Summer lunch in **Le Languedoc Restaurant,** where
you can enjoy French country elegance and superb
cuisine at midday prices.

Browsing two favorite year-round bookstores—
Mitchell's Book Corner and **Nantucket Bookworks,**
different in atmosphere and selection; similar in the
expertness of staff people who read!

"Watching the pass" (Nantucket slang for people
watching from sidewalk benches) in front of the

side-by-side, old-fashioned drugstores on **Main
Street.**

Meditating in the stark beauty of the **Friends
Meeting House.**

Visiting in one day all three historic lighthouses,
each for their own unique character: **Brant Point,**
rotund and welcoming at the entrance to the harbor,
Sankaty Head, the peppermint striped sentinel on
the eastern shore, and **Great Point,** standing in
isolation miles out on a fragile spit of beach.

Favorite simple Nantucket food treats: warm
doughnuts from the **Downy Flake,** Nantucket
Portuguese bread from **Something Natural,** sweet
harbor scallops with a wisp of lemon on the first day
of commercial scalloping season, sautéed venison
tenderloin with a side of Wauwinet eggs in hunting
season, Nantucket Nectars juices and teas, and
Nantucket Coffee Roasters brew.

The classic beauty of the **Great Hall** of the
Nantucket Atheneum where the old meets the new
in a tranquil setting surrounded by China Trade
paintings and 19th-century art, artifacts, and books.

Tom Congdon
Editor/Author

For cheap, simple food in a plain place with the
Nantucket locals, the **Downy Flake** restaurant; try
the crab cakes and the pastry called "scotch irish."
Downy Flake also has an open-air branch down by
Children's Beach.

On a chilly day, onion soup at **Le Languedoc
Restaurant.** On a sunny day, clam rolls at **The
Rope Walk,** at the end of **Straight Wharf.**

Wonderful restaurant: **India House.** Lovely old
rooms and great food. Don't miss the swordfish
encrusted with pecans.

Most tourists get no farther than the **Pacific Bank** at
the top of **Main Street,** but you should keep going,
branching off upper Main Street with its famous old
mansion into the little lanes to the left and right, with
their pretty gardens and picturesque glimpses.

Take a brisk walk along a dirt road in the **Polpis
Moors,** ending up at **Altar Rock,** the island's highest
point. Wonderful sunrises and sunsets, and
mysterious vistas as the fog rolls in.

Rent a jeep and drive seven miles up the beach
to the tip of **Great Point.** Fishing, bird watching,
seals (in winter), and a stunning lighthouse.

View the star-stuffed summer skies through the
telescope of the **Maria Mitchell Observatory.**
Great natural-science exhibits for every age.

Bird-watching walks every Sunday at 8AM. See
newspaper for location.

Nantucket is Mr. Rogers's neighborhood in the
summer; you might see him at any time, so mind
your behavior. Also often visible, Jerry Stiller,
George Costanza's irascible father on *Seinfeld.*

eslie Linsley
uthor, *Nantucket Style*/Store Owner

he best kept secret on Nantucket is **Old South Wharf.** This is the only downtown area closed to ars and off the beaten path. The crushed-shell romenade is lined with fishermen's shanties–urned–artists' galleries, and tiny shops selling nusual handmade items you won't see anywhere lse. At night we always stroll along the pier, ecoming voyeurs, peeking into the most exquisite rray of boats that have pulled into the harbor during he day.

lost romantic thing to do on Nantucket: watching he sunset from **Madaket Beach** with a good bottle f wine, a sandwich, and a significant other.

oller skating on the **Sconset Bike Path.**

inner at **West Creek Cafe,** because it's out of town, way from the summer crowds.

pending a leisurely hour browsing in **Mitchell's ook Corner,** where there's a better selection of style nd decorating books than you can find in any ookstore five times its size.

rainy day at the **Nantucket Atheneum Library.**

Saturday morning ritual for islanders in pursuit of reasures is going to yard sales. Look for the listings Thursday's *Inquirer* and *Mirror.* An interesting way discover different areas of the island.

lat Philbrick
irector, Eagan Institute of Maritime Studies/Author

njoying the view from **Altar Rock**—one of the ighest points on the island.

ayaking up the creeks of **Monomoy Island.**

ailing a Sunfish on the island's ponds.

njoying a good book at the **Nantucket Atheneum.**

Vatching the stars from the **Maria Mitchell bservatory.**

rowsing for books at **Mitchell's Book Corner** and lantucket Bookworks.

oogie boarding at **Surfside Beach.**

ane Booth Vollers
hotographer

hatham Municipal Airport—Take a sight-seeing de up, over, and around **Chatham.**

Carol Richardson, Orleans—Around Thanksgiving, hey have a buy-it-for-nothing clothing sale.

Great Island, Wellfleet—Even in summer you can nd a place on the beach all your own.

ld Village, Chatham—Walking quiet roads with eat old houses.

lot Chocolate Sparrow, Orleans—Ohh yumm, an spresso milk shake. Be ready to express yourself or a fast walk after this rush!

'Alouette, Harwichport—Great French cuisine open year-round).

Nauset Beach, Orleans—Walking the cold, cold windy beach in snow squalls, exhilarating.

Art's Dune Tours, Provincetown—Take a cruise out to the **Province Lands** dunes at sunset, a magical place.

Titcomb's Book Shop, Sandwich—Good poking around on three floors.

Addison Holmes Gallery, Orleans—Great stuff including my fine art photographs!

Cape Cod Museum of Natural History, Brewster—A great gem, especially if you have kids. Come to hike the path through the marsh or out to the beach and come to learn from their exhibits.

Wellfleet Bay Wildlife Sanctuary, Wellfleet—Take all their trails, through the woods, past the pond, and the boardwalk to the bay.

Atlantic White Cedar Swamp Walk, Wellfleet—A dark mysterious and beautiful place to hike.

Green Briar Nature Center & Jam Kitchen, Sandwich—Bring money to buy some great old-time jams and jellies, hike the trail, and visit the gardens.

Heritage Plantation of Sandwich—A Shaker roundhouse barn full of an amazing collection of cars, a beautiful carousel, a fantastic collection of miniature soldiers, and rhododendron bushes galore.

Red Maple Swamp Trail, Fort Hill, Eastham—In the fall run the boardwalk under flame red maples and continue up the hill to a beautiful view of **Nauset Marsh.**

Susan Baker Memorial Museum, North Truro—She's alive and well and making crazy incredible art. She opened her own museum as she thought it was the only way (at one time) to get her work into a museum.

Silk & Feathers, Provincetown—An interesting collection of ladies' clothes.

Sandy Neck, Barnstable—Hiking the marsh trail and cutting through into the dunes of a four-wheel track and heading back out to the bay.

Land Ho!, Orleans—Atmosphere atmosphere atmosphere. Go early for lunch.

Janice Hewins
Sales Manager, Cape Air/Nantucket Airlines

Body surfing at **Nauset Beach**—the water is never warm, but waves are consistently big!

Concerts under the stars at the **Heritage Plantation of Sandwich.**

Biking along the **Cape Cod Canal.**

The wading pools at **Corporation Beach, Dennis.** Great for toddlers!

> When farmers who lived in the area of Nantucket called Polpis came into town, local folks dubbed their difference in behavior "polpisy," which came to be the Nantucket term for country hick.

Detours

If approaching the Cape from the north or west, you'll pass within minutes of **Plymouth** and **New Bedford**, two towns intimately linked with its history, and deserving of a stopover. As the launching pad of US history, Plymouth has been a long-time tourist mecca. Aside from the rather underwhelming **Plymouth Rock**, the main attraction here is **Plimoth Plantation**, a "living history" museum that convincingly recreates the early days of colonization. Maritime history buffs will want to make a brief detour to New Bedford, on **Buzzards Bay.** During the early 19th century, New Bedford vied with the Islands for preeminence in the whaling trade; its glory days are long gone, but a few vestiges remain. A ferry from New Bedford serves **Cuttyhunk**, outermost of the **Elizabeth Islands**, which trail off the Cape's southwestern corner; it's close enough, and unusual enough, to make an appealing day trip. Fourteen miles out to sea, the island is primarily a nature preserve, where deer roam the streets. To read up on the sights before heading off to these towns, obtain brochures from the **Massachusetts Office of Travel and Tourism** (100 Cambridge St, 13th floor, Boston, MA 02202, 617/727.3201, 800/447.6277) and the regional tourism offices listed below.

Plymouth

Calling itself "America's Hometown since 1620," Plymouth has not exactly been shy about courting tourists. The harborside community is a curious amalgam of breathtaking historic homes and garish commercial properties. If you overlook the architectural mishmash, there are several sites worth seeking. Note that virtually all the attractions close from Thanksgiving to late May (and most of the historic houses shut their doors even earlier, around Labor Day or Columbus Day). Call ahead to **Destination Plymouth** (747.7533, 800/872.1620) to check schedules if you plan to visit off-season.

As many as a million visitors a year make a beeline for **Plymouth Rock** (Water St, opposite North St, 866.2580), a glacial boulder of at best apocryphal authenticity. No one knows for sure whether this chunk of rock was indeed the spot where the *Mayflower* passengers first alighted on 20 December 1620 (neither William Bradford nor Edward Winslow, who wrote detailed accounts of the colonization, mention it), but in 1741 a 95-year-old man claimed one of the "first comers" had told him this was the very stone. If it looks a little puny, that's because hordes of souvenir-seekers reportedly chipped away some 3,000 pounds, or three-quarters of its bulk, before it was placed under protective custody (**Pilgrim Hall Museum** (see below) has a good-size sample). The rock was also moved around town quite a bit between the 1870s and the tricentennial year of 1921, when—with the help of the National Society of the Colonial Dames of America—it finally found a home under an elaborate Neo-Grecian portico designed by **McKim, Meade & White.** The monument today is the centerpiece of Massachusetts's smallest state park. That large, gaudily painted vessel at the end of State Pier is the *Mayflower II* (State Pier, off Water St, 746.1622), a full-scale (106.5-foot) replica made in England and sailed over in 1957; the passage took two months, as did the original one. The reproduction is accurate, down to the last detail; and so skilled and well schooled are the actors playing passengers and crew, you'd swear they were

the real thing too. On board, time is seemingly frozen to February 1621, two months after the Pilgrims arrived in Plymouth; most still live on the ship, as they work to build their colony. You can ask them all manner of questions, such as why they came and what they hope to gain, and get thoughtful and often humorous responses, full of the feel of real life. There's an admission charge. The *Mayflower II* is a harborside extension of **Plimoth Plantation** (see page 192), 2.5 miles down the coast; combination tickets are available.

From the pier, hop aboard the *Plymouth Rock Trolley* (747.3419), which offers a narrated tour of town at 20-minute intervals; you can get off at will, and then catch another trolley. Or you might head off under your own steam; all the major sights are within a two-mile radius. Start by scaling **Coles Hill,** where half of the Pilgrim community were buried that first bleak winter—secretly, at night, so the natives wouldn't learn how severely the colonists' numbers had shrunk. The hill is now topped by a handsome statue of the great sachem Massasoit, erected by the Improved Order of Red Men in 1921; the treaties he agreed to in the spring of 1621 held for decades, until his death, permitting the Pilgrims the stability they needed to establish themselves and prosper in the New World.

These stories and two dozen others are depicted nearby at the corny but colorful **Plymouth National Wax Museum** (16 Carver St, between Middle and North Sts, 746.6468). In the spookily lit tableaux, the Pilgrims' linens may look a little too clean and crisp, but for a young audience, this is a fun way to take in the basic facts. The museum is open daily March through November, and there's an admission charge. Also on this bluff are two historic houses to tour (call for hours; admission charge for both): the humble 1749 **Spooner House** (27 North St, between Carver and Court Sts, 746.0012), packed with the belongings and tales of five generations of the family who built it, and the **Mayflower Society House Museum** (4 Winslow St, between North and Water Sts, 746.2590), headquartered in the 1754 home of

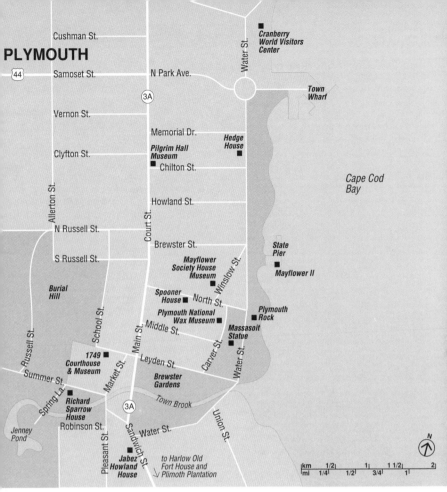

PLYMOUTH

Cushman St.

44 Samoset St. N Park Ave.

3A

Vernon St.

Memorial Dr.

Clyfton St.

Pilgrim Hall Museum ■

Hedge House ■

Chilton St.

Howland St.

N Russell St.

Brewster St.

S Russell St.

Mayflower Society House Museum ■

State Pier ■

Mayflower II ■

Burial Hill

Spooner House ■

North St.

Plymouth National Wax Museum ■

Plymouth Rock ■

Massasoit Statue ■

1749 **Courthouse & Museum** ■

Leyden St.

Brewster Gardens

Summer St.

Town Brook

Richard Sparrow House ■

3A

Robinson St.

Jenney Pond

Water St.

Jabez Howland House ■

to Harlow Old Fort House and Plimoth Plantation

Cranberry World Visitors Center

Water St.

Town Wharf

Cape Cod Bay

N

km 1/2 1 1 1/2 2
mi 1/4 1/2 3/4 1

---

dward Winslow, great-grandson of Governor dward Winslow. This magnificent white Colonial ouse contains a gravity-defying double "flying taircase," and nine rooms of 17th- and 18th-century urnishings, including some items once owned by the ilgrims. Next door is a delightful bed-and-breakfast, he 1782 **Jackson-Russell-Whitfield House** (26 North St, between Winslow and Court Sts, 746.5289; ax 747.2722). Behind its pretty brick Federal facade urk elegant/cozy common rooms and three idyllic edrooms with antique bedsteads and hand-tenciled walls.

Two blocks south on Main Street is the **1749 Court-house & Museum** (Town Sq, between Market and School Sts, 830.4075). Before becoming president, John Adams argued a few cases here, in the oldest wooden courthouse in America. Today, the building ouses various artifacts, including an elaborate 1740 hand-carved oak bench and an 1828 fire pump. It is open daily 10AM-4PM July through September; Saturday and Sunday only in May, June, and October; here is no admission charge. On **Burial Hill** behind he courthouse, you can wander among centuries-old graves and gaze down on the harbor, where the mast of the *Mayflower II* sports a British flag.

On the southern slope of the hill is the modern **John Carver Inn** (25 Summer St, between Market and

Russell Sts, 746.7100, 800/274.1620; fax 746.8299), complete with outdoor pool and the **Hearth 'N Kettle Restaurant.** Across the street is the 1640 **Richard Sparrow House** (42 Summer St, between Pleasant St and Spring La, 747.1240), Plymouth's oldest surviving home, and thus one of the oldest in the country. Inside this plain frame house (donation recommended; by appointment only) with diamond-pane windows is a pottery shop where resident artisan/caretaker Lois Atherton creates richly glazed stoneware for **Plimoth Plantation** and others. Watch her work, and then visit the keeping room and upstairs bedrooms, where a remarkable 1649 wooden wingback "master chair" (the wings were intended to block drafts) is on display. Around the corner, stop off at the country-style **Run of the Mill Tavern** (6 Spring La, off Summer St, 830.1262), offering reasonably priced sandwiches, burgers, and fish entrées. Or follow Town Brook (the source of the Pilgrims' drinking water) through Brewster Gardens down to the harbor to **Cafe Nanina** (14 Union St, between Barnes La and Water St, 747.4503), where the close-up view of the harbor—including the *Mayflower II* in full profile—is complemented by hearty Italian country cuisine served in a sophisticated setting.

Heading north along the harbor, past the pier, you'll see **Hedge House** (126 Water St, between Chilton St and Memorial Dr, 746.9697), an 1809 Federal home refurbished with period antiques, including Chinese porcelains and local textiles, as well as exotica ranging from wallpaper bandboxes to a "magic lantern." Call for hours; there's an admission charge. Beyond, in a former clam factory on the harbor, is the **Cranberry World Visitors Center** (225 Water St, north of Town Wharf, 747.2350), which features a scaled-down demonstration bog, exhibits on the history of cranberry cultivation, and free samples from Ocean Spray, the center's sponsor. It's open daily May through November; admission is free.

On Court Street (Route 3A), parallel to Water Street and one block west, is the **Pilgrim Hall Museum** (75 Court St, at Chilton St, 746.1620). Operated by the Pilgrim Society, the oldest public museum in the nation is housed in an 1824 Greek Revival building designed by **Alexander Parris** (the Bulfinch protégé who, two years later, completed Boston's Quincy Market). No high-tech interactive exhibits here, just an astounding haul of Pilgrim artifacts—including John Alden's halberd and Bible, William Brewster's wooden chair, and the hooded wicker cradle of Peregrine White, who was born aboard the *Mayflower* while it was anchored in Provincetown. Among the other fascinating objects, rather stodgily displayed, are the remains of the *Sparrow-Hawk,* the first recorded shipwreck off Cape Cod. This 40-foot bark, its hull constructed from naturally curved tree trunks and branches, struck Chatham Bar around 1626 en route to Virginia and lay on the ocean floor until 1863, when it surfaced after a storm. It was displayed on Boston Common and went on tour before coming to rest here in 1889. The museum is open daily except in January when it is closed; there's an admission charge.

South on Route 3A toward **Plimoth Plantation,** two more historic houses await. There's an admission charge for both. Just past Town Brook, the **Jabez Howland House** (33 Sandwich St, between N Green and Pleasant Sts, 746.9590) is the only surviving house to have been inhabited by *Mayflower* Pilgrims (Howland's parents, John and Elizabeth). Built around 1667, it more than doubled in size over the next 80 years. Today, it's maintained by the Pilgrim John Howland Society, a group of descendants, and

contains period furnishings. Call for hours; there is an admission charge. The 1677 **Harlow Old Fort House** (119 Sandwich St, between Stephens and South Sts, 746.0012) was built with timbers from the original 1622 fort that stood atop Burial Hill. Here, you can observe and even participate in 17th-century homemaking crafts, such as spinning and candle-making. Call for hours; there is an admission charge.

Any visit to Plymouth must include a stop at **Plimoth Plantation** (entrances on Rte 3A and at Exit 4, Rte 3, 746.1622), a few miles south of the center of town. Start at the quadrangular **Visitors Center** designed in 1986 by Cambridge architect **Graham Gund** to house changing exhibits and an introductory video. Then it's off to the reproduction 1627 **Pilgrim Village,** where, according to the museum's roadside signage, "history repeats itself." (On the way, you can watch artisans demonstrate pottery, weaving, joinery, and basketry at the **Crafts Center.**) Once you enter the wooden barricades of the village, a kite-shaped compound of thatch wattle-and-daub houses set on slanting hillside overlooking the sea, you're on your way to a full sensory appreciation of another age. Here, skilled actors portray specific colonists going about the business of daily life: tending the livestock and herb gardens, performing military drills, cooking and eating (ubiquitous flies notwithstanding), and gossiping over the split-rail fences in the dialects of the time. They'll engage your participation whenever possible and entertain endless questions—as long as they're not anachronisms (any mention of post-1627 events will only elicit bewilderment). So comprehensive is **Plimoth Plantation**'s portrayal of the past (even the farm animals have been back-bred to the 17th-century norm), the illusion is eerily convincing; you'd swear you were conversing across the centuries. There's an admission charge.

On the way back to the 20th century (i.e., the **Visitors Center**), you can visit a re-created Wampanoag camp, **Hobbamock's Homesite.** Hobbamock lived alongside the colonists in the 1620s and helped them to adapt. Though some of the staff members dress like the Wampanoag of old, they do not impersonate the original residents. But they're happy to provide information on the bark-covered huts called *wetus* and on the crafting of dugout canoes.

Open from April through November, **Plimoth Plantation** mounts a full schedule of special reenactments, such as trials and weddings, as well as concerts, workshops, and authentic colonial dinners. You might want to call ahead to see what's up. But even an impromptu visit is sure to be rewarding. Allow yourself at least a couple of hours to get into the 17th-century spirit.

The first product, other than salted cod, that English explorer Bartholomew Gosnold brought back to England from the New World was sassafras. It was an expensive medicine in England but very plentiful on Cuttyhunk.

Map labels:
Elm St.
Mechanics St.
William St.
New Bedford Visitors Center
Bethel St.
Johnny Cake Hill
Rodman St.
Centre St.
Water St.
Front St.
Frontage Rd.
Piers 3 & 4 ■ New Bedford Visitors Center
City Hall
Union St.
Seaman's Bethel
The Whaling Museum
State Pier
Acushnet River
Zeiterion Theatre
Spring St.
Pleasant St.
Purchase St.
Acushnet Ave.
2nd St.
MacArthur Dr.
School St.
7th St.
6th St.
Homer's Warf
Walnut St.
Leonard's Wharf
William Rotch Rodman Mansion
Madison St.
Rotch-Jones-Duff House and Garden Museum
Cherry St.
18 JFK Hwy.
MacArthur Dr.
County St.
Russell St.
New Bedford Fire Museum
Bedford St.
Conway St.

km / mi   1/4 / 1/8   1/2 / 1/4

N

New Bedford

Charted by Bartholomew Gosnold in 1602 and settled in 1652, New Bedford, located at the mouth of the **Acushnet River,** got a slow start as a boomtown—a century later, it was still a sleepy hamlet, an outpost of Dartmouth, harboring a dozen or so farming families, mostly Quaker. Its deep waters, however, had caught the eye of early whaler Joseph Russell, who in the 1740s renamed the port for the Duke of Bedford. The first ship launched was the *Dartmouth,* in 1767; six years later, it was among the vessels whose cargoes were dumped during the Boston Tea Party. The British demolished the town in 1778, but in 1787 it was rebuilt on the western side of the river. (The original site, now the town of Fairhaven, boasts a residential area, **Poverty Point,** dating from the 18th century.) In the heyday of whaling, New Bedford competed with Nantucket for the title of whaling capital, finally taking the lead in 1857, just before the industry went bust.

The town may have lost much of its affluence, but not its will to live. Today, it's an active fishing port (with the largest commercial fleet on the East Coast) and an industrial center with a great deal of civic pride. Townspeople have worked for over a decade to restore more than a hundred buildings of historic significance, partly in hopes of luring visitors to their shores. The odds they face are considerable but they were helped in 1966 by passage of National Park status for the 22-block historic district. The integrity

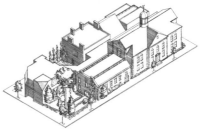

of the downtown area has been compromised by some rather hideous 20th-century additions, including intrusive roadways seemingly designed to discourage pedestrians. Yet admirers of old architecture will find much to savor, and the city offers perhaps a more realistic glimpse of seafaring life today than do the carefully preserved, fantasy-fulfilling towns along the Cape. At the very least, you'll want to stop to enjoy the collections at **The Whaling Museum** and visit the nearby **Seamen's Bethel,** immortalized in *Moby Dick*.

To get your bearings, stop at the **New Bedford Visitors Center** (33 William St, at N Second St, 991.6200, 800/288.6263), which is open daily 9AM-4PM year-round; or the new branch (on Pier 3 in the Wharfinger Building, 979.1745, 800/508.5353; fax 979.1763), which is open daily 9AM-4PM April through October. Both are maintained by the **Bristol County Convention & Visitors Bureau;** they'll provide suggestions and brochures, including a series of walking itineraries prepared by the New Bedford Preservation Society. Guided one-hour tours of the **Waterfront Historic District** are offered in summer, or you can wing it on your own. You might start by repairing to **Freestone's** restaurant (41 William St, at N Second St, 993.7477) to plot your course while enjoying affordable seafood entrées and a drink; this 1833 Richardsonian Romanesque brownstone once housed a bank. A few blocks toward the water is **Candleworks** (72 N Water St, at Rodman St, 997.1294), an elegant Italian trattoria that extends, conservatory-style, from the cellar of an 1810 factory decorated with graceful Federal ornamentation (quoins and lunettes); the patio is an oasis in summer.

One block south is **The Whaling Museum** (18 Johnny Cake Hill, at Union St, 997.0046), which houses a fully rigged half-scale model (89 feet long) of the 1826 whaling bark *Lagoda;* you can climb on board the ship, or get a good view from the balcony. Other nautical treasures range from figureheads, models, and trade signs to sea chests, paintings (including an extraordinary naïf triptych by whaler-turned-painter C.S. Raleigh), and outstanding examples of scrimshaw. The museum also boasts a collection of dolls and toys, along with holdings from the now-defunct **New Bedford Glass Museum.** The museum is open daily and there's an admission charge.

When you've exhausted the possibilities, head across the street to the refreshingly spare **Seamen's Bethel** (15 Johnny Cake Hill, between Union and William Sts, 992.3295). Herman Melville visited this 1832 Greek Revival chapel when it was still relatively new, and noted: "Few are the moody fishermen shortly bound for the Indian or Pacific oceans who failed to make a Sunday visit to the spot." Although it has been architecturally amended over the past century and a half—the bow-shaped pulpit didn't exist in Melville's day—it remains a poignant monument to those lost at sea. Touching cenotaphs surround the upstairs assembly room ("In his coral grave he's left to rest / with no Urn or willo tree"); horrific tales are hinted at, and yet the place has a peaceful and consoling air. Donation is requested.

One of New Bedford's architectural treasures began as an instant failure. The **Zeiterion Theatre** (684 Purchase St, between Spring and Union Sts, 994.2900) was built in 1923 to host vaudeville shows; George Jessel was the opening act. Within months, the stage was dark, a victim of bad timing. That fall, however, the tapestry brick building with its opulent ivory-and-rose interior and gilded Grecian frieze reopened as a movie house. Over the next six decades it hosted five world premieres—including the 1956 *Moby Dick.* A 1971 renovation completely obscured the theater's original charm, but with the help of local benefactors, it was restored in 1982 and donated to the town as a not-for-profit performing arts center. Throughout the year it puts on a multicultural array of concerts, plays, dance, and educational programs.

The 19th-century nabobs of New Bedford built their mansions away from the wharf, along the ridge of **County Street,** originally a native trail. Some of the residences, like the private **William Rotch Rodman Mansion** (388 County St, between Madison and Walnut Sts), resemble institutions more than homes. Now an office building, this granite Greek Revival structure, designed by Providence architect **Russell Warren** in 1833-36, was rumored to be the most expensive house of its time. It's still an imposing sight. On the next block, the **Rotch-Jones-Duff House and Garden Museum** (396 County St, at Madison St, 997.1401) is open for tours Tuesday through Sunday from 10AM to 4PM year-round. There's an admission charge. This 22-room clapboard-brick Classical Revival mansion was commissioned by whaling merchant William Rotch Jr. and built by English carpenter/architect **Richard Upjohn** in 1834. It changed hands only twice over the next 150 years. In 1981, it was bought by the Waterfront Historic Area League (WHALE) and preserved as an architectural sampler of the many periods it survived—there's a Greek Revival sitting room, a Victorian parlor, and upstairs, the 1940s bedroom of the last owners, appended by an enviable full-size dressing room with hatboxes going back two centuries. The grounds are particularly appealing, and encompass a wildflower walk, a dogwood allée, and a boxwood parterre, culminating in a lattice pergola clustered with red, white, and pink roses. In summer, a steady stream of inexpensive concerts draws appreciative crowds.

Families with restless young children in tow might enjoy the **New Bedford Fire Museum** (Bedford and Sixth Sts, 992.2162). The museum (open weekdays in summer; there's an admission charge) is maintained by firefighters at the oldest active station in Massachusetts. It houses an array of restored fire trucks, including an 1840 hand-pump engine; visitors are invited to slide down a brass pole, try on uniforms, and ring bells. If you've time to spare and more energy to burn, the **Buttonwood Park Zoo** (Hawthorne St, between Rockdale and Brownell Aves, 991.6178) is a fun place to roam around while marveling over mountain lions, black bears, harbor seals, and other animals. Set within a 970-acre park designed by noted landscape architect **Frederick Law Olmsted,** the 1894 zoo does not quite measure up to his original design and features none of the natural-habitat settings of more contemporary zoos, but little kids won't mind. It's open daily April through October, and admission is charged.

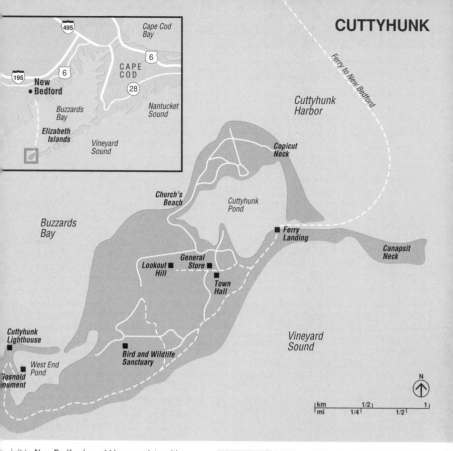

CUTTYHUNK

visit to New Bedford would be complete with-
t trying the local ethnic cuisine. **Antonio's** (267
ggeshall St, at Rte 18 Washburn St Exit, 990.3636)
ts the best recommendation for those wishing
sample such classic Portuguese specialties as
calhau assado (baked cod), *carne de porco a
atejana* (marinated pork stew with littleneck clams),
d *paelha* (a flavorful fish and rice dish). The prices,
ppily, are geared to workers, not tourists.

uttyhunk

/ou're longing to "get away from it all," there is no
tter place than this final link in the Elizabeth Islands
ain. In summer, at least one ferry a day makes a
und-trip, a little over an hour each way, to the tiny
and (2.5 miles long and less than a mile wide)
ated 14 miles out to sea (its native name meant
thing that lies out of the water"). Off-season, from
lumbus Day to Memorial Day, there are only two
ries a week, to accommodate the 30 or so year-
und residents.

July and August the population expands to all of
0, mostly habitual summerers descended from the
rly settlers of 1688. It's quiet. Deer roam the
eets, all 1.3 miles of them. There's one general
re, and that's it. More than half the island is a
ture preserve. The principal entertainment,
turally, is a long, bracing walk. Leave behind your
efcase, beeper, and woes, and come
encumbered, to enjoy an elemental encounter
h an island scarcely touched by the 20th century.

The first duel in the New World took place on a
Plymouth beach. Stephen Hopkins, a leader in
the Plymouth Colony, had brought with him his
daughter Constance and two servants, Edward
Dotey and Edward Leister. On the morning of
18 June 1621, the two Edwards fought with swords
and daggers for the love of Constance. Both were
wounded and ordered by Governor Bradford "to
have their Head and Feet tied together, and so to
lie for 24 hours without Meat or Drink."

One of the instruments of courtship in Puritan
Plymouth was a courting stick. This was a hollow
tube six or eight feet long with openings at both
ends through which a young man and woman
could whisper to each other while in the presence
of their elders. The lovers would be seated on
either side of the fireplace and whisper sweet
nothings through this early manual telephone.

In *Cape Cod Pilot* (1937), WPA writer Josef
Berger provided this assessment of putative
Mayflower relics: "The only thing to bear in mind
is that Lloyds of London has the measurements
of the *Mayflower* on record as 90 feet from stem
to stern and 20 feet in the beam, with a depth of
hold of 11 to 14 feet, and that enough objects
have already been established in this country as
genuine *Mayflower* cargo to fill a warehouse of a
hundred times this cubic area."

Pilgrims' Progress

The Puritans (so-called because they wanted to "purify" the Anglican church) were Protestants—mostly farmers and craftsmen—who bridled at what they perceived as corruption in the Church of England. They viewed the hierarchy, with its elaborate ceremonies and trappings, and the intermingling of religious and secular power, as a replay of what they considered to be the excesses of Roman Catholicism. After convening secretly in Scrooby, England (under threat of imprisonment) in 1606, the Puritans emigrated to Leyden in the Netherlands in 1607 and 1608, but never fully adjusted to life in exile. The Dutch, though tolerant, were even more worldly than the English, and not only did the Puritans experience difficulty securing work, they also did not want their children to grow up in a foreign culture.

Not surprisingly, then, the Puritans leapt at the proposal made by the Merchant Adventurers, a company of speculators who offered New World colonists financial backing in exchange for a share in the natural riches sure to be found overseas. A contingent of Puritans (or "separatists," as they were called by less rebellious Protestants) sailed for England aboard the *Speedwell,* there to link up with the *Mayflower* and head overseas. Twice forced back into Plymouth, England's port because of leaks, the *Speedwell* had to be abandoned. On 6 September 1620, 102 passengers (including 34 children) crowded onto the 90-foot *Mayflower.* Of the adults, about half were Puritans seeking religious freedom, the other half seeking economic betterment. Collectively, they would come to be known as Pilgrims, for their long and arduous journey.

The 66-day crossing, undertaken in hurricane season, was indeed horrendous. Aiming for the mouth of the Hudson River (then part of the Virginia colonies), the *Mayflower* was blown off course, at length dropping anchor off the tip of Cape Cod at sunrise on 11 November. The Pilgrims had to put off debarking because of insurrection among their ranks. The indentured servants, no longer bound for the households of an established colony, insisted they be granted freedom if they were to participate in the risks and rewards of settlement; and mutiny seemed likely if they could not be appeased. Before going ashore, the Pilgrims drafted the Mayflower Compact, a precursor to the US Constitution, which asserted a belief in self-rule and made the servants full citizens of the community. Thus the Pilgrims helped set the course for the colonies' ultimate independence.

Meanwhile, the group faced more pressing needs. The day after their arrival, while the women washed clothes in saltwater, the men went ashore to collect firewood and reconnoiter. What they found was utter desolation.

One lucky scouting party, led by the group's military officer, Captain Myles Standish, found a cache of Indian seed corn at the site now known as **Corn Hill** in **Truro.** They took 10 bushels, without which they might never have survived the next season. Pressing on in search of a place to settle, they met up with a band of hostile natives at what is now called **First Encounter Beach** in **Eastham.** The natives had reason to be hostile, since two dozen of them had been captured by Captain Thomas Hunt during an expedition in 1614, and sent to Spain to be sold into slavery. This time the Indians attacked with arrows, and the Pilgrims retaliated with musket fire. While no lives were lost, the Pilgrims had second thoughts about the area.

Within five weeks of landing, increasingly harsh weather impelled the settlers to cross the bay in search of a more protected port. On 20 December 1620, they landed in what was to become Plymouth, Massachusetts, where they found a plot already cleared, at a relatively safe, high location near freshwater springs. The Indians who had cleared the land had been decimated by plague the preceding year and were scarcely to be seen. Of the handful remaining, one astounded the Pilgrims by walking into their compound and addressing them in their own language: "Welcome!" This was Samoset, who had picked up a bit of English from cod fishers and would be of great help as the Pilgrims adapted to their strange new world. Six days later he returned with another invaluable aide, Squanto—who had traveled to London and back, and been among those kidnapped by Hunt in 1614.

For the Pilgrims, wrote Bradford, Squanto "was a speciall instrument sent of God for their good beyond their expectation. He directed them how to set their corne, wher to take fish and to procure other commodoties and was their pilott to bring them to unknowne places for their profitt, and never left them till he dyed." he succumbed to a fever in 1622, Bradford records, seeking prayers that he might "goe to ye Englishmens God in heaven." The peace treaties Squanto had helped secure between the settlers and the Indians lasted for half a century.

The Pilgrims needed every advantage. In their first winter half died from scurvy, pneumonia, and other diseases. Come spring, the natives helped the survivors plant crops. A three-day harvest celebration was held that fall; 90 natives attended, far outnumbering their hosts. They feasted on turkeys, geese, duck, lobsters, clams, oysters, fish, eels, fruit tarts and beer. The natives brought five deer, corn, and popcorn.

Such bounty notwithstanding, the New World never yielded the riches anticipated by the Merchant Adventurers. The Pilgrims dutifully sent all they could gather to England, but their backers, who had invested $34,000, were inclined to end the venture. The Pilgrims, for their part, were ready to cut loose. In 1627, eight Plymouth leaders, purchased the Londoners' share in the company for $9,000. They were officially on their own.

Three years later, 1,000 more Puritans on 11 ships landed at Salem during the "Great Migration," and worked their way south to Boston to take advantage of its well-protected harbor. By 1636, another 12,000 immigrants arrived. In just 16 years, the colonists had secured their foothold in the New World.

ndex

Restaurants

Only restaurants with star ratings are listed below. All restaurants are listed alphabetically in the main (preceding) index. Always call in advance to ensure a restaurant has not closed, changed its hours, or booked its tables for a private party. The restaurant price ratings are based on the average cost of an entrée for one person, excluding tax and tip.

Index

Hotels

The hotels listed below are grouped according to their price ratings; they are also listed in the main index. The hotel price ratings reflect the base price of a standard room for two people for one night during the peak season.

$$$$ Big Bucks ($225 and up)
$$$ Expensive ($150-$225)
$$ Reasonable ($75-$150)
$ The Price Is Right (less than $75)

Features

Bests

Maps